A. Kupiek
Fall 2011
HIST 246-1
Frederick Campus

EVERYDAY LIFE IN BRITISH GOVERNMENT

WS or TWS
→ The Westminster Story
MS or TMS
→ The Managerial Story

EVERYDAY LIFE IN BRITISH GOVERNMENT

R. A. W. RHODES

OXFORD
UNIVERSITY PRESS

OXFORD
UNIVERSITY PRESS

Great Clarendon Street, Oxford OX2 6DP

Oxford University Press is a department of the University of Oxford.
It furthers the University's objective of excellence in research, scholarship,
and education by publishing worldwide in

Oxford New York

Auckland Cape Town Dar es Salaam Hong Kong Karachi
Kuala Lumpur Madrid Melbourne Mexico City Nairobi
New Delhi Shanghai Taipei Toronto

With offices in

Argentina Austria Brazil Chile Czech Republic France Greece
Guatemala Hungary Italy Japan Poland Portugal Singapore
South Korea Switzerland Thailand Turkey Ukraine Vietnam

Oxford is a registered trade mark of Oxford University Press
in the UK and in certain other countries

Published in the United States
by Oxford University Press Inc., New York

British Library Cataloguing in Publication Data
Data available

Library of Congress Cataloging in Publication Data
Data available

Typeset by SPI Publisher Services, Pondicherry, India
Printed in Great Britain
on acid-free paper by
MPG Books Group, Bodmin and King's Lynn

ISBN 978-0-19-960114-1

1 3 5 7 9 10 8 6 4 2

To Jenny
Of the many men who I am, who we are,
I can't find a single one,
they disappear among my clothes,
they've left for another city.
(Pablo Neruda, 'We are Many' in *The Poetry*
of Pablo Neruda. Edited with an introduction
by Ilan Stavans. New York, Farrar Straus and Giroux,
2003: 474).

Contents

Tables and Figures

TABLES

FIGURES

Glossary of Terms

1:1	One-to-One
APS	Assistant Private Secretary
BSE	*Bovine spongiform encephalopathy* (or mad cow disease)
CMPS	Centre for Management and Policy Studies
CPAs	Comprehensive Performance Assessments
CRB	Criminal Records Bureau
DCMS	Department for Culture, Media and Sport
DEFRA	Department of the Environment, Food and Rural Affairs
DETR	Department for the Environment, Transport and the Regions
DfES	Department for Education and Skills
DoH	Department of Health
DS	Diary Secretary
DTI	Department of Trade and Industry
DWP	Department of Work and Pensions
ESC	Education and Skills Committee
ESRC	Economic and Social Research Council
EU	European Union
FWNB	Fieldwork Notebooks
FMD	Foot-and-Mouth Disease (*Aphtae epizooticae*)
GCSE	General Certificate of Secondary Education
HMC	Headmasters' and Headmistresses' Conference
JCGQ	Joint Council for General Qualifications
KiT	Keep-in-Touch
MAFF	Ministry of Agriculture Fisheries and Food
MoD	Ministry of Defence
NAO	National Audit Office
NDPB	Non-Departmental Public Body
NFU	National Farmers Union
NWPLP	North-West Parliamentary Labour Party
OCR	Oxford, Cambridge and RSA Examinations
ODPM	Office of the Deputy Prime Minister
OfCom	Office of Communications

Ofsted	Office for Standards in Education, Children's Services and Skills
OPSR	Office for Public Service Reform
PAC	Public Accounts Committee (strictly, Committee of Public Accounts)
PASC	Public Administration Select Committee
PQs	Parliamentary Questions
PBR	Pre-Budget Review
Perm Secs	Permanent Secretaries Group (Wednesday morning meeting)
PLP	Parliamentary Labour Party
PMDU	Prime Minister's Delivery Unit
PMFSU	Prime Minister's Forward Strategy Unit
PO	Private Office
PPS	Principal Private Secretary
PQ	Parliamentary Question
PS	Private Secretary
PSA	Public Service Agreement
PSG	Public Services and Growth directorate (Treasury)
PUSS	Parliamentary Under-Secretaries of State
QCA	Qualifications and Curriculum Authority
SEU	Standards and Effectiveness Unit
SHA	Secondary Heads Association
SpAd	Special Adviser
TI	Transcribed Interview

Preface and Acknowledgements

Normally, I would use the preface to provide a short summary of the book. Thus, I would say that the book reports my shadowing of ministers and senior civil servants in British government and seeks to answer the question 'what do they do?' It draws extensively on my fieldwork notebooks, supplemented by interviews, to describe their everyday life.

This starting point has the virtue of telling the reader what question I will try to answer and how I will try to answer it. What it does not tell the reader is how nervous I was in writing this book. Like Gustave Flaubert 'giving the public details about oneself is a bourgeois temptation that I have always resisted', but I am present throughout the stories I tell. So, the book is also a journey on which I try to find a way of incorporating me in these stories of everyday life at the top. Given that I am present in my story, it behoves me to tell how I came to be in it. The starting point is a lifelong fascination with bureaucracy and how, in all its manifestations, it shapes our lives. There were, however, three more specific wellsprings; my work on governance, the Economic and Social Research Council's (ESRC) Whitehall Programme, and my collaboration with Mark Bevir.

It started back in 1991 when I was on the ESRC committee responsible for research programmes. I argued for both a local government and a central government programme. With Gerry Stoker, I set up the local governance programme. I then stepped down from the committee so I could be director of the central government programme that became known as the Whitehall Programme. I first used the term 'governance' for the launch of local governance initiative when I wrote a short piece entitled 'Beyond Whitehall: Researching Local Governance' in the *Social Sciences* (No. 13, February 1992, 2). Then I expanded on that in an invited lecture for the Royal Society of Arts on 24 January 1995, which was published as an RSA/ESRC pamphlet 'The New Governance: Governing without Government'. A revised version was published in *Political Studies* in 1996.

This work on governance was a logical extension of my previous work on policy networks. It came out of my reappraisal of *Beyond Westminster and Whitehall* (1988), which was necessary after Thatcher's reforms. That reappraisal was *Understanding Governance* (1997), which was one of the wellsprings of the Whitehall Programme.

Had I not been Director of the Whitehall Programme (see Rhodes 2000*b*), I doubt I would have written this book. The appointment gave me access to senior civil servants and then ministers. Also, under the funding rules prevailing at the time, it gave me money. The University of Newcastle rewarded its staff for successful grant applications by returning a proportion of the grant's overheads to them to spend on research and research related activity. I saved this money and used it to fund my fieldwork. So, I must thank the ESRC and the University of Newcastle for financial support, although neither knew they were funding this book.

Finally, for a decade now, I have been working with Mark Bevir on an interpretive approach to political science (see Bevir and Rhodes 2003, 2006, and 2010). We stress the importance of historical and ethnographic analysis. This book demonstrates their value in the study of British government. My aim is to describe the changing world of permanent secretaries and ministers through an account of their daily life in government. I seek to provide my interpretation of their interpretation of what the world looks like through their eyes. So, I watched people in their everyday office life. I relied on what they said and did, on their reasons for their actions. In a short phrase, I aimed at a 'thick description' of office life.

I incurred the usual debts while writing the book. I owe the greatest debt to the senior civil servants and ministers who helped in many ways. I would prefer to thank everyone by name but the protocol dictates they remain anonymous. Where I name anyone in the text, it is with their express permission. I thank each and every one for their invaluable contribution. Without their cooperation there would be no book. I apologise for the long delay in publication. I can only plead that, when I started the project, I did not expect to spend five years in senior management posts at the Australian National University.

Many colleagues and friends have commented in whole or in part on the manuscript. My thanks to: Paul Fawcett, Bob Goodin, Brian Hardy, Paul 't Hart, Carolyn Hendriks, Evert Lindquist, Kevin Orr, Alison Procter, John Wanna, and Pat Weller. I am responsible for any remaining errors of fact or judgement. Two individuals made special but different contributions. Mark Bevir has shaped my beliefs and practices in almost as many ways as he believes! Jenny Fleming is the reason I moved to Australia. As every writer knows and invariably says in the preface, he or she could not have written the book without the loving support of their partner. Well, it's true.

1

Observing Government Elites

It is one of those grey London days where the colour of the sky matches the buildings. I am sat in a ministerial car in Parliament Square. By London traffic standards we make good time, although we don't have far to travel. I wonder if London itself contributes to the air of rush and stress that surrounds the Minister. It is such a big, noisy, dirty, congested place. There must be corners of peace and quiet but I see none of them in the square mile of Westminster and Whitehall. I just see people and traffic rushing in every direction. London is a metaphor for the Minister's lifestyle. I miss the peace and quiet of my Canberra suburb with its gum trees and views over the Brindabellas where the noisiest thing is the kookaburras arguing over territory, mates, and food. There is no stillness here, only the privilege of a chauffeured limousine and the demands of the unrelenting diary.

Why study government elites? As citizens, why do we care about the everyday life of ministers and civil servants? We care because the decisions of the great and the good affect all our lives for good or ill. For all their personal, political, and policy failings and foibles, they make a difference. Forget about grand acts of parliament. Relatively minor decisions can change people's lives. For example, the literacy and numeracy rates among 5–11 year-old pupils were low. So, the Secretary of State for Education decided that improving these rates was a priority. He set targets and this ostensibly boring act triggered a massive improvement; the policy was an 'unadulterated success' (Barber 2007: 38). The government made a difference to children's achievements.

So, we want to know what ministers and bureaucrats do, why, and how. In other words, we are interested in their beliefs and practices. This book ploughs virgin territory in the analysis of British central government because it is an exercise in political anthropology. I apply the observational methods of the anthropologist to explore the reasons and actions of the ministers and permanent secretaries of three British government departments. I describe the government elites' world through their eyes, focusing on beliefs and everyday practices. I explore how their beliefs and practices create meaning in politics, policy making, and public service delivery. I analyse how such beliefs and practices are embedded in traditions; in webs of routines, rituals, and languages. I provide case studies of specific 'events' to show ministers and civil servants 'in action'. I challenge conventional views of British government and governance with their focus on constitutional norms, institutions, and managerialism. Instead, I paint the portrait of a storytelling political-administrative elite with beliefs and practices rooted in the Westminster model that uses protocols and rituals to domesticate rude surprises and recurrent dilemmas. This chapter outlines the organizing ideas used to present my empirical observations, describes how I observed everyday life in a government department, and provides a summary of the rest of the book.

ORGANIZING IDEAS

As John Stuart Mill (1969 [1840]: 119–20) remarked:

> By Bentham . . . men have been led to ask themselves, in regard to any ancient or received opinion, Is it true? And by Coleridge, What is the meaning of it? The one took his stand outside the received opinion, and surveyed it as an entire stranger to it: the other looked at it from within, and endeavoured to see it with the eyes of a believer in it . . . Bentham judged a proposition true or false as it accorded or not with the result of his own inquiries. . . . With Coleridge . . . the very fact that any doctrine had been believed by thoughtful men, and received by whole nations or generations of mankind, was part of the problem to be solved, was one of the phenomena to be accounted for.

In this book I ask, after Coleridge, 'what is the meaning of it?' where 'it' refers to the working life of political and other governmental elites. I concentrate on meanings, beliefs, and practices, not laws and formal rules, correlations between social categories, or deductive models. I look at the ways in which practices are produced, reproduced, and changed through the particular and contingent beliefs, preferences, and actions of individuals.

With Mark Bevir, I have already written a detailed account of both an interpretive approach in political science and its key concepts of beliefs, practices, traditions, dilemmas, and narratives.[1] This book serves a different purpose. I focus squarely on empirical observations and their implications for how we think about British government, not on theory and method. The aim is to show how much work can be done with a small conceptual and methodological toolkit. However, I must describe each concept if only briefly because they provide the organizing framework for the empirical observations.

Beliefs

An interpretive approach argues it is not possible to identify people's beliefs by appealing to the allegedly objective social facts about them. Instead, we must explore the beliefs and meanings through which they construct their world. These beliefs and desires are inextricably enmeshed with theories. When we say that a civil servant in charge of a department has a vested interest in increasing that department's budget and employing more staff, we use a particular theory to identify their interests from their position. Someone with a different set of theories might believe that someone in that position has different interests; for example, loyalty to their politician and implementing his or her policies as efficiently and speedily as possible. The important point here is that how the people we study see their position and their interests inevitably depends on their theories, which might differ significantly from our theories. Officials might possess theories that lead them to see their position as administrators serving the public interest, rather than as chief executives employing the best managerial practice of the private sector. Or they might see their interests as sustaining best professional practice, not maximizing the turnover of clients. I stress decentred analysis; that is, focusing on the social construction of a practice through the ability of individuals to create, and act on, meanings. It is to unpack a practice as the disparate and contingent beliefs and actions of individuals. Political scientists cannot read off beliefs and desires from objective social facts about people. Instead they have to interpret beliefs by relating them to other beliefs, traditions, and dilemmas.

I can illustrate the difference by comparing the mainstream and an interpretive approach to the study of institutions. Institutions are said to take a concrete, fixed form; that is, they have operating rules or procedures that govern the actions of the individuals. This notion is unacceptable. It leads political scientists to ignore the effects of contingency, internal conflict, and the several constructions of actors in an institution. If we think of institutions in this way, we do not interpret what institutions mean to the people who work in them. Rather we assume the allegedly objective rules prescribe or cause behaviour. There are two problems with this assumption. First, people not only wilfully choose to disobey a rule, but also, they subvert, ignore, avoid, and redefine them. Second, we cannot read off people's beliefs and desires from their social location. Rules are always open to interpretation. It is not just a question of literal meaning but also a question of whom the rule applies to, and applying the rule in any given situation.

On the other hand, if institutions are said to include cultural factors or beliefs, then rules do not fix such meanings or the actions of its members. Now we must ask how beliefs and actions are created, recreated, and changed in ways that constantly reproduce and modify institutions. Of course, an institution understood in this way poses the question of whether the approach remains, in any significant sense, institutional. Explanations are no longer cast as if behaviour were the result of rules but of the multiple, diverse ways in which people understand, and react to, conventions. The purpose of these reflections is not to undermine all appeals to institutions or rules. These reflections suggest only that we need to tailor appeals to institutions to recognize that political science is an interpretive discipline focused on the beliefs of the relevant actors.

Practices

When we leave the micro-level of individual beliefs and actions for the macro-level, I think of social objects such as the state as practices rather than institutions or structures. A practice is a set of actions, often a set of actions that display a pattern, perhaps even a pattern that remains relatively stable across time. Practices consist simply of what a group of people do, and the unintended consequences of these actions. So, the state or a government department is a set of embedded practices. Such notions as institution and structure can be used as a metaphor for the way activity coalesces into practices. I avoid this metaphor because all too often it has a bewitching effect, leading people to treat institutions or structures as real, reified entities (see Marsh 2008*a*).

Practices often help to identify beliefs. I interpret people's actions by ascribing beliefs to them. Nonetheless, practices cannot explain actions because people act for their own reasons. I explain their actions by reference to the beliefs and desires of the relevant actors, not by reference to the practice itself. I unpack a practice as the disparate and contingent beliefs and actions of individuals. It is possible to explain people's beliefs (and the practices to which their actions give rise) only by locating them in a wider web of beliefs.

Traditions

I need a concept such as tradition to explain why people come to believe what they do. People understand their experiences using theories they have inherited. This social heritage is the necessary background to the beliefs people adopt and the actions they perform. I define a tradition as a set of understandings someone receives during socialization. So, a governmental tradition is a set of inherited beliefs and practices about the institutions and history of government (Perez-Diaz 1993: 7). Although tradition is unavoidable, it is only a starting point, not something that determines later actions. Traditions are an unavoidable presence in everything people do, but they are mainly a first influence on people.

Social contexts only ever influence, as distinct from determine, the actions of individuals. Traditions are products of individual agency. When people confront the unfamiliar, they have to extend or change their heritage to encompass it, so developing their heritage. Every time they try to apply a tradition, they have to reflect on it, they have to try to understand it afresh in today's circumstances. By reflecting on it, they open it to innovation. Thus, human agency can produce change even when people think they are sticking fast to a tradition they regard as sacrosanct.

A particular relationship must exist between beliefs and practices if they are to make up a tradition. For a start, the relevant beliefs and practices must have passed from generation to generation. As well as suitable connections through time, traditions must embody suitable conceptual links. The beliefs and practices a teacher passes on to a pupil must display a minimal consistency. A tradition could not have provided someone with a starting point unless its parts formed a minimally coherent set. Traditions cannot be made up of purely random beliefs and actions that successive individuals happen to have held in common.

I see tradition as a starting point, not a destination. Traditions do not determine the beliefs that people go on to adopt or the actions they go on to perform. They are diverse. In any society there is a multiplicity of traditions. I adopt a pragmatic notion of tradition. Investigators choose a particular tradition to explain whatever set of beliefs or practices happen to be of interest to them. Traditions are essentially artefacts. The justification for any choice of traditions lies in the claim that they best explain what is of interest, in my case the beliefs and practices of central political and administrative elites, not in the claim that such traditions are given or natural.

In conventional social science terms, I am recasting the problem of structure and agency. It is our ability for agency that makes tradition a more satisfactory concept than rival terms such as structure, paradigm, and episteme. These latter ideas suggest the presence of a social force that determines or limits the beliefs and actions of individuals. Tradition, in contrast, suggests that a social heritage comes to individuals who, through their agency, can adjust and transform this heritage even as they pass it on to others. This idea of tradition also differs from political scientists who associate the term with customary, unquestioned ways of behaving (Oakeshott 1962: 123 and 128–9) or with the entrenched folk-lore of pre-modern societies. At the heart of this analysis of tradition is the notion of *situated agency*: of individuals using local reasoning consciously and subconsciously to reflect on and modify their contingent heritage.[2]

Dilemmas

A dilemma arises for an individual or institution when a new idea stands in opposition to existing beliefs or practices and forces a reconsideration of these existing beliefs and associated tradition (Bevir 1999: ch. 6). Or as MacIntyre (1996: 552), would have it: 'traditions, when vital, embody continuities of conflict'. Political scientists can explain change within trad-itions by referring to relevant dilemmas. Dilemma provides a way of under-standing the role of individual agency in developing traditions. Whenever someone adopts a new belief or action they have to adjust their existing beliefs and practices to make way for the newcomer. To accept a new belief is to pose a dilemma that asks questions of existing traditions.

It is important to recognize that we cannot straightforwardly identify dilemmas with allegedly objective pressures in the world. People vary their beliefs or actions in response to any new idea that they come to hold as true. They do so irrespective of whether the new idea reflects real pressures, or, to be precise, irrespective of whether it reflects pressures that political scientists as observers believe to be real. In explaining change, we cannot privilege our academic accounts of the world. What matters is the subjective, or more usually, intersubjective, understandings of political actors, not our scholarly accounts of real pressures in the world. The task of the interpretive political scientist is to recover the shared, intersubjective dilemmas of the relevant actors. The task is not to privilege scholarly accounts, although, of course, the pressures political scientists believe to be real often overlap with the actors' perceptions of the relevant dilemmas.

Dilemmas do not have given, or correct, solutions. It might look as if a tradition can tell people how to respond to dilemmas. At most, however, it provides a guide or hints to what they might do. The only way to check if an individual's actions are consistent with the beliefs of a tradition is to ask whether other adherents of the tradition are happy with those actions. Even when people think they are merely continuing a settled tradition or practice, they could well be developing, adjusting, and changing it. Change can occur when people think they are sticking fast to a tradition. Traditions and practices could be fixed and static only if we never met and faced novel circumstances. But, of course, we are always meeting new circumstances. People can integrate a new belief into their existing beliefs only by relating themes in it to themes already present in their beliefs. Change thus involves a pushing and pulling of a dilemma and a tradition to bring them together. Beliefs about the state and political institutions are in such perpetual flux.

Narratives

I use the term 'narrative' to refer to the form of explanation that disentangles beliefs and actions to explain human life.[3] Narratives are the form theories take in the human sciences.[4] I explain actions by reference to the beliefs and desires of actors, and I explain these beliefs by reference to traditions and dilemmas.

It is often claimed that positivist political science provides causal explan-ations while interpretive approaches provide understanding of beliefs, motives, and actions. Not so. Narratives explain actions. Scholars from all sorts of disciplines use the word 'cause' to signal there is a significant relationship between people and events. Narrative is a form of explanation that works by relating actions to the beliefs and desires that produce them. Narratives depend on conditional connections. When individuals act on their beliefs and desires, there is a conditional connection. Conditional connections are neither necessary nor arbitrary. Because they are not necessary, political science differs from the natural sciences. Because they are not arbitrary, we can use them to explain actions and practices.

So, narratives identify the conditional connections that link people, events, and ideas to one another and explain actions and practices. Although these narrative structures also appear in works of fiction, we need not equate political science to fiction. Political scientists offer us narratives that strive, to the best of the narrator's ability, to capture the way in which events did happen in the past or are happening today, whereas writers of fiction need not do so. Political scientists cannot ignore the facts, although we must accept that no fact, agreed or otherwise, is simply given to them.

METHODS

Anthropology or ethnography—the two terms are commonly interchangeable—reconstruct the meanings of social actors by recovering other people's stories from practices, actions, texts, interviews, and speeches. Hammersley and Atkinson (1983: 2) claim the method 'captures the meaning of everyday human activities', and encourages the researcher to get out there and see what actors are thinking and doing. It is exploratory—'unstructured soaking' (Fenno 1990: 57)—and characterized by deep immersion in social worlds so we can understand day-to-day practices, and how these practices become meaningful.[5]

Political anthropology encompasses many ways of collecting qualitative data about beliefs and practices. For example, Cris Shore's (2000: 7–11) cultural analysis of how EU elites sought to build Europe defines ethnography to include participant observation, historical archives, textual analysis of official documents, biographies, oral histories, recorded interviews, and informal conversations as well as statistical and survey techniques. I am not a methodological missionary, but I do want to argue the case for *observation* as an important addition to the political science toolkit. As Fenno (1990: 128) observed 'not enough political scientists are presently engaged in observation' and his remark is accurate whether we are talking of Australia, North America, or the United Kingdom (Rhodes 2002). Observation is conspicuous for its absence in the political science armoury of research methods.[6]

For Geertz (1973: 9), ethnography is about 'thick descriptions', about explicating 'our own constructions of other people's constructions of what they and their compatriots are up to'. So, we seek to understand the webs of significance that people spin for themselves. The everyday phrase is 'seeing things from the other's point of view'.[7] The key point is that the ethnographer provides his or her own interpretation of what the informants believe they are up to, so his or her accounts are second- or even third-order interpretations. It is a soft science that guesses at meanings, assesses the guesses, and draws explanatory conclusions from the better guesses. Yet it is still possible for ethnographers to generalize. Theory provides a vocabulary with which to express what symbolic action has to say about itself. Although ethnography rarely aims at prediction, theory still has to 'generate cogent interpretations of realities past' and 'survive . . . realities to come'. The task of the ethnographer is to set down the meanings that particular actions have for social actors and then say what these 'thick descriptions' tell us about the society in which they are found. The ethnographer will never get to the bottom of anything. Ethnography is a science 'marked less by a perfection of consensus than by a refinement of debate'—'what gets better is the precision with which we vex each other'.[8]

To write a story that vexes the reader, I draw on three sources of information:

> the pattern of practice, talk, and considered writing—the first is the most reliable, the second is the most copious and revealing and the third is the most difficult to interpret. (Oakeshott 1996: x)

Oakeshott would turn in his grave if I described this approach as triangulation, but my account is based on these three sources of information. On practice, I observed the office of two ministers and three permanent secretaries for two days each, totalling some 120 hours. I also shadowed two ministers and three permanent secretaries for five working days each, totalling some 300 hours. On talk, I had repeat interviews with: ten permanent secretaries (2 × 2-hour taped and transcribed), five secretaries of state and three ministers (1 × 2-hour taped and transcribed); and 20 other officials (1 × 1-hour taped and transcribed), totalling some 67 hours of interviews. On considered writing, I had copies of speeches and public lectures; committee and other papers relevant to the meetings I observed; and newspaper reports. I report such details as the number and length of interviews and the total hours of observation to increase confidence in the results just as, when reporting a survey, I would include various details such as the sample size and the response rate (Yanow 2006).

My interviews and fieldwork observations were for citation but not for attribution without the interviewee's permission. I interviewed three female ministers and two female permanent secretaries. There were so few women that if I gave the person's gender, in effect, I identified them. So, I use the male pronoun throughout. The Private Offices were more equally divided between male and female and with 20 interviews it does not compromise a person's identity if I use the correct gender. I anticipated that at least some parts of the story would have to be anonymous. I chose three departments similar in size and status, so I could talk about the composite minister, department, or permanent secretary and remain plausible.[9] Had I sought to draw a composite based on departments as unlike as the Treasury, the Foreign Office, and the Department for Work and Pensions, the result would have been implausible. I conducted the interviews in 2002. The fieldwork was carried out in 2003. There were several repeat interviews and occasional visits in 2004.

There is a conventional stereotype of ethnography that sees the researcher moving to a single location for a long time. But as it spread beyond social and cultural anthropology, ethnography came to encompass more varied forms of field involvement. Following the established practice of latter-day ethnographers, for this book I undertook 'yo-yo fieldwork'; that is, I repeatedly went back and forth, in and out of the field (Wulff 2002: 117). I also went to more than one fieldwork site because I was 'studying through'; that is, following a policy process through the 'webs and relations between actors, institutions and discourses across time and space' (Shore and Wright 1997: 14; see also Marcus 1995). Most of the research reported in this book used a combination of elite interviews and fieldwork observation conducted during repeated visits to several locations.[10]

I told every participant I would not write up the research during the life of the 2001–5 parliament. I calculated that everyone would have a different job when I told my story, thus minimizing, if not removing, any political sensitivities surrounding the events I describe. When I cannot attribute a quote, I use the phrase 'Transcribed Interview' (TI). It does not mean 'something someone's told me some time'. All such information is from a taped and transcribed interview. I give the position held by the individual—minister, permanent secretary, and so on. For the quotes from ministers there are eight possible sources, and for permanent secretaries there are ten. In every other case, there will be at least three possible sources for the quote. When it is consistent with protecting the anonymity of the individual, I also give the individual's departmental affiliation.[11]

One of the advantages of not publishing straight away is that I also had several insider accounts of the period to draw on (see Chapters 2 and 3 below). So, I supplemented the fieldwork and interviews with the primary sources listed in the bibliography and with the several insider accounts now available.[12] Throughout, whether drawing on my fieldwork or other primary sources, I stress the views of insiders because I am trying to describe their world through their eyes. Finally, nowadays, senior civil servants speak in public almost as often as ministers. Moreover, the speeches of both are easily available from the Internet. I also attended many lectures and seminars under the Chatham House rule,[13] which offered the opportunity to hear many senior public figures speaking, often frankly, off the record. I found this combination of talk and considered writing a valuable primary source, which I commend to colleagues.

Perhaps the most intractable problems arise not from the fieldwork but in finding a way to provide an authoritative account of that work. Van Maanen's (1988: 8) observation that 'there is no way of seeing, hearing, or representing the world of others that is absolutely, universally valid or correct' is probably now the conventional wisdom of anthropology. There is no agreed way of representing the world of others. His aspiration is to find 'more, not fewer, ways to tell of culture'. He uses the term 'tale', 'quite self-consciously to highlight the presentational or, more properly, representational qualities of fieldwork writing' (Van Maanen 1988: 2, 8, and 14) and he identifies several ways of telling: realist tales, confessional tales, and impressionist tales.

Realist accounts are dispassionate, third-person documentary accounts of everyday life. The story is told from the native's standpoint but the author has the final word, both selecting the standpoints and pronouncing on the meaning of their culture. Van Maanen (1988: ch. 3 and pp. 54 and 64–6) concedes that realist ethnography has 'a long and by-and-large worthy pedigree', although its writing conventions are now seen as 'embarrassing'.

The characteristics of a *confessional* account are that it is an autobiographical, personalized story, which tells the tale from the fieldworker's perspective; and aims for naturalness and getting it right in the end. Confessional tales are first-person and anecdotal. All too often the storyline is that of 'a fieldworker and a culture finding each other and, despite some initial spats and misunderstandings, in the end, making a match' (paraphrased from Van Maanen 1988: ch. 4 and p. 79).

Impressionist tales take the form of a dramatic storyline, with a fragmented treatment of theory and method, because they focus on characterization and drama (Van Maanen 1988: 103–6). Impressionist tales 'highlight the episodic, complex and ambivalent realities that are frozen and perhaps made too pat by realist or confessional conventions'. Their accounts are 'as hesitant and open to contingency and interpretation as the concrete experiences on which they are based' (Van Maanen 1988: 119).

This book presents mainly a confessional and impressionist narrative and I am present throughout. The worlds I present are complex, episodic, ambivalent, and contingent. I had to decide the extent to which I should be present in the story. Normally, I seek refuge in the language of the social science and avoid talking in the first person. The first challenge was to write an account with narrative drive in both everyday English and the language of those being watched. The second challenge was to incorporate the narrator as an observer. I am present throughout the text and the reader is continuously made aware of both the involvement and detachment of the researcher that lies at the heart of observation. That admitted, I insist that every scholarly attempt to make sense of politics in all its many shapes and forms involves a blend of personal involvement and scholarly detachment.

Finally, as White (1973: 7) argues, the meaning of my stories will depend on the way I tell my story:

> Providing the 'meaning' of a story by identifying the *kind of story* that has been told is called explanation by emplotment.... I identify at least four different modes of emplotment: Romance, Tragedy, Comedy, and Satire.

So, the choice of language, whether romance, tragedy, comedy, or satire, emplots different explanations in the text. My story encompasses comedy and tragedy. It is a comedy in that the desire of ministers to make a difference holds out the prospect of 'the temporary triumph of man over his world by the prospect of the occasional *reconciliations* of the forces at play'. So, 'the condition of society is represented as being purer, saner and healthier' because 'seemingly inalterably opposing elements' can be reconciled. In Tragedy there are terrible, inalterable, eternal divisions. Reconciliations are sombre; we are resigned to the conditions under which we labour, limiting what we can aspire to (White 1973: 9). Such is the story of the minister and permanent secretaries; oscillating between comedy and tragedy.

I adopt several storytelling devices: chronology, scenes, asides, and dialogue. In Chapters 4 and 5, I tell mainly chronological stories. In Chapters 6–8, I rely more on scenes, or story segments, that I use as building blocks to develop specific themes. Throughout, I use dialogue, or reciprocal conversations, sometimes in the form of semi-structured, transcribed interviews but also, during the observational fieldwork, they were part of everyday conversations at the office. The stories, scenes, and dialogue took place mainly in the offices of the public servants. I wrote them mainly from the viewpoint of, and sometimes in the words of, their inhabitants. On occasions, I use long extracts from the transcribed interviews so the reader can 'hear' the voice of the interviewee, not just my voice. Stories cover days and weeks. Scenes cover moments in time; there is no unfolding storyline or character development as in the chronological stories. I present dialogue from the interviews in italics. Observed practices from the fieldwork notebooks (FWNB) are in roman font. Quotes from the FWNB are in inverted commas. To show that my stories are plausible, and to guard against the criticism that I have picked only juicy quotes from interviews and fieldwork notebooks, I cite other insider accounts whenever possible. Most of these citations are in the endnotes and are illustrative, not comprehensive. Other quotations are attributed in the usual way. I follow my own advice and compare observed practice (from FWNB), talk (from interviews and conversations), and considered writing (from autobiographies, memoirs, diaries, speeches, and lectures). Also, readers always know my sources.

I also triangulate my three sources of information—'the pattern of practice, talk, and considered writing'—to increase confidence in my stories. As Sanjek (2000: 281) argues, observation is an essential complement to interviews. Finally, I provide multiple quotes to demonstrate a point. Such detail is endemic in observational fieldwork; it is a defining characteristic of 'thick descriptions'.

I am well aware of the limits of ethnography. The most important limitation to the analysis in this project concerns my role as non-participant observer. I report the interviews as if I am neutral and as if the data are given to me in a pure or unmediated form. I am not that naive. All observers construct their material drawing on their prior theories. I accept that the several stories are *my* construction of how my interviewees see their world and that it is crucial to locate people's beliefs and practices against a background of traditions.

Also, how do we keep our distance from the people who are under observation? You see a lot of each other and you get to like each other. I admit to warm admiration for all three permanent secretaries. But it is just as likely you will come to dislike the people you observe. Some politicians made that all too easy. Either way, academic detachment can be compromised. It is a tricky balancing act to remain both distant and to keep their confidence; to keep critical detachment and empathize and not go native. That said, the ersatz native eventually withdraws from the field and a reflexive stance to one's work should enable the researcher to become a 'professional stranger' (Agar 1996).[14]

A third question is how to manage the control that government elites can exercise over the research. They can restrict, even deny, access at will. They can delay, even prevent, publication. They can refuse permission to attribute quotations from interviews. What will they allow? What will we settle for? The problems should not be overstated. Almost everyone was willing to speak on tape. At the end of most long interviews, the elite were relaxed, willing to chat about anything, historical or present-day. Many have a need to talk. As Rawnsley (2001: xi) observes 'they have to tell an outsider because they are so worried about whether it makes sense or, indeed, whether they make sense'. For most of the research, most of the time, there was no issue. I report the few issues that arose in Chapter 10 as part of the elites' reflections on my work. The brute fact is, of course, that when problems arise, they win.[15]

Finally, how do we know that our research is objective? How do we interpret our interpretations of elites? How do we know are findings are reliable and valid? How do we know the few days we spend observing and interviewing our subjects are typical days? How do we make sure the observed behaviours remain natural? Our presence as researchers influences the behaviour and reasoning of our subjects, consciously or unconsciously, and provides us with a potentially flawed picture of their actions and thinking. Subjects may engage in impression management for the researcher rather than going about their usual business. Such issues arise for many varieties of social science research. The differences are ones of degree, no more. Anthropologists have argued over these issues for decades, and developed intelligent and widely accepted ways of dealing with them.

I see no point in trying to pretend the ethnographic approach and its distinctive research methods is just a 'soft' version of the positivist approach with its penchant for 'hard' quantitative data. They are simply different in both the aims and knowledge criteria they employ. In his defence of case studies, Flyvbjerg (2006: 224) argues 'concrete, context-dependent knowledge is . . . more valuable than the vain search for predictive theories and universals'. He argues for the primacy of 'thick descriptions'. So does this book. 'Thick descriptions' produce data that are as valid as that of any social survey. Neither method is any better than the research question it seeks to answer.

I also see little virtue in abstract arguments about method. Grounding in fieldwork, and not in abstract argument, is the best way to assess methods. As Wright Mills (1970: 136) suggested, we should pay 'serious attention . . . to general discussions of methodology only when they are in direct reference to actual work'. I incline to Fox's (2004: 4) practical and pragmatic assessment:

> While participant observation has its limitations, this rather uneasy combination of involvement and detachment is still the best method we have for exploring the complexities of human cultures, so it will have to do.

In short, what works is best, so I became a *bricoleur*—less a handyman and more a jack of all trades—gathering material when, where, and how I could (Levi-Strauss 1966: 16–17).

Finally, I adopt an intersubjective agreement approach to assessing research findings.[16] In other words, objective knowledge arises from the comparison of rival stories. The political science community's continuing debates define and redefine the criteria by which we judge the knowledge claims of individual members of that community. It is not self-referential because the knowledge claims can be 'reconfirmed' by encounters with practitioners and users. So, I translate abstract concepts into conversations in fieldwork. These encounters and their conversations produce data which I interpret to produce narratives which are then judged by evolving knowledge criteria of the political science community. Reconfirmation occurs at three points.

- When I translate my concepts for fieldwork: that is, are they meaningful to practitioners and users and if not, why not?
- When I reconstruct narratives from the conversations: that is, is the story logical and consistent with the data?
- When I redefine and translate my concepts because of the academic community's judgement on the narratives.

Reconfirmation is an iterative process. We translate our concepts into conversations in fieldwork, and these conversations produce data that we interpret to produce narratives that are then judged by the evolving knowledge criteria of our academic community (see also Giddens 1993: 170).

Bevir (1999: ch. 3) identifies the criteria for judging any narrative, referred to as the rules of intellectual honesty. They include a willingness to take criticism seriously; a preference for established standards of evidence and reason; and a preference for speculative theories that suggest exciting new predictions. So, because we respect established standards of evidence and reason, we prefer webs of interpretation that are accurate, comprehensive, and consistent. Objectivity is, therefore, a product of 'local reasoning' in that it arises from the critical comparison of narratives within an academic community, reconfirmed in debate between communities, where all debates are subject to the provisional rules of intellectual honesty.

I try to put this approach to objectivity into practice. The draft manuscript was sent to all the major figures in the study for comment, and I have cited their advice and criticisms both in the text and in Chapter 10. I also presented the findings at various workshops and conferences and I benefited from the advice and criticisms of my academic colleagues. Finally, in Chapter 10, I discuss what we know from being there and focusing on everyday practices. I identify my key findings and describe how my account differs from the conventional narratives of British government with their focus on constitutional norms, institutions, and managerialism. I seek to highlight how my observations alter our view of British government. This narrative can then be critically compared to others.

SUMMARY

Before I tell my stories, I must describe their setting. That is the task of Part I. Chapter 2 provides a short survey of British government and its key domestic policies and politics between 2001 and 2005, the parliament during which I undertook the fieldwork. The Labour government's second term was a turbulent affair scarred, for example, by the Iraq war. I sketch the main events of the period as the backcloth against which my actors played their parts. My focus is domestic politics, and foreign affairs only intrude as they affect domestic politics. My aim is to contrast the excitement of high politics as presented in the newspapers and on television (see, for example: Rawnsley 2001 and 2010) with the low politics of everyday life in the government departments. I also introduce three narratives that will recur. The Westminster or constitutional story stresses that British government is hierarchical with a strong executive. The public management story focuses on the managerial, market, and delivery reforms of the past two decades. The governance story looks at the horizontal and vertical networks in which the core executive and the departments are embedded.

Chapter 3 describes the ministers' setting. I studied three ministries: the Department of Trade and Industry (DTI), the Department for Education and Skills (DfES), and the Department for Environment, Food and Rural Affairs (DEFRA). All three are middle-ranking ministries. I provide short portraits of each, describing: where people work, who holds the key positions, and what they do. I provide a brief account of the buildings in which the events take place with an outline of the internal organization of each ministry. I describe the roles of ministers and permanent secretaries. I describe what departments do by describing their traditions (or departmental philosophies) and their present-day policy agendas. Finally, running through these portraits is an analysis of the dilemmas that confront the departments; between Westminster roles and relationships and managerialism; between constitutional bureaucracy and political responsiveness; and the unintended consequences of neo-liberal policy agendas and metagovernance.

In Part II, I describe the everyday life of the main actors; the ministers and the permanent secretaries. Chapter 4 provides portraits of secretaries of state and ministers of state at work. My account is based on an analysis of their engagement diaries, repeat interviews with ministers, and a qualitative analysis of their work drawn from my fieldwork notebooks. In this chapter, as in all others, when I write 'I will describe' or an equivalent phrase, it means that I provide an account 'in the words of the main actors'. I seek to present their world as they see it. I describe their everyday working life inside and outside the department.

Chapter 5 provides a portrait of the permanent secretaries and describes their working day. Again my account is based on an analysis of the diary, repeat interviews with permanent secretaries, and a qualitative analysis of their work drawn from my fieldwork notebooks.

Part III introduces the notion of the 'departmental court' and explores scenes of comedy and tragedy. The everyday practices of departments, their protocols, rituals, languages, and their links with the rest of Westminster and Whitehall are the stuff of jokes much loved by *Yes Minister*. It has its amusing side, but the purposes of their protocols and rituals were all too serious. They routinized, even domesticated, everyday life. When they could not cope with a crisis, a political tragedy took place and the minister resigned. The stories move from comedy to tragedy.

Chapter 6 looks at the central secretariat or the departmental core executive, which I describe as the 'departmental court'. All ministers and permanent secretaries are supported by a court. For ministers, it comprises the Private Office, ministerial advisers and the press office, and junior ministers. For permanent secretaries, it comprises the Private Office, senior management team, and director generals (or equivalent). I describe the roles, responsibilities, and relationships of the court inside the department. I describe the work of the principal private secretary (PPS), the private secretaries (PS), and four aspects of the everyday life of the departmental court: recruitment and training, internal management, office tensions, and internal networking.

Chapter 7 focuses on the practices of the departmental court; its protocols, rituals, and languages that make up the willed ordinariness of everyday life. Administrative protocols are the sedimented or codified practices of civil servants because they are written down. I describe the protocols around: the diary; the red box; telephone; correspondence and filing; travel and hospitality (including drivers); meetings, committees, and briefings; submissions and policy advice; and speeches. Rituals are habitual practices that are not written down. I describe the rituals of politeness, gossip, and humour. Finally, I distinguish between, and discuss, the traditional or classical Whitehall language, and managerialism.

The traditional Westminster story about British government and the challenge from managerial, market, and delivery reforms of the past two decades dominate the book to this point. In Chapter 8, I turn to the governance story; to the horizontal and vertical networks that criss-cross Westminster, Whitehall, and beyond. Every department is part of a web of links encompassing: the central agencies (Number 10 Downing Street (hereafter No. 10), the Cabinet Office, and the Treasury); other functional departments; parliament and the political parties; and broader links beyond Westminster and Whitehall. Moreover, the several actors know they are part of a web and deliberately build links, play games, and otherwise manage their networks. This chapter also tells the departments' stories about 'outsiders', not the outsiders' stories of the minister and the department.

Chapter 9 turns to tragedy, in particular Estelle Morris' resignation at the Department for Education and Skills. I describe how the Department strove to domesticate a rude surprise. I look at the incidence and effects of stress on ministers and permanent secretaries, and at their reasons for doing the job. Finally I reflect on how storytelling, a siege mentality, performing, and the media shaped the ways in which the Department coped with this 'rude surprise'.

Finally, in Chapter 10, I summarize the beliefs, practices, traditions, and dilemmas that make up everyday life at the top using the Westminster, public management, and governance stories. There was no shared story of how British government worked. Yesterday's story remained an important guide to today's practice. So, the managerial story (in its various forms) and the governance stories have been grafted on to the Westminster narrative with all the attendant dilemmas. I argue that my account of how willed ordinariness and storytelling domesticate life in the goldfish bowl provides a distinct and distinctive account of British government. Second, I discuss the advantages of political anthropology, of 'being there', for studying British government. Third, I report the comments of the ministers and permanent secretaries on my research. Finally, I reflect on the ways in which inherited traditions as myths continue to shape British government, and on the world we are losing.

In sum, this book aims to understand the ways in which the political and administrative elites of central government departments make sense of their worlds; to provide 'thick descriptions', or my constructions of their constructions of what they are up to, through an analysis of their beliefs and everyday practices; and to show that observation is not an optional but an essential part of any toolkit for studying British government.

NOTES

1. I describe briefly the ideas I need to organize my stories, no more. I do not pretend to offer an account of the interpretive approach. I have done so elsewhere at length with my friend and colleague Mark Bevir. Those readers interested in theory should look at Bevir and Rhodes 2003, 2006, and 2010; and the debate with our critics in *British Journal of Politics and International Relation* 6 (2) 2004: 129–64; *Political Studies Review* 6 (2) 2008: 143–77; Bevir and Rhodes 2008 and Marsh 2008*a* and *b*; and the special issue of *Public Administration* 89 (1) 2011.
2. Local here means 'local to a web of beliefs', not necessarily 'local to a geographical area'. See Bevir and Rhodes 2010, ch. 4.
3. I use stories and tales as synonyms for narratives both for stylistic reasons—the everyday phrase is storytelling—and because members of the Whitehall village talk about 'getting their story straight'. I am not trivializing the notion of narratives or the activity of storytelling, which I consider, along with game playing, integral to all human social behaviour (see Huizinga 1955).
4. There is a massive literature on narratives. Alvermann 2000 provides a short introduction. I found the following helpful: Barthes 1993; Bevir 1999: 252–62 and 298–306; 2000, and 2006; Ricoeur 1981, ch. 11, and 1991, ch. 6; and White 1987.
5. As with theory, I describe my methods so readers know how I collected the data for my stories. For a detailed discussion of observation and its limits see Rhodes 2002, 2005 and Rhodes, 't Hart, and Noordegraaf 2007, chs 1 and 9. For general surveys of qualitative methods, see: Denzin and Lincoln 2005; and Hammersley and Atkinson 2007.
6. Even in the study of British government, there are honourable exceptions; see, for example, Burns 1977; Dargie 1998; Faucher-King 2005; Hall et al. 2000; and Heclo and Wildavsky 1974. Also my comment applies to political science only. Observation is an increasingly common tool in organization studies. For a brief overview see Czarniawska 1998; and for public sector examples, see: Maynard-Moody and Musheno 2003; Mintzberg and Bourgault 2000; and Noordegraaf 2000.
7. The parallel in fiction is with the story told from the vantage point of its several participants as in Lawrence Durrell, *The Alexandria Quartet* (1957–60), William Faulkner, *The Sound and the Fury* (1929), and Mario Vargas Llosa, *The Real Life of Alejandro Mayta* (1986).
8. This section is paraphrased from Geertz 1973: ch. 1. The quotes are from pages 9, 20, 26, and 28–9.

9. When I refer to a specific Minister, Permanent Secretary, or Department, I capitalize the first letter. When I am talking generally about ministers, permanent secretaries, and departments, I use lower case. I also follow everyday language conventions and refer to the Secretary of State as Minister, unless clarity requires the full form of address.

10. On observation see: Adler and Adler 1987; Fenno 1990; Geertz 1973 and 1983; Hammersley and Atkinson 1983; Punch 1986; Sanjek 1990; and Van Maanen 1988.

11. In earlier articles reporting the fieldwork, I gave the date of the interview or of the fieldwork observation. I have not done so here simply because there were too many dates. They littered the text and made it more difficult to read.

12. For the period 2001–5, Michael Barber 2007, Alastair Campbell 2007, and David Blunkett 2006 were especially useful, while Tony Blair 2010*a*; Cherie Blair 2008, Lord Michael Levy 2008, and John Prescott 2008 were less so. Some historians and journalists should also be included in this list because of their impeccable off-the-record sources. Anthony Seldon's (2004 and 2007) two-volume biography of Blair has a staggering array of insider interviews. Peter Hennessy (various), Andrew Rawnsley 2001 and 2010, and Robert Peston 2005 are not far behind; the latter had the best access to Brown and his court. Less consistently useful contributions were: Beckett and Hencke 2004, and Pollard 2005. Other memoirs, diaries, biographies, and autobiographies were of episodic use and are listed in the bibliography.

13. Although we usually say 'Chatham House Rules' (plural), in fact there is only one rule: 'When a meeting, or part thereof, is held under the Chatham House Rule, participants are free to use the information received, but neither the identity nor the affiliation of the speaker(s), nor that of any other participant, may be revealed'. See: http://www.chathamhouse.org.uk/about/chathamhouserule/ (accessed 9 November 2010).

14. I have much sympathy with Watson's (1986) prayer, 'make me reflexive—but not yet'. I sought to remain a 'professional stranger', so I had to strive for both detachment and critical self-awareness.

15. These issues are a matter of longstanding debate; see Punch 1986; and Mitchell 1993.

16. For a detailed defence see: Bevir 1994; 1999: ch. 3; and Rhodes 1997*a*: ch. 9.

Part I

The Setting

2

The Governmental Setting

Government departments are part of a web. At the centre of the web are No. 10 and the Treasury. The departments with their departmental courts and policy agendas are the inner ring. The next ring is Westminster or domestic politics, especially parliament and the media. Finally, the web is suspended in world events. Of course, life is nowhere near this neat and tidy but the metaphor helps define the scope of this chapter. I describe the outer rings of domestic and world politics. I am not providing a history of the Blair government but selectively describing the events that exercised a major influence on the departments between 2001 and 2005. I am looking at the world through the eyes of the three departments, not the prime minister. Clearly the Iraq war was the major event of Blair's second term but I do not provide an account of, or commentary on, the UK's involvement. It is important here only when it distracts the Prime Minister from his domestic policy agenda or when it changes the policy agendas of the domestic departments. So, I move from an account of the government's domestic policy agenda to the diversions of domestic politics, covering world events only as they impact on domestic politics and policy.

The events I describe took place during the second parliamentary term of the UK's Labour government, which began on 8 June 2001 and ended in May 2005. The Prime Minister and head of the government is Tony Blair and his official residence and office is No. 10, Downing Street. The Prime Minister appoints all ministers: Secretaries of State who are in the cabinet, Ministers of State who are not, and makes the junior appointments of Parliamentary Under-Secretary of State and Parliamentary Private Secretaries. Most are from the majority party in the elected House of Commons. Some junior ministers come from the non-elected House of Lords. The rules about ministerial conduct and about ministers' duties and responsibilities to, for example, parliament, are set down in the *Ministerial Code*.[1] The cabinet is the fulcrum committee of British government, although its role and importance varies with the whims and wishes of each prime minister. The other key coordinating central bodies are the Treasury, which holds sway on all matters financial, and the Cabinet Office, which is home to a ragbag of central functions, unkindly referred to as the rest home for the pet projects of past prime ministers. No. 10 and its various units, cabinet, the Treasury, and the Cabinet Office are the heart of the British government machine; its core executive coordinating policy and resources and managing conflict.

THE DOMESTIC POLICY AGENDA

Odd though it may sound, 'it was only at the beginning of the second term that he really identified what it was he wanted to do' (Blair aide cited in Seldon 2007: 42). Blair mused, 'There is an irony that everyone said we hit the ground running in 1997' but that was not so because 'the real work, that's only beginning now' (cited in Hyman 2005: 175–7). No. 10 knew the second term would be tough not only because they were taking on doctors, teachers, police, and judges but also because they would be accused of 'destroying the public service ethos', although the aim was to modernize it (Campbell 2007: 522). The new, overarching theme was 'delivery'. The core aim was to improve public service delivery, especially in crime, education, health, and transport. But this aim was clearer in 2005 than in 2001. The work of the departments continued against a backcloth of an unfolding delivery agenda.

My construction of ministers' and civil servants' constructions of their world revolves around three commonly told stories. The Westminster or centralization story claims the changes sought to centralize power in the Prime Minister at the expense of cabinet and the departments. The public management story claims the delivery agenda foundered on Blair's lack of policy making and management skills. The network governance story argues the Prime Minister locked into webs of dependence that undermined his initiatives.

The danger in any account of these three narratives is that it will read as if they have essentialist characteristics. But there is no list of general features or essential properties that characterize them in every instance. Rather, there are diverse practices of multiple individuals acting on changing webs of beliefs rooted in overlapping traditions. Westminster, managerialism, and network governance arise as the contingent products of diverse actions and political struggles informed by the beliefs of agents as they arise against a backcloth of traditions. It is futile to search for the essential features of an abstract category that denotes a cluster of human practices. We can only define them as a series of family resemblances, none of which need always be present. Wittgenstein (1972) famously suggested that general concepts such as 'game' should be defined by various traits that overlap and criss-cross in much the same way as do the resemblances between members of a family—their builds, eye colour, gait, personalities. He considered various examples of games to challenge the idea that they all possessed a given property or set of properties—skill, enjoyment, victory, and defeat—by which we could define the concept. Instead, he suggested the examples exhibited a network of similarities, at various levels of detail, so they coalesced even though no one feature was common to them all. So, each of the following general accounts of Westminster, managerialism, and network governance should be understood as a set of family resemblances.

The Westminster story

The Westminster narrative is the classical constitutional view of British government. Its core tenet is a belief in centralization or hierarchy, with its roots in the royal prerogative and the monarchical origins of British government. Birch (1964: 244–5) argues this tradition of 'a strong leader' willing to make 'unwelcome decisions' determines the nature of political responsibility in the British constitution.

The belief in strong government unpacks into several specific beliefs about the British constitution: strong cabinet government, ministerial responsibility, a constitutional bureaucracy based on a neutral civil service, and parliamentary sovereignty.[2] Perhaps the most famous debate surrounds the claim that the prime minister has grown more powerful at the expense of the cabinet. The debate recurred under New Labour in the guise of the presidentialization thesis.[3]

I doubt anyone would dispute that centralization was part of the socialist tradition or that it was on New Labour's agenda before they came to power. For example, Peter Mandelson and Roger Liddle (1996: 240) argued there was a need 'for a more formalised strengthening of the centre of government' that 'provides the means of formulating and driving forward strategy for the government as a whole'. Journalists, academics, and insiders also agreed that Blair sought to centralize power in No. 10 (see Bevir and Rhodes 2006). Structural changes to both the Prime Minister's Office and the Cabinet Office were the main ways in which Blair sought to centralize policy making. These included an increase in special advisers (SpAds), a strengthening of the Prime Minister's Office's role in policy making and the emergence of 'a Prime Minister's department that would not speak-its-name' (Hennessy 2000a: 388).

Special advisers (SpAds)

In March 2003, there were 27 SpAds in No 10. The most senior was the Chief of Staff, Jonathan Powell. He had line management powers over civil servants and, while the post was not new, the role that Powell played as Head of the Prime Minister's Office was unprecedented in scope. The Prime Minister also appointed unpaid advisers who reported directly to him. The most notable example was John Birt. He was the Prime Minister's part-time strategy adviser, located in No. 10. Special advisers were also appointed by secretaries of state, who were normally restricted to two. In March 2003, there were 54 special advisers in departments. There was a cross-Whitehall network of SpAds. I will describe their role in Part 2 so it will suffice to note that individual No. 10 advisers played a prominent role in departmental policy deliberations. For example, Andrew Adonis of the Prime Minister's Policy Directorate often intervened to influence education policy making, although some insiders opined acidly that 'if anyone knew Andrew was behind a policy, it immediately made people suspicious' (Seldon 2004: 642).

Strengthening policy making

In 2001, the Prime Minister's Private Office was merged with the Policy Unit to form a new Policy Directorate. Its key functions were day-to-day liaison with Whitehall departments and writing briefs and speeches for the Prime Minister. It was also involved in developing short-term policy in the Prime Minister's priority areas.

The Cabinet Office was always a ragbag of functions. Blair added to the ragbag, although he broke with tradition in the number of units created and the speed of change. Most of these units changed their name to reflect changed priorities or responsibilities and many were transferred out of the Cabinet Office to other departments. For example, the Social Exclusion Unit started life in the Cabinet Office at the beginning of December 1997, transferred to the Office of the Deputy Prime Minister at the end of May 2002, only to return to the Cabinet Office in June 2006, with a revised name and remit. These changes show Blair seeking to control government functions without bothering himself with too many of the operational details. As Peter Hennessy (1998: 15) noted, 'Number 10 is omnipresent'.

The second wave of initiatives sought to develop strategic policy for the Prime Minister. Initially, Blair set up the Performance and Innovation Unit (PIU) (and the Prime Minister's Forward Strategy Unit (PMFSU)). In June 2001, they were merged to form the Prime Minister's Strategy Unit (PMSU). It had three roles: strategic reviews and policy advice on the Prime Minister's domestic policy priorities; helping departments develop effective strategies and policies; and identifying and disseminating thinking on emerging issues and challenges. It worked in project teams organized around five clusters: public service reform, home affairs, economy and infrastructure, welfare reform, and social justice and communities. At its peak, there were no more than 90 people working in the Unit and by mid-May 2005 it contained some 55 people. The workforce was drawn from the civil service, the private or voluntary sectors, and the wider public sector.

It is difficult to assess the impact of the PMSU. It had a growing role. It was responsible for developing reform of the public services. By the prevailing standards for such units, its position was secure (Public Administration Select Committee (PASC) 2007). However, it is hard to judge its effectiveness because it was not the only strategic unit in the core executive undertaking such work. The Treasury always played an important role (see below).

Supporting the cabinet

The Cabinet Office under Blair had the usual secretariats: economic and domestic, European, defence and overseas, and intelligence. There has been a tendency for commentators to focus on the glamorous strategy units and ignore the long-standing, even dull, work of the Cabinet Office. That is a mistake. Contrary to assertions about the 'death of cabinet', the Cabinet Office Secretariat continued to perform its traditional coordinating role. Of course, it was subject to the same pressures for change. For obvious reasons, after 9/11, there was a major expansion of the Cabinet Office's work in both intelligence and security, and emergency planning. In July 2001 the Cabinet Office merged its existing emergency planning units with those from the Home Office. The new post of Permanent Secretary, Intelligence, Security and Resilience, was created as a link between these two areas of work.

It is hard to escape the conclusion that here was a government intent on centralizing policy making. The aim of No. 10 and the Cabinet Office, as a Prime Minister's Department in all but name, was to allow Blair to remain on top, if not in detailed touch. However, it became abundantly clear the Prime Minister 'never [really] succeeded in finding a structure that suited him' (Seldon 2004: 694). So, the various reforms made 'the centre more powerful but not necessarily more effective across government' (cited in Campbell 2007: 606).

The managerial story

The managerial narrative, also referred to as the new public management, is a set of inherited beliefs about how private sector management techniques would increase the economy, efficiency, and effectiveness—the 3Es—of the public sector. Initially the beliefs focused on managerialism or hands-on, professional management; explicit standards and measures of performance; managing by results; and value for money.[4] Subsequently, it also embraced marketization or neo-liberal beliefs about competition and markets. It introduced ideas about restructuring the incentive structures of public service provision through contracting-out, quasi-markets, and consumer choice. The civil service was to shrink because it had shed responsibilities to the private sector and its function was now to negotiate and manage contracts (Davis and Rhodes 2000; Rhodes 1997*a*: 48–9). Margaret Thatcher introduced both these managerial and neo-liberal ideas and both were adopted by New Labour, with a twist. New Labour had a distinct and distinctive response to the dilemmas posed by neo-liberal reforms. It introduced a third strand to managerialism, focused on service delivery, consumer choice, and joined-up government. The earlier stands of managerialism had their roots in management theory and neoclassical economics. This strand drew on different types of social science, mainly new institutionalism and communitarianism (Bevir 2005: chs 2 and 3). The Prime Minister was both blunt and clear: 'the world has changed and the civil service must change with it' (Blair 2004*a*).

So, between 2001 and 2005, the key development was the evolution of managerialism into the 'delivery agenda'. It sprang from frustration. Blair spoke of the 'scars on my back' left by trying to change the public sector and his conviction that such reform was 'the core of what the government is about' in improving public services (cited in Richards and Smith 2004: 107). The government presented the shift to choice and diversity as a naturally evolving process, and it led to further reform at No. 10.[5] Two new units were created in the Cabinet Office—the Office for Public Service Reform (OPSR) and the Prime Minister's Delivery Unit (PMDU).

The OPSR developed and promulgated the 'philosophy' of the delivery agenda. It also advised the Prime Minister on the ways of implementing reform in the public services and the civil service. It covered all public services including local government. It was at the heart of the delivery agenda. Nevertheless, the lack of a white paper underpinning the delivery agenda means that its development has to be tracked through a series of policy papers, speeches, and statements (OPSR 2002). So, the principles of the delivery agenda were not always clear, mainly because they evolved over time. Even at the start, the Cabinet Office website was less than specific in announcing the end of the Modernising Government programme and the arrival of the delivery agenda:

> Thus delivery of better, modern public service is the Government's *key* priority for its second term. This is not easy; one commentator has said, 'There is no drama in delivery . . . only a long, grinding haul punctuated by public frustration with the pace of change.' Failure will not be tolerated, nor will mediocrity. (Cabinet Office 2002, emphasis in original)

The clearest statements of the principles underpinning the early phase of the delivery agenda can be found in two separate documents. The first document, *Reforming Our Public Services: Principles into Practice* outlined the 'Prime Minister's four principles of public sector reform': national standards to ensure that people have the right to high-quality services wherever they live;

devolution to give local leaders the means to deliver these standards to local people; more flexibility in service provision to meet people's rising expectations; and greater customer choice (OPSR 2002: 3). The second document, *Putting People at the Heart of Public Services* (OPSR 2005) contained much of the same rhetoric. In July 2004, each of the main delivery departments also published their own five-year strategies, which sought to identify how the Prime Minister's principles of public sector reform could be incorporated into the front-line delivery of services. Alas, the reform was beset with the usual problems. As Jill Rutter, Head of the Strategy and Sustainability Directorate at the Department for Environment Food and Rural Affairs commented, one of the main shortcomings of the five-year strategies was the persistent problem of a 'lack of integration' (PASC 2007: Q. 444).

The general principles informing the delivery agenda were outlined by Michael Barber, the Prime Minister's former Chief Adviser on Delivery in his comments about education:

> Between 2001 and 2005 what Blair increasingly hankered after was a way of improving the education system that didn't need to be constantly driven by government. He wanted to develop self-sustaining, self-improving systems, and that led him to look into how to change not just the standards and the quality of teaching, but the structures and incentives. Essentially it's about creating different forms of a quasi-market in public services, exploiting the power of choice, competition, transparency and incentives, and that's really where the education debate is going now.... At the political level Blair really understands this challenge, but it is highly controversial—within the Labour Party and nationally. (Interview with Michael Barber, 13 January 2006; see also Barber 2007: ch. 3)

And in February 2004, the Prime Minister outlined what delivery meant for him:

> The principal challenge is to shift focus from policy advice to delivery. Delivery means outcomes. It means project management. It means adapting to new situations and altering rules and practice accordingly. (Blair 2004*a*)

The delivery agenda received its fullest elaboration in 2006 as the 'self-improving' model of reform. It had four components: top-down performance management; greater competition and contestability in providing public services; greater pressure from citizens through choice and voice; and improved management capability and capacity by civil servants (see PMSU 2006: chs 4 and 7; PASC 2005).

For the departments, the core element of the delivery agenda was performance management, especially targets (Barber 2007: 73 and 79–101). For service deliverers and middle-level managers, the focus was on delivering against performance targets. As the Prime Minister's policy review stated: 'to drive up standards, and to tackle inequalities, the immediate focus was on stronger top-down performance management' (PMSU 2007: 23). The Prime Minister's primary institutional mechanism for doing this was the PMDU. It began life tracking how well departments were performing against their Public Service Agreement (PSA) targets in 'key delivery areas' (see below pp. 31–2). These key areas included health (waiting times for in-patient treatment and accident and emergency), education (levels of secondary school performance, including GCSE results), transport (cutting train delays) and criminal justice (including street crime and the flow of illegal asylum-seekers). It ran the regular prime ministerial stocktakes, provided progress reports to the Prime Minister on each of the priority areas, and intervened if it felt departments might fail to deliver. Over time, the Unit's remit extended to cover all PSAs, although it continued to focus on the Prime Minister's top priorities. The Cabinet Secretary also gave it oversight of the Capability Review programme, which assessed the capacity of departments to deliver their objectives (see below). The problem in assessing the PMDU is that it was only one of several mechanisms used by the core executive to track progress against PSAs. Barber (2007: 287) concluded 'the Delivery Unit had a substantial impact... in spite of the incoherence and weakness of the Cabinet Office of which it was a part'. Seldon (2007: 304–5) agrees there was 'real progress' but notes the time lags in improvements, the unevenness across the country, and the hostility of the public service unions (see also Blair 2010a: 338–9 and 503; Richards and Smith 2006). We will see what impact it had on the Department for Education and Skills later.

Running alongside the delivery agendas was an ever-present desire to improve public sector management. All Blair's cabinet secretaries entered office with new ideas on the best way to reform the civil service. The Prime Minister delivered several speeches on the subject (see, for example: Blair 2004a; Turnbull 2005; Wilson 2003). So, civil service reform was always been high on the agenda and there was a general concern to improve leadership and professional skills.

Throughout, many civil servants and policy advisers saw the problem as a Prime Minister who had no clear idea of how to bring about that improvement. Blair made it clear that leadership was central to public service delivery and, where successful leadership could not be found in the public sector, then government would look to the private or voluntary sectors irrespective of the policy area in question. There was also a general belief that the private sector performed better than the public sector, but there was no clear direction that successive cabinet secretaries could follow.

The result was a constant stream of individual reform initiatives clustered around five themes: leadership; skills training and employee secondments; individual performance management and reward; diversity; and better recruitment practices and career development. Few of the initiatives stood the test of time.

The plethora of reform initiatives was not always seen as significant in the departments (see Chapter 5). The pressures for a 'new professionalism'

(Wilson 2006) were relentless but its form was uncertain. It remained so throughout Blair's second term because of the 'central flaws' of prime ministerial 'inexperience', 'lack of clarity about both means and ends', and 'confusion about the role of central government' (Riddell 2001: 38–9; and 2005: 41). As Richard Wilson observed to Blair back in 1997, 'your problem is that neither you nor anyone in No. 10 has ever managed anything' (cited in Seldon 2004: 629). Baroness Jay of Paddington, former Labour Leader in the House of Lords, observed 'Blair wasn't the least interested in management. He had the "Blair garden look," where his eyes glazed over and he looked out at the No. 10 garden whenever the word "management" was used' (cited in Seldon 2007: 41). The same point was made at the end of the second term by Michael Barber (2007: 304–5) who argued that a 'major', 'self-imposed' constraint was that:

> he had never run a government department, or even been a junior minister. Neither did he have experience of running a major organisation outside government. . . . As a consequence, as Prime Minister he had a huge amount to learn about how organisations, especially large bureaucracies, work.

Barber (2007: 287) also wonders how much could have been achieved if 'the drive for delivery had been part of a coherent approach to transforming the performance and health of the civil service'. It was not to be. Blair's weaknesses included a lack of follow-through: 'He intervenes, persuades, and then forgets'. He lacks 'policy making and management skills' (Seldon 2004: 692). His 'style of management has not always maximised his influence' and he did not recognize that what he saw as the failings of others were 'a consequence of his own unique style of management' (Barber 2007: 305). His 'erratic management style' remained 'as impervious as ever to systematic planning' (Seldon 2007: 224). So, although he wants results 'he finds it hard to understand why things can't happen immediately' and he is frustrated when 'waiting for the pay-off and he doesn't have time' (Official cited in Hennessy 2000c: 10). Blair was dissatisfied with the performance of the civil service but he never knew what he wanted (Rawnsley 2010: 291–2). He was a Prime Minister aware of his government's limited achievements in domestic policy (Seldon 2007: 114) and searching for a toolkit for steering the heart of government.

The network governance story

The network governance story highlights ideas about policy networks, the hollowing out of the state, the segmented nature of the core executive, and the shift from government to network governance.[6] The idea of network governance is associated with the changing nature of the state following the neo-liberal public sector reforms of the 1980s. The reforms are said to have precipitated a shift from a hierarchic bureaucracy towards a greater use of markets, quasi-markets, in the delivery of public services. The effects of the reforms were intensified by global changes, including an increase in transnational economic activity and the rise of regional institutions such as the European Union. The resulting complexity and fragmentation are such that the state increasingly depends on networks of other organizations to secure its intentions and deliver its policies. This first wave of network governance evokes a world in which state power is dispersed among a vast array of spatially and functionally distinct networks comprising all the public, voluntary, and private organizations with which the centre now interacts (see Bevir and Rhodes 2010: ch. 5). It focuses on the ways in which the informal authority of networks supplements and supplants the formal authority of government.

These ideas have important implications for understanding the role of the executive. The phrase 'the core executive' always sought to broaden the notion of executive power beyond a narrow focus on prime minister and cabinet (Rhodes 1995). It stresses the interdependence of the *several* actors at the heart of government. The executive is no longer seen as a single decision centre focused on the prime minister but as the set of institutions that coordinate central government policies and act as final arbiters of conflicts between different elements of the government machine. These functions can be carried out by prime minister, cabinet, the Treasury, and the Cabinet Office. The executive is segmented and its core is embedded in horizontal and vertical networks of interdependence. As one actor among many, the executive cannot rely on hands-on control.

The second wave of governance was a response to the segmented centre's perceived control deficit. The state resorted to indirect or hands-off management. This distinction is commonly described as a shift from rowing to steering. Confronted by fragmented service delivery systems, the Blair reforms sought to impose the desired degree of coordination but central fragmentation confounded central intervention and coordination. The attempts to improve coordination are an example of metagovernance.

The two waves of governance were a response to the dilemmas confronting government actors. Neo-liberal ideas about marketization undermined existing departmental policy agendas and their underpinning philosophies. The resulting fragmentation begat network governance as governments sought to put together packages of organizations to deliver services. But multiplying networks and the ensuing central control deficits prompted a search for better coordination. Metagovernance was the response to this dilemma as central government sought to improve its capacity to steer.

Different parts of the core executive responded differently to this challenge. The Cabinet Office and No. 10 relied on soft levers, such as influence, support, and partnerships. The Treasury controlled with hard levers, most notably the power of the purse. It was, and will remain, a prominent actor in the core executive. The different responses were not just about levers. The centre was also riven by court politics, which undermined its search to steer.[7] Many newspapers thrived on the copy provided by the long-running disputes between the Prime Minister and his Chancellor of the Exchequer, Gordon Brown (see below). Importantly, these differences were also given an institutional expression. Court politics were entwined with institutional change, so there was both a second centre of coordination and a second wellspring of civil service reform.

As soon as he took up office, the Chancellor, Gordon Brown, made it clear that he wanted the Treasury to extend its reach far beyond its traditional Ministry of Finance role. He outlined what he expected his department to do in a speech to the Institute of Fiscal Studies:

> A Labour Treasury would need to be not just a Ministry of Finance, but also a Ministry working with other departments to deliver long-term economic and social renewal. (Brown 1999)

The department fleshed out these comments in a memorandum that it submitted to the Treasury Select Committee:

> With the macroeconomic framework now firmly established, more resources can be directed towards examining microeconomic issues. Evidence-based microeconomic and distributional analysis is essential to underpin the Treasury's output—from Budget tax measures through developments in competition policy and analysis of poverty issues to work on reform of the legal aid system and deciding transport priorities. (Treasury Select Committee 2000)

This theme became constant. As the former Treasury Permanent Secretary, Terry Burns, explained colloquially: 'macro-economic policy is very boring . . . so . . . we are getting very interested in social policy' (Treasury Select Committee 2001: para. 39).

The Brown chancellorship was notable for the reform of public expenditure control. He introduced both biennial Spending Reviews, which set expenditure limits for departments over the ensuing three years, and a new performance management framework of Public Service Agreements. These PSAs set targets for key areas in the departments. In theory, future funding hinges on meeting the targets. Performance against them is monitored by several parts of the core executive: the PMDU in the Cabinet Office; the spending teams based in the Public Services and Growth (PSG) directorate of the Treasury; the PSX Cabinet Committee; and separate departmental stocktakes involving the Prime Minister, the minister, the permanent secretary, and the Chief Secretary to the Treasury.

The PSAs were a tool providing the Treasury with a 'legitimate' reason for continued or extended intervention in departmental affairs. They also provided the Treasury with a reason to demand an unprecedented amount of data from departments. As a Senior Treasury official explained, the effect is that the Treasury 'plays a much more proactive and strategic role in the development of policy in Whitehall'. Of course, the Treasury would not be the Treasury without acerbic asides, so he added: 'This, of course, has had a positive impact on this enthusiasm for "joined-up" government.'[8] Given the increased spending on health and education, the Treasury saw this role as a natural extension of their powers and a necessary control on departments.

The Treasury was also heavily involved in public service reform through its efficiency programme. It was a different agenda to that of the PMSU but just as important. The efficiency programme can be traced through several reports commissioned by the Treasury. They included: the Gershon Review (2004), the Lyons Review (2004), and the Hampton Review (2005). The overall aim was to achieve the headline target contained in the Gershon Review of £21.5 billion of efficiency savings by 2007–8. Subsequent reports looked at particular ways of achieving that aim. More recent reports, starting with the Cabinet Office's (2005) *Transformational Government*, combined the efficiency drive with a renewed emphasis on joining-up front-line services. In the lexicon of management-speak there is little that is new.

Clearly the efficiency programme was a Treasury driven agenda. It wrote the reports. It chaired the two main cabinet committees (on Efficiency and Relocation and Electronic Service Delivery). The scope of the efficiency programme was broad, so it had important consequences for all the public sector. In short, the PMSU and the Treasury each ran their public sector reforms concurrently. They coexisted. They were not coordinated, nor could they be, because one agenda was driven by Blair and the other by Brown.

Finally, the Brown chancellorship also played a strategic policy role with its internal reviews focusing on cross-cutting issues of government policy, reporting to the Chief Secretary to the Treasury, but sometimes published in partnership with another department. There were typically six or seven reviews for each Spending Review. Eight policy areas were the subject of multiple reviews. They accounted for 37 of the 42 policy reviews, including: seven reviews on young children and older people; six reviews each on crime (including drugs), and the voluntary sector.

In sum, the Treasury sponsored much strategic work that would normally have been produced by a central strategic unit in the Cabinet Office. The Chancellor or the Chief Secretary to the Treasury, rather than the Prime Minister or cabinet, were directly associated with these reviews. The Treasury and not the Cabinet Office provided the secretariat support for these reviews. As the former Cabinet Secretary Andrew Turnbull (2007) explained, the consequence was that the Treasury became a policy department:

> The reviews have varied a lot in quality. Some are actually quite good. But a lot of them are HMV—His Master's Voice—and are really written to order. The

Wanless report on health spending was a good example of that. And that has changed the relationship between the Treasury and colleagues, and changed the way the Treasury works, making it a policy department.

As one member of the Prime Minister's Strategy Unit put it, 'Gordon does have a strategy unit, it is called the Treasury'. These changes were as much about the court politics of Blair and Brown as they were about public sector reform. In an unguarded moment, Andrew Turnbull (2007) commented on Gordon Brown's 'Stalinist ruthlessness' and 'the more or less complete contempt' with which the Treasury treated ministerial colleagues. Treasury control had come: 'at the expense of any government cohesion and any assessment of strategy'. No matter how commentators interpret either the court politics of the two rivals or Brown's Treasury reforms, it is clear the Treasury's redefinition of its role altered the way central government worked. Central coordination was undermined by competing centres of policy making. It caused 'dilemmas and sometimes downright confusion' in the departments because ministers and officials had 'to pick their way across a minefield'.[9]

No. 10 and the Cabinet Office compounded the problem. Geoff Mulgan's[10] assessment of No. 10 was it had lost authority, and its 'overall narrative was no longer clear' (Campbell 2007: 707). The Capability Review of the Cabinet Office (2006a: 14) found its overall performance 'variable' and reflected on 'the gap between the current capability of the Cabinet Office and the task it faces in the future'. It concluded there was both 'ambiguity over the scope of its role and powers' and 'overlap between the work of various units' (Cabinet Office 2006b: 17). In a similar vein, the Public Administration Select Committee (2001a: para. 42) commented on the 'difficulty in determining priorities' in the 'highly complex organisation of the Cabinet Office itself, with a profusion of small units and divisions all exercising surveillance and issuing instructions from the centre of government'. It was not only a divided centre but in key respects a weak one, constantly looking for new ways to steer departments.

THE 'DIVERSIONS' OF DOMESTIC POLITICS

This selective account of domestic politics focuses on the events that exercised a major influence on my case study departments between 2001 and 2005: the court politics of Blair and Brown, the cabinet and its resignations and reshuffles, parliament and backbench revolts, the media and New Labour, covering various scandals, sleaze, and controversies.

The court politics of Blair and Brown

The standing of Gordon Brown as Chancellor of the Exchequer means there is no tale of a Blair presidency. Rather, between 2001 and 2005 the story is about a dual monarchy: 'Brown conceived of the new government as a dual monarchy, each with its own court' (Rawnsley 2001: 20; 2010: ch. 4; Barber 2007: 307). This notion has its roots in the 'infamous' Granita restaurant story—a meeting between Blair and Brown in Islington on 31 May 1994.[11] 'Brown believed that he had his wish granted to be the central figure over economic and social policy in the future Labour government.' There is much disagreement about, and little documentary evidence on, the degree of control ceded to Brown, 'but there is no doubt that substantial if imprecise control was granted to Brown' (Seldon 2004: 193–4). James Naughtie (2002: 71) believes command over economic policy and 'significant chunks' of social policy were conceded.[12] While there is no documentary evidence to support a deal on when Brown would take over as prime minister, there is some evidence on the policy deal (*The Guardian*, 6 June 2003). Michael White, political editor of *The Guardian*, concludes that 'Blair had effectively ceded sovereignty to Brown in the economics sphere' (cited in Seldon 2004: 669; see also Peston 2005: 67).

The second term exemplifies the TeeBee-GeeBees of New Labour.[13] There were endless disagreements; 'while Blair aimed . . . to limit Brown's authority over domestic policy, Brown fought to increase it' (Seldon 2004: 627). The result was two men presiding over territory ever more jealously guarded. Brown was 'immovable', 'dominating his own territory' with 'jagged defences designed to repel any invader, including the Prime Minister'. As Naughtie (2002: 352) claims, 'they were not interested in submerging their differences in outlook, but in making an exhibition of them'. It is a fine example of the politics of political space. Brown commanded most of the domestic political space, forcing Blair almost by default into overseas adventures, simply because of his inability to carve out some domestic political space.

By 2005, their relationship had deteriorated to an all-time low; 'Gordon hates his guts' (cited in Seldon 2007: 228). Brown believed Blair had torn up their deal with his announcement that he would stand for a third term (see Peston 2005: ch. 10). Brown was reported as saying to Blair that 'There is nothing you could ever say to me now that I could ever believe' (Peston 2005: 349). By the end of the second term, Brown was now 'the official opposition to Blair within the very heart of the Cabinet' (Peston 2005: 13 and 353).[14] The ministerial claim that 'our second term political project is comparable to Thatcher's second term' [Minister FWNB DTI] seems more like aspiration than description. Rather, the key characteristic of 2001–5 was the court politics of the duumvirate. The result was, as John Birt[15] put it, a second term that was 'reactive, short-termist and Treasury driven' (cited in Seldon 2007: 332).

Court politics are not confined to Blair and Brown. Ministers remain 'medieval barons' who preside over their 'policy territory' forming alliances, competing, and defending their turf (Norton 2000: 116–17). The rivalry between Brown and Mandelson is a constant: 'one of the great laws of British politics . . . is that any action by Mandelson causes an equal and opposite reaction by Brown' (Peston 2005: 223; see also Rawnsley 2001: 20; Seldon 2004: 162).[16] There have been other major running conflicts; for example, between Brown and Alan Milburn, Secretary of State for Health, over foundation hospitals; and between David Blunkett and Charles Clarke, Jack Straw, and John Prescott (see Blunkett 2006: 218, 261, 285, 340–1, 546, 588, 604, 784, and 820). Ministers struggle to become heavy hitters. Ministerial standing rises and falls. Gossip records their fortune (see Chapter 7 below). But despite the incessant media focus on the prime minister, it remained the case that 'a Secretary Of State who knows what he wants and is prepared to argue it can say No to Number 10' (SpAd cited in Blick 2004: 276). Barber (2007: 311) gives the example of Charles Clarke (Education) who believed 'Prime Ministers . . . should appoint powerful secretaries of state and leave them to get on with it'.

The story of Blair and Brown, and their ubiquitous court politics, shows how misleading it is to focus only on the prime minister. Political power is not concentrated in the prime minister, but more widely dispersed. It is contested, so the standing of any individual—minister, prime minister, or chancellor—or collection of individuals—cabinet or department—is contingent. The role of the cabinet is also contingent, and it too changed while Blair was Prime Minister.

The cabinet, resignations and reshuffles

Blair's No. 10 aides asserted that 'Cabinet died years ago', claiming they wanted 'to replace the department barons with a Bonapartist system' (Kavanagh and Seldon 2000: 291). Blair's ministerial critics do not demur. Mo Mowlam (2002: 356, 361), former Secretary of State for Northern Ireland, claimed 'more and more decisions were being taken at No. 10 without consultation with the relevant Minister or Secretary of State'. She criticizes 'the centralising tendency and arrogance of No. 10', especially 'their lack of inclusiveness of the cabinet, MPs, party members and the unions leads to bad decisions. Try as I might, I got no indication that their views or behaviour would change.' Similarly, Clare Short (2004: 278) talks of 'the concentration of power in No. 10', criticizing 'his personal entourage of advisers' because it 'enhances the personal power of the Prime Minister but reduces the quality of decision-making'.

Tony Blair did not agree:

> To my certain knowledge that has been said about virtually every administration
> in history that had a sense of direction. I remember that people said that back in
> the Eighties about Thatcher. Of course you have to have Cabinet Government.
> (*The Observer,* 23 November 1997; see also the citations in Hennessy 2000c: 11,
> and n 70)

His Chief of Staff, Jonathan Powell, was as vigorous in defence of sofa
government:

> I don't think it matters whether a meeting takes place in the Cabinet room, where
> John Major used to hold meetings, or in the sitting room, where Mrs Thatcher or
> Tony Blair used to hold their meetings. I think the key thing is that you have the
> right people there, the people who need to be involved in a decision, that they are
> properly informed, have the proper material before them, in written or in oral
> form, and that decisions are taken, then recorded, and then distributed to
> government to be followed up. As long as that happens, I think it doesn't really
> matter if someone is sitting on a sofa or sitting round a table. (Powell 2010: 8)

Indisputably, Blair preferred an informal, personal, bilateral style of working.
He said: 'I think most Prime Ministers who have got a strong programme end
up expecting their Secretaries of State to put it through; and you've always got
a pretty direct personal relationship.' Also, he would not expect ministers to
raise matters in cabinet: 'look I would be pretty shocked if the first time I knew
a Cabinet Minister felt strongly about something was if they raised it at the
cabinet table'—'I would expect them to come and knock on my door' (cited in
Hennessy 2000c: 12). 'Sofa government' was the order of the day and the
commentary on it was 'ludicrously overblown' (Blair 2010a: 18).

In fact, as Seldon (2007: 287) concludes there was 'a limited revival of
cabinet government' during the second parliament. On Iraq, there were 25
pre-invasion cabinet discussions and 28 ad hoc ministerial discussions (Blair
2010b: 227). Also, as Rentoul (2001: 544) observes, 'a lot of the business of
government continued to be done in cabinet committees'. So, during the
second term of government, there were some 66 cabinet committees and
Tony Blair chaired 10 of them. Similarly, ministers play their traditional
roles. John Prescott as Deputy Prime Minister felt that 'it was vital that all
important things should be discussed openly in cabinet' (Prescott 2008: 255).
Alastair Cambell (2007: 625) records Prescott saying: 'He [Blair] has to do
things through Cabinet and his ministers'. He wanted the outside world to
take cabinet 'seriously' (Blunkett 2006: 611). As Michael Barber (2007: 311)
points out, everyone putting a proposal to cabinet has to consider whether it
will get through. It is no surprise that most do—the rule of anticipated
reactions holds sway. Or, if it is judged there will be serious opposition,
proposals are held over until 'the time is ripe'.

Individual secretaries of state are as much a constraint on the prime minister as the cabinet. The traditional view is that you appoint a minister and leave him or her to get on with it. Gerald Kaufman (1980: 78) advises that ministers 'need to take a close interest in what the prime minister says and does' but 'do not be foolish enough to believe that he is keeping a close check on your every move' because 'he has given you a job to do and simply, expects you to get on with it'. David Blunkett would be adjudged of this persuasion. He rationed his contributions to key issues. He did not interfere in the affairs of other departments, although there were spats over turf with John Prescott (Blunkett 2006: 578–9). However, he brought sensitive political issues such as introducing identity cards to cabinet where they were fully aired. The policy was also run through cabinet and interdepartmental committees (Blunkett 2006: 542–3, 551, 632, 701; Pollard 2005: 26 and 305–6). He presented the Home Office's strategic forward look to cabinet, noting how much better he performed when he had his colleagues' support (Blunkett 2006: 644). If the decline of cabinet government refers to the meetings of full cabinet, then that specific meeting is no longer the forum for policy making, if indeed it ever was (see Weller 2003). If cabinet government refers to the cabinet *system* then it is still active, even thriving, and desuetude is not yet cabinet's fate. Tony Blair discovered that collective government was a useful security blanket. He recognized that 'government is a collective exercise and what you need to do is harness the collective responsibilities that different ministers have and also the collective experience they bring with them' (*The Guardian*, 24 May 2005). It would seem that the apogee sofa government was the first term and that it supplemented rather than supplanted cabinet government in the second term (see Prescott 2008: 205–8).

Nothing illustrates the contingency of political life at the top better than ministerial resignations and the ensuing cabinet reshuffles. Between 2001 and 2005, there were several high-profile ministerial resignations—David Blunkett, Stephen Byers, Estelle Morris, and Alan Milburn—as well as several ministers who were not in cabinet. These four resignations were a particular blow to Blair because he lost his chosen secretary of state in each of his priority 'delivery' areas. The plan had been for them to stay for the duration of the parliament. None survived.[17]

These four resignations were caused by domestic policies and politics. There were also resignations caused by world events in the guise of the war on Iraq. The high-profile resignation was Robin Cook. The botched resignation was Clare Short who dithered for so long she lost credibility. The lesser lights who also resigned included junior ministers John Denham (Home Office) and Lord Hunt (Health) and six parliamentary secretaries. By any standards, these events were bad news. It was the first time since 1914 that two ministers had resigned on a foreign policy issue. The rights and wrongs of any particular resignation are not important here. What matters is that such resignations are invariably a massive distraction. Commonly, there was an extended media campaign against the individual concerned and, after the resignation, there was an equally distracting ministerial reshuffle. There were also the periodic reshuffles caused by general elections, slumps in opinion poll ratings, and other political considerations. Blair was 'uninterested' in reshuffles (Seldon 2007: 214) and they were often messy. As Campbell (2007: 621) observes:

> Reshuffles, like pregnancy, dentistry and exams, were further proof that pain has no memory . . . until a new one starts you forget how awful the process is. . . . With each reshuffle came the realisation that the PM's power and room for manoeuvre is more limited than people might think. (see also Blair 2010a: 269 and 528–9)

There was a window of opportunity to remove Brown in the cabinet reshuffle following the 2005 general election (Peston 2005: 329; Seldon 2007: 33). Blair did not take it. There was always the need to strike a balance between the Blairites and Brownites. The reshuffle of June 2003 was messy, complicated by the resignation of Alan Milburn (Rawnsley 2010: 197–202). It was nothing compared to the reverberations of Milburn's return in September 2004. Brown was furious at the return of his arch rival, seeing it as an attempt to exclude him from the election campaign. He was not soothed by Blair promoting Brown's ally Ruth Kelly. Combining media coverage, ministerial rivalries, and the court politics of No. 10 can be a distracting witches' brew of toil and trouble. And even the dismissal of lesser lights can and does fuel backbench dissent because they have a greater propensity to vote against the government.[18]

Parliament and backbench revolts

It is commonplace to point to the over-mighty executive and the inability of parliament to hold it to account. It is an oversimplification. Managing the two Houses of Parliament is a major call on the government's time and skill. Conventionally, parliament has four main functions—legitimation, recruitment, socialization and training, and decisional or influence functions (Norton 2005: 9). For ministers and departments, the key activities fall in the decisional category. It covers: law making (for example, taking a bill through its committee stages); conflict resolution (for example, managing the Parliamentary Labour Party); and scrutiny (for example question time and the investigations of select committees). All consume large amounts of ministerial and official time. I describe these facets of everyday life in Part II. However, I need to say a few words about the Commons' function in conflict resolution.

At first glance this task might refer to managing the official opposition in parliament or, less commonly, to the demands of interest groups or conflicts in society over such ethical issues as abortion or euthanasia. However, the government rarely had any problems dealing with the Conservative opposition. The most effective opposition, and the conflict that had to be resolved, came from the backbenches of the Parliamentary Labour Party (PLP). Although there were backbench revolts in the first term, the war on Iraq fuelled dissent and it was not confined to that issue. On 18 March 2003, 139 Labour backbenchers voted against the government on Iraq. It was the largest backbench rebellion since the nineteenth century Corn Laws. It followed an earlier rebellion in which 121 MPs voted against military intervention in Iraq. There were also substantial revolts against foundation hospitals (61) and top-up fees for universities (72).[19] Cowley (2005: 241) concludes that the 2001–5 parliament had 'a higher rate of rebellions than in any other postwar Parliament', and only the longer 1974–9 parliament had more rebellions. It also had the 'two largest rebellions against the Whips by MPs of any party for over 150 years'. Ministers have to manage the PLP and ensure that it feels involved in policy making. The prime minister promising to listen is not enough. To alienate the mainstream of the party is to invite a backbench revolt.

The media

Prime ministers and ministers live in a '24-hour media churn' (Alastair Campbell cited in Barber 2007: 301). The media love a scandal, whether little or big, trivial or important. So, although the New Labour government had relatively favourable coverage from the media for much of its first term, especially compared with the fate of their predecessor John Major, the media returned to its regular diet of scandals, sleaze, and campaigns. It was the era of professional news management, referred to pejoratively as spin (Jones 1999), but not for long. When Lance Price (2005: xv) left his post as Alastair Campbell's deputy, the 'media's relentless attention on spin had rendered it useless'. Perhaps the most notorious example came from Jo Moore, a special adviser to Stephen Byers, Secretary of State for Transport, Local Government and the Regions. She said that 9/11 was 'a very good day to get out anything we want to bury'. The statement was seen as typifying the cynicism of spin under New Labour.[20]

The media's growing distrust of spin coupled with criticisms of the way the government handled such issues as the outbreak of foot-and-mouth disease in the summer of 2001 led No. 10 to develop a siege mentality. Campbell became increasingly abusive towards the media. From the media's standpoint: 'If it was necessary to obstruct, bully or mislead reporters in the course of his duties, Campbell would do so ... Campbell stopped at nothing to protect the Prime Minister (Oborne and Walters 2004: 198). For Campbell, the epithets for the press ranged from the mild 'hacks' to the abusive 'fucking wankers'. Blair's views were as critical but expressed in more temperate language. He attacked the media because, to 'a dangerous degree', it is driven by 'impact':

> The damage saps the country's confidence and self-belief; it undermines its assessment of itself, its institutions; and above all, it reduces our capacity to take the right decisions, in the right spirit for our future. (Blair, 2006)

The relentless drive for the story leads on the one hand to sensationalism and on the other to a disregard for accuracy. It also leads to an inability to identify the important. Michael Barber (2007: 225–6) describes a press conference with Tony Blair on the delivery agenda. As they went through the slides, a journalist from 'a well known tabloid newspaper' greeted each slide with 'Bullshit . . . bullshit . . . bullshit . . .'. After the presentation, the journalists questioned Blair about whether Peter Mandelson would be the UK's new European Commissioner. At the end, to wind them up, Blair said: 'Anyway, just before you go, because I know you really enjoyed it, Michael is going to repeat the presentation.' For most citizens, whether violent crime is rising or falling is probably of greater concern than Peter Mandelson's next job.

Whatever the faults of the 'hacks', New Labour provided them with many an opportunity for caustic and cynical coverage. After reading Iain Dale and Guido Fawkes' *The Little Red Book of New Labour Sleaze* (2006) or visiting the Iain Dales' blog with its misnamed 'top 50 or so' scandals (in fact it is nearer a 100),[21] it was clear that New Labour fed the feral beast. When Blair attacked the media, he would have had these stories in mind as much as the war in Iraq.

The stories are many and various, although most encompass sex and money; the favoured cocktail of the English tabloid press. Thus, there was a furore when Lakshmi Mittal donated money to the Labour Party and Blair then wrote to the Romanian Prime Minister supporting Mittal's takeover bid for a Romanian steel company. Sleaze allegations about Labour Party funding would escalate (see Levy 2008: ch. 9). Closer to home was 'Cheriegate'. Cherie Blair purchased two flats in Bristol. Unfortunately she used her confidant's lover, Peter Foster, to negotiate the price. He was a convicted con artist. At first, Cherie Blair denied he was her financial adviser but the *Mail on Sunday* had e-mails showing the contrary. The tone of the ensuing few weeks is effectively communicated by Alastair Campbell (2007: 647–53):

> I . . . said to him the real problem was that whether you liked it or not, you are linked to a conman. He said I resent that. 'You are. You're married to a woman who is determined to protect and keep a woman who is in love with a conman so you are linked to a conman.' . . . And everyday it's like that, it hits your authority more, both with the rest of the government and with the public. TB was having none of it. 'We have a fundamental disagreement. You think Cherie has done something monstrous and I don't.' (Campbell 2007: 652)[22]

And this exchange was between allies, not No. 10 and the media. In this frenzied climate, prime ministers (and ministers) have to make decisions. Controversy around the personal lives of family and colleagues never went away. The media were wild dogs in a bear pit when one of its own, Kimberly Quinn (also known as Fortier), the editor of *The Spectator*, had an affair with David Blunkett, the Home Secretary (Pollard 2005: 308–17).

Scandals and sleaze were, however, 'minor' distractions. The never-ending controversy was the war on terror. The domestic implications reverberated. It not only fuelled backbench revolts and ministerial resignations (see above) but it also led to both the Hutton Inquiry into the suicide of Dr David Kelly and the Butler Inquiry into the intelligence on weapons of mass destruction. These events reduced the government's relations with the media, from the grubbiest tabloid to the BBC, to an all-time low.

The Hutton Inquiry into the suicide of Kelly is part of a larger story—the decision to invade Iraq in 2003. Part of that process was to gather evidence on the military threat posed by Saddam Hussein's regime. A key claim in that assessment was that Iraq had weapons of mass destruction that could target the West. David Kelly was an official in the Ministry of Defence (MoD). He was a biological weapons expert who had worked for the United Nations in Iraq. In 2002, he advised on, but did not write any part of, the dossier compiled by the Cabinet Office's Joint Intelligence Committee which advised the Prime Minister on weapons of mass destruction in Iraq. He did not accept the claim in the dossier that Iraq had the capability to launch battlefield biological and chemical weapons in 45 minutes. Kelly's job involved briefing the media and on 22 May 2003 he met Andrew Gilligan, a BBC journalist. The meeting was on a 'not for attribution basis' and Kelly voiced his doubts about the 45-minute claim. Gilligan broadcast this claim on 29 May on the *Today* programme, but crucially made the additional allegation that 'Downing Street . . . ordered it [the dossier] to be sexed up' by including the 45-minute claim (see Rogers 2004: App. 1 and 2). All hell broke loose.

On 30 June, as the political furore showed no sign of abating, Kelly told his manager at the MoD about his meeting with Gilligan. The ensuing meetings, and who said what to whom, matter not because the result is clear.[23] The MoD decided to admit the source of Gilligan's story worked at the MoD and gave enough information for journalists to make an informed guess as to Kelly's identity. Contrary to their normal practice, the MoD confirmed Kelly was the source when journalists asked the direct question. Michael Evans, defence editor of *The Times*, put 21 names to the MoD to get Kelly's identity confirmed (Rogers 2004: i).

Although Blair claimed 'Nobody was authorised to name David Kelly', Sir Kevin Tebbit, Permanent Secretary of the MoD, told the Hutton Inquiry the decisive meeting took place at No. 10 on 8 July 2003:

A policy decision on the handling of this matter had not been taken until the Prime Minister's meeting. It was only after that that any of the press people had an authoritative basis on which to proceed. (see also Rawnsley 2010: 222)

The meeting also decided the MoD should prepare both a press release with details of Kelly's background; issue a question-and-answer briefing that provided more clues to Kelly's identity; and confirm Kelly's name if it was put to them (Rogers 2004: 6). In the purple prose of his diaries, Alastair Campbell (2007: 713) admitted these actions would 'fuck Gilligan'. In short, Campbell had declared war on the BBC.

The public pressure on Kelly was unremitting. The MoD gave him a formal warning for his unauthorized meeting with Gilligan. On 15 July he appeared before the House of Commons Foreign Affairs Select Committee. On 16 July he appeared before the Intelligence and Security Committee. On 17 July he went for a walk in the woods near his home where he committed suicide by cutting his left wrist.

The government responded by setting up an inquiry chaired by Lord Hutton. His report concluded no one could have anticipated Kelly's death and the MoD behaved properly in confirming Kelly's identity (Hutton 2004). Ministers could not believe their luck. Although Hutton agreed that Blair chaired meetings about naming Kelly, he still concluded it 'was not part of a covert strategy to leak his name'. To use *The Spectator*'s rhetorical question: 'What did he [Lord Hutton] think was discussed at these meetings?' (31 January 2004). For the government that was the end of the matter. For David Kelly's family it was clear 'the government made a conscious decision to cause Dr Kelly's identity to be revealed and it did so to assist it in the battle with the BBC'. They were not alone in their disbelief.

For many, the Hutton Report bordered on official apologia; a whitewash (Kuhn 2005: 103–5; Rawnsley 2010: 237–41). The issue did not go away. Media pressure was unrelenting, alleging that parliament and the public had been knowingly fed misleading information. So, Lord Butler was appointed to review the intelligence supporting the decision to invade Iraq. Butler (2004: 110) concluded there was 'no evidence of deliberate distortion or of culpable negligence', although he did suggest the government exaggerated the quality of the intelligence. When interviewed later, Butler forswore the measured tones of his report and said Blair had 'misled the public, Parliament and the world' (7 February 2007, cited in Seldon 2007: 286).

My concern is not the accuracy of the dossier on Iraq, or whether the Hutton Report was a whitewash, or why Kelly committed suicide. My main point is that the issue ran and ran. Gilligan's initial claim was made on 25 May 2003, Kelly committed suicide on 17 July, the Hutton Inquiry started work on 1 August and it reported on 28 January 2004. The Butler Inquiry was appointed on 3 February and reported on 14 July 2004. For almost 15 months,

No. 10 faced a constant barrage of media criticism on the domestic impact of the war on Iraq while confronting the problems of fighting that war. The consequence was an often frenetic air in No. 10 and much soul-searching (see Campbell 2007: 722–4). Seldon (2007: 221) reports that Campbell 'never fully recovered from the shock of Kelly's death'. Cherie Blair (2008: 357) reports of her husband that: 'I have never seen him so badly affected by anything.'

It is scarcely surprising, therefore, that the war on Iraq and its domestic ramifications diverted Blair's attention from his core domestic policy; 'just getting meetings into his diary for domestic policy was a great struggle after 9/11. He was very distracted by the international scene' (No. 10 aide quoted in Seldon 2007: 47). Barber (2007: 119, 175, and 205) observes that Blair was 'distracted and less than attentive', 'clearly had less and less time to devote to the delivery agenda', and 'it was harder to get his attention'. It also exacted a personal price. Although Blair is said to cope well with stress, for Campbell, Blair was 'haggard'; for Tessa Jowell, Iraq 'turned his hair grey'.[24] The issue is captured well by Blunkett (2006: 537):

> The problem is that when Tony is put under too much pressure, he doesn't have time to prepare. He came into the meeting and, although he handled it with great professionalism and expertise, it was absolutely clear that nobody had worked through the agenda with him. Just before the end, he handed over, as he had a couple of international calls coming in. Lord knows how he manages to keep his mind on one thing when another is just about to come up.

Oborne and Walters (2004: 296) conclude the second term failures of the Blair government lie not only with the lack of management skills but also in the emphasis on communication and presentation. They claim Blair's 'closest advisers . . . were experts in presentation, not policy' and that Blair's policy advisers were 'secondary figures'. Campbell's diaries do nothing to dispel that view. The media lived down to New Labour's expectations; it was 'caustic, often cynical and destructive' (Barber 2007: 301). Most ministers would agree with the view from No. 10. For example, Blunkett (2006: 307 and 745) observes there has never been an era when the media had such an impact and rails against the 'gross intrusion' into the private lives of family and friends when there is no effective remedy against their 'lies'. After weapons of mass destruction, Hutton, Butler, spin, scandals, and sleaze there was, to put it mildly, 'a breakdown of trust' on both sides (Phillis 2004). If New Labour's first term of office was a long honeymoon, then the second term was adversarial and acrimonious (Kuhn 2007).

CONCLUSIONS

This chapter describes the web, the broader political setting, in which the three departments work. I have described domestic policy, focusing on the TeeBee-GeeBees, the cabinet, parliament, and the media. I also identified the impact of world events on domestic politics. I will trace the influence of this context on everyday life at the top of the department in Part II. The next chapter outlines the specific departmental context in which ministers and senior civil servants worked. I describe where they work; structure, people, politics, and policies. There are common analytical threads. The Westminster, public management, and network governance narratives recur because I discuss the dilemmas these conflicting stories pose for the individual departments.

NOTES

1. On the development of the code see Baker 2000. For the rules operating between 2001 and 2005 see Cabinet Office 2001*b*. On developments since 2005 see Gay 2007*a*.
2. For more discussion of the Westminster story and its inherited beliefs, see: Gamble 1990; Rhodes and Weller 2005; and Verney 1991. On the constitution, see: Bogdanor 2003; and Marshall 1986.
3. For a summary of the debate and citations see Rhodes 1995 and, more recently Blick and Jones 2010. Specifically on the presidentialization thesis see Foley 2000; and Poguntke and Webb 2005.
4. On the deep roots of managerialism see Chapman and Dunsire 1971: 17; and Thomas 1978. For a more detailed discussion of today's version of managerialism, see: Hood 1991; and Pollitt 1993. For 'a state of the art' compendium on public management see: Ferlie et al. 2005.
5. On the reforms see: Bovaird and Russell 2007; Fawcett and Rhodes 2007; Hodgson et al. 2007; Rhodes 2001; and Richards 2008.
6. On the inherited beliefs about governance see: Harris 1990; Lowe and Rollings 2000; Rhodes 1997*a* and 2007*a*.
7. I prefer the term 'court politics' to 'bureaucratic politics' (Allison 1971) because it evokes the monarchical tradition which cloaks the game playing of ministers and civil servants. Also, in sharp contrast to other accounts of 'administrative politics' in British government (Gray and Jenkins 1985), I stress the network context of court politics.
8. Personal communication.
9. Support for Turnbull's views can be found in Barber 2007: 114, 217, and 308; Campbell 2007: 615; and Seldon 2007: 229.
10. Geoff Mulgan was co-founder of the Demos think-tank, Director of the Prime Minister's Strategy Unit, and Director of Policy at Number 10.
11. Peston (2005: 57, 58, and 60) claims that: the key meeting took place on 15 May at the home of Nick Ryden in Edinburgh, two weeks before the meeting at Granita; Brown was promised 'total autonomy over the social and economic agenda'; and negotiations continued over the next two weeks culminating in the Granita agreement.
12. Support for Naughtie's views can be found in Keegan 2003: 124; Peston 2005: 58; and Rawnsley 2001: 20, 111.
13. If 'heebie-jeebie' refers to a state of nervous apprehension, then 'TeeBee-GeeBees', formed from the respective initials of the two protagonists, refers to their state of

apprehensive antagonism and their regular spats. On the court politics of No. 10, see: Hennessy (2000b: 493–500), who has conscientiously mapped Blair's inner circle and its changing membership. Memorably, Beckett and Hencke (2004: ch. 14) describe the 'oestrogen-fuelled', 'Girl's Own', comic book' view of life at the No. 10 court (see also: Blair 2008; Oborne and Walters 2004).

14. See Blair 2010a: 114 and *passim*, especially ch. 16, and his summary views on Brown on 616–17. See also: Bower 2007: 475–6; Rawnsley 2010: ch. 4.

15. John Birt was Director General of the BBC (1992–2000) and personal adviser to Tony Blair (2001–5). His task was 'blue skies thinking' and attracted attention because his role was shadowy. His advice was not published. He was not a civil servant. He was not accountable to anyone other than the Prime Minister.

16. Peter Mandelson, Gordon Brown, and Tony Blair were the architects of New Labour's victory in 1997. Brown and Mandelson split when Mandelson supported Blair's bid for the leadership. Initially, he was Minister without Portfolio (1997–8). His subsequent career is chequered with two resignations and a spell in the European Commission. It admits of no brief summary. It is worth noting that in 2008, after years of enmity, Gordon Brown, on becoming Prime Minister, brought him back into the cabinet as Secretary of State for Business, Innovation and Skills.

17. On ministerial resignations the *locus classicus* is Finer 1956. See also: Dowding and Dumont 2009; Dowding and Won-Taek Kang 1998; and Woodhouse 2004.

18. There were 45 members of the so-called 'ex-ministers' club' in the 2001–5 parliament. Six voted against the government on 10 or more occasions. See Cowley 2005: 211–12.

19. See Cowley 2005: Appendix 3 for a list of the major rebellions of the 2001–5 parliament. See also: http://www.revolts.co.uk/. It is the best single source of information on backbench behaviour in the British parliament. I last accessed this web site on 6 October 2009.

20. On the Jo Moore affair see: PASC 2002; and Kuhn 2005: 106–7. For general accounts of New Labour and the media at the time, see: Kuhn 2007; Scammell 2001; and Seymore-Ure 2003.

21. See: http://iaindale.blogspot.com/2006/04/top-50-or-so-labour-sleaze-scandals.html. Of course I refer to the 2001–5 period. It just became worse during the next parliamentary term with the exposé by the *Daily Telegraph* of MPs' abuses of expenses. See: http://www.telegraph.co.uk/news/newstopics/mps-expenses/. Both last accessed 6 October 2009.

22. See also Beckett and Hencke 2004: 273–8; Blair 2008: chs 27 and 28; Oborne and Walters 2004: 312–20; and Seldon 2007: 132–4.

23. See Hutton 2004. Rogers 2004 provides a convenient digest of the roles of the key actors in 'outing' Kelly. For Tony Blair's version see pp. 182–7; for Geoff Hoon's version (Secretary of State for Defence) see pp. 163 and 166–7; for Sir Kevin Tebbit's version (Permanent Secretary, MoD) see pp. 294–6; and for Lord Hutton's conclusion see p. 318. Full transcripts can be found on the Hutton website: http://www.the-hutton-inquiry.org.uk/. Last accessed 6 October 2009. See also: Blair 2010a: 455–6; Campbell 2007: 742–54; Seldon 2007: 218–20, 254–6, and 284–7.

24. See: Blunkett 2006: 441; Campbell 2007: 724; Seldon 2007: 174–5 and 270.

3

The Departmental Setting

This chapter provides the context for understanding everyday life in a department. I describe the departments, key positions, traditions or departmental philosophies, and their main policies between 2001 and 2005. I observed three ministries: the Department for Education and Skills (DfES), the Department for Environment, Food and Rural Affairs (DEFRA), and the Department of Trade and Industry (DTI). I answer three questions. Where do they work? Who holds the key positions? What do they do?[1]

WHERE DO THEY WORK?

The Department for Education and Skills (DfES)

I was based in the Sanctuary Buildings, head office of the DfES in central London. In total, DfES has eight buildings on six sites, mainly in Darlington. The Department moved into Sanctuary Buildings from its sixteen-storey office 'slab' over Waterloo Station in 1992. It moved into a modernized office block built around a refurbished Park House, which was a nineteenth-century denizen of Great Smith Street. It incorporated Number 9, Great Smith Street, which was formerly the London Reformatory for Adult Male Criminals. The façade of Park House was preserved because it was a Grade II listed building. So, the building combines historic-style meeting rooms, although their chandeliers have now been removed, with regular office accommodation.

When you arrive, the building has several immediately striking features: its original big wooden doors in their nineteenth century-brickwork, the extensive use of marble, the arboretum with its fountains on the ground floor, and the hollow centre surrounded by seven atria or Aztec balconies forming extensive and attractive planted terraces. The building was refurbished for an international banking organization, so 'it looks rather grand with the atria and fountains and suchlike . . . which we wouldn't have put in out of choice if it had been our call'.[2] The offices are spread over eight floors with lifts, or 'scenics', that face into the central area giving a splendid view of the terraces and their foliage. There are about 1,700 people working in the building out of a total staff of some 3,600. There are over 30,000 visitors a year. The upper floors provide a light, airy working environment, a mix of open-plan and private offices. Ministers and senior civil servants have an especially grand vista of the Houses of Parliament, Westminster Abbey, and the surrounding area. The lower floors are less appealing and the National Audit Office thought the buildings 'difficult to use efficiently because of its irregular shape and the mix of open-plan and irregular-sized offices'.[3]

The internal structures of the three departments had some important common features: the central secretariat, the Management Board, and the functional directorates. The central secretariat encompasses the private offices of the secretary of state, the ministers of State, and the permanent secretary and commonly it has a section specializing in parliamentary and other correspondence. The private offices support both ministers and permanent secretaries. Civil servants staff both offices. A principal private secretary (PPS) heads each office. I refer to the central secretariat as the departmental court and I describe its work and inhabitants in more detail in Chapters 6 and 7.[4]

However, there was one distinctive feature of the departmental court that warrants an early introduction—the special (or ministerial) advisers (SpAds). SpAds were political appointments, not career civil servants, and at the time there were two, at most three, in any department. In 2003 there were 43 in the departments in total. Their role was controversial.[5] The Public Administration Select Committee's (2001b) report on special advisers expressed concern over their recruitment, pay, and accountability. The Committee on Standards in Public Life (Committee on Standards in Public Life 2000 and 2003) similarly sought to clarify their roles and accountability. So, the government introduced a *Code of Conduct for Special Advisers* and a model contract of employment. The *Code* made it clear that SpAds were accountable to the minister. According to the *Code*, SpAds helped ministers 'where the work of Government and the work of the Government Party overlap'. They were a 'politically committed and politically aware' resource carrying out tasks inappropriate for neutral civil servants. These tasks included reviewing papers, checking facts and research findings, preparing speculative policy papers, increasing the policy options available to the minister, liaising with the party, helping to brief party MPs, attending party functions, speechwriting, and representing the views of their minister to the media. As Sir Richard Wilson (2003: 373–5), former head of the Home Civil Service, observed, SpAds are 'a proper and legitimate feature of the constitutional framework within which Cabinet Ministers work'. He preferred to talk about what SpAds must not do. For example, they must not do anything that undermines the political impartiality of civil servants, or play any role in their recruitment, promotion, and line management. However, phrases in the *Code*, like 'give assistance on any aspect of departmental business' opened the grey area of whether SpAds can give 'instructions' to civil servants or simply make 'requests'. I will explore the relationship between civil servants and SpAds in Part II.

Finally, most ministries are divided into functional directorates, headed by a Director-General (DG). Each DG will be a member the department's Management Board (MB). The Board will also have a handful of non-executive lay members appointed for their external experience and expertise. It will be chaired by the permanent secretary or, on occasion, the secretary of state. Its role is to provide strategic direction and advise ministers on allocating resources and monitoring performance.[6]

DfES (excluding employment services) had some 4,200 staff. Its running costs were low but it was responsible for managing a budget of some £64 billion. It had a Management Board comprising the permanent secretary, the six DGs and two non-executive directors. The six directorates comprised: strategy and communications; schools; youth; lifelong learning; corporate services and development; and financial and analytical services. The Schools Directorate was the largest.

DfES also had nine English regional offices and 13 non-departmental public bodies and training boards. Two of these bodies will crop up in later chapters. Ofsted is the Office for Standards in Education, Children's Services and Skills. Its head is Her Majesty's Chief Inspector of Schools, at the time Chris Woodhead, and it inspects and regulates mainly schools. It aims to promote service improvement; to ensure services focus on the interests of their users; and to see that services are efficient, effective, and promote value for money.[7] The Qualifications and Curriculum Authority (QCA) accredits and monitors school qualifications. All departments, and DfES is no exception, are multifunctional. They encompass many and diverse tasks. If anything DfES is one of the less complex departments. Even so, my account focuses on education, not employment, and on education in schools rather than one of the other directorates. I also focused on the central secretariat.

The Department for Environment, Food and Rural Affairs (DEFRA)

As the name suggests, DEFRA was formed in 2001 from three separate ministries: the Ministry of Agriculture, Fisheries and Food (MAFF), parts of the Department of Environment, Transport and the Regions (DETR) and a small part of the Home Office. Its head office is in Nobel House in Smith Square; and both the house and the square have a noteworthy history.

Smith Square was the home of the Conservative Central Office between 1958 and 2003 and of Transport House, the headquarters of the Labour Party between 1928 and 1980. Nobel House is Number 17, Smith Square. It was built in 1928 as the headquarters of the newly formed Imperial Chemical Industries (ICI). ICI was formed from a merger of four companies including Nobel Industries. This company was founded by Alfred Nobel, of Nobel Prize fame, to manufacture dynamite. ICI leased it to the British government in 1987.

Nobel House became the headquarters of MAFF in 1997 when ministers and senior civil servants moved there from Whitehall Place. MAFF's Whitehall buildings were deemed unsatisfactory for ministers. In evidence to the Select Committee on Agriculture, MAFF commented that the rooms in Whitehall Place were 'at the lower end of what Ministers were entitled to expect' and the 'private offices for officials were also cramped' while the 'media and conference facilities were inadequate' (Select Committee on Agriculture 1998, Annex A, para. A3; Donoughue 2003: 338 and 343).

Nobel House is a vast improvement. It is a Grade II listed building. Because it housed ICI's senior management, it has some grand rooms that were deemed suitable not only for ministers and the permanent secretary but also of sufficient architectural distinction for European Union (EU) visits. There was some concern that ministers would be inconvenienced because the new building was further from parliament and Whitehall and the increased distance did, as we shall see, produce some amusing moments.

When you arrive at Smith Square you are struck first by St John's church. My interest in and knowledge of architecture is limited but I am told it is one of the finest works of English baroque. The entrance to Nobel House is tucked away in a corner and is overshadowed, even overawed, by St John's. On arriving at DEFRA, or any of my three departments, it is immediately clear that I am entering the land of the official and the powerful. There are security guards on every door and everyone has to check in at the front desk to get a security pass. The pass is issued provided you are booked in already by your host. There is a large board displaying today's security level; normally black, the lowest level. Commonly, there is also a table with more security guards who randomly check visitors and their bags.

Once you have your pass, DEFRA has tubular, glass, security doors. The guard opens one door to let you into the tube and closes it, so you are encased in a glass tube. It feels like Star Trek and 'beam me up, Scotty'. Then the guard opens the second glass door to let you into the building. You are invited to sit down while your host comes to collect you. The process is not unfriendly but it is as impersonal as it is implacable, with social comments limited to the formal 'good morning'. Flippancy is just ignored, cheeriness is tolerated, and brevity and politeness are preferred. No matter how many times I went to one of my departments, and it was often enough to be recognized by surname, the process was the same and I was not allowed to walk through the building unescorted. My status as a professional stranger (Agar 1996) was all too clear. I was not one of them.

The corridors are wide enough and long enough for a cricket net. The rooms are indeed grand and of suitable distinction for a secretary of state with major responsibilities in the EU. So, the Minister's office is spacious with high ceilings, wood-lined walls even when there are no bookshelves, walnut veneer furniture, and large charcoal etchings of nudes. One feature caught my attention more than any other—the private lift. Originally, it was reserved for the top brass of ICI. It goes only to floors 6 and 8 and it is bombproof. The doors and walls are made of steel and Prince Charles commented 'it was like a bathroom' because the walls acted as mirrors. Nowadays it is used only by ministers and their visitors; for example, international delegations and, of course, royalty. I was allowed a ride in it but clearly they were stretching the meaning of the phrase 'ministerial visitor'. The lift, like the secretary of state's room, is part of the pomp and circumstance that is an integral function of many government departments.

DEFRA employed some 10,000 core staff. It had a budget of some £5 billion. It was a complex, multifunctional department, covering subsidies to farming, animal health, food safety, the Kyoto Protocol, environment, conservation, waste management, floods, fisheries, and rural development. Indeed, the Environment Food and Rural Affairs Committee of the House of Commons (2002: 5) wondered if its remit was too broad and if it could give priority to all its policy areas. The composition of the Management Board gives some indication of the organizational priorities. The main directorates were: environment; food, farming, and fisheries; legal services; land use and rural affairs; operations and service delivery; chief veterinary officer and director-general of animal health and welfare; finance; planning and resources; chief scientific adviser; communications; and policy and corporate strategy. There were also three non-executive directors.

DEFRA's complexity reaches challenging proportions when one turns to its external arms. It had eight regional offices based on Government Office regional boundaries; although this varied between functions as does the number of sub-regional offices.[8] There were six executive agencies (for example, the Central Science Laboratory and the Rural Payments Agency); 21 executive non-departmental bodies (for example, the Countryside Agency, the Environment Agency, English Nature, the Meat and Livestock Commission); 28 advisory non-departmental public bodies (for example, the Advisory Committee on Pesticides and the Royal Commission on Environmental Pollution); two public corporations (for example, British Waterways); five tribunals (for example, the British Wool Marketing Board), and 12 other advisory bodies and stakeholder groups (for example, National Parks and Broads Authority). Moreover, ministers had responsibilities across DGs; one Minister of State was responsible for, among other things, rural affairs and local environmental quality (for example, air pollution in cities). I focused on the work of the central secretariat and on rural affairs.

The Department of Trade and Industry (DTI)

This department has a long and proud history. Its origins lie in the seventeenth century as the Board of Trade and the President of the Board of Trade is one of the oldest offices in British government. This lineage is celebrated in the corridors of the present-day building with portraits of former Presidents. The original functions of the Board were broad, covering all forms of economic activity but over the centuries that remit changed with great regularity.[9] The first Department of Trade and Industry was created by Prime Minister Edward Heath in 1970. It not only inherited the functions of the Board of Trade but the new secretary of state was also president of the Board of Trade, although there was no longer any such department. The latter-day version of the DTI was created by Margaret Thatcher in 1983. The allocation and reallocation of specific functions continued unabated; for example, in 1995 the DTI inherited industrial relations from Employment but lost science and technology, and deregulation to the Cabinet Office. And for the sake of completeness, the DTI disappeared in 2007 when it became the Department for Business, Enterprise and Regulatory Reform (DERR)—and, yes, regulation had returned from the Cabinet Office.

Unfortunately, and in sharp contrast to DfES and DEFRA, the DTI building is a letdown. It occupies an undistinguished glass and concrete office block in busy Victoria Street. Both DfES and DEFRA are off the main road. I suppose it is symbolic that the department responsible for industry should be next to a busy highway and live amid the constant drum of traffic.

The Office of the Secretary of State is also in the modern office style, light and airy with pastel yellow walls, and cream and oatmeal furniture. It is separated from the main office by glass panels decorated with frosted waves. The various shelves have a selection of modern vases and bowls, abstract modern pictures hang on the walls, and a large tree separates the desk and the window. The window frames the front towers of Westminster Abbey. Alan Johnson, who was a Minister of State (Employment) at DTI and succeeded Patricia Hewitt as Secretary of State, commented that 'this office has been feminised . . . Patricia's influence'.[10] To me, the overall effect is 'Habitat' with a big budget.

DTI employed some 4,000 core staff with a budget of some £6 billion. It had the usual Management Board (originally Strategy Board). It comprised: UK trade and investment, chief scientific adviser and Office of Science and Technology, innovation, business, energy, fair markets, services, with the head of the strategy unit and legal services. There were also seven agencies (for example, Companies House, the Patents Office); 13 executive non-departmental public bodies (for example, the Advisory, Conciliation and Arbitration Service, Equal Opportunities Commission, United Kingdom Atomic Energy Authority); seven research councils (for example, the Medical Research Council); eight Regional Development Authorities; 25 advisory non-departmental public bodies (for example, the Low Pay Commission, Women's National Commission); and eight tribunals (for example, Employment Tribunals). It also had residual responsibilities for four public corporations (for example, British Coal and British Shipbuilders). I focused on the work of the central secretariat and on the industry side.

WHO HOLDS THE KEY POSITIONS?

The main characters in my departmental tales are the elected politicians who head central government departments and are known as 'the Secretary of State', referred to in everyday language as the 'Minister'.[11] The top official in the department is known as 'the Permanent Under-Secretary of State', referred to in everyday language as the 'Permanent Secretary'. I provide a résumé of the conventional account of their roles.

The Minister[12]

Conventionally ministers' roles fall into four groups: policy; political; managerial; and diplomatic.[13] I describe each role and give examples from my departments. Just in case it is not obvious, let me say ministers commonly play all of these roles in differing combinations. The separate categories are for ease of exposition.

Policy

The policy role comes in many guises. Heady (1974: 58) distinguishes between the minimalist who has little or no impact on policy, the policy selectors who probe and choose between departmental policy proposals, and policy initiators who set departmental objectives. Among the policy initiators, Marsh et al. (2001: 133–4) proffer a useful distinction between those ministers who set the broad policy agenda and those who introduce specific policy proposals. For example, David Young was determined to change the interventionist, protectionist philosophy of the DTI. It was to forsake corporatism and become the ministry promoting enterprise. He rewrote the objectives of the department on one side of paper. In place of words like subsidy, there were phrases about producing a more competitive market and creating a larger market through privatization and regulation (Young 1990: 250). As he told Marsh et al. (2001: 136): 'I went into politics, not because I wanted to be in politics but because we wanted to institute change.' David Blunkett was just as determined to change DfES. However, he inclined to specific policy initiatives such as improving literacy and numeracy standards in schools rather than such 'big' issues as the reorganization of the education system with its age-old controversies around comprehensive schools and selection. In the era of endless reform:

> reordering the engine room is no substitute for politicians on the bridge who know where they want to get to, and who have the nerve and application to select the course, and stick to it. (Bruce-Gardyne 1986: 246)

And as Roy Jenkins' (1971) makes clear, a minister does not have 'to batter his head against the brick wall of determined departmental opposition'. Rather, 'if he knows what he wants to do he will not in general have much difficulty in getting his policy carried out' because civil servants believe that 'if a Minister is putty in their hands they have a nasty suspicion that he will be putty in the hands of everybody else too'.

Politics

The political role of ministers is to stand up for, or to employ less combative language, advocate the interests of the department in its dealings with cabinet, parliament, and the majority party. It may also involve, depending on the department, managing links with the EU.[14] In all of these relationships, the minister is expected to display political skill and sound judgement.

The key political role of the minister is winning resources for the department in cabinet; 'your Minister...should be able to get his way in Cabinet' (Heclo and Wildavsky 1974: 133; see also Marsh et al. 2001: 142). The minister has to win support for the department's policies by getting a slot in the parliamentary timetable and resources allocated by the Treasury. Where he wins support includes, but is not confined to, 'cabinet'. The minister deals with the heart of the machine or the core executive. The minister will represent the department's interests on interdepartmental committees and cabinet committees, with the prime minister in person, and with the Treasury, the Cabinet Office, and No. 10's various units.

Ministers also have to perform in parliament. As Kaufman (1980: 98) observed, 'Treat the House cursorily or insultingly, and it will punish you.... Treat the House with courtesy and take it seriously...and you will earn respect even from those who disagree most strongly with you.' How well they do in the gladiatorial arena of question time, debates, and adjournment debates will not only affect their standing in the party but also in the ministerial hierarchy. They also have more mundane tasks: appearing before select committees, piloting legislation through both Houses, and appearing in the tearoom for a friendly chat with backbenchers. There are also meetings of the parliamentary party and of regional groupings of MPs. Whatever one's assessment of the influence of the House, indisputably it makes heavy and routine demands on ministerial time and energy. If there is a backbench revolt over a piece of legislation then the demands are even heavier, the reputational costs even higher.

Management

To talk of the minister's managerial role in the climate of the 1990s and the 2000s is to talk about strategy and performance measurement. Some ministers, although by no means all, are managers in this sense. When at DTI, Michael Heseltine saw himself exercising not only strategic direction but also instituting more detailed management reforms. Similarly Patricia Hewitt took a keen, and at times hands-on, interest in the strategic management of her department. Others are less enamoured of the role. Bruce-Gardyne (1986: 233–4) claims it is a 'misconception that Ministers are, or ought to be, in the business of management'.

Ministers do manage in the old-fashioned sense of executive work. The volume of paperwork is intimidating. The red box of work to take home (see below) is usually boxes, and they are always full. The correspondence by both e-mail and snail mail is mountainous. Despite the support of junior ministers, SpAds, and the private office, there are still many letters to sign; for example, replies to MPs. Speeches have to be topped and tailed if not redrafted. At DfES, David Blunkett (2006: 168 and 225) complained about the need 'to keep an eye on the minutiae because if I don't, I know that days will be spent picking up the pieces'; and about 'going over, again and again, anything that was to emerge publicly'. Moreover, any speech or other publicly available document takes much longer to prepare than to deliver or read.

Diplomat

The diplomat role has become more and more important as the influence of the media has grown. I outlined in Chapter 2 the effects of the 'electronic glut' (Seymour-Ure 2003: 9) on the government in general and the prime minister in particular. The pressure is not always so great on every minister, but none escape. Compared with the ministers studied by Heady (1974), ministers in the 2000s are more exposed and spend much more time on their image in particular and public relations in general.

Ministers also have a diplomatic role in the classical sense of that term. They represent their department to the outside world on visits to conferences, professional associations, businesses, and schools; on overseas trips; and on EU business. Kaufman (1980: 39) urges all ministers to 'inform the Diary Secretary that nothing whatever can go into your diary without your own express permission'. Failure to do so leads to both congestion and indigestion from innumerable lunches and dinners. As we will see, a diary full of 'back-to-back' engagements is an indicator of both ministerial machismo and of exhaustion.

Finally, there are the junior ministers. The species comes in three guises. The most important, and they have grown in importance since the 1970s, are the ministers of state who are now routinely allocated a substantial block of work, especially in the large multifunctional departments. They are appointed by the prime minister although he can and does take the advice of the relevant minister. Tony Blair discussed such appointments with Gordon Brown. They are responsible to the minister, not parliament but bound by collective cabinet responsibility. They have been described as political eunuchs. However, their authority is 'informal and indeterminate, depending on personal and political, not statutory, factors' (Theakston 1987: 67). So, the key determinant of their role is whether the secretary of state trusts them. In a government split between Blairites and Brownites, junior ministers could become part of the balancing act between the two factions. As with so much of life at the top, the junior minister's role is contingent; it depends on the personal and on events.

Belying the permanent secretary cited in Theakston (1987: 176), ministers of state are not 'one of the lowest forms of political life'. As Shirley Williams (1980: 86) recognizes, that distinction belongs to the parliamentary under-secretaries of state, or PUSS, and the unpaid parliamentary private secretaries. The former assist a minister of state on particular subjects, often the chores the minister does not want to do. The latter are the minister's eyes and ears in the House of Commons, planting questions, garnering opinion, and otherwise nurturing the minister's relations with his party's backbenchers.

It has been said the House of Commons is a small talent pool. Tristan Garel-Jones (Conservative whip) recalled 'a list of fifteen candidates for a junior ministerial post and thinking... "I wouldn't appoint a single one of them"' (cited in Paxman 2002: 209). The numbers are daunting. From (say) 350 MPs, not all of whom are sane or sober, a government has to fill some 90 posts. So, ministers come in all shapes and sizes with greater and lesser talents. Given the disdain in which politicians are held, I should make it clear that I do not share this view. Rather, and with apologies to Samuel Johnson, I observe that if the minister's job is not done well, I am surprised it is done at all.

The Permanent Secretary[15]

Britain has an uncodified constitution and its provisions are not embedded. So, there is always a penumbra of uncertainty around the position of civil servants. The civil service is a 'constitutional bureaucracy', a term which refers to a permanent, neutral, anonymous, generalist body of officials. It is:

an unpolitical civil service whose primary connection is with the Crown, and which, while subordinated to party governments, is unaffected by their changes: the two permanent elements, the Crown and the civil service, which not by chance together left the political arena, supply the framework for the free play of parliamentary politics and governments. (Sir Lewis Namier cited in Parris 1969: 49)

According to *The Civil Service Code* (Cabinet Office 1999*a*: 1): 'The constitutional and practical role of the Civil Service is, with integrity, honesty, impartiality and objectivity, to assist the duly constituted Government' and 'the accountability of civil servants (is) to the Minister'. Ministers come and go. Permanent secretaries are loyal to every one of them. Conversely, the duty of the minister is 'to give fair consideration and due weight to informed and impartial advice from civil servants . . . in reaching policy decisions' (Cabinet Office 2001*b*: para 58). These constitutional statements seem reasonably clear but the notion that civil servants have a larger 'public duty' persists even if contested (see, for example: Chapman and O'Toole 1995). However, the constitutional position is clear on one key point; ministers are the fulcrums of departments.

So, what do permanent secretaries do? Permanent secretaries sit at the top of a hierarchy where three main tasks come together: political advice (to ministers), management (of their departments) and diplomacy (or managing external relations). It is a singular combination. This job description would be instantly recognized by earlier generations.

Advising

Advising the minister is the classical Westminster role of permanent secretaries. They must know the mind of their minister. The relationship is a close one (see Chapter 5). The simple point is that all permanent secretaries must establish a working relationship with every minister with whom they work.

Advising the minister cannot be reduced to giving policy advice. Indisputably some departmental secretaries bring cerebral, analytical qualities to policy making in their department. But both minister and permanent secretary live in a complex political environment and the permanent secretary must help the minister to manage that environment. So, advice is about support and fire-fighting, not policy, and can extend to the grey area of party politics. Ministers now draw on several sources of policy advice; political advisers, think-tanks, consultants. The civil service in general no longer has a monopoly. Even inside the civil service, advice can come from any member of the senior civil service with the appropriate expertise, not just the permanent secretary who may not even see the advice going to the minister. Barberis (1996: 42) concludes they are now 'policy managers rather than makers or originators'.

Managing

Many of the reforms of the civil service since the 1980s fall under the rubric of 'management', whether performance management or marketization. Both Conservative and Labour governments want the department to implement their policies effectively. The permanent secretary must get on with the job of ensuring the department 'delivers', a phrase which covers both organizing the department and managing its human resources. However, it does not mean operational management; the day-to-day running of the department is increasingly and extensively delegated. The focus is strategic management and a key challenge is fragmentation. Many departments have several agencies. There is no simple hierarchy. The permanent secretary is more like a chair of the board—a facilitator and co-ordinator—and the challenge is to impose some coherence on a complex organization and its many policies. Views differ on the extent to which departmental secretaries have acquired more than a veneer of the managerialism. Sir Richard Wilson (1998), looking back, observes that 'Twenty years ago senior civil servants only had to take an interest in legislation, policy advice and bonding with Ministers' but 'wave after wave of initiatives battered Permanent Secretaries until . . . we found ways of . . . bringing our management up-to-date.' One point is clear. The classical Westminster roles of advising and diplomacy were challenged by the rise of managerialism and all senior civil servants had to confront the dilemma it posed.

Diplomacy

I use this term to cover all the external relations of the department; that is, other central departments, other public agencies (including local authorities), parliament, the media, and the EU. Permanent secretaries are the public figureheads of their departments. Part (1990: 66 and 69) comments on the Department of Education's negotiations with local education authorities, 'we felt that there must be more in common between the Home Civil Service and the Diplomatic Service than we had at first supposed'. It was crucial to be friends with key people in other organizations and to ensure that everyone gained some advantage. Such skills are not new although they are now used in new contexts. Thus, departments have always had to square policies with the Treasury and other affected departments and agencies, including No. 10, while I have been studying British central government. There have been legendary turf wars between departments when diplomacy failed and the never-ending search by No. 10 to strengthen 'central capability' testifies to the difficulties of coordinating them.

Permanent secretaries have to exercise their diplomatic skills in several arenas, most notably parliament. Warren Fisher fought a long battle to make

departmental secretaries the accounting officers for their departments reporting to parliament (O'Halpin 1989: 48–55). Since then appearances before the
Committee of Public Accounts (universally known as the PAC) have developed
into grand drama with dress rehearsals in the departments and questioning
which resembles bear-baiting. No permanent secretary wants to be shown up
by the PAC and much time is devoted to preparing for the experience.[16]

Select committees are not as venerated, even feared, as the PAC but they too
can make heavy demands on a permanent secretary. When appearing before
the committee the permanent secretary appears as a spokesperson for the
minister. He or she must not contradict or compromise the minister. Diplomatic skills can be strained to breaking point when committees smell ministerial blood.

Such appearances are now on television. They are an indicator of an
important change in the working context of permanent secretaries; greater
visibility. They have to manage their links with the media. In the 1960s, few
outside Whitehall could name a permanent secretary. They may still not
be household names but they are not anonymous and can get their Warhol
15 minutes of fame by being 'economical with the truth'. Media skills are part
of the repertoire, whether giving an interview explaining policy or relaxing in
swimming trunks by the pool for a documentary.

There is a danger in these introductory remarks of wrapping changes up in
neat little parcels. For all their commonality of background, they remain a
mixed breed. Richards (1997: ch. 9) distinguishes five types of senior civil
servant in the Thatcher era. First, there were the 'managerially oriented can-
doers', the new breed of permanent secretary brought on by Thatcher, sometimes from outside the public sector. Second, there were the 'overtly political'
appointees, who can be seen as evidence of the party politicization of civil
service appointments. Third, some were 'blackballed' for clashing with the
government of the day and were told further promotion was unlikely:

> I crossed swords badly with the person at No. 10. I was seen as backing
> nationalisation trying to resist privatisation, which was not true. But as a result
> of that I think I was sidelined at that time, and until Thatcher was out of the way,
> there was no possibility.[17]

Fourth, there were the also-rans who did not adjust to the Thatcher changes.
Finally, there were the 'traditionalists' who demonstrated that outstanding
individuals could still get the top job. In updating his account for the Blair
years, Richards (2008: 171–2) concludes there was no Blair effect on the
senior civil service. He was willing 'to adopt, or at least accept a traditional
role and accept the status quo'. There was no increase in either rapid
promotions or outside appointments. If there is such a being as the 'typical'
permanent secretary, he is a white male over 50, with an Oxbridge degree in
the humanities who has worked in the civil service for 25–30 years, serving in

a central as well as a functional ministry, and who will retire at 60 after 5–10 years in the top job. However, to read biographies of twentieth-century civil servants is to encounter individuals who are by turns eccentric, laudable, unconventional, overbearing, charismatic, even ones who evoke an empathetic sorrow for their fate. There are outsiders as well as members of the 'old boy network'. There are men and women who oil the machine of state and men and women with grand ideas who make a difference. I explore some of these differences, especially the rise of the 'managerially oriented can-doers', in Part II.

So, who are the ministers and permanent secretaries in this study? I observed and interviewed five secretaries of state (three women). I interviewed or observed eight ministers of state (two women). I interviewed ten permanent secretaries (one woman) and observed three. I undertook to protect the anonymity of individuals, so, I give only the position of an interviewee. As a result, there are several possible sources for any quote. Between 1997 and 2005, DfES has had four secretaries of state, two permanent secretaries, and, while I was in the department, there were also two ministers of state. DEFRA and its main constituent department MAFF had three secretaries of state between 1997 and 2005. While I was in the department, there were two ministers of state and two parliamentary under-secretaries of state. At DEFRA and MAFF, there were two permanent secretaries. Finally, ministers changed almost as regularly as functions at DTI.[18] Between 1997 and 2005, there were seven secretaries of state. While I was in the department, there were also four ministers of state and three parliamentary under-secretaries of state. I interviewed two former permanent secretaries.

WHAT DO THEY DO?

Departments initiate, implement, and evaluate policies. Such work takes place against a backcloth of both departmental philosophies, or the inherited ideas and practices that are specific to the department, and the policy agenda of the government of the day. As Kaufman (1980: 50) observed, 'what Whitehall does believe in, for better or for worse, is continuity'.

Departmental philosophies

In Chapter 1, I stressed the importance of traditions and dilemmas in understanding the origins of, and changes in, beliefs and practices. The civil service respects tradition and codifies much of it in rules and procedures. They refer to it as the departmental philosophy. The notion is captured by a former Head of the Home Civil Service, Sir Edward Bridges (1971: 50–1) (see also Wass 1984: 49–50):

> The departmental philosophy is the result of nothing more startling then the slow accretion and accumulation of experience over the years.... [B]y trial and error something has come about which differs greatly from the original plan.... [I]t is less logical but wiser and more comprehensive.

He sees it as 'the essence of a civil servant's work'; the 'slow accretion and accumulation of experience'. A departmental philosophy contains knowledge about what worked and what did not work, what aroused public criticism and what did not. It is thus 'the duty of the civil servant to give his Minister the fullest benefit of the storehouse of departmental experience; and to let the waves of the practical philosophy wash against ideas put forward by his ministerial masters'. Here Bridges identifies four 'skills or qualities' needed by civil servants. First, they must have 'long experience of a particular field'. Second, there are the specialized skills of the administrator:

> perhaps it should be called an art—the man or woman ... who will be a good adviser in any field because he or she knows how and where to go to find reliable knowledge, can assess the expertise of others at its true worth, can spot the strong and weak points in any situation at short notice, and can advise on how to handle a complex situation.

Third, the civil servant should possess the qualities associated with the academic world: 'the capacity and determination to study difficult subjects intensively and objectively, with the same disinterested desire to find the truth at all costs'. And, finally, the civil servant must 'combine the capacity for taking a somewhat coldly judicial attitude with the warmer qualities essential to managing large numbers of staff'. Hence, administration was, for Bridges, not a science but an art, and recruits would acquire the relevant qualities by learning on-the-job. What the administrator needed was 'a general understanding of the main principles of organisation' or 'a kind of rarefied common sense'. The permanent secretary was a 'general manager', comparable to 'the conductor of an orchestra'. The analogy was with rowing. You cannot become a good oarsman by studying diagrams and angles. You learn to row 'from the mere fact of rowing in a good crew behind a really good oarsman, for the good style and rhythm proved as catching as measles'.[19] These characteristics of civil servants are summed up in the description 'generalists'. This strand of the Westminster narrative persists today. Simon James (1992: 26), a former civil servant, sums it up succinctly:

> What matters is ... the capacity to absorb detail at speed, to analyse the unfamiliar problem at short notice, to clarify and summarise it, to present options and consequences lucidly, and to tender sound advice in precise and clear papers.

This tradition has great strengths. I have met many departmental secretaries. Almost without exception they are talented individuals; intellectual, adaptable, resilient, and collegial. And the tradition persists. David Blunkett in an interview on 19 January 2007 commented:

> I think the inherent departmental view, and departmentalism of the defence of the department and the concern about the department, have not changed. There has been restructuring to the point where the sense of loyalty to the department by staff, other than the Treasury and the Foreign Office, in my view has diminished. So the civil service within the upper echelons continue to be departmental in their outlook but less in terms of their commitment.

However, there has been no scarcity of critics of the generalist tradition since the Fulton Committee Report (1968) instituted 'the managerial revolution'.

First, governments of all political persuasions have railed against bureaucracy and its inefficiency. Staffing cuts recur. The government rids itself of functions by contracting out; the neo-liberal or market strand of managerialism. Second, both Conservative and Labour governments complain that civil servants are poor managers who fail to deliver; the performance management strand of managerialism. Third, commentators claim there has been a politicization of the civil service, arguing there are more accelerated and outside appointments than previously and too many SpAds. Finally, ministers claim the civil service is not responsive and resists change.

We encountered these criticisms earlier. In Part III, I will explore the dilemmas posed for the generalist tradition by its critics. The impact of managerialism, or the public management story, will be a recurrent theme. These criticisms also posed a further dilemma; between constitutional bureaucracy and political responsiveness.

The constitutional bureaucracy strand of the Westminster narrative views the relationship between ministers and civil servants as a close partnership. For example, Heclo and Wildavsky (1974: 2 and 36) refer to *both* ministers and civil servants as 'political administrators' to stress their mutual dependence and overlapping roles and responsibilities. However, ministers, especially but not exclusively in the Thatcher years, viewed civil servants with distrust. Thatcher saw them as part of the problem because they saw their role as 'the orderly management of decline'. She believed permanent secretaries saw themselves 'mainly as policy advisers, forgetting that they were also responsible for the efficient management of their departments'. So, she took a 'close interest in senior appointments' and some commentators claimed her reforms and appointments politicized the civil service (Thatcher 1993: 46–7). For example, Hugo Young described the service as 'a thoroughly Thatcherised satrapy'.[20] It is, however, more productive to move beyond the idea of politicization with its pejorative undertones to a different idea—responsiveness (Wass 1984). In other words, ministers were asserting control over the policy agenda and wanted a civil service that could respond to that agenda and implement it effectively. So, permanent secretaries were, and are selected, and kept in part because their style and approach 'fits' the government's style and approach, in part because of their expertise whether understood as policy implementation or can-do managerialism, and in part because ministers are comfortable with them (Weller and Rhodes 2001: 238).

Whether the label is politicization, personalization, or responsiveness, one point is clear; ministers wanted change, and ministers get what ministers want. They got their way by preferring 'can-do managerialists', and increasing the number of special advisers. The effects of these changes remain to be seen because there are dilemmas great and small here; between beliefs about constitutional bureaucracy and the call for greater political responsiveness; between permanent secretaries as 'administrative conservators' (Theakston 1999: 257) and as implementers of change. Parts II and III explore how these dilemmas play out in the three departments.

One response to decades of challenge to the generalist tradition has been to use codes to protect the civil service and its traditions. There were some early efforts by Heads of the Home Civil Service (see Butler 1992: 8) and the core values have been set out in the *Civil Service* Code (Cabinet Office 1999*a*). It adumbrates integrity, honesty, impartiality, and objectivity. Civil servants should also deal sympathetically with the public and make effective and efficient use of public money. The *Code* also stipulates what civil servants should not do. They should not take part in political activities, misuse their official position or information for private gain, or disclose official information (see also Jary 2008: ch. 7 and pp. 85–7).

The inherited beliefs and practices about everyday life, or the departmental philosophy, shape the everyday lives of civil servants. It will embrace, even articulate, the high moral ground of the *Code* at times of crisis but in the main it comprises lessons learnt by trial and error; by incremental decision making. A core policy task of civil servants is to ensure policy proposals are feasible. Jary (2004: 21) warns his civil service colleagues that 'our interpretations and opinions can be invaluable, but they should be clearly identified as such, and not be confused with the facts'. But, when spotting snags, civil servants can and do elide fact and interpretation. The department's accumulated wisdom is the guide. Departmental philosophies are the institutional memory or repository of folklore for the organization.

Policy agendas

Elected governments have manifestos and new policy ideas. Ministers want to make a difference. Departments also have preferred policies and trusted stakeholders. The tensions between the two are a common characteristic of decision making in departments. What was New Labour's policy agenda? What dilemmas did it pose for existing departmental philosophies and their established agendas? For each department I provide a brief account of the inherited policy agenda before summarizing New Labour's new policies.[21]

The (old) Department of Education and Science was the heart of a strong policy community; a troika comprising the department, the teachers' unions, and the national associations of local government. Its view of policy was to go where the arithmetic led; that is, pupil and student numbers (Rhodes 1988). For example, when Margaret Thatcher became Secretary of State for Education and Science in 1970, she inherited a department with an 'entrenched culture' and 'a settled agenda of its own'. She was deemed a successful minister because she won resources for the department. She was an ideal minister for her civil servants because she was hard-working, a good advocate for the department, and at the time had no education agenda of her own. She was 'a high spending minister with a reputation of having "gone native"'. This reputation was an 'embarrassment' for her that 'never ceased to rankle' (Campbell 2001: 212–15; Thatcher 1995: 190–1).

The 1980s saw the teaching professions 'hand bagged', the introduction of neo-liberal policies, and the department playing a more directive role with local government. As Ranson (2008: 201) points out the Education Reform Act (1988) gave parents more information and the right to choose while delegating finance to schools. It sought to create a quasi-market in which competition between schools improved performance and made the education service more accountable to parents. New Labour accepted the Conservative government's broad policy thrust and accentuated the shift to users or consumers; standards, diversity, and choice were its watchwords.

The initial thrust was to improve standards of numeracy and literacy in primary schools. The Standards and Effectiveness Unit (SEU) in DfES was the forerunner of a government-wide 'deliverology' agenda. Ambitious targets were set and at first there was clear improvement. There were more and better paid teachers. However, by 2001 it was clear there was 'slippage' and improvements had reached a plateau. Some 25 per cent of pupils left primary school without adequate reading, writing, and numerical skills. The results of the push to improve standards in secondary schools were similarly mixed. The numbers of pupils meeting key targets and passing the GCSE rose but the proportion leaving with little or nothing had also risen.

The second thrust was diversification, described by Alastair Campbell with his usual verbal felicity as 'the end of the bog standard comprehensive' (Barber 2007: 38). Blair's key policy advisers were Andrew Adonis and Cyril Taylor. The central idea was specialization. So, England got Foundation Schools, which were non-selective state schools that received extra funding to add, for example, sport, business studies, science, or languages to the national curriculum. Then there were city academies, which were new schools partly funded by the private sector that would replace failing inner-city schools. Add to the mix the independent sector, faith schools, and existing state schools and, in principle, parents had a choice of secondary schools for their children.

However, the third thrust was muddle. The initial changes were imposed. Central direction was the means. Diversification saw a shift of emphasis to parental choice.

The department confronted two dilemmas. Neo-liberal ideas of choice challenged the department's alliance with long-standing stakeholders. From Thatcher onwards, the drive had been to marginalize key stakeholders like the teachers. Now, if the delivery agenda's changes were to stick, there had to be a change from below with the centre switching from direct to indirect tools of steering. Such indirect steering, referred to in the academic literature as metagovernance (see Chapter 8), posed new challenges. No one was sure how to do it. It required the cooperation of stakeholders, but reconciling the hand bagging of the professions with diplomacy and cooperation was a hard ask. The problem was intensified by the second dilemma: the resurgence of the professional.

By 2005, the Prime Minister's commitment to 'education, education, education' had waned because of more pressing issues such as the war on terror, Iraq, Northern Ireland, and an impatient heir presumptive. Education policy was beset by a procession of ministers; between October 2002 and May 2005, there were three secretaries of state or one every 11 months. There was much controversy over the funding of higher education, which prompted a major backbench revolt. The resulting policy muddle is not surprising; for example, Charles Clarke abolished that beacon of the standards revolution, the SEU. Also, the contradictions in the diversity policy became clear. As Smithers (2007: 380) puts it: 'what happens when more parents want their child to go to a school than can be accommodated?' The use of entrance examinations was an option too far even for the Blairites. In fact, there was no answer beyond local happenstance; parents confront 'a confusing and incomplete mix of specialist schools . . . without a fair way of deciding who gets into where' (Smithers 2007: 380). So, the Prime Minister still complained about the failure to give greater choice to users of the service. Observers noted the new self-confidence of teachers (Toynbee and Walker 2005: 89). Others commented on the lack of policy substance (Smithers 2005: 282). The department remained cautious; there were snags. The dilemmas posed by neo-liberal policies in a policy network with a powerful producer group, the contradictions between diversity and inclusion, the splits in the Parliamentary Labour Party over education, and the search for effective tools for indirect steering, were all too clear to them. As Michael Barber (2007: 144 and 314) observes, after 2001 there was 'a loss of pace and direction' because 'officials returned power to the professionals' and 'the official view prevailed once more'.

The Ministry of Agriculture Fisheries and Food had a close, symbiotic relationship with the National Farmers Union (NFU). For most of the post-war period agriculture would be seen by most commentators as the paradigm policy community (see Smith 1993). Its core policy was to maximize food production and its policy instrument of choice was farm subsidies. It was 'dominated by farming and agrochemical clients', and it 'exuded a mentality of welfare subsidy and protectionism'. It did not care for 'management efficiency', it was incapable of 'speedy reactions', and it was 'hostile and negative to new policy approaches'. It was also 'secretive' with a 'bunker and often hostile attitude to other departments' (Donoughue 2003: 358). The EU perpetuated the subsidies and protectionist policies albeit with some different instruments and emphases. The standing of this tight-knit closed policy was neatly captured by Gillian Shephard, a former Secretary of State:

> It [MAFF] was regarded by smart political commentators as dull, and by other departments as incomprehensible. Therefore the Minister was left alone for the most part to get on, which is certainly in its way a form of power. It worked particularly well with the Treasury, whose clever officials knew nothing about agriculture and who usually gave in during public expenditure rounds out of boredom. (Shephard 2000: 22)

There have been several pressures for change: the environmental lobby, food safety and quality, the costs of the EU's Common Agricultural Policy, and changes in EU trade policies mainly with the USA (see Grant 2005: 16; Smith 1993: ch. 5). For example, such food crises as salmonella in eggs and BSE fuelled criticism of intensive, industrial farming methods. MAFF was seen as incompetent in its handling of both the BSE and 2001 outbreak of foot-and-mouth disease (FMD). So, in 2001, MAFF was replaced by DEFRA. The intention was to give greater priority to environmental concerns, food quality, and the consumer. The farmer's pre-eminence was under direct and immediate threat. It was not, however, at an end. As Grant (2005: 23) points out 'farmers continue to be more heavily subsidised and protected than any other group in society' and 'in an era in which neo-liberalism has supposedly triumphed . . . agriculture remains a conspicuous exception'. It was an era of transition for the department and for the agriculture policy community.

DEFRA sought an identity that was greater than the sum of its former parts. In its search to reinvent and integrate its disparate departmental philosophies, it lapsed into grandiloquence:

> Our *vision* of the future is of a world in which climate change and environmental degradation are recognised and addressed by all nations and where low carbon emissions and efficient use of environmental resources are at the heart of our whole way of life. A future where, here in the UK, rural communities are diverse, economically and environmentally viable, and socially inclusive with high-quality public services and real opportunities for all. A country where the food, fishing

and farming industries work closely together with Government and are not dependent on output-related subsidies to produce safe, nutritious food which contributes positively to consumer choice and the health of the whole nation. A place where the land is managed in such a way as to recognise its many functions, from production through to recreation; where we seek to promote biodiversity on land and in our seas; and where the promotion of animal welfare and protection against animal disease is at the core of the way in which we farm and live. The pursuit of sustainable development, which means a better quality of life for everyone, now and for generations to come, is central to achieving this vision. (DEFRA 2004: 14, emphasis in original)

Only a final 'amen' is missing, and I doubt the message was received with many hallelujahs from the department's diverse and competing stakeholders. In fact, for all the care and attention devoted to its strategic planning process, and to managing organizational change, the policy outputs of DEFRA between 2001 and 2005 differ but incrementally from those of its predecessor departments.

DEFRA lived a life of routine punctuated by unwelcome crises. Much of DEFRA's routine work is carried out through the agencies and non-departmental bodies noted earlier, and in the EU. While I was there, the priority task was to meld the new department into a single, coherent entity. The Environment, Food and Rural Affairs Select Committee (2002) was critical of the early efforts. It felt the twin challenges of sustainable development and promoting rural interests required the department to undergo structural and cultural change. It concluded that cultural change 'has barely begun'; and that 'much needs to be done' to bring the parts of DEFRA together (para. 38). It had 'doubts about the abilities of management to oversee such a period of change' and 'its strength in depth to administer complex programmes' (p. 4 and para. 42). It cites with approval the Anderson Inquiry report (2002), which criticized 'decision taking by committee, and fear of risk taking'. It called for better skills in operational and project management (para. 40). The report was not a vote of confidence. A former minister, Bernard Donoughue (2003: 363) similarly thought the 'agricultural divisions may be reasserting their undoubted skills at the Whitehall office games to reimpose their old culture on the new department'.

The task of transition was not helped by recurring crises.[22] The earlier crises of FMD and BSE, which led to the abolition of MAFF, refused to go away. The department was dealing with their aftermath well into 2003.[23] New crises came along, including such 'doosras' as: the ban on fox hunting with dogs, which led to the cabinet giving in to backbench pressure and passing the Hunting Act 2004; the Chinese cockle pickers who drowned in Morecambe Bay, which led to the Gangmaster Licensing Act 2004 and the Gangmasters Licensing Authority; and genetically modified crops, which led to . . . nothing as the government opted for passivity in the face of consumer resistance and open hostility from radical environmental groups on one side and the GM crop lobby on the other.

As Winter (2003: 52) points out, creating DEFRA brought three contentious issues together in the one department: hunting, FMD, and the (mis)fortunes of farming. So, the Countryside Alliance's 'Liberty and Livelihood' campaign could 'focus its ire' on DEFRA. It made my 22 May 2002 visit to the department an adventure. I was greeted by a couple of riders in full, red-coated hunting garb with their hounds, and two pipers, obviously protesting about the efforts to end fox hunting with the pipers there to declare solidarity with the Scottish hunts. They added a boisterous air to the day, although to be honest, there were probably more police there than there were protesters!

Toynbee and Walker (2005: 247) argue DEFRA 'failed to brand a Labour image on environmental policy'. They do not see DEFRA's work as 'incremental' but as 'incoherent' because:

> Margaret Beckett was a political firefighter whose main strength was to minimise trouble. She gradually dropped from view until, with the hunting demonstrations in 2004, she had disappeared completely, leaving her unfortunate colleague, Alun Michael, to face the flak.

In a similar vein, David Blunkett commented:

> There are people who are just doing their jobs like Margaret Beckett, who are really just holding the ring; they're solid but they are not going to come up with anything radical or new. (Pollard 2005: 27)

Many would see that as a summary of the department, not just its secretary of state. However, it is worth pondering whether DEFRA was 'in any position to influence, let alone deliver on the policies'. The key levers for effective policies on sustainable development lay with the Treasury (Toynbee and Walker 2005: 247); and the lead for major reforms to agricultural subsidies lay with the Commission of the EU.

In DTI, 'there was a great difference in philosophy between the Trade people and the old Industry people' (Young: 1990: 244). In shorthand, Trade favoured free trade while Industry favoured intervention. Between 1979 and 1997, there was much continuity on the Trade side with its belief in trade liberalization. However, the Industry side changed dramatically. Its policy focus shifted from intervention and by 1997 it had experienced a cut of some 65 per cent in its budget. The focus now was competition, deregulation, and advice to industry (Marsh et al. 2001: 80–4). There were also significant changes in other facets of the department's culture. A former Permanent Secretary claimed that 'management scarcely existed within the service' when he joined the Board of Trade. By the late 1990s, 'DTI probably embraced managerialism more wholeheartedly than most of Whitehall' (DTI officials, both cited in Marsh et al. 2001: 85). With its neoliberal economics and commitment to managerialism, in matters trade and industrial, it is the very model of a modern government department.

Its specific areas of responsibility are diverse and include company law, trade, business growth, innovation, employment law, regional economic development, energy, science, and consumer law. Most of the specific services were delivered by its agencies and non-departmental bodies. In 2002–3, DTI undertook a wondrously ornate strategic planning process to rationalize both its services and its internal organization. In brief, DTI advises, promotes, and regulates industry at home and represents British interests in EU and other international trade forums.

However, the department struggled to overcome a basic problem; the Treasury, which directly steered the department's policy agenda. As Crafts (2007: 276 and 286) cogently argues, 'the Treasury rather than the DTI has dominated' industrial policy and 'its metamorphosis into productivity policy . . . has been controlled by Gordon Brown'. The consequence is that key Public Service Agreement (PSA) targets are not in its control; for example, it was charged with raising the UK's productivity and narrowing the productivity gap with the USA, France, and Germany. As its Capability Review for the 2001–5 period concluded:

> The Department's overarching aims are highly aspirational and long term. They are achieved through complex delivery mechanisms in which DTI's influence can, at times, be limited and unclear. The baselines, outcomes and the link between inputs and outcomes are often unknown, and the costs and benefits of delivery are difficult to track. DTI has to work through and with others in loose partnerships, making appropriate links amongst the government departments, stakeholders and agencies with which it deals. (Cabinet Office 2006c: 15)

All DTI could do was follow where the Treasury led. It is a department that has been downsized, rationalized, and reduced to carrying out prosaic if necessary work. The DTI's own list of highlights in 2003 illustrates this point. It includes: UK Trade and Investment helped to develop over 1,150 successful new exporters and 2,900 firms to trade successfully in markets new to them; a new consumer and competition regime under the Enterprise Act 2002 and the Communication Act 2003; the Consumer Credit White Paper; the EU's Better Regulation Plan; UK-wide consultation on the future of the Structural Funds post-2006; raising the national minimum wage to £4.50 an hour; 107 investments in 83 companies; new fireworks safety regulation; and the Sunday Trading Regulatory Reform Order 2004. The contrast between DTI and the other departments is sharp. Industry was rarely a priority, and when it was the Treasury took the lead. Education was a priority policy for the government, so DfES had a starring role. Even DEFRA was more politically visible.

CONCLUSIONS

There are some recurrent themes in my account of what departments do. First, and most notably, there is the challenge from neo-liberal beliefs about competition and empowering the users of the service.[24] The transformation of old departmental philosophies by neo-liberal ideas of markets and competition is most complete at DTI. Such beliefs had deep roots in the old Board of Trade laissez-faire tradition. The challenge was acute in education as government policy sought a shift from state provision to the mixed economy of state, church, community, and business. The challenge was most muted in agriculture. Second, in multifunctional departments, it can be a mistake to talk of a single departmental philosophy. Trade and Industry were different for more than a decade. Agriculture may prove to be the cuckoo in DEFRA's nest bringing old beliefs and practices to the new department. Finally, the contest of ideas was complicated by powerful producer groups outside the department but allied with it or parts of it. In education and agriculture, caution was not the sole preserve of the civil service. Their stakeholders were as resistant to change, and one can only marvel at the ability of farmers, with EU support, to maintain agricultural subsidies.

The aim of Part I has been to outline the setting of everyday life in my ministries. I intend to feed off the contrast between the high politics of the New Labour government and the low politics of everyday life in a service delivery department. Also, I do not want to interrupt my account of everyday life with explanations of broader features of the British political landscape. That task is now complete. Chapter 2 provided a short survey of British government's key domestic policies and politics between 2001 and 2005. It also introduced three narratives that will recur: Westminster, managerialism, and network governance. This chapter described the immediate context of ministerial life in DfES, DEFRA, and DTI. I described where they work, who works there, and what they do. I also identified the dilemmas that confront the departments between the classical Westminster roles of ministers and permanent secretaries and managerialism; between constitutional bureaucracy and political responsiveness; and between the departmental philosophy, the neo-liberal policy agenda, and indirect steering or metagovernance. One of the distinct advantages of observation is that it is well suited to identifying and unpacking departmental traditions—their folklore and folkways—and to teasing out the dilemmas that confront inherited beliefs and practices. In Part II, I turn to the folklore and folkways of the ministers, permanent secretaries and their respective courts. I start with the everyday life of the minister.

NOTES

1. My description covers 2001–5 only. DfES is now the Department for Children, Schools and Families. DTI is now the Department for Business, Innovation and Skills. The top political and administrative personnel in all three departments have either retired or moved to a new department.

2. Facilities Manager, TI, 25 February 2002.

3. National Audit Office Press Notice 65/94, Department for Education: Management of Office Space, Report by the Comptroller and Auditor General, HC 72 1994/95, 15 December 1994.

4. Initially, I used such phrases as 'research subject' to refer to ministers and permanent secretaries, treating them as objects of enquiry. Eventually, I chose 'inhabitants' because I like the analogy with Westminster and Whitehall as a village. The description 'village' is also used by the inhabitants; see, for example: Bruce-Gardyne 1986: 2.

5. For a history of SpAds, see: Blick 2004. For a brief survey on developments in the 2000s, see: Gay 2007*b*. On the arguments about their roles and accountability, see the reports of the Public Administration Select Committee 2001*b* and the Committee on Standards in Public Life 2000 and 2003. On the views of civil servants, see: Wilson 2003. For the various codes, see: http://www.cabinetoffice.gov.uk/propriety_ and_ethics/special_ad-visers/code.aspx Last accessed 6 October 2009.

6. Most departmental organization charts, or organograms, show it to one side of the line hierarchy and it advises key actors in the departmental court. There are some minor variations in nomenclature and procedures of no great import.

7. See: http://www.ofsted.gov.uk. Last accessed 5 November 2009.

8. As an illustration of the organizational complexity of DEFRA see the listing of organizations involved in rural service delivery in Haskins 2003: Annex 2.

9. For a summary chronological account of the changes undergone by the department see: http://www.berr.gov.uk/about/about-berr/history/index.html. This website is evidence of the department's continuing pride in its evolution. It is the only one of the three departments to provide a public digest of its history. Last accessed 11 November 2010.

10. *The Observer*, 16 October 2005.

11. I follow everyday usage. For clarity, I sometimes use Secretary of State.

12. Several commentators have noted the lack of research on British ministers (see, for example: James 1999: 251; Norton 2000: 101; and Marsh et al. 2001: 1). There are many ministerial biographies, autobiographies, memoirs, and diaries but, as James (1992: 254) notes, 'ministerial memoirs proliferate, but are often not much use to a student of Whitehall'. However, there are some important exceptions to these general conclusions. Among political scientists, the work of Heady 1974; Heclo and Wildavsky 1974; Marsh et al. 2001; and Rhodes and Dunleavy 1995 are important sources on ministers and their departments. Theakston 1987 is the best book on junior ministers. Among politicians, Kaufman 1980 is funny as well as informative on being a minister and Bruce-Gardyne's (1986) comparable effort deserves more attention than it gets. The undisputed classics among ministerial diaries are Benn 1990 and 1991; Castle 1984; and Crossman 1975; and Blunkett 2006 will join them. Among ministerial memoirs, Jenkins 1991 is worth consulting and Lawson's (1992) detailed account of economic policy is impressive. Gamble (1994: 38) notes that few memoirs set out to describe ministerial policy making. However, there is some relevant material in Fowler 1991 and Young 1990, while Blunkett 2006 is a goldmine. Among journalists, the doyen of Whitehall watchers is Hennessy 1989. Others rarely descend from the Olympian heights of prime minister watching and when they do the results are commonplace (for example Paxman 2002), although Peston 2005 is an important exception. For comments on the diaries and memoirs covering the second Blair government see Chapter 1, note 12 above.

13. For other discussions and typologies of the roles of ministers see Headey 1974: ch. 3; James 1999: ch. 2; Marsh et al. 2001: ch. 6; and Norton 2000.

14. In DEFRA, the EU workload is heavy for farming but variable elsewhere. For DTI, the effects of the EU are widespread across the several directorates and the workload is growing. For DfES the effects and the workload are light. During my fieldwork, the EU did not figure prominently, so it is largely missing from my account of everyday life.

15. Barberis (1996: xvi) expresses surprise that 'there has never been a book specifically devoted to permanent secretaries' and argues we know little about these officeholders beyond the popular television programmes, *Yes Minister* and *Yes Prime Minister*. There are a few memoirs by senior civil servants but all too often they are 'unintentionally revealing of the more tortuous cast of mandarin mind' (James 1992: 255). There have been some recent, useful additions to the literature. See: Barberis 1996; Denham 2002; Packer 2006; Rhodes and Weller 2001; Richards 2008; and Theakston 1999 and 2000.

16. One Permanent Secretary pointed out correctly that the role of accounting officer was not limited to his or her personal accountability to parliament for the use of taxpayers' money. It suffuses departmental management, especially the oversight of spending and value for money.

17. Permanent Secretary, TI, 5 June 1999.

18. One former Permanent Secretary estimated he had served '29 secretaries of state during my 37 years in the civil service'. And it matters because 'the transition between ministers of the same administration can be almost as great as the transition from one administration to the next' (Permanent Secretary, TI, 5 June 1999). For the turnover of ministers at the DTI in its various guises since 1970 see: http://www.berr.gov.uk/aboutus/corporate/history/ministers/page19800.html Last accessed 6 October 2009.

19. The quotes in this section are from, in order: Bridges, 1950: 50, 51, 52 and 55-7, and Bridges, 1956: 6, 14, and 23. On the origins of this generalist tradition, see: Beloff 1975; Bevir and Rhodes 2003: ch. 8; Chapman 1988; Chapman and Greenaway 1980; and O'Halpin 1989.

20. Cited in Hennessy 1989: 631 and Plowden 1994: 104 respectively. For a review of the politicization debate, see: Rhodes and Weller 2001: ch. 8; and Richards 1997: ch. 9 and 2008: ch. 6.

21. In the era of managerialism, all departments must have an explicit strategic plan of some sort. They come in various guises—strategic plans, annual reports, mission statements, and even visions. Most of the fieldwork was done in 2003, so I use the 2004 annual reports because they report the work of the departments in 2003. They are glossy documents laid before parliament, which provide a mix of advertisement, aspirations, and hard data summarizing achievements against PSAs and other targets. They tell parliament what the department is doing, why it is doing it, and how they got along implementing it. I draw on them for summaries of the departments' work in their several policy areas. I also draw on the Capability Reviews published on the three departments, although these documents are more about aspirations than information (see Cabinet Office 2006c, 2006d, and 2007).

22. On the several crises see: Anderson 2006; Grant 2005; Greer 2003; McConnell and Stark 2002; Taylor 2003; Toke and Marsh 2003; and Winter 2003.

23. See, for example: BSE Inquiry Report (Phillips) 2000; The (Curry) Policy Commission on the Future of Farming and Food 2002; and the Anderson Inquiry 2002, into FMD.

24. Neo-liberal thought comes in various guises. The term is used here to refer to that set of ideas about the role of the state that focus on privatization, regulation, managerialism, markets and quasi-markets, productivity, and residual welfare. For more discussion see Coates and Lawler 2000; and Gamble 2006.

Part II

The Actors

Secretary of State is a cabinet minister; a minister of state is a secretary of state in waiting (p. 101).

4

ministers of state do not sit in the cabinet.

The Minister

SofS and MofS are appointed by the PM — (see p. 21)
they are elected MPs for the most part or from the HoL.

The chapter has three-parts. I provide an overview of a year in the life of a Minister to provide a context for a detailed description of a day in the life of both the Secretary of State and the Minister of State. I provide a chronological account based on my fieldwork notebooks. I then seek to show this account is reliable by drawing on my interviews with three secretaries of state and three ministers of state about their daily lives. I provide further support from published diaries and memoirs. In short, I juxtapose practice, talk, and considered writing, a procedure I follow throughout Parts II and III of the book.

SS
+
MS
why?

THE WORKING YEAR

Of course there is no such thing as a typical day. All days come with a surprise, with stress, with last-minute changes. If there is a typical day, it is long, with many meetings, few breaks, unexpected and possibly unwelcome changes, an evening engagement usually a speech or dinner, and a red box or two for late-night relaxation. To provide some context for my story of a day in the life, Figure 4.1 illustrates the range of tasks in a year.

I had access to only one Minister's diary for a whole year, although I had the engagement diary for parts of the year for another (for Chapter 9 below). Nonetheless, Figure 4.1 provides a believable outline. The obvious conclusion is that ministers have many demands on their time. Although most ministers spend over a third of their time on departmental matters, especially speaking for the Department in meetings with other departments, they spend more of their time on other, diverse tasks. The minister spends on average twelve hours a week in formal discussions with officials, with a roughly similar amount of time a month spent in formal discussions with other ministers and special advisers (SpAds). A further half-day a month is spent on political contacts. The 'Other' category refers to a miscellany of entries, some indecipherable even by the Diary Secretary and the Private Office.

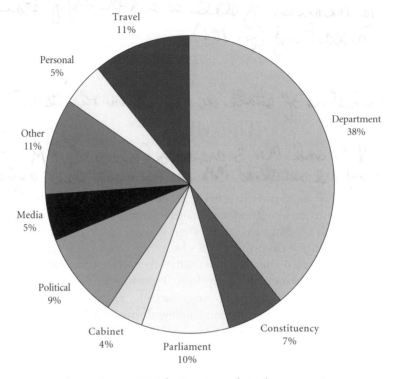

Figure 4.1 The Secretary of State's year

The data drawn from the diaries of both ministers and permanent secretaries (see Chapter 5 below) have some important weaknesses. The diary secretaries in the private offices keep the diaries. There is no standard method of recording appointments. So, a meeting with a named individual in one Department will be recorded as a 1:1 (one-to-one) in another diary. While I coded the Permanent Secretary's meetings with the Minister as policy, that meeting could be about anything. Similarly a meeting with an official colleague could have much policy content and nothing in the diary would show that. Each Diary Secretary went through their Permanent Secretary's or Minister's diary with me but obviously could not remember the topic of every meeting. The diary is an incomplete record in other ways too. There are many unplanned meetings—colleagues pop in for a quick chat. The diaries are not clear on whether other people were present at these meetings or about the extent of informal contact. We did not always agree on how to code some work. For example, I thought trips to agencies located outside London should be coded as representational while permanent secretaries thought it should be coded as internal management. As the project is about how ministers and permanent secretaries see their world, their views prevailed. We agreed to show them as 'external relations'. Indeed, the Private Office did most of the work in coding the Minister's diary. Finally, the list of specific tasks is less diverse than the diaries reveal simply because I had to limit the categories to get a clear picture and, for permanent secretaries (see Chapter 5 below), a degree of comparability. In brief, the portrait is broad brush. It is an estimate of their workload.

A DAY IN THE LIFE OF A MINISTER

As I looked at both the annual outline and the official engagement diary for the week, it was clear the pace was unrelenting. My story is one of the inhabitants seeking to contain their complex and changing world within their diaries. I describe one day—see Table 4.1.[1]

I had been in and around the Department on several occasions and for two lengthy stays. So I have been briefed about today and I do not go direct to the Department but to a breakfast policy launch at the Institute of Mechanical Engineers in George Street.[2] It is a grand old Victorian building, chosen because it is adjacent to both parliament and the Department. The room is grand with all wood walls and floor to ceiling pillars. There is a massive chandelier in the middle of the room. The walls are covered with portraits of nineteenth-century engineers looking, as they often do, self-satisfied and self-important. It is a suitable setting for a government event. It has the right trappings of grandeur. Mind you, it is snowing outside and high ceilings may be grand but they are bad for keeping the room warm. I do not take my coat

Table 4.1 The Secretary of State's engagement diary

TIME	ACTIVITY—planned	ACTIVITY—unplanned
8.00–9.30	Breakfast policy launch	
10.00–11.00	Cabinet	
11.00–11.30		Bilateral meeting with cabinet colleague
11.35–11.45	Return to Department	
11.45–12.15	Opening speech at conference	
12.30–13.30	Lunch with father	
14.00–15.00	Meeting about Department's budget attended by Treasury official	
15.00–15.30	Telephone interview with *The Guardian*	
15.30–16.00	Strap	E-mails and diary
16.00–16.30	Bilateral with Minister of State	
16.30–17.00	DG: external appointment	Telephone call with cabinet colleague
17.30–18.30	Reception (House of Commons)	
About 18.00	Three-line whip, then home and red box	

off, and I am not the only one. It is mingling time and there is a continental breakfast of coffee, croissants, and Danish pastries. The Danish pastries provide the expected sugar hit but the croissants are the English variety, neither light nor crisp. A Private Secretary (PS) mutters to me, 'there is an office cold and it keeps on doing the rounds—no wonder', referring to our chilly surroundings.

The platform speakers have to take off their coats. They are on public display and must present themselves accordingly. They don lapel microphones and get a level with the usual '1, 2, 3, testing'. The event is a public relations exercise to improve links between government, business, and higher education. There are two secretaries of state, one minister of state, and a senior business spokesperson on the platform. The audience comprises senior business executives, vice-chancellors, and the professoriate. So it is a high-powered affair. The room is full and the PSs and SpAds have to stand at the back. I stand with them.

Looking at the platform, once again I am struck by the different expectations of men and women. I saw eight ministers and ten permanent secretaries in action and the majority took care over their public appearance. However, today, one Minister wore a crumpled black suit that looked as if he had worn it all week. It had many creases and none were in the right place. He had stubble and was overweight. The impression is one of a careless, untidy dresser. Most take much more care over their appearance no matter what the event. The Permanent Secretary was going on a visit to a client organization. He was discussing the logistics with his Principal Private Secretary (PPS). 'You can't dress down', he said, 'you have to manage the impression you make.' When he wanted to appear less formal he wore a blue rather than a grey or black suit. Of course, like most of the men, he dressed in a boring way. It was invariably dark suits with white shirt and tie. I came across the occasional marker of the florid handkerchief, the hand painted silk tie or even the Paul Smith designer suit. The more distinctive clothing was worn by strangers. There was a marked gender dimension to appearance. The women were not limited to dark suits. One PPS dressed in a fawn trouser suit with a three-quarter length coat with black V-necked wool sweater and black accessories. She typified the phrase 'power dressing' but 'in an understated way'. One Minister was most stylish. She wore a lilac trouser suit with a three-quarter length jacket with a dark purple hip-length top. The outfit was by Jean Muir, an upmarket designer label specializing in 1960s and 1970s styles and available only at the top stores. The accessories caught the eye. She wore a string of pearls with matching earrings, a gold watch and man's style signet ring. The style is loose, draped, and striking. I know the female ministers are aware of the difference. As one said, 'women have to take care over their wardrobe. Men are so lucky.' She was correct, but most ministers, irrespective of gender, consciously managed their appearance most of the time.[3]

The Minister in the chair makes a few opening remarks, explaining there will be no speeches. It will be a question and answer session on ways to improve links between the several parties in the room. Various briefing documents have already been circulated but extra copies are available. The second Minister then makes some general, positive comments about British business with examples of successful collaboration between industry, government, and higher education. The business spokesperson then gives a speech! It is a cheerful, amusing discussion of, among other things, business attitudes to higher education. It is well received. We then turn to questions and the Chair tells the audience that journalists are present, so we are not on the Chatham House rule.

The opening moments are stiff and the Minister asks the audience questions rather than the expected way round. The early speakers make statements and take positions, rather than asking questions. The Chair collects several questions and comments before inviting members of the panel to respond. Their replies are brisk, clear, and even efficient. As at all these big events the questioning is all over the place. It is hard to see any coherent themes. The universities defend themselves and give examples of effective working with business. Small business expresses concern that, yet again, it will be overlooked. The Chair attempts to give it a sense of direction by asking for proposals on improving relationships. The various proposals from the floor are discussed, most in a cursory fashion. Then the platform sums up. So, they tell the audience, 'it is a two-way street', and stress the need to counter prejudice on both sides by disseminating examples of 'best practice'. They identify a couple of areas where they want to 'go forward' and 'make a small difference'. The secretaries of state agree they will drop one another a note about taking the discussion forward after Easter. The business spokesperson comments: 'It is symbolic and significant that we have big companies, government and academics here.' The PS thinks the meeting is 'excellent'. Above all, it is 'an event' and what is important is that it took place. Whether there are any specific outcomes is less important.

As the meeting breaks up, people mingle again. They add new contacts to their personal networks and reinforce existing ties. The SpAds from the three Departments are gossiping with one another, especially DfES and DTI. The PSs are not. Afterwards, I ask them why. The answer is simple: 'we are working'. The reply is accurate. They took notes of suggestions that might require action and, towards the end, collect coats and summon the cars to the front of the building.

My Minister zooms out of the building. I have to run to keep up and he grins at me as we speed off, 'still with us then?' I am part of the scenery. The PS passes the Minister a file for a later speech. The Minister says, 'It's OK, I don't need it', but he glances at it all the same. When we arrive at the Department, we are whisked in and I do not have to collect my usual daily pass. We have travelled less than a mile. The walk is much shorter.

The Minister is just passing through on his way to cabinet. There is a call waiting, which he takes before heading off for No. 10. I am not allowed to attend cabinet, nor am I allowed to see any of the papers. That said, there was no evidence of any papers. Neither the Minister nor the PS were carrying files as he left the building. Cabinet is scheduled for one hour only. I am told it is because there has already been a meeting devoted to the budget. So, this meeting is for briefings, especially about the war in Iraq. On his return the Minister describes cabinet meetings positively: 'There is a very strong sense of cabinet as a collective entity' because 'we've all worked together for so long. It's cosy.'

Apart from cabinet and its committees, there are few things from which I have been excluded. I have not been allowed to attend one-to-one perform-ance appraisals unless the staff member agrees. Most did not. I have not been allowed to shadow any of the Minister's personal engagements with family and friends. Selectively, I have been excluded from bilateral meetings between cabinet ministers. I could claim that I had such privileged access because I was trusted. That helped. But I suspect the real reason is that much of the work is routine and boring. The media are interested in about 5 per cent of what goes on; high politics, big policy initiatives, personal indiscretions. Regulating business is essential. Reviewing the continuing relevance of such regulations is also necessary. The work is unglamorous and time-consuming; the minutiae of government. Most of the time, the media see it as boring if they are aware it is going on. Much Department work is of this nature. So, if I am odd enough to want to see the machine in its everyday detail, and provided I do not get in the way too much, they will let me follow them around.

I use this downtime productively. With the PPS, I go through my notes for the previous day, filling gaps, translating acronyms, and correcting the spelling of full names. I also interview one of the private secretaries. The context is the usual office conversation; frustration that they cannot get through on the phone, badinage about almost anything. Today's main topic of concern is an away day to Southend. One of the PSs does not want to go and asks, 'what's wrong with Marbella?'

Then to my chagrin, the Minister does not arrive back at 11 a.m. There is a mobile phone call. He will be delayed because he is having a chat with a cabinet colleague. I curse my luck. I have little enough time shadowing him. I do not want to lose any of it. Cabinet was bad enough. To make it even more irritating, I discover later that I could have listened in because it was not about the budget or the Iraq war or any other matter of high politics. It was about low politics; the imminent local government elections. The two secretaries of state agree they will go to my Minister's local constituency on Friday—by tradition, constituency day—to campaign in the local elections. They discuss the trip and what each will do. On his return, the Minister briefs the Diary Secretary, who will liaise with the Minister's constituency office about the trip (see Chapter 8: 233).

Reception calls; 'the Minister is in the building'. But he doesn't arrive in the office, and there is more frustration for me. He is delayed briefing his SpAds on what happened in cabinet, and what he has agreed with his ministerial colleague. More conversations I do not hear. There is barely time for any conversation at all once he gets to the office because he is on his way out again. A PS hovers with files to take him to his next engagement, delivering the opening address to a conference.

The Queen Elizabeth II (QE II) is a massive modern conference centre and the conference room holds over 500 people. It is walking distance but the driver is still on hand. He gets the Minister's coat, which was left in the car. The Minister is waited on hand and foot. He is also never alone. This time he is escorted by a PS and two members of the Press Office until we get to the conference centre when the Minister's party acquires two more members from the conference organizers. The Minister gets the red-carpet treatment and my hosts take him off to his personal dressing room. There, he adjusts his appearance and has a light dusting of face powder to make sure he does not shine on camera.

Work on the speech began several days before (see Chapter 7). On the day, there is a last quick read through in the car from the breakfast engagement. Of course, there is the usual disclaimer on the text: 'check against delivery'. I never saw a Minister deviate from the written text and, if they did, they were usually some pleasantries at the beginning and end, rarely matters of substance. Today is no different. The Minister stands at a lectern with a big screen behind him. The lights are dimmed. He is well trained. He knows that little gestures go a long way on screen, so he restricts himself to the occasional hand movement. The speech is listened to in a hushed, respectful silence. It is delivered slowly, clearly, and firmly. It contains all the buzz words of the day but it is made palatable by the occasional use of everyday language. There are no dramatic pauses for laughter or acclamation as at a party conference. As delivered, the speech has a conversational feel but it is not a laugh a minute. The applause is polite but not sustained. There is an opportunity for questions but there are only a couple—rehearsed and from the Chair. The point is not what the Minister says but the simple fact that he is there. It is an example of the ceremonial functions of members of the government; it is about the appearance of ruling.

Once again I am stood at the back with the PS and, as the Minister finishes, we rush to meet him off the platform. It is but a short walk from the QE II to the House of Commons where he is meeting his father for lunch in the Strangers' Dining Room. I walk back to the Department with the others. I have a quick sandwich lunch in the office, and then interview the administrative officer in charge of correspondence and get a quick briefing from the PPS about the meeting scheduled for the Minister's return.

The budget is imminent. Various members of the Department have been discussing its contents with the Treasury off and on for several weeks. Today's meeting could be contentious because it is about extra funds. The Minister is back a few minutes before the meeting and skim reads the briefing document. He asks, 'Is there anything hidden in here which we will scream about?' 'Yes', is the reply, but it is from the Treasury spokesperson at the meeting who has just walked into the room.

Such visits have their own mythology in Whitehall. For example, Shriti Vadera was a banker with UBS Warburg recruited by Gordon Brown ostensibly for her Third World expertise. The prized skill of Gordon Brown's 'excitable aide' was that of 'assassin'. In a meeting, she could switch from a 'lengthy monologue' to an abrupt 'no' (Bower 2007: 312, 313, and 486). So, her visits were anticipated with some apprehension by civil servants, not only because she spoke with the authority of the Chancellor but also because her interventions were seen as unpredictable.

Today's Treasury spokesperson is neither excitable nor lethal nor unpredictable nor witch-like. His role is exactly what I would expect from a Treasury spokesperson at a departmental meeting. He asks analytical questions about the economic merits of the proposed expenditure. The tone of the meeting is civilized; the everyday conventions of polite behaviour prevail.

The issue is whether to pay a subsidy to a loss-making executive agency. The Director General (DG) believes the agency's management can turn it around. Others are less sure and want to know what has gone wrong and why before agreeing. Yet others are concerned about the public reaction to the agency failing. Discussion revolves around the costs of exit compared with the subsidy. There is general agreement that 'we are good at keeping the damper on these crises'. They are right. The story does not make the newspapers until much later. But the Treasury is unhappy about the subsidy and the brief is to impress this simple fact on the Department. The spokesperson argues that 'the rate of return' on the expenditure is 'poor'. He wants to compare the costs of keeping the agency with 'outsourcing' and he wants to know if outsourcing will get rid of the risk for government. It is a focused, analytical discussion. It goes nowhere because, in effect, the Treasury is saying 'no' to the subsidy and wants the Department to look at other options. In my notebook I summarized his position as: 'I am talking for the Chancellor of the Exchequer who has authorised me to say there is no more money for a bailout and there will be no long-term commitment of public funds' (FWNB). The 'no' is polite, even gentle. To this outsider, it is a classical example of Treasury–Department relations. Nobody says it but the Treasury's word is final. The frisson of apprehension is not specific to any single spokesperson. It is a common reaction to Treasury visitations.

The meeting breaks up. Some hurry off. The DG is talking to the Treasury official, no doubt about what to do next. The Minister is talking to his PPS. The PPS did not attend the meeting. A PS took notes. As the office is open plan with much glass, the PPS can visibly hover when the next appointment is due.

He stands quietly in the doorway. He does not have to say anything. Everybody knows why he stands there. The Minister has a booked telephone call with a journalist from *The Guardian*.

Nothing, absolutely nothing, is left to chance if it can be avoided. So, the journalist has submitted the list of questions beforehand. The article is about the Blair generation of politicians, their influences and their ambitions. It is hard hitting and path breaking journalism. Who was the greatest influence for the work you do? What is your greatest professional achievement? How hard is it to balance personal and professional lives? What are your favourite treats, luxuries, and self-indulgences? The Minister gave outline answers and the Private Office did a draft for him to read aloud over the phone. The replies are as inspired as the questions. So, the luxury is a weekend away with the spouse. The professional ambition is to make lasting change through building consensus. And so on. The journalist rings. Pleasantries are exchanged. The journalist reads the questions. The Minister reads the answers. It is priceless. I struggle not to laugh aloud. You can't make this stuff up. But, there is an important side to it. *The Guardian* is an important broadsheet. It has to be treated with respect. It cannot be fobbed off with e-mailed answers.

The interview does not last the allotted half-an-hour, so the Diary Secretary pops in to discuss changes in the diary and future appointments. The visit to the constituency is top of the list. The Minister does some personal e-mails. He grabs every available opportunity to do so, otherwise the backlog becomes impossible. The PPS pops in with the straps.

I am intrigued. I saw the item on the calendar but had no idea what it was. The PPS asks me to leave the room. When we are outside, I ask why. I did not want to appear to argue about leaving in front of the Minister. He tells me that straps are top secret documents for the Minister's eyes only. Each strap is in a red plastic folder with a large cross on the front. It is numbered, not named. I ask why they are called straps. The PPS does not know. I speculate that the cross represents the original strapping that sealed the folder. The PPS shrugs his shoulders. Today the straps are Joint Intelligence Committee briefings on the war in Iraq. They must be read in the Office, and it is only recently they have been given diary space; 'before the war I didn't keep up'. On occasion, there is an urgent strap that is supposed to get immediate attention. It doesn't. It arrived at 2.15 p.m. but it is not read until an hour later. And nothing happened. There was no telephone call, no e-mail, after reading it. I suspect straps are a throwback to the days when messengers scurried between government buildings with urgent messages. It is another face of the appearance of governing. But for whose benefit? Does it reinforce the sense of being a privileged insider; that Ministers are important people?

No time for such musings. The next appointment has arrived. It is the Minister of State. The topic is the Department's review of its regulations. This Minister of State is well liked by both the Minister and top civil servants. He is widely seen as destined for higher office. They sit next to each other and there is some idle chit-chat about the progress of legislation through parliament—it is proceeding smoothly. The PPS is not in the room but the Minister wants him there. He sits apart with his ubiquitous notebook. It seems that only some 20 regulations have been rescinded but the Minister wants 60. The discussion is detailed. The Minister has mastered a detailed brief and comments, 'I've had another look and I really think we have to end this.' The Minister of State is not convinced. They argue politely back and forth.

> MINISTER: The Treasury and No. 10 are placing us under great pressure
> MINISTER OF STATE: I want to see EU progress before we end it
> MINISTER: Can we put a time limit on it?

They are looking for some compromise but the Secretary of State insists, 'I want to get rid of it'. And they do, by reclassifying it. It is no longer a regulation, but 'it must end in its current form'. So the Minister of State agrees to redraft it. The PPS makes a note of the agreement and will chase the redraft. This meeting could appear unusually detailed, even unproductive. Why are two senior people wasting time over one regulation? In fact, the PPS tells me the Minister often gets his way by arguing from, not for, a detailed case. He has made the general point that the Minister of State needs to do more about scrapping regulations. More pleasantries, the Minister of State departs, and the next appointment is waiting.

It is a DG who needs to discuss an appointment to a regulatory body. The PPS has returned to his desk. A PS attends. The DG talks the Minister through a list of possible candidates, commenting on their suitability—'insufficient experience'; 'probably a first reserve'. After about ten minutes we get to the nub—'the Treasury is briefing against us'. So, the Department has a preferred candidate but the Treasury prefers someone else. The Minister is happy with the Department's candidate. He is not happy about Treasury interference. He agrees he will ring the SpAd at No. 10 'and talk him through it'. In practice, that means the Minister's SpAd will do it. More important, the Minister will 'meet' Ed Balls (Chief Economic Adviser, Treasury, and Gordon Brown's *consigliore*) 'and tell him to stop it'.

There is just time for a quick telephone call. A cabinet colleague called about the planned constituency visit. The Minister returns the call (see Chapter 7 on the protocols about such calls). They talk about travel arrangements, who will talk about what, and other details of the trip. When you hear only one side of a conversation, it is hard to know what you miss. Now we are on the move again, this time to the House of Commons for a constituency event.

The Sikh Society of the United Kingdom is celebrating *Vaisakhi*—roughly the equivalent of harvest festival—in the House of Commons. The event is hosted by several MPs with Sikh communities in their constituency. The Minister makes a few opening remarks in Gujarati, expands on the theme of multiculturalism, and receives a garland. It is a cheerful event—noise, bright colours, and the smell of exotic food. I eat a selection of Indian nibbles as the Minister mingles, shaking hands and smiling. He then moves to one side and gives a telephone interview to his local radio station on *Vaisakhi* and Britain as a multicultural society. At least I think that is what it is about. It is noisy. I enjoy the food but the event drags on. The Minister's thoughts have also turned to home. It is 6.10 p.m. as he escorts me out. He is heading home for dinner and the red boxes—'I am grateful for the early night'.

I head back to the Department. I have arranged to see the PPS for an interview at 6.30 p.m. I am out of luck. He has been summoned by the Permanent Secretary and when he gets out it is 7 p.m. and he is determined to go home. I can't say I blame him. I am tired too and I don't do this day in and day out. He suggests a telephone interview. I ask if I should submit the questions in writing beforehand. Will he read his replies to me? We laugh and head off out—me to a pub to read through and check my notes for tomorrow. It will be an early start for the Private Office and, therefore, me.

WHAT THE MINISTER SAYS ABOUT HIS DAY[4]

Ministers have differing understandings of their job. In this section, I explore these different understandings and how they affect everyday life. These interviews with four secretaries of state reveal a sharp contrast between the Westminster or traditional beliefs and practices and managerial beliefs and practices.[5] I report only the Ministers' views (see Chapter 5 for the views of civil servants).

Westminster beliefs and practices

The traditional or Whitehall conception sees Ministers as 'good generalists':

We understand current affairs, the subtext, the great political issues, but we're not specialists and I think if you pretend to be a specialist you're fooling yourself.

The key to success is:

Cooperative working, I wanted understanding of the briefs and the issues, I wanted politeness and respect and I didn't want my weight thrown around.

In return, ministers had to be 'willing to learn, and willing to listen' [Minister, TI]. Most ministers had close relationships with their Permanent Secretary:

I see a lot of the Permanent Secretary and the other senior officials. In fact I liked him . . . . They knew what they were doing, and I had confidence in them, and my approach would not be 'we are going to do this', it would be 'what do you think we should do?' I would listen to them, and then I would talk to the two political advisers who would have a political take on it. [Minister, TI]

Ministers wanted two things from their civil servants:

They've got to be the master of the brief, they're my specialist adviser, and honestly I don't expect them to withhold things from me, because they'll think I'll make a decision they don't like, and bluntness. I'd much rather they said, 'No, don't do that in my opinion you would be wrong', and then talk me through why. I'd much rather they did that than just let me go off and say 'did you see what this stupid blighter's done?'. [Minister, TI]

The Minister's account of his relationship with his top civil servants is classical Westminster model.[6]

RAWR: So, civil servants would say 'No Minister I'm sorry but . . .'
MINISTER: They certainly did, the Permanent Secretary did it all the time. He had very strong views himself which I liked. I mean he's conservative not Labour but he's blunt, he's very intelligent, he's very honest, to the point, and I like all that.
RAWR: But at some point you didn't agree with him.
MINISTER I'm not a tyrant. This isn't some medieval court. If the answer is no, you've got to have a reason and it's got to be an intellectually defensible reason that others would say on balance you've got a point, or that's a sensible, or that's a reasonable decision, you know that a reasonable person could make.
RAWR: How often would that happen?
MINISTER: Very, very rarely. [Minister, TI]

The same pattern was reported in the other departments.

RAWR: Would you discuss with the Permanent Secretary how things were going? Are we doing OK?
MINISTER: Oh yes, exactly in that language. Not 'am I doing OK?' but 'are we doing OK?' [Minister, TI, emphasis in original]

The consequences of this view of a minister's role are that he or she is cocooned by the civil service. The traditional style encourages such briefings and meetings. I have already described the official working day. Here a Minister describes the long, informal parts of his day that are not in the diary.

Oh God the workload is phenomenal. My pattern is fairly regular I suppose. I am at work by 9 a.m. because I swim beforehand. I didn't want to swim at 7 a.m. to get in by 8 a.m. I saw no reason for that, so I swim at 7:50 a.m. [and], I am ready for working at 9 a.m.

[. . .]

My pattern of work used to be that I didn't have meetings in the diary after 6.30 p.m. but maybe after 6 p.m. I wasn't overly keen on a timetable meeting after 6 p.m. But I use the 6 p.m. and beyond slot. Civil servants like to 'pop up' and see you, so they would call in during the day and say can I have five minutes. So 6 p.m. onwards became 'could you fit so and so in?' So that was a bit of an 'open door policy', which I quite liked. If people did want to wander up, they usually knew that it wasn't a meeting time at 6:00 p.m. So, I stayed in the Department and, given that the meetings I attended were often 'back-to-back', there had not been a break at all during the day, I would then do paperwork. Even if you did go home, you still had to do it. I did low-key work. I either signed letters or more often than not I read my papers for tomorrow's meetings. I did not do policy stuff when I went home at night. I couldn't do it. Past it. Absolutely past it.

I went home Thursday night, constituency day Friday, but constant phone conversations. Box arrived Saturday morning. The box has to go back on Sunday lunchtime, Sunday afternoon. So you have only got Saturday and Sunday to do the box. And the problem is the box has got all Friday's day work in as well as the stuff that is there for the weekend. As Minister of State, when I left on Thursday night, including the train journey home, I aimed to have cleared all the work that was on my desk from the Monday–Thursday, so it didn't run in to the Friday box. I couldn't do it as Secretary of State. On Sunday, apart from big documents that are with you for a week or two, I aimed to clear the weekend box work by the time I got in Monday morning, so it didn't bump into the Monday work. That's the only way I could cope. So, by the time I got on the train on the Sunday there was stuff that hadn't gone back in the box and I have kept for the train journey or for a little time back in the flat on Sunday. And apart from that, say you've got a draft of the Green Paper which is with you for a few days. I wasn't bad at keeping to that routine, but the trouble was you have a weekend off or a day off and it absolutely went 'up the shoot'. [Minister, TI]

It is also linked to an incremental view of what can be done:

the trouble is, we were boxed in, the room to manoeuvre was pitiful, the room for discretion very, very small. [Minister, TI]

So, the Department may cocoon the Minister but he has to work hard. Not everyone wants to play this game. Some secretaries of state are relatively detached from their departments. One Minister of State explained, when asked how frequently he saw his Secretary of State, that because there was *'such pressure of international events'*, because *'DEFRA's remit is so broad'*, and because *'each of the ministerial team is pretty strapped'*, he saw the Secretary of State infrequently for *'an informal chat over dinner'* [Minister, TI]. The Permanent Secretary saw the same Secretary of State for a 30-minute briefing each week. Other permanent secretaries had the equivalent meeting but they also had regular informal chats. This Secretary of State was more detached from the internal running of the Department, focusing on international events and playing a role *'in the cabinet in addition to his portfolio'*. But at least the Private Office knew where the Minister was and organized his day and the trips. Others were not so much detached as absent. Here a ministerial colleague comments, not a civil servant. One Minister:

> had a very bad reputation in the Department. Most of the time he wasn't <u>in</u> the Department and the Private Office didn't know where he was because he wouldn't tell them. So there were quite basic relationship breakdown issues. A lot of the time he was doing political stuff and there was a real problem. [Minister, TI]

I saw the Private Office fret when the Minister was delayed. It is hard to envisage the levels of concern when the Minister would not tell them where he was! Also, some ministers chafe at the traditions embedded in the diary and the cocoon. They seek reform and managerialism holds out the prospect of change.

Managerial beliefs and practices

Alongside the traditional beliefs and practices, I encountered managerialism. There is no choice to be made. All ministers speak both languages, although not everyone took a hands-on interest in managing the Department. For one Minister, it was his major contribution.

> I knew the first thing we had to do was just review the Department and sort it out because it was obviously not a functioning Department. [It] still operated as silos. I'd worked out we had to have a review. We needed the help of external consultants but we couldn't hand it over to external consultants partly because we couldn't afford it and partly because we needed to learn to do it ourselves. I hadn't really done terms of reference for the review but had an idea of where I wanted it to go, plus some other stuff. So when the [Permanent Secretary] came in for our very first meeting and said, 'Do you think it would be a good idea if we sort of looked at what the Department does and how it works?' I said, 'Absolutely, we are going to have a review.' In fact, I did give him the draft terms of reference. That's right, I said, 'Here are the draft terms of reference. I want consultants but not to do the whole thing, we will have to have a good review team.' And he said, 'Oh right.' He said, 'Very well, shall I draft some terms of reference and kick these around and so on.' [Minister, TI]

The Department underwent a year-long review devising a new internal structure and writing a new strategic plan.

> [The Permanent Secretary] very quickly put together the internal review group and then we brought in consultants to reinforce it. And he found a PPS and another chap. Very bright, very bright, committed to change, good, good people. Really

pleased. And I was having practically weekly meetings on various aspects of the review. And really 'hands-on', driving the thing forward, working with the consultants, we had a Review Board with some outsiders on it to steer the thing. I was really involved in it. Then we got to the point when we were putting the new organisation in place, getting all our new people and so on, and I felt able to step back, anyway I needed the time for other things. [Minister, TI]

The Department replaced most of its top management team:

It was clear we had to have a smaller DG group and a much better DG group. But it took us a bit of time to get there because we had to reorganise the Department.

It was a clear out:

RAWR: So you have put together your own top team and it's basically completely different from that which you inherited.
MINISTER: There is nobody doing the same job. I don't think. Nobody at all, from what I inherited. Still a few of the same people but in different jobs. So it's a big change [Minister, TI]

The Minister was hands-on, with opinions on the strengths and weaknesses of top staff, so individuals were moved on through early retirements and secondments. The Minister did not want what he saw as the typical civil servant:

Most of the DG's are introverted, thinking, analyse 'till the cows come home', you know, rather than the extrovert, 'make it happen' end of things, which is very much the typical civil servant. So there's just too much analysis, too many meetings, too much process, too much 'oh goodness me, we can't upset XYZ'.

It might be Margaret Thatcher's phrase but it is still beloved by many politicians today; Ministers want 'can-do' civil servants. This Minister preferred the shorthand description of 'hands-on' or 'make it happen', but he was alluding to the same decisive style. He was enthusiastic about the new DGs; '*very* good' and '*very bright, very capable*' were at the bottom end of the fulsome scale that encompassed '*she's doing wonderfully, absolutely wonderfully*', '*just super*', and '*an absolute star*' [Minister, TI].

Of course, reform is neither a one-off event nor without its problems:

About six weeks ago something like that, some quite big alarm bells starting ringing. The consultant said, 'No no we are doing it as fast as we can.' But then they started saying, 'It's getting bogged down.' I could see it was getting bogged down. The business planning stuff was turning into a kind of mega industry of its own and getting bogged down. And I started picking up just the odd little bits of feedback that the senior people felt change was happening, but not down there. So I thought, 'Right we'll have to up the input here.' So I got for instance the head of HR to come in, and we had a very frank debrief on what was really going on. I got the chief consultant in to tell me what was really going on. So I have been doing quite a

lot. So I have really stepped up the effort and I will continue from now [on] ...
*I will put a lot more effort into the change process. Because it's very clear if it doesn't
get another mega injection of energy, it's going to sink back a bit.* [Minister, TI]

Management reform was at the heart of this Minister's agenda (and see
Chapter 5 for more details). Such reforms are not unusual. In DEFRA, the
Permanent Secretary was driving a major internal reform. What is noteworthy
from this interview is the central role of the Minister. It is not unique. Michael
Heseltine was an enthusiastic advocate of management reform when at
the Ministry of Defence and the Department of the Environment.[7] But as
Sir Frank Cooper, former Permanent Secretary at the Ministry of Defence
observed with characteristic vigour:

> Personally, I regard the minister-as-manager as nonsense. Ministers are not
> interested. It's not part of the Minister's stock-in-trade. . . . It's not what they
> went into politics for. (cited in Hennessy 1989: 609)

Many ministers in the 2001–5 Blair government would still agree with Sir
Frank. As my interviews illustrate, the world of Whitehall changes so there are
ministers who manage but they remain a minority (see also Marsh et al. 2001:
145–7).

A DAY IN THE LIFE OF A MINISTER OF STATE

Secretaries of state and ministers of state come in all shapes and sizes from the
stalwart being rewarded for years of service to the rising star being blooded for
even higher office. Parliament is a small talent pool (see Chapter 3: p. 55). One
Minister recollected being told by Tony Blair, 'we are going to be a bit short of
Ministers, find a seat' [Minister, TI]. Prime ministers incur debts, which are
discharged in making appointments. Departments pay the price of his or her
choices. As Kaufman (1980: 38) observes:

> The new Minister may turn out to be rude, lazy, irascible, dirty, a drunkard or—
> worst of all—stupid. And they are stuck with him. . . . To begin with, they operate
> on the safest principle, namely that he is an imbecile.

The department should start with low expectations. They all live in a gossipy,
bitchy world. There is no shortage of critics. Yet it is relatively rare for
secretaries of state to attract the odium of their permanent secretaries (see
Chapter 5). If there is mutual trust then many a foible will be forgiven.

However, some secretaries of state distrust the civil service and the consequences of distrust can be severe for everyone. There was much gossip that
Stephen Byers, when Secretary of State for Trade and Industry, held secret and

unreported meetings with his political advisers and used spin and leaks as his preferred tools of policy making. It was not without foundation. There was much distrust on both sides (Blunkett 2006: 351–2) and the Department was *'pretty demoralised and unhappy and confused'* [Permanent Secretary, TI]. Byers left to much *'rejoicing'*, and a general air of vindication when the scandal over the attempt to use the 11 September 2001 attacks on the twin towers as cover for bad news blew up in Byer's face at the Department for Transport, Local Government and the Regions. It was not a good day to bury anything! The ruckus served only to reveal that Byers again had an inner cabal, and a poor relationship with his career civil servants, who suspected him of embroiling the Department in party politics (see also Chapter 7).[8]

Ministers of State, judging by the comments of both senior civil servants and Ministers, can be a mixed blessing. Some are just unpleasant people. One Permanent Secretary looked back on his time in the Private Office of the Minister of Housing and called it 'easily the shittiest job I ever had' because the Minister was abusive and a bully. He admitted he gained credit from his colleagues for surviving [Permanent Secretary, TI].

Some are time-servers. One Minister of State's remit was government reform. A white paper was promised. It was delayed repeatedly. His Permanent Secretary insisted they:

> *were very nice to each other'* [but he was] *a nonentity . . . obsessive and deeply suspicious of a machine that he thought was out to get him; he despised Peter Mandelson and officials in equal measure.* [Permanent Secretary, TI]

Whitehall is gossipy. You laugh at such stories. You know they will enliven the book. But you keep a question mark in the back of your head. I came to share the Permanent Secretary's view. I had a long conversation with this Minister of State on a train journey. I thought it would be a great opportunity to talk about civil service reform. Not everybody's cup of tea, I concede, but I was interested and he was supposed to be. He was more interested in the trappings of office. So, the conversation revolved around the ministerial car and, obviously his great love, international visits. He mentioned he did not fit in with the London set but when I pressed by sharing his distaste for 'southerners', he moved on. So, I never knew whether he was airing his northern preferences, or his Old Labour views on New Labour, or his distrust of officials.

Some ministers of state hold office mainly because of their party political alignments. The tussles between Tony Blair and Gordon Brown extended to ministerial appointments at all levels. I asked a PPS about a Minister's standing because he seemed 'off-side' at the ministerial meeting. He is 'not a team player'. He had a poor reputation compared with other ministers; a state revealed in the way officials addressed him as '*Mr* [Smith]. Other ministers of state were often called Minister or, in the confines of the Private Office, referred to by their first name. Using the title of 'Mr' speaks volumes. The PPS 'hopes' he will go in the next reshuffle, but that is a civil servant speaking. When I discussed this Minister with one of his ministerial colleagues, I was told with much merriment that he would stay because 'he is harmless, a Brown-ite, and everybody has to have one'. The unkind barb of 'lackey' was never far away in any conversation about this Minister.

One Junior Minister gave me the run around. His time was so important that he cancelled, rearranged, and rearranged again on a whim. When I saw him, the interview was interrupted regularly by phone calls, the Private Office, and short car trips to the Commons to vote. I was convinced it was a show designed to impress me that he was a busy and important person. I just sat still or followed him as appropriate and carried on with the interview when I could. Slowly he realized the interview was about him and I got his attention. As I left, and the PS escorted me from the building, I said the interview was fine once he started talking about himself. The PS was indiscreet; 'heaven forbid I should use the word ego', he pauses and corrects himself, 'no, posterity'. I conclude that for some ministers, self-importance triumphs over substance; hence this vignette of self-importance.

Ministers can be most vociferous in their complaints about ministerial colleagues:

> [He] was an absolute disgrace. I mean how he ever got into the Lords I do not know but to be made a Minister; he just wouldn't do any work. All he wanted to do was to get on foreign trips. [Minister, TI]

Others, such as Alan Clark, also '*didn't do much*' but bring an affectionate smile to faces because he '*was outrageous but very funny*' [Permanent Secretary, TI].

Finally, some ministers of state are out of their depth. They exemplify the Peter Principle of promotion to their level of incompetence. One Minister of State put off his interview with me three times. I know they are busy, but the permanent secretaries and secretaries of state are busier and they cancelled their meetings with me rarely. When we were finally in the same room at the same time, he brought along his PS, in effect, to hold his hand. We were not long into the interview before he was deflecting questions to the PS. It became brutally clear that he was 'lost' when I asked about the Department and his policy area. So, an interview with me was threatening. When we talked about his daily life and his external role representing the Department, he became more relaxed. Departmental gossip confirmed my impression that he 'struggled', although his Private Office went to great lengths to protect him. After all, any gaffe by him reflected badly on them.

Accuracy dictates I note the ministers who struggle for whatever reason but my story is not about them. I have chosen a Minister of State who was widely regarded as successful. I record events drawn from two days to avoid undue

now two days' work of an MS widely regarded as successful...

Table 4.2. The Minister of State's engagement diary[9]

TIME	ACTIVITY—planned
7.00–9.30	'Doing the rounds', early morning TV interviews with GMTV, ITV, and Sky
10.00–11.00	Ministerial meeting with Secretary of State
11.00–12.30	Meeting–building renovation
12.30–15.30	Running Whip with various meetings at House of Commons
15.30–17.00	Committee Meeting, House of Lords
17.00–19.30	Third Reading of Bill, several votes, 1:1 meetings with officials, paperwork,
17.00	Privy Council—on hold
18.30–20.30	Reception—Natural History Museum

overlap with the Secretary of State's day (Table 4.2). My aim is to show the variety of ministerial work.

It was an early start to the day with an activity that is often undertaken but not well loved—doing the rounds of the TV studios. I am collected from the front steps and we are driven in turn to GMTV, ITV, and, our last stop, to Sky News' subsidiary studio on Millbank. Like every such studio, all are a tip. Newspapers and boxes of videos are jumbled everywhere. Whichever way you turn, there is a television screen, commonly with the sound muted. Telephones, desktop and mobile, ring. People pace around. It is the amiable anarchy popularized in *Drop the Dead Donkey*. Some find it appealing. The Minister finds it frustrating. Nothing ever starts on time. You are always kept waiting. It is a rush from building to building. And when the interview starts, they ask you about today's headlines, not the topic you came into the studio to discuss. So, the Minister finds himself answering questions about a ministerial colleague at the Home Office, Beverley Hughes. During March there had been a running controversy about granting visas to migrants from Romania and Bulgaria. It was alleged that bogus applications were being rubber-stamped by officials in the UK against the advice of officials on the ground. The Minister claimed she had not been warned. Correspondence was found that demonstrated she had been warned. She resigned. The rights and wrongs of this affair are not germane. The point is that the Minister had to answer questions on a topic which was no part of his Department's brief. With no notice or briefing, he was a spokesperson for the government on immigration. The Sky interview broke this camel's back and it is an angry man who leaves the building heading for the Department.

There is time for a cup of coffee, a whinge about the media, and a catch-up chat with the PS before we go to the early morning meeting with the Secretary of State. The meeting starts as a briefing, update session for the ministerial team. For example, they discuss whether the Minister should be granted reserve powers in the bill before parliament. The PPS is present, making a note of any items that need action. Either I am sleepy from an early start, or the discussion becomes unfocused, because I rapidly become lost. I am not sure why we have turned to the topic of building local communities. There is much chatter about 'value added', 'reaching out into real communities', and the Secretary of State seems to be engaged in a pep talk; he wants 'exciting and innovative proposals'. It would also seem that the voluntary sector has irritated him; 'outdoor relief for the unemployable'. My Minister of State has said nothing after nearly 45 minutes of discussion. Conversation turns to the war in Iraq and the traffic in Whitehall.

There is nothing unusual about this meeting or my response to it. Updating sessions move quickly and everybody in the room has a good idea of what is going on in the Department and the government. Background knowledge is just assumed. But I do not have that local knowledge, so I can and do get lost. I am reminded that I am a stranger and it is not my world. As we head back to his office, I tell the Minister of State I did not follow the discussion. He is not surprised. The Secretary of State wants to involve local communities in the Department's initiatives but other ministers and their officials do not. So, the meeting between, for example, the affected officials, had been cancelled. The Secretary of State was frustrated by such delaying tactics. He wanted an end to inaction; hence the pep talk. I asked the Minister of State why he had not spoken. It was because the topic had 'little impact on his area of responsibility' and he did want to get caught in the 'crossfire'.

We stop in the office long enough to collect the Minister's coat and a PS and we head off to the car. The next meeting is with the building managers of an eighteenth-century building owned and managed by the Department. The agenda is not riveting. They cover the various uses of building space; subletting to the nearby university, the programme of maintenance, modernization of the east wing, installing a café in the ground floor, and so on. The Minister of State 'ums' a lot. The building managers call him 'Minister'. They never use his name. The problem is that part of the building is occupied by another government department. If that tenant would move, they could redevelop the building but . . . the building managers want the Minister to get the other department to move. The plans for the building are 'exciting' and they want a decision by the autumn. I smile, envisaging the SAS moonlighting as Rackmanite enforcers.[10]

The PS is hovering. Hovering is an art form. It is physically interrupting a meeting by walking into the room. It is just standing in the door. It is putting a call though when you have been asked to hold calls. It is standing up in a meeting. It is moving to the Minister's side. It can be pre-arranged or automatic. The PS, who has been in the room taking the occasional note, is now stood by the Minister. 'I'm coming, I'm coming,' he says. Everyone knows he has to leave but the conversation continues. 'We can't get to the House in eight minutes,' says the PS. We hurry but we are late and now we are stuck in traffic at Trafalgar Square. We are due at the House of Commons for a three-line whip on the Higher Education Bill. The Minister is running through his folders for the various meetings he will have at the Commons. He is also concerned he will be caught out if the Conservatives call a snap vote. We are delayed further by an accident. A scooter knocks over a pedestrian, who gets straight up and continues running for the bus. The Minister is harried. He does not want to work at the Commons and when I see the room, I know why.

It looks and smells like the 1950s office in which my father would sometimes work. The dominant colour is the ubiquitous House of Commons green. The chairs have the portcullis insignia. There is no computer and only one picture but there is a phone, a fax, and a speaker for the division bell. There is a dark wood corner desk and, despite the glass bowl on the meeting table, the overall impression is impersonal, dark and inspissated gloom.[11] Should I attribute any significance to the broken House of Commons TV screen that is supposed to display the sessions?

The Minister cannot find his spectacles. The PS rings the office. They are in the briefcase! The Minister has a one-to-one with a DG until the division bell rings. The vote is on the Higher Education Bill, which controversially seeks to introduce top-up fees, which allow universities to charge different fees for different courses, although the bill sets limits. There will be votes on amendments to specific clauses all afternoon; there are five. The corridor is wide with glass fronted bookcases and it has become a busy thoroughfare. The Minister returns after five minutes. The corridor is once more deserted. He carries on where he left off with the DG. It is one of the innumerable updating briefing sessions. Where are we now? What are the problems? What do you need me to do? What are you going to do? It is not a decision making meeting as such, although decisions will be made about the best way of making progress. Phrases like 'keep at them' and 'shepherd them' abound.

The afternoon is turning into a seamless procession of DGs—it's another DG, another one-to-one, and we are discussing the Department's non-departmental public bodies (NDPBs). There is one difference. The Minister has sent out for some sandwiches and a member of the Private Office arrives with them. I pay for mine and drop one of the coins. In this environment, it rings like a bell and I get a 'look' from the Minister. The Minister discusses alternative ways of consulting NDPBs; 'I'm not as on top of this as I need to be.' He asks for a note on the issues. The problem is that the new proposals for consultation break the direct line between the Minister and the NDPBs. They 'feel threatened' because they will 'lose status'. But officials think the system is too fragmented and needs rationalizing before they can plausibly ask the Treasury for more money. The discussion is desultory and interrupted by another division bell.

On the Minister's return a team of three officials arrives to discuss a Private Finance Initiative (PFI). This discussion is lively. The PFI is in the Minister's constituency and he is gung-ho for it. His officials are cautious. They are not hostile or even defeatist but it is plain the Minister will struggle to get his way. They think it is an example of shameless lobbying, and they are probably right. The Minister wants them to meet the Lord Mayor to discuss the proposal. They think such a meeting would be 'inappropriate'. It would mean they were not being 'even handed'. They have to keep a 'level playing field'. They explain 'we offer guidance on bids at a technical level. So, we are happy to see officials and it is OK for you to see politicians. But don't mix them up.' 'OK', says the Minister, 'I'll get the chief executive to come down'. As they leave, one of the officials grins at me and says 'we welcome a top-level steer.' I choke back the guffaw. The Minister chips in, 'You are just so cautious, why won't you meet [the Lord Mayor]?' It is all good-natured. Equally, the meeting is ruled by the officials' sense of propriety.

We are on the move to the 'other place'. It is a complex trek into the depths of the House of Lords to a committee room where we will discuss planning for existing new towns. It is an interdepartmental meeting with six departments represented by 18 ministers and MPs and nine officials. The Office of the Deputy Prime Minister (ODPM) is in the lead and Lord Jeff Rooker, Minister of State at ODPM, is in the chair. Various outside interests are also present; for example, the Local Government Association. Because the meeting is large, everyone has nameplates on a large horseshoe table. It is an example of the drive for joined-up government (see Chapter 8 below). My Minister points out that this is exactly the kind of meeting he is sent to. The Secretary of State would never attend.

There are three presentations. They are all about the partnership between central and local government to develop sustainable communities in the new towns. The room is hot, the atmosphere soporific, and people are yawning. This meeting is typical of a way of life in British government. Its kith and kin take place across Westminster and Whitehall every day of the week. The language is also permeated with New Labour-speak. So, his Department has 'a role that sits with the grain of policy'. It will be 'inclusive'. There are many calls for local level leadership; for civic entrepreneurs. We need effective governance, 'engagement at an early stage', partnerships, and joined-up government. For all the snide comments, this language is widely used in White-hall. The partnership approach was clearly the new conventional wisdom of the moment, and it will not happen unless there are these kinds of meetings. And the eyes glaze and the heads nod until one official launches a gratuitous attack on academics. I wake up, but the Chair shuts him up.

The meeting ends in disarray. There is no summation. No one seems to have taken notes but I could be wrong. It was a large group. The room was hard to find. There have been late arrivals and early departures almost throughout. The Chair is cross because it has been hard to both cover the ground and to let everyone contribute. Indeed, there were few questions. Most of the time was taken up with the presentations. The Chair leaves muttering,

'I told you we had to keep to time.' I suspect the meeting was ill-fated and that it was talked to an inconclusive end because the departments judged the time was not ripe for any significant action.

So, circuitously, we return to the Commons, and the Minister rings the constituency to arrange his Friday visit. I muse on what a hopeless place the Commons is for working. It seems designed to hinder busy people from doing their work. The PS was waiting for us with the red box. The Minister reads through, corrects and signs letters. There are long silences while the Minister reads submissions. He is redrafting a letter to the Treasury. He doesn't like the current version because, by implication, it blames the Treasury. He discusses his diary for the rest of the week. The PS will take the letters and other correspondence back to the Department. He knows the vote is due and is listening for the division bell. He organizes all of us, we hasten off to the Chamber so the Minister can vote. The corridors are heaving. There is a rush to the main chamber. On his way back to the Department, the PS takes me to the Public Gallery. He fills in forms for me to visit and tells me to meet the Minister in the Central Lobby afterwards. The Serjeant at Arms is responsible for security and signs me in. The vote is expected about 6 p.m.

With about eight minutes to go before a vote, the Speaker calls 'lock the doors'. There is general mingling on the floor of the Chamber while everyone waits for the division. After eight minutes, there is a vote on the specific amendment. Just after 7 p.m., the Minister moves the third reading of the bill. Although this bill has not had an easy passage, with 72 Labour MPs voting against the bill and 20 abstaining at the second reading, the atmosphere is friendly (for the story of the bill's passage, see Cowley 2005: ch. 7; and Rawnsley 2010: 230–6). The cliché is 'club-like', and it fits. Ian Paisley is there looking like one of his cartoon caricatures. I was a great fan of Runrig[12] and their former keyboard player, Peter Wishart, is a Scottish National Party (SNP) MP. I see him on the floor of the House. As I spot celebrity MPs, my Minister is mingling. The students in the Public Gallery are quiet. I am sure the foreigner seeing these events would consider it very English. I do. Voting doesn't take long and, obviously, the Minister played no other part in the proceedings. The government wins comfortably with the Ayes 309, and the Noes 248 (*Hansard*, 31 March 2004: 1715–23). The debate started at 12.45 p.m. It ended at 7.20 p.m.

While I witness these momentous events, the Minister was supposed to attend a Privy Council meeting to approve a senior appointment to the BBC. It was put on hold because of the anticipated third reading vote. Indeed, there were sharp words with the Diary Secretary—brave man—when the Minister told her he did not want to do it. Eventually, it was agreed that only Privy Council members in the House of Lords would attend. It was a ten minute meeting. The Minister was also supposed to attend a reception at the Natural History Museum. The organizers were told the Minister would be late and the day's working assumption has been that he would drop in on the way home. I have been included in the official party. Although it has been a long day, I am looking forward to it. I don't go to many grand receptions. Unfortunately the Minister does and, in the car, he decides, as it is 7.30 p.m., he has had enough for today. He rings the Private Office on his mobile. I ask him about his workload. He does not think the job is particularly demanding. It is more frustrating than demanding because 'he fills in around the Secretary of State'. He gets the jobs the Secretary of State does not want to do. He is not complaining, although he was this morning. It is more an observation on his current status. He knows he has to make a decent fist of this job if he is climb further. He does, and he climbs.

WHAT THE MINISTER OF STATE SAYS ABOUT HIS DAY

As with the secretaries of state, ministers of state have different understandings of their work. I explore their understandings and how they affect everyday life. Again I explore the contrast between the Westminster traditional beliefs and practices and managerial beliefs and practices. Nowadays, most ministers of state have a designated area of work delegated to them by the secretary of state. So, with due apologies to the Austin Powers' movies, they are mini-ministers. The question is whether they are also a mini-me; there to do the bidding of the Secretary of State.

Westminster beliefs and practices

By tradition, ministers of state had three broad areas of work: departmental work including interdepartmental committees; parliament, especially parliamentary bills; and external representation, especially supporting the Secretary of State by attending meetings at home and abroad on his or her behalf (see, for example: Theakston 1987). They were often at the mercy of the whims of their secretaries of state (and for examples see, Clark 1993). Times change. Nowadays most ministers of state are no longer 'the fags of Whitehall' (Jenkins 1991: 184) who should be 'seen and not heard' (Heseltine 1990: 12). They have a substantial area of responsibility delegated to them.[13] It is today's norm, and they are *'expected to get on with it'* [Minister, TI]. Similarly,

> RAWR: *I'm putting words in your mouth so please correct me if I'm wrong—you're giving me the impression that you actually have got your own piece of turf and you run it.*
> MINISTER: *By and large that is true.* [Minister, TI]

Finally, in more dramatic vein:

Obviously you have to get on with your work and there has to be some delegation by Secretaries of State to their Ministers of State. If you don't, Secretaries of State who don't do that, will end up in a mental home because they'll be—deprived of sleep. . . . Good Secretaries of State know how to delegate but at the same time keep their tabs on what's happening. And good Ministers of State will keep their Secretaries of State informed about what they're doing, either by sending them notes or by meeting with them. [Minister, TI]

All had regular meetings with the Secretary of State. The ideal ministerial team recognizes that:

Politics is a team game and, you know, you help your colleagues, you expect your colleagues to help you. I find that mostly you get back what you give out. [Minister, TI]

So, there are regular ministerial meetings that all ministers attend. Normally the PPS is the only civil servant present. Such meetings discuss the current concerns of the Secretary of State and his colleagues, but the common theme is to '*discuss issues and debate them in the political context*' [Minister, TI]:

They are informal, sitting round, and [the Secretary of State] talks to us about what's happening, what's going on across the Government, what his current priorities are. We report on what we are doing, but in pretty brief form, so typically there might be just four items that I will report on that are going on at the moment, and there might be a discussion prompted by one of those around the table. We alternate between meetings which are only Ministers, plus the Government Whip, and meetings at which [the Permanent Secretary] is present and some of the senior officials. Now they don't actually happen every single week, I have to say. There are sometimes gaps in them for a variety of reasons, but I guess you would expect two weeks out of three to have one of those meetings with just Ministers and one with officials. [Minister, TI]

Normally, the Secretary of State does not:

lay down the line and we go away and do it. On the whole, for most of the work we do, given that it's relatively detailed, we are autonomous and take it forward in discussion with the officials. At times there will be a need for me to go and speak to *[the Secretary of State]* about issues. It's quite rare but sometimes it will need to be done. [Minister, TI]

There are, however, limits to both autonomy and trust. One Minister of State claimed credit for IT improvements in the Department in a letter to the Treasury. The Permanent Secretary 'formally objected'. He did not accept that the Department's IT was poor, he did not agree that the Minister of State did anything other than take an interest, and he had no intention of letting such a letter sit in a Treasury file. As they were attending the same dinner later that week, the Permanent Secretary had a quiet word and the letter was redrafted. It was an example of 'self-aggrandisement by a junior minister'

[FWNB]. It is a recurrent tension. Junior ministers want to rise. As one Permanent Secretary put it, junior ministers 'will take actions that are eye-catching that may not be wholly compatible with [the Department's] strategic direction' [Permanent Secretary, TI]. I came across one dramatic illustration of this gentle rebuke. All of one Minister of State's letters with political or policy implications were sent through the Secretary of State. The Minister was not trusted to stick to the agreed policy line [FWNB]. Some Ministers of State have a precarious hold over their job and secretaries of state will actively try to get rid of ministers of state (Campbell 2007: 622). Some junior ministers find they are condemned to routine and chores with little scope for exercising autonomy and no role in developing policy.[14]

Although for some the work is '*challenging*' because they have '*to move intellectually from one area to a quite different area of responsibility*' [Minister, TI], there is also detailed progress chasing. It is tedious work, which explains the infrequent contact with the Secretary of State:

> *Without saying anything disrespectful about the Department, I was a number two, in a much bigger department with much bigger budgets, [and] it was prosaic. I was going through the motions. I wasn't stretched.* [Minister, TI]

Some Ministers have heavy workloads. So, there is '*constant pressure*', and '*you have to jump from issue to issue and sometimes aren't able to focus sufficiently and consistently on something to get the change right*' [Minister, TI]. The daily grind of seeing a bill through parliament is taxing and ministers of state lead on bills: '*in my first year there I did four pieces of legislation*' [Minister, TI].

For such work, as with much of the rest, most contact is with the DG and his or her officials.

> *I meet the Director-General fairly regularly and fairly briefly for perhaps a half-an-hour, half-past 8 in a morning perhaps once a month, something like that, just to make sure we're keeping closely in touch.* [Minister, TI]

> *I had <u>endless meetings</u> with them to discuss particular things.* [Minister, TI, emphasis in original]

This Minister of State illustrates one effective working relationship.

> *It's very important for ministers to develop a good relationship with officials. You can't do it without them. You're not going to be there that long, and they know that. So you need to be persuasive and you need to be considerate. And far too many ministers are not. But at the same time, you need to be punishing when they don't deliver. I always worked on the basis of demanding high standards from officials, being very nasty if they weren't being provided. And I know some people thought, you know, I was frightening and very formidable. But I also feel that I gave praise, too, which is terribly important, when praise was merited. So I didn't have a problem for the most part with working with officials. Sometimes, I thought that civil servants could be a bit risk-averse and sometimes I felt that behind your back*

there could be ways of blocking what we wanted to do. But not very often. Most of the time I felt we worked as a team; that I had their confidence, they had mine; and that was the best way of doing it. [Minister, TI]

For many ministers of state, work in the Department can pall into insignificance besides their task of representing the Department both to the rest of Whitehall and to the outside world. Here the Minister of State relieves the Secretary of State of much work and tedium. Some ministers of state do not feel put upon:

RAWR: What I'm really interested in is to what extent you control your own diary and to what extent you are there to help the Secretary of State cope with his workload? MINISTER: I would say that I am pretty much in control of my own diary, with the exception of a fairly small number of occasions when [the Secretary of State] *will say 'Can you do this for me?' and I'll say 'Yes', unless it's impossible.* [Minister, TI]

Although he found on: '*looking through my diary over the weekend, that I am delivering three speeches tomorrow morning*' and he did not remember agreeing to doing three [Minister, TI]. Another talked of the committee work '*allocated*' to him [Minister, TI] and some pick up onerous tasks:

I was responsible for international work. The Secretary of State gave it to me as he didn't have time to do a lot of travelling. So, I did all the European meetings. And that involved about six meetings a year, something like that. [Minister, TI]

There were so many dinners and so many forced, even artificial, conversations that my reaction was one of horror. But I'm the odd one. Ministers loved it.[14]

I actually enjoy doing it. I find it helpful—I like meeting people, talking to people, getting some sense of what people in the industry are saying. So I'm actually quite keen to get out of the building and talk to people. [Minister, TI]

What is the reward of the Minister of State for this endeavour? It is to bask in the reflected glory of the Secretary who will take centre stage for the big announcements; for the policy successes. It is to wait for that telephone call from No. 10 and the next promotion. To be a Minister State is to be a Secretary of State in waiting. The job is a proving ground.

Managerial beliefs and practices

Since the 1970s, the main change in the job of the minister of state is in the delegation of important responsibilities to them. Other than that, their workload is similar to that of their predecessors. There is a conspicuous lack of interest and involvement in managerial reform. No minister of state was involved.

> *RAWR: To what extent as a Minister were you involved in implementing the [management] change programme as it was usually referred to?*
> *MINISTER: Not much at all really. [Minister, TI]*

When asked about performance indicators, a Minister of State could not remember any discussion of the subject [Minister, TI]. One Minister conceded he had been asked, but commented, *'the fact I can't remember it shows I wasn't involved'*. [Minister, TI]. One Minister of State noted this lacuna:

> *We had in the Department a sort of business meeting system that means that the ministers meet fairly frequently as a ministerial team followed by a business meeting that involves the members of the Board of Management. I think that has been very good in terms of dealing with the immediate. It is not as good for dealing with long-term strategy and one of the things I still find difficult—I gather that it is general across government—is clarity about what the Management Board is meant to do and what the interface with ministers is meant to be. I do think there is a real deficit in governance understanding there. [Minister, TI]*

He also observed:

> There are all sorts of expectations placed on boards of management to operate in a more businesslike way and at the same time there is an expectation on ministers to be accountable for everything that happens in the Department when actually the relationship between the two is far from clear. *[Minister, TI]*

In sum, managerialism was peripheral to the world of the Minister of State and their occasional brushes with it were more confusing than helpful.

CONCLUSIONS

What does my account of the day tell me about the Minister? It tells me about coping, about Westminster beliefs and practices, and about the appearance of rule.

Coping

One conclusion is all too obvious. Ministers work long hours and are subject to great stress; the pace of their daily lives is unrelenting. One has only to compare the fresh-faced youth that was Tony Blair in 1997 with his drawn features on standing down in 2007 to realize that high office exacts a high price. The relentless pace and pressure must adversely affect the quality of decision making. A DTI briefing for new members of the Private Office tells them that Secretaries of State have a 15-hour day with 12 hours devoted to constituency, parliament, visits, and functions, and cabinet and other committees, 'There are *at most* about **3 hours a day** for Ministers to consider your input on policy issues' (dual emphasis in original). And if anything that overestimates the time available. They have three hours a day for **reading** and that covers letters, e-mails, briefings, and submissions. So, policy issues are but a part of the three hours.

The Minister openly admits to the pressure. 'Phew, I'm so tired. I didn't sleep well last night.' And my heart goes out to the Private Office, whose pay and status are not remotely acceptable for their hours. They are unflaggingly cheerful. Their rationale is simple: 'It's ever so difficult to give a bollocking to a cheerful person.' It isn't, but it makes them feel better.

There is also the challenge of wearing many faces. I made a note that 'he's good at spotting a familiar face and attaching it to a bit of personal information; the master of instant sociability' [FWNB]. At various points in my story I have provided several examples of the contradictory roles the Minister plays (see also Rhodes 2007*b*). In the Department, he is all powerful, waited on hand and foot. Ceilings are mended without having to ask, coats are fetched from cars. But he is also dependent on prime ministerial whim, attending meetings of no great significance at his behest. He is all too human, banging tables because of delayed phone calls. He is both a key decision maker, driving through organizational change, and an automaton, chairing committees on autopilot because he has to be there. He has a public face of polite interest in the people he meets and the private face, tired and in need of dental care. I intend no criticism, no implication of insincerity when I describe him as an actor. Rather, I express admiration for his dexterity, for his skills. He is convincing in these several roles. I am impressed by the way the Minister slips between his roles. One minute he is chairing a committee, the next he is chatting away socially about breakfast at No. 10 with Tony, Cherie, and little Leo. Normally, being a cynic, if I saw such transparent glad-handing on television, I would find it off-putting, but it is done with great skill and conviction.

The boredom of endless committees and meetings, the tyranny of the engagement diary, and the routines of the Private Office are all examples of the protocols of the bureaucracy. They are used to domesticate the turbulent working environment of the Minister. So, my protestations of boredom miss the point. If issues are political and volatile, then emotions can also run high. So, the Private Office sets up meetings, tea is drunk, matters are discussed through the Chair, the Private Office synthesizes material for the red box, there is a further round of meetings, by which time there is an air of dispassionate consideration verging on boredom. Such routines also matter even when there is no big issue. The pace of events is unrelenting and the Private Office, the diary, and the red box are the way of organizing, even disciplining, events. Political life may be 'events, dear boy events' but they are coped with using bureaucratic rituals. The Private Office is the efficient cocoon that helps Ministers to cope. Its many protocols for domesticating everyday life are so central to managing the Minister and his day that I consider them in more detail in Chapters 6 and 7.

Beliefs and practices

Ministers and officials talk to one another in ways that are striking to outsiders. There is no one set of beliefs, no one vocabulary that dominates. There are overlapping, competing webs of beliefs that vie with one another. Westminster or traditional beliefs persist. They define the relationship between ministers and civil servants (see Chapter 5) and accountability to parliament (see Chapter 8). But they are overlaid with managerial beliefs or, as they are referred to by some, critically, 'New Labour-speak'. Management is not new. Replacing 'administration' with 'management' may signify a desire for change but it merely relabels much of the work of the Department, which carries on as before. It is not clear to this 'professional stranger' that the language of management has become the dominant discourse. You have to be fluent in it but, at times, it seemed more like a veneer. Expressions like 'drilling it down' suggest that reform has not penetrated far down the hierarchy. The world I visited was a world of process, of committees, not a world of output measurement. Officials talked the management talk with ease. But to use some of the more cringe inducing phrases, it was not clear they 'walked the walk' and delivered 'more bang for the buck'. So, my account of the Minister's work has as many examples of old beliefs and practices as of new ones.

The obvious examples of everything remaining the same are the work of the Private Office; committees; and the role of ministers of state. The Private Office runs the Minister's day in a hundred small ways, which I describe in detail in Chapters 6 and 7. Another obvious continuity is working in committees. It may be obvious, but given 20 years of management reform it is worth stressing that committees remain the main decision making vehicle. The Minister's diary is made up of back-to-back committee meetings. They come in various forms, their purpose is not always to make decisions, but the next one will be along very soon. Finally, ministers of state may be responsible for a delegated block of work but they are still there to help secretaries of state by doing the work they do not want to do.

The obvious examples of new practices are the departments' business plans with their stress on objectives, targets, performance, outputs, cost containment, and evaluation. The layer added by New Labour uses such words as joined-up government, delivery, and value driven. Recent candidates for inclusion include leadership and civic entrepreneurs. I will discuss the civil service and management in Chapter 5. Now I look at the role of minister as manager and it is a brief examination because it forms but a small part of most Ministers' daily lives.

According to Foster (2005: 204), ministers have become 'progress-chasers', and a 'fundamental flaw' of Blair's reform was to expect ministers to become managers. He need not have worried. Only one Secretary of State saw management as a significant part of his job. The others devoted themselves to their constituency, parliament, visits and functions, and cabinet and other committees, just as they have always done. They think in these categories. Their diaries are organized using this terminology. If anybody is a progress chaser, it is the ministers of state. Their main task remains to ease the burden on the Secretary of State. But they are not managers. None had any role in managing or reforming the Department and few had any grasp of managerialism and its language of performance indicators and targets. The rhetoric of managerialism and its practice diverge for most politicians for the simplest of simple reasons; it is not why they sought office and it is not why they were elected.

Rule or the appearance of rule

The Westminster story tells us the role of the Minister is to make policy, individually and collectively, and to be held to account for it in parliament. The managerial story tells us the job is to run the department, making sure that services are delivered. Ministers make and implement policy, but only some of the time. Many ministers spend much of their time doing neither. They represent the Department, the ruling party, and the government to the world. As we will see in Chapter 8, they work long and hard at maintaining networks across Westminster, Whitehall, and beyond. Their work is about the appearance of rule; 'about stability. Keeping things going, preventing anarchy, stopping society falling to bits. Still being here tomorrow' (Lynn and Jay 1984: 454).

Of course ministers can and do make policy. Some even run their departments. But as my account of their daily life shows, it is not their main activity. They are mainly the public face of government. They represent its authority. They must appear as men and women of stature and standing. The Minister is the Queen's Minister and accorded due homage. His office has a long history of grandeur. The Minister is called Minister or Secretary of State and rarely addressed by his first name by officials. Outsiders display equivalent verbal and physical deference. He is the centre of attention and this simple fact is displayed in language, beliefs, and practices. The monarchical tradition of hierarchy lives on as a central characteristic of the Westminster model and ministerial practice. The point is that the Minister is a celebrity, if not royalty. As one Departmental induction video put it: there 'is a bit of mystique around Ministers and they make you feel inferior'. Most dress to reinforce the appearance of rule.

As a celebrity, he is escorted everywhere in a chauffeur driven car, greeted at doorways on red carpets by respectful hosts.[16] He is a godfather, recipient of homage from expectant interests. In their self-mocking manner, civil servants refer to this as the *Courtier Syndrome*—the civil servant who 'tip-toes round (and sucks up to) the Minister, rather than serving him or her professionally. Apart from being unutterably sick-making, this distorts the true purpose of the relationship and damages advice and decision-making'.[17] Others are even less polite: 'brown nosed crawling creep' [FWNB]. There is a buzz around the office when the Minister arrives at work. I thought, 'Ladies and gentleman Elvis Presley is in the building.' Everyone seems to change gear; they process their e-mails a little more quickly.

At times, one can feel sorry for ministers because of the constant media scrutiny (see Chapter 9). Any such sentiment must be tempered by recognizing that many welcome their celebrity. They encourage the media. Alastair Campbell opined, 'we had created this monster, seen it as a beast and we fed it well' (Campbell 2007: 711). Ministers also fed the media beast often and well. They welcome the visibility that comes from celebrity just as they enjoy their ministerial trappings.

All governments need their symbolic trappings. The Minister sweeping into a public meeting with his entourage and the media are one example. This representative work is onerous. I do not mean it is onerous to meet people's expectations—it may well be. Rather, I refer to the time he has to spend on it. If the work representing the Department and the government to the outside world was subject to output measurement, it would be hard to identify the value added, especially given the wear and tear on the Minister. Yet the appearance of rule is a central part of ruling because it enacts daily the authority of the government. For citizens, public appearances are the government. One Minister was described as 'imperious', and he was. When schoolchildren assemble to welcome the ministerial visitor to their school, they see the pomp and circumstance of the official car, the deference of the head and teachers, and experience the excitement of the event. They see the mystique, the appearance of rule that legitimates government.

Finally, there is also a gendered side to the appearance of rule. It is probably a mistake for a man to comment on how being a woman affects her role as Minister. Wajcman (1998: 159–60) argues that 'senior women managers manage in much the same way as senior men within the same specific context'. 'The norm for the managerial occupation remains male' and 'women who have made it have done so by adopting the male model' and 'are still expected to "manage like a man"'. However, female ministers were meticulous in the ways they presented. The clothes and accessories were expensive and carefully chosen. Some male colleagues were a disgrace—fat, in ill-fitting suits with stubble chins and wispy hair in desperate need of styling. The women knew men were lucky. Casualness bordering on careless was not an option for them. I noted other differences. In various small ways, the Minister supported women at work. Her Private Office was mainly female. She had a female PPS. It was no accident. Only one (of six) other private offices I visited had a female PPS. She supported events such as 'Bring a daughter to work', and striking a better work–home balance. She gave interviews on New Labour's approach to women's issues. She was more concerned about her work–home balance than any male minister or permanent secretary I spoke to. Homework, the Scouts, and making breakfast did not figure in any interview with a man.

In sum, this thick description in the form of a confessional and impressionistic narrative describes the complex, episodic, ambivalent, and contingent everyday life of a Minister. It is my interpretation of the Minister's interpretation of his everyday experiences and encounters. But the Minister does not act alone. He works closely with the Permanent Secretary and the Department; they constitute his life-support system. In the next chapter I look at the everyday life of the Permanent Secretary and in Part III, I look at the rest of the Minister's life-support system.

NOTES

1. Rhodes 2007*b* also describes a day in the life of a Secretary of State. Here I report a different day in the diary with a different mix of activities. Consequently, in my general remarks, I can draw on both accounts and cover the diverse range of ministerial work.
2. The following account is from FWNBs Nos 9 and 10, dated 7/8 April and 9/10 April 2003 respectively.
3. On the argument that recruitment to, resource allocation by, and the rules and relationships of the core executive are gendered see: Annesley and Gains (2010).
4. The everyday life of British ministers has not been a topic of academic concern, although Theakston's 1987 account of junior ministers is a partial exception. The best accounts of the ministerial day and workload can be found in the diaries of former secretaries of state. See, for example: Blunkett, 2006; Castle 1984; Crossman 1975; and Lawson 1992.
5. See Chapter 2 above for a summary of the Westminster, managerial, and governance narratives. The *governance* beliefs and practices of secretaries of state, ministers of state, and permanent secretaries are the subject of Chapter 8.
6. For ministerial views similar to those expressed in my interviews see: Bruce-Gardyne 1986, ch. 7; Donoughue 2003: 362–3; Fowler 1991: 111–13 and 327; Heseltine 1990: 11; James 1999: 36–47; Jenkins 1975 [1971]: 218–19; and Kaufman 1980: ch. 5. Labour ministers have often been trenchant critics of their allegedly obstructive civil servants; see, for example: Benn 1991: 138–9 and *passim* but see the exchange of letters on 409–10; Castle 1973; Crossman 1975: 614–28; Sedgemore 1980: chs 3–6; and, more recently Blunkett 2006: 352 and *passim*. For academic studies of the relationship between ministers and civil servants see: Barberis 1996: chs 2 and 10; Campbell and Wilson 1995: ch. 2; Foster 2005; chs 14 and 15; Heady 1974; chs 5 and 6; Hennessy 1989: ch. 11; Marsh et al. 2001: ch. 7; Rhodes and Weller 2001; and Richards 2007.

7. On Michael Heseltine and management reform see Hennessy 1989: 607–8; Heseltine 1990: chs 1 and 2, and 2000: 190–4 and ch. 14.

8. On the Jo Moore affair see: Kuhn 2005: 106-7; PASU 2002; and Chapter 7 below. For general accounts of New Labour and the media at the time, see: Kuhn 2007; Scammell 2001; Seymore-Ure 2003; and Chapter 9 below.

9. The following account is from FWNB No. 11, dated 30/31 March 2004.

10. Peter Rackham was a London landlord. His notoriety was such that 'Rackmanism' entered the Oxford English Dictionary as 'exploitation or intimidation of a slum tenant by an unscrupulous landlord'. His other claim to fame is that both Christine Keller and Mandy Rice Davis of Profumo fame were his mistresses (see Green 1979).

11. An archaism for 'dense', which is so apt for the bowels of the House of Commons.

12. Runrig are a Scottish folk-rock band; see Morton 1991; and http://www.runrig.co.uk/. Last accessed 6 October 2009.

13. Michael Heseltine (1990: 12) attributes this delegation model for running a Ministry to Peter Walker, former Secretary of State for the Environment (1970–2); Secretary of State for Trade and Industry (1972–4); Minister of Agriculture, Fisheries and Food (1979–83); Secretary of State for Energy (1983–7); and Secretary of State for Wales (1987–90). See also Walker 1991: ch. 7.

14. Bernard Donoughue (2003: 352–7) talks of a junior minister 'exclusion zone' at MAFF and claims there were no regular meetings with junior ministers and that 'effectively I had no ministerial role'.

15. This representative work or networking was ubiquitous among all senior politicians and civil servants. The Department has links with No. 10 and the Treasury, with other departments, with parliament, with the political parties, and with outside interests. It is a major part of everyone's working life. In this chapter, I have focused on Westminster and managerial beliefs and practices. I provide a detailed account of this networking, or governance beliefs and practices, in Chapter 8.

16. In Goodin's (1980: 165–7) terms, they are 'constitutive rituals'; that is, they are rules about formal ceremonies that invest an individual with authority. For further discussion see Chapter 10 below.

17. Personal communication, 8 August 2009.

5

The Permanent Secretary

This chapter parallels the chapter on the Minister. It has the same three-part structure. I provide an overview of the permanent secretaries' working year followed by a chronological story based on my fieldwork notebooks of a day in the life of the Permanent Secretary. I observed three permanent secretaries at work for between three and five days each. I then juxtapose their practice with talk by drawing on my interviews with ten permanent secretaries. Finally, I draw on published memoirs.[1]

THE WORKING YEAR

I was given access to the engagement diaries of all three permanent secretaries, so, before telling the story of a day in their life, I outline briefly their broad pattern of work. The same limits apply to this broad-brush analysis as applied to the Minister's diary that I described in Chapter 4.

The work of a permanent secretary is divided conventionally into the policy, management, and diplomatic or representational roles. Figure 5.1 shows that most time is spent on departmental management and external relations with politics and policy a long way behind in third place. Although I have no numerical time series data, the interviews (below) support the conclusion that the time spent on

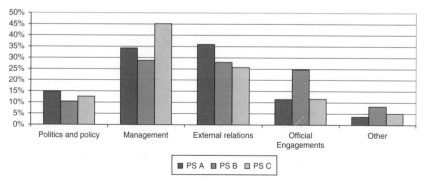

Figure 5.1 The Permanent Secretaries' year

management is a large increase on 20 years ago. The increase reflects a shift of time and effort from policy related work to managing their departments. However, and perhaps more significantly, it reflects the longer hours worked. All my interviewees knew they worked longer now than at any other period in their career. Most were reluctant to compare their workloads with that of their predecessors but, when pressed, thought life in early times was less pressured. Some thought a five-year stint was enough given the demands of the job.

To some extent it is seasonal—the budget comes but once a year. Accountability to parliament is a core doctrine of the Westminster model but it accounts for precious little of a permanent secretary's time, although appearances before the PAC (commonly Public Accounts Committee, although strictly the Committee of Public Accounts) involve intensive dress rehearsals. Here, however, the diary is misleading. The departments all have elaborate procedures for processing parliamentary questions. They involve the permanent secretary only rarely (see Chapter 8 below).

Perhaps most dramatic is the finding that they spend between 3 and 10 per cent of their time on strategy and thinking; working alone, reading, and preparing papers.[2] This figure is misleading because it refers only to time allocated in the diary. Much reading and writing is done in the early evening when the diary is empty and outside office hours, travelling to and from work.

> *Two hours on a train, you can think. Or I get in about half past eight, and it may well be that, after mulling over something in the car, if I have made sure I haven't got a meeting until about 9.30 that day, I can open up the Dictaphone having mulled.* [Permanent Secretary, TI]

It is not just the minister who has to consume endless towers of paper. It is the lot of permanent secretaries also, only they have a briefcase not a red box.

It is worth stressing the unrelenting pace of work. There is a culture of long hours in the departments and it is the inescapable fate of the Private Office (see Chapter 6 below). Most permanent secretaries work a 50-hour week routinely, and it is often much more. Official engagements in the evening consume large chunks of time. They can lead to behaviour akin to a 'grumpy old man' because they have been bored too often for too long.

In sum, as with senior managers in the private sector, permanent secretaries spend their time communicating, not thinking; meeting people, not writing papers or developing strategy.

A DAY IN THE LIFE OF A PERMANENT SECRETARY

Turning from the general particular, I can now tell the story of a day in the life of a permanent secretary.[3] For Peter Barberis (1996: 140), permanent

Table 5.1 The Permanent Secretary's engagement diary

TIME	ACTIVITY—planned	ACTIVITY—unplanned
9.00	Diary followed by 1:1 about colleague's pension	Arrives late so there is no diary meeting
10.00–11.00	KiT with Treasury and Board	
11.00–12.30	Regular meeting with DGs	
13.00–14.00	Lunch at QE II Conference centre	
14.00–15.15	PBR @ Treasury	
15.30–16.00	Interview with journalist	
16.00–16.45	Office work including photo competition	Rearranged diary meeting
16.45–17.40		MoD and contracts
18.00 to late	Ballet, Covent Garden	

secretaries are: 'resilient, mentally and physically'; 'good team players'; able 'to work with ministers of almost any hue or persuasion'; have 'a bit of "fizz"' or 'a leadership style that inspires others'; 'assimilate and analyse vast amounts of material'; able 'to seize upon the central issues and see the way forward'; 'good at problem solving'; 'sound in their judgement'; and 'quick to spot trouble'. They also 'imprint their personalities' on their departments and 'develop their own styles'. It is a formidable set of characteristics. However, William Plowden (1994: 74) points to their conservatism, caution, scepticism, elitism, and arrogance. Did I encounter the paragon or the elitist while observing daily life?

The Permanent Secretary had a 'slow, slow, quick, quick, slow' week. He worked in his office, at the Treasury, and attended a departmental workshop (see Table 5.1). Here I describe a day in the office and meetings with the Treasury. I describe the departmental workshop in Chapter 7. Of all the permanent secretaries I observed, he was the one most likely to arrive at work between 9 and 10 a.m., mainly because he had a hectic evening calendar. Over the course of the year, he spent just under 25 per cent of his time at conferences, working lunches, and evening engagements. He took his diplomatic role seriously.

This morning he is late because his train from the Home Counties was delayed. I am reminded of Reginald Perrin's encyclopaedia of excuses for being late, ranging from 'seasonal manpower shortages, Clapham Junction' to the bizarre 'badger ate a junction box at New Malden'.[4] In this case it is a prosaic signal failure and he is now in a rush. He is supposed to do the diary but instead he goes straight into a meeting with an old colleague who has complaints about his pension. It is a personal matter and I am excluded.

The Diary Secretary is having a stomp. She needed to talk to the Permanent Secretary about the diary but now will not see him again this morning. She is being pressurized on the phone but will not agree to a meeting until she has spoken to him. She is gatekeeping and words are exchanged. The caller provokes a 'don't get ratty with me' response and 'if you complain to your Permanent Secretary, I will tell mine what really did happen'.

The Permanent Secretary emerges from the meeting laughing. He announces to no one in particular, 'he won't shut up or give up and he's going to appeal'. There is no time to expand on this remark. The Private Secretary (PS) hovers and off we go to the lift and a windowless, basement room for the usual Monday morning meeting with his Directors-General (DGs). Only it is not the usual meeting. The usual meeting is an informal round-up of issues of the week; there are no strangers present. Today, three members of the Treasury attend. My Permanent Secretary is in the chair. There are no papers. The PS takes the minutes of the meeting and a note of any matters requiring action. The aim is an informal round-up of shared concerns. Of course, if the Treasury is concerned, then any department will share that concern.

The Permanent Secretary welcomes the Treasury; 'it was an opportunity to discuss matters of mutual interest, and help both departments move away from some historic "problems of mistrust"'.[5] It is a wide-ranging discussion dominated by the Permanent Secretary and the Treasury, who makes the opening presentation. The key phrase is 'delivery is working through others'. So, the discussion focuses on the 'joint agenda', 'shared analysis' and, one of the era's key phrases, 'evidence-based policy making' (FWNB). They roam broadly over various matters such as the pre-budget report (see below); pay, pensions, and an ageing workforce in the Department, higher education, and their respective contributions to a white paper on energy policy.

It is not a meeting in the sense of a group discussion. Rather it is a series of bilateral exchanges within a meeting. It is a group Keep-in-Touch (KiT). Everyone is polite and restrained. The tone is agreeable. They are sharing information. But there is an undercurrent. The Permanent Secretary makes jibes at the Treasury's expense: 'not one of your winners there', 'that puts your pro-business stance in jeopardy'; the Treasury can take care of itself: 'your stakeholders are our vested interests'. They may be sharing information but in the process they are highlighting differences. The Treasury intimates 'this raises a general issue on which we would be grateful for your views' but it doesn't come across as an invitation. It sounds more like an instruction to pay attention. The minutes also record that 'the department's positions were still a very long way apart'.

Of course, there is common ground. Both sides are concerned about their ageing workforces. The Treasury feels impelled to point out that only 43 per cent of its workforce is over 45 years old whereas the Department has 79 per cent. It wasn't necessary. It provokes the response from the Department that it means their workforce is 'more experienced'. They agree on some matters. The Treasury praises the Department's internal management reform programme. The minutes record that the Treasury was 'firmly behind Andrew Turnbull's (Head of the Home Civil Service) efforts to push the civil service change agenda'. He wanted to 'get away from people who write wonderful essays'. He wanted better project management and more use of external analysts. He noted the 'changes [the Department] had made—and were continuing to make—were of great interest to the Treasury'. My fieldwork notes added he believed, 'we can learn from each other' and find out 'what works and what doesn't'.

It is an agreeable note on which to end. The Treasury describes the meeting as 'constructive and useful'. He continues, 'we need to get out and see you more', but spoils the effect by adding 'not necessarily at this level', then adding 'next time it should be smaller and more focused'. I was not the only one who saw an implicit criticism in these remarks. The whole meeting had this sparring quality and they talked past one another as often as not.

The Treasury officials get up to leave and there is the usual gossiping in the margins of the meeting. I catch snatches of conversation. The Permanent Secretary says to the Treasury: 'Ed [Balls] comes round to see [the Minister]'. The Treasury comments it is 'an unusual way of working'. They turn to higher education policy and the Treasury opines, 'It's becoming a debate about where's the "Labour" in "New Labour".' They agree, 'It's messy'.

The DGs stay behind for the more conventional Monday morning meeting (and for which there is no summary note). The chair rotates among the DGs. There is the usual round-up of the week ahead. For example, they discuss internal charging for legal services, which is considered a 'leap in the twilight if not in the dark'. Normally, there is also a more detailed discussion of two management issues (with papers). This week the issues are performance pay and accommodation. Today's euphemism is 'making space'. It refers to using performance assessment to cull staff, especially by early retirement. Human Resources have produced a plan to improve poor performers or get them to leave or retire. The group agree 'we have to do it but it will be enormously difficult'. They recognize they cannot target individuals because it would be against the law. They can use performance assessment but, assuming the individual appeals, this process takes at least 12 months. They cannot offer retirement packages without Treasury approval and the Treasury are sceptical there will be a significant improvement in performance. They discuss ways of helping people to leave by outplacement services and counselling. They decide to centralize all vacancies and not to replace anyone unless it is a departmental priority area.

For such a potentially emotive topic, the meeting is low key. The Permanent Secretary says nothing, fidgets, and keeps looking at his watch. The various speakers talk quietly and to the floor. They are hard to hear. There is little eye contact. There is some agreement that they need 'tougher performance management' and they decide to take a paper to the Management Board. The Permanent Secretary agrees but urges decisive action now; 'we must get 58-year-olds who want to go, out now'. He also tells them the matter is confidential. So far there is no Treasury money to pay for early retirements. Also, the Department must have a communication strategy to explain the scheme to all staff. They nod.

Accommodation takes less time. The Business Plan calls for a 25 per cent saving from accommodation and the aim is to move some 25 per cent of head office staff (some 1,000 people) to other London offices or to the regions. Human Resources raises specific implementation problems. The Permanent Secretary is not sympathetic. He bites his tongue to hold back some acid remark. He frowns. He contents himself with the observation that we can shed staff from those who don't want to relocate. Human Resources are undeterred. They want to redesign the work environment and make it open plan. Their 'soft' management style is to the fore. The Permanent Secretary has switched off. He is resting his chin on his hand and staring at the far wall. The Chair tries to steer them along but the meeting drifts to an end.

We return to the Private Office only briefly. The Prime Minister is speaking on e-government at the QE II Conference Centre. The Minister is also attending and will take part in a panel discussion answering questions. He wants the Permanent Secretary to go with him. It will be an opportunity to network with other senior officials, industry, even academia, but there is a conspicuous lack of enthusiasm about meeting Tony Blair; 'hopefully he won't stay for lunch'. I walk across to the QE II with the Minister's party but I am supernumerary, no more than another member of the audience. I don't get backstage. I am not invited to lunch. I do not meet the Prime Minister. I am parked in a quiet corner. It has happened before. It reinforces a feeling of dependence on the goodwill of others. I get to see what I am allowed to see. Sometimes I feel as if I am under everybody's feet. I asked the Permanent Secretary if he was comfortable with me around; 'I forget you're there', he replied. That was mildly reassuring. Indeed, I was pleased to become part of office humour. I am greeted with 'bet you thought you were in some seedy nightclub' when the meeting could not have been more prim and proper. But they pay more attention than they let on. I am greeted with 'How's day 5'—so, they are counting the days to my departure.

I grab a sandwich, check my notes, and wait for the Permanent Secretary. When he emerges we get into the car and drive the short distance to Great George Street and HM Treasury. I have been looking forward to this meeting. It is a pre-budget review (PBR) at which the Treasury discusses with the Department its budget for the following year. Conversation in the margins of the meeting seems interesting but it is episodic, hard to hear, and impossible to reproduce coherently. It sounds to me like the Permanent Secretary warming up to the task ahead. The Permanent Secretary grumbles about the Treasury because its interventions are seen as too detailed, too controlling; 'we need another action plan like we need a hole in the head'. Much of the Department's submission is agreed quickly. There have been several meetings and now there are only a few outstanding matters to discuss. However, as soon as the meeting turns to these matters, the Permanent Secretary criticizes the scrutiny process rather than discussing them. He compares the Treasury to the Delivery Unit; 'it's feeling worse than Barber' because it is getting more and more rule bound. He tells the Treasury that 'it is prescriptive, not enabling' and the Treasury is 'not following the five principles of Blair's public sector reforms'. He is laughing as he speaks. The Treasury is much more subdued and soft spoken. The Permanent Secretary calls the process 'terribly old-fashioned' and tells the Treasury, 'I don't want to do this every year'. The Treasury makes it clear, however, that he is keen on a prescriptive regime. He steers the conversation around to the outstanding budget item and asks the Permanent Secretary, 'shall we get [Smith] to look at it?' He must know the Permanent Secretary would rather put his eyes out with red-hot needles. The Treasury opines gently that 'we are all after the same thing'. The Permanent Secretary concedes [Smith] has relevant expertise but he does not want [Smith] as part of the process. He agrees to look again at the item and get back by Monday provided [Smith] is excluded. In return, the Treasury promises 'a lighter touch'. They agree 'our people had better get together'.

The tone of the meeting is affable and business-like. The Permanent Secretary tells me the Treasury is a 'nice bloke, relaxed'. He thinks they get on well; that they are like-minded. The Treasury says, 'good doing business with you'. They both seem pleased. Yet, most of the conversation was disagreements—over money, process, and people. It is a good example of how the civil service's conventions of polite behaviour smooth over potential trouble. The Permanent Secretary laughs as he criticizes. The Treasury is sweet reasonableness as he suggests the unacceptable. No one raises their voice. No one talks over or otherwise tries to dominate the speaker. There is no ill feeling. Points have been registered by both sides. The Department knows it will have to revise its budget. The Treasury knows it is now time to back off. Everyone has their take-home message.

The pace is frenetic. The car takes us back to the Department for an interview with a journalist. The first point to note is that the Permanent Secretary is giving the interview, not a minister. There are four observers, including a Special Adviser (SpAd) and a member of the Press Office. The aim is to provide a 'half-term report' on the Department. The Permanent Secretary insists on checking any quotes and on anonymity; 'I told the Secretary of State it was off the record.' He wants to make sure the interview is risk free; that is, it will not embarrass the Minister. So, the Permanent Secretary runs through the major changes of the past year. He claims there was a consensus on the need for change; 'it's what most staff want'. He is confident the changes are 'locked in' and he praises the Minister for his leadership. The questions take the form, 'it is said that . . .'; 'it has been said . . .'. So, it has been said that the Department is weak in its dealings with the Treasury. The Permanent

Secretary claims the two departments are 'aligned'. It is a calm, measured presentation of basic information about the Department. The Permanent Secretary is restrained. He can be boisterous, but not in this forum. He is careful to make eye contact with the journalists. He feeds them little catch-phrases for their copy; 'the shift from regulation to innovation'. Afterwards he explains he was a tad more careful than usual because a SpAd was there. He was not always so 'low key'. The modern Permanent Secretary numbers working with the media as one of the essential skills. The Permanent Secretary does at least one interview a month. He also has lunch meetings with senior journalists, mainly but not exclusively from the broadsheets and 'trade' jour-nals. It is hard to envisage the grand old mandarins of yesteryear, Edward Bridges or Warren Fisher, even condescending to be interviewed let alone getting the necessary skills. Lunch with the editor might be an option.

Spot on 4 p.m. who should appear at the door but the PS, the conventional signal that time is up. The journalist leaves to the usual 'good to see you', 'I'll hear from you soon, 'happy to help'. The SpAd stays behind for a 'debrief'. He is pleased with the catchphrase on innovation and will get the Minister to use it. The Diary Secretary hovers. She wants her 'missed' meeting of this morning. She takes the Permanent Secretary through the various changes to get his approval. He agrees with all her suggestions, which means she can now return the 'ratty' telephone call. It begins with a triumphal, 'The Permanent Secretary says ...' Never, get on the wrong side of the Diary Secretary. It will only delay your appointment. She then contacts the Cabinet Office because one of its deputy secretaries[6] wants to speak to the Permanent Secretary about transparency and the Department's appointments to non-departmental public bodies; and about more private sector appointments to the Department's management board. The Permanent Secretary protests that a quarter of the Management Board is already from the private sector. He also resists the notion that such appointments should be regulated by the Cabinet Office. He does not linger over the call. Now, he must turn his attention to the Depart-ment's photography competition.

There is much badinage in the Private Office about this event. The PS calls for 'no sniggering', but his effort is futile. 'I bet there's one of the [Westmin-ster] Abbey bathed in sunlight,' howls the Diary Secretary. An office has been given over to the competition and there is a large entry. Twelve postcards and nine posters have been designated finalists. The judging panel, including the Permanent Secretary, look only at the finalists. He mutters to me, 'I had to do this last year' but concedes 'you have to do these things.' He does not express many opinions. He goes with the flow. He is there to lend his imprimatur to the event. He knows his job is to agree with the others. He does just that.

If the day seemed to be tailing off, it springs to life unexpectedly. The Permanent Secretary at the Ministry of Defence (MoD) has rung about problems with a contract. It would seem that No. 10 has suggested that the MoD should get another department to act as a third-party arbiter. My Permanent Secretary says, though I paraphrase, 'I would not touch this with a bargepole.' He advises his colleague 'to get better control systems in his department'. He is laughing as he says it. Nonetheless I am sure the remark went down like a lead balloon. He also points out that 'we're not getting the full facts from your lot'. This statement means he cannot possibly make any decision until he has the full facts. They do agree on one point: 'zero communication', 'complete media blackout'.

The Permanent Secretary calls in the Principal Private Secretary (PPS) and the relevant DG. They want to get the story straight—'what did we know and when did we know it'—so they can brief the Minister. They want to establish a paper trail. They agree the MoD must have known first. They also agree that the MoD is sharing information parsimoniously. MoD assured the Permanent Secretary that it would sort the problem but clearly MoD is looking for a joint approach to No. 10 and the Treasury. So, No. 10 will get a briefing on all the options. The PPS thinks the Department should help to sort the problem out. The Permanent Secretary does not agree; 'it's their problem' and 'they can sort it out'. However, 'we'll help on request'. He has niggling doubts on whether this crisis can harm his Department. He asks, 'Am I lulling myself into a false sense of security?' The PPS is also prominent in the discussion, in effect speaking for the Minister. They mull over the implications but the Permanent Secretary insists that 'I can't see why we have a major role'. The PPS is 'amazed it hasn't leaked'. That prompts the Permanent Secretary to stress that we 'keep stum'. He does not want to be a source of a leak either. Caution and risk avoidance pervade the conversation.

WHAT THE PERMANENT SECRETARY SAYS ABOUT HIS DAY

Westminster beliefs and practices

The permanent secretaries were fast streamers in the 1970s and 1980s. They were the classical generalist but they were also the generation that had to confront managerialism for most of their careers. They were probably the last generation to receive the traditional training. None of the permanent secretaries had any formal management training beyond the two courses of ten weeks each run for Administrative Trainees and Higher Executive Officers (A) Scheme (AT/HEO). After two to three years, the promising individuals would be designated 'fast streamers'; that is earmarked for promotion. It is a moot point that these courses provided management training (Rhodes 1977), although the permanent secretaries made career-long friends, acquaintances, even wives. One Permanent Secretary described the ten week course '*as essen-tially a bridge school*'; '*it was enjoyable*' but '*I did not learn an awful lot*'. Another described it as '*pretty patchy*'.[7] Some 20 years later, when on the fringe of promotion to senior posts, two of them went on the civil service's Top Management Programme (TMP). It was seen as '*enjoyable*' and '*stimulating*', but there was '*about three weeks work*' in the six week course and '*it wasn't a vintage one*'.

Most had a mentor:

> *She was terrific, enthusiastic, inspiring. She probably turned me into a career civil servant. I definitely decided I wanted to be like her. She brought much more spice and brio into the thing.*

On-the-job learning and the mentor did not give them specific policy expertise. Rather, 'it was more general skills', such as drafting letters and briefs. His mentor:

> *was adept at using what appeared to be tiny stokes of the pen to turn it [my draft] into something that was good, and again I learned quite a lot of classic drafting skills.*

The permanent secretaries built work and social networks in their depart-ments and gradually extended them to other departments. They did not see it as a grand activity such as building networks; it was just the accepted way of doing business. It was part of learning on the job, moving to a new job every year.

They had the traditional aspirations; '*once I got fast streamed, I was aiming for Private Office*'. Conventionally, their aspirations would also include a stint in either the Treasury or the Cabinet Office. The posting allowed the most senior civil servants and the prime minister to test their metal and it further extended their Whitehall network. One Permanent Secretary on his posting to the Cabinet Office reported travelling around regularly with the prime minis-ter, providing him with four or five briefings a week; '*I saw a lot of him*'. He was '*part of the No. 10 extended family*'. He was also convinced he would not have become a permanent secretary so early but for this experience: '*I was in the right place at the right time, doing the sort of things [the Prime Minister] needed*', '*so I got noticed*'. For most, their lives were lived in the square mile of Westminster and Whitehall; '*I don't think I ever went out [of London] at all*'. A *stage* in Brussels, the city, or industry was still the exception, not the rule.

They took pride in their generalist skills. One Permanent Secretary remem-bers his (then) boss saying:

> *if you think you are as hot shit as you say you are you should look at this. I know you don't know anything about it, but you say you are Rolls Royce. OK, put the foot down.*

So he was:

> *'persuaded' [said with irony], it's the Secretary of State's first priority and I was obviously the boy to deliver it. I remember being a bit nervous because I knew <u>absolutely</u> nothing by then, I <u>seriously</u> knew nothing, and in so far as I have thought about it, which probably wasn't much, I was not at all sympathetic. [emphasis in original]*

These statements are from a classical generalist; I can master any policy brief, even when sceptical.

They see it as a generic skill. One Permanent Secretary helped to write a green paper about which '*I didn't know the policy issues deeply*' but '*I did know a lot about those sorts of subjects*':

> *what you know about from your own experience is, you know about how to analyse policy, you know you have a lot of experience of the issues. You get to know quickly how ministers are likely to react on particular things, so you bring a lot of things which are not policy specific but which help. You are a senior person with the judgements and abilities to advise on policy and as time goes on you obviously develop knowledge in particular areas.*

Such analysis is also produced rapidly. One Permanent Secretary commented:

> *One learns an awful lot, such as the phone call I had at home, 9 o'clock one evening from a man called Nigel Wicks, who at that point was the Principal Private Secretary in No. 10, to say the Prime Minister would like a note on subject X by nine o'clock tomorrow morning. I phoned two, what we now call Grade 3s, who had the relevant coverage. I well remember saying, could they come up with material for Edmund Dell's arrival in the office for half past eight tomorrow morning? And one of them doing the understandable grumbling and moaning and how difficult it was, and the other just saying, 'Hell's teeth'. And of course we didn't get the note across by nine, but by about half past ten there was a paper. So you learn that sort of skill, you learn.*

They also held the conventional Westminster view of their relationship with the minister. Michael Heseletine[8] was admired as a minister because '*once he trusted you he trusted you completely*'. When '*he made a decision, he made a decision, but he was quite prepared to listen and to be argued with up to that point*'. However, although '*he was prepared to be argued against*', nonetheless he '*dismissed us quite shortly*'. Above all, '*he gave instructions and you had to obey them but they were clear instructions and they were coherent instructions*'. Michael Heseltine could be just as appreciative of his civil servants:

> I freely admit to the moments when the pure gold of the permanent secretary shone though. . . . You are tired. It is late. The issue is of secondary importance, only half understood, and you know in your heart of hearts that you have lost control of the meeting of civil servants waiting for the firm hand of government. You ramble, hesitate and suddenly the voice at your elbow takes over: 'I think that

is most helpful Secretary of State. We'll proceed as you have outlined which, if I follow you correctly, I would summarise as follows . . . ' And the permanent secretary pours out a string of elegant phrases and concise instructions as tears of gratitude well up within you. And private secretaries . . . make no mean fist of the same process. (Heseltine 1990: 11)

Working out how to get on with your minister is a core skill. If a permanent secretary could not build a working relationship with his or her minister, it was a black mark against their professionalism: it is '*a relationship that needs to be worked at to make it work*'. The same is true for the PPS and the PS. All pride themselves on their ability to work with any minister put in front of them; '*learning how to work with ministers is what it is all about*'. They do not have to like them; '*they are not our friends*'; '*it is not a close relationship*'. This story captures the preferred relationship:

> *He invited me around his house to watch the football with his political advisers, with a beer. And I couldn't make it. So I said, 'I'll tell this to [the Head of the Home Civil Service].' And he said, 'That's exactly right, he should invite you and you should refuse.'*

Much time and effort is spent on making it work. It starts even before the minister takes office;

> *[The Permanent Secretary] did an <u>awful</u> lot of briefing of [the Minister] in the permitted period before [the election], probably more than most and the relationship with [the Minister], which became the bedrock of the Department after the election, was forged there. I remember when the whole of the opposition team met the whole of the senior team. It was quite a formal occasion but they were sort of 'sizing us up'. And they had done a lot of work on who we were and had chatted to people outside and had picked up all sorts of vibes about us. It was very funny. They got all sorts of messages about who were the good guys and who were not.*

If the relationship can encompass friendship, it is not necessary. However, a professional, business relationship is essential (Barberis 1996: 34). Sometimes the relationship can seem too close. One Permanent Secretary mused: '*we certainly got along very very well . . . it was a marvellous atmosphere*' but he thought that '*better analysis and less can-do approach*' would have led to better outcomes. I tell the Permanent Secretary that such terms as 'husband and wife' and 'father confessor' have been used to characterize the relationship with the minister (see, for example: Barberis 1996: 33–4; Theakston 1987: 105; and Wass 1984: 58). He dislikes them. He describes his role as:

> *I'm either a fixer or I'm a prodder or I'm a bit of both. So, either he will ask me to arrange something, which I will do—change of personnel or sorting out a stakeholder, expediting this or something like that. So it's like a fixer or a sort of plumber,*

as it were. Or I am a prodder urging him, beguiling him into doing something which might be in his interest and the Department's interest.

Others admit to a more personal relationship. The wife of a Permanent Secretary told me that, when she met the Minister, she was told 'the biggest thing your husband can do for me is build up my self-confidence'. When I quizzed the Permanent Secretary, he admitted that the Minister's confidence could drop sharply and quickly.

They also acted as political antennas for their minister:

that's the sort of thing we talk about in our twice weekly meeting with [the Minister] *and indeed I have Monday morning meetings with the Management Board team at which we discuss topical issues, challenges, and dangers. So I've got that as an absolutely critical function of the senior civil service.*

In particular the Permanent Secretary wants to avoid the Department speaking with two voices. It doesn't matter 'whether it's bad or good news', it's 'just news' and 'for me it's consistency as much as anything else. When the Department's caught acting inconsistently, I think that's mis-management by me.'

Of course, secretaries of state vary greatly. Recognizing they will be there for only a short time, some secretaries of state have tunnel vision; '*he didn't care about anything to do with [the Department] apart from green matters*'. But this extract from an interview captures many shared beliefs about ministers.

RAWR: What do you expect from your Secretary of State?
PS: [long pause] Well I expect . . .
RAWR: Presumably you have got expectations about what you are supposed to do out there . . .
PS: Yes.
RAWR: . . . and therefore you expect the Secretary of State to support you?
PS: Yes I expect that. You said something earlier about holding civil servants to account for delivery but I expect the Secretary of State to take ultimate responsibility for the success of our operations.
RAWR: That's for the public presumably? In private they are going to hold you to account.
PS: Yes they are but I expect us to share that responsibility, which my Minister has done. I expect the Minister to give clear leadership about what they want. I expect an engagement with us on the difficult issues, the willingness to listen to us, and then clarity of decision. And I have certainly got that from my Minister. But you also get a willingness to listen, which is legendary. So I want that. I want my Ministers to be influential with their colleagues because I need them to go out there and argue for resources and so on, of course. And because in our world the ability to persuade and communicate is so important to getting everybody to go along with you, I need ministers who are good publicly and good at connecting with their audiences and communicating. I don't know what else I need from them.

RAWR: It's not quite the same question but it is going to sound like it. What do you like in your Secretary of States?

PS: What do I like about the Minister? The Minister has an almost unique ability to connect with the audience. That is something quite special about the Minister, which people don't see on these big occasions but the Minister has that ability. The Minister is somebody who listens intently to others and to civil servants and respects the advisers, all of them. And the Minister is someone who trusts people and enters genuinely into a debate. The best debates I have had about policy, in my entire career, are around the Minister's table because the Minister is in an equal position where, you know, together we are exploring the solution.

RAWR: Yes okay.

PS: And of course eventually, the Minister then takes the decision but the Minister is able to create a sense of a teamworking towards the Minister's achievements.

RAWR: You've worked with several Ministers over the years.

PS: Yes and I've liked a lot of them.

RAWR: What do you dislike about Ministers?

PS: [long pause] [sound of drinking]

RAWR: You can always edit it out.

PS: I know that. It's difficult. I was trying to think of the ones I didn't like and then trying to generalize what I didn't like about them. What I most dislike is when all they are interested in is themselves. That is the moment which I have disliked most and when it seems that everything that they do is not for the public good but for their own position and career, self-advancement. That is what I have most disliked and occasionally that has been so. There is something of that in a lot of Ministers. It is in all of us isn't it—in civil servants too. But just occasionally there have been people who have put that a long way ahead of anything else and I disliked that.

I dislike it when you can't get them to think straight. Oh I have some civil servants like that as well. You know, I think Ministers are just human beings like all the rest of us. They share exactly the same range of strengths and weaknesses as the rest of us. Sometimes, because of the position they occupy, myths develop about them that magnify their strengths and weaknesses. There aren't a lot of things I don't like about Ministers.

RAWR: Short-termism?

PS: I am tolerant of that because it is sort of in the nature of the beast. Of course I mean the changes, the chopping and changing and the short-termism. I'm afraid I accept that as part of the political process and maybe I am too tolerant of it but I just accept it goes with the territory. I am sometimes amazed that governments are as long term as they are. The Prime Minister said the other day about something which will remain nameless, 'It's amazing isn't it that we are investing in this, the benefits are probably coming in about 25 years time.' [PS laughs]. Some of the benefits of policy now are the result of decisions taken a long time ago.

Other permanent secretaries held similar views. One wanted:

a frank relationship, one that can develop mutual trust, a recognition that we are in this together.

Another said:

> *I always like ones who are honest. I hate those who are secretive. It's just if they don't talk openly with officials then you don't maximize the relationship. So, say, Nicholas Ridley[9] was entirely and totally open as far as I can see. In Nicholas Ridley's case [he was] completely open with officials, would listen, discuss, nothing was held back, there was no secret agenda. There was no secret other concourses in which final decisions get taken. So that's where I think the system worked best or that's where I worked best in the system. I would get rather frustrated and have got frustrated, in the past, with ministers where you have discussions for the sake of 'form', as it were, and then the real decision was taken somewhere else, and maybe that's the Byers' problem. It's not a way in which to get the best out of civil service, if you ask me.*

Inevitably there are other prized qualities: '*politeness*' and '*a sense of humour*' (see Chapter 7 below). There are also some clear 'don'ts' for permanent secretaries: '*How not to handle [a Minister] when you are head of department in a crisis—keep on telling him what's difficult and what can't be done.*'

I asked what the Permanent Secretary could do if, like the aforementioned Minister of Housing (see Chapter 4), there was boorish behaviour.

> *RAWR: Is it not possible to speak to them and say look folks this is not the way to do it?*
> *PS: It certainly is and that's my job. I do have fatherly talks with the junior ministers, not with [the Secretary of State] with junior ministers, but they don't necessarily take it from me.*

Others are less formal. One Permanent Secretary had regular one-to-ones with junior ministers and '*I will use that occasion to make a legitimate criticism of their behaviour.*' They also try to help. One political adviser was off-side with the Minister and sought the Permanent Secretary's advice. He was told his manner was patronizing. Of course, any such advice is governed by the civil service's codes of politeness (see Chapter 7). Equally obvious, advice is not always acted on. Managing relationships at the top of the Department is a core activity of the departmental court (see Chapter 6).

Managerial beliefs and practices

All three permanent secretaries faced the managerial challenge as their careers developed and were managing change in their departments. It is not a new task:

> Then, as now, the administrative class spent most of their time initiating or implementing changes. It was—and is—their characteristic function, a point that has been overlooked by a number of prominent people who ought to know better. (Part 1990: 20)

The difference today is the focus on management reform, with an emphasis on stakeholders, consumers and, increasingly, delivery. The balance between policy advice and management has shifted:

> *the job divides into the policy advice, accounting officer role, delivery, and leading the change programme.... There is a policy advice bit. Although my job title implies, and the job description indeed states, that I am the Secretary of State's principal policy adviser, I hope none of my colleagues in other departments, or I, interpret that as meaning I am the adviser. I guess my role is to quality proof, if you like, the advice ministers get at a broad level, and be on hand to discuss particular policy issues with ministers.*

On policy advice, he thought he '*added value*' where issues cut across several DGs and he '*ensured the links were made*'. But for the most part he did not provide policy advice for the Minister. Nonetheless, the push and pull between the policy and management sides of their job was constant. As another Permanent Secretary pointed out:

> *Most difficult for any permanent secretary I think, is you want to be involved in the policy because that is what your Secretary of State is doing and the more distant you get from that, the less able you are to be an influence on how the department operates. But of course to keep abreast of all the key policies is almost impossible and you have to be selective in that. What you want, I mean when you get deep down, what you really enjoy, a lot of the time, is being at the table when big decisions are being taken about policy. But of course I now have somebody else to do that. [So you are] trying to keep your eye on the big picture and spotting what may or may not be going well and intervening early enough to be an influence on that and, therefore, being selective about where your intervention is but in being selective, you have to know what the big picture is, to know where you should be intervening. I guess that's the constant pressure.*

The priority for all three permanent secretaries was change management.

> *It matters to me that the public services deliver for this government. I mean there is a big issue here about the confidence of this government in the civil service and if I could play a part in building that confidence, I think that would be something of longstanding importance.*

All of them had some management experience deliberately built into their career development. All described themselves as managers. They had grown up with management. As one observed;

> *this was one of the times, when, one of the sort of phases in Whitehall, it was thought to be, a quote 'good thing' unquote, for so called 'high-flyers' to do jobs in internal management of one sort or another; personnel, finance.*

One Permanent Secretary had extensive management experience. He had set up a new agency separate from his home department. He had to meet specific targets when implementing the policies of that organization. He enjoyed doing it from scratch, putting a team together, and making it work. He was *'completely devastated'* when he was promoted to the Minister's Private Office. Later he was responsible for 500 job centres and 8,000 staff and still he *'had no formal management training'*. This management experience stood him in good stead for the changes to come. He also sought experience in the human resource management and corporate services DGs, convinced these skills were essential to his career. In the past, such areas of work were the death knell of a career, not its making. The comment that he *'wanted the personnel function to be a true support for better management in the line'* marked him out as *'unusual'*. He was convinced his *'leadership and management skills, built on my real experience of delivery'* marked him out for promotion and at his promotion interviews he *'played very hard'* his *'real experience of delivery, my experience of being an area manager and managing large numbers of people in the region and delivering through others'*.

In one department, and only one, was management the priority for *both* the Permanent Secretary and his Minister.

> So [the Minister] and I made a point of focusing both on the customer focus, the purpose of the Department, the new objectives and the vision of the Department <u>and</u> the internal management as part of the <u>same</u> agenda and he went out of his way to say that, unlike his predecessor, he was going to work with the civil service and was keen and is and remains very keen on internal management issues. [emphasis in original]

This Department launched two reviews in the first week in office of its new Minister and

> Everything that came out about the reviews was jointly signed by [the Minister] and me to try to show a new joint approach to management here. We set up two review teams, one of the support schemes and one of the ways of working and structure and vision. Sent out questionnaires. Internally we had a <u>huge</u> staff questionnaire on the same basis and then went out to all the stakeholders, the senior ones, the most important ones.

So, the Permanent Secretary was *'driving down'* *'a customer focused change management programme'*. The Department was *'still in the middle of a huge, huge change programme, which will drive through new ways of working, project teams, team working, horizontal communication, less vertical'*. The Permanent Secretary was spending *'more than half my time doing change management in one guise or other'*. He was convinced that:

> I spend much, much, much, much more time on people and change management than my predecessor would have done. I am certain that 25 years ago, management wasn't a very trendy thing. I think, it is a whole new ballpark and to do it effectively

we have to learn leadership, change management, and persuasion skills, which
were not what I was taught.

Of course, in this context, management means strategic management:

the role is getting the Board to show collective leadership, then getting the board
members as DGs to drill down to their areas and to play a corporate role.

One Permanent Secretary told his DGs: '*as Permanent Secretary I can't do*
anything you lot would recognize as operational'. They are not only strategic,
they are also selective about both their policy interventions and in managing
the Department:

we had a systematic look at what was taking up time in my diary to see if we could
shift some things out so I could focus a bit more on big policy issues and big delivery
issues.

So, they are not involved in operational management but in supporting their
DGs in implementing strategic decisions. To make this happen, the Permanent Secretary stresses his '*visibility*'. He holds open meetings, and visits the
regions and the Department's agencies on what he calls, laughingly, '*royal*
tours'. It is the planned, deliberate selling of his Department's change
programme. Also, it is a way of tailoring the changes to the several bits of
the Department because he gets to know their work and its distinctive features.
He takes the view that

virtually everything I do concerns management unless it's a meeting with Ministers,
or a meeting with an external body. But every meeting I take in my office is
management of one sort or another.

The permanent secretaries disagree on the extent of the change. A few
permanent secretaries thought that the permanent secretary as mandarin
remained alive and well and was still not persuaded by managerial reform.

The idea of the mandarin is used here as a synonym for the old ways (see
Chapter 7) and, indisputably, some permanent secretaries of this generation
never made the transition to manager:

[He] had many strengths, but 'people leadership', empowering people and connect-
ing the department to the rest of Whitehall, were not his strengths. His strengths
were policy and clarity of the view on things.

The reservations of others are expressed as criticisms of the Blair version of
managerialism.

The critique of Blair might be that they haven't got enough underlying principles. If
you look at Ridley or Thatcher or Heseltine they had complete clarity of outcomes

and ways of achieving it. A critique of the current government is that they don't have that particular characteristic about ways of achieving something and what they want to achieve, apart from delivery, which is of only limited help.

And there is the frustration with how long it takes to change things:

It is the frustration of changing things, round here. I suppose any leader says this, you know what you want to have happen, but somehow it doesn't seem to happen. I heard the Prime Minster say, 'I pull a lever and nothing seems to happen.'

It is essential to me that my senior colleagues understand about how you manage people to achieve results, that is what I look for most. And the people I get most frustrated by, inside and outside, are people who don't understand about how you manage and deliver things, who have no instincts about that; that is a problem. Some of my permanent secretary colleagues are like that, and I have people like that inside and I think that is where there is a weakness in the civil service. The instinct about how something is going to work or operate or be implemented isn't there. So people blunder about and take a long time to get to decisions and then don't know, don't understand, that the decision taking point is the easy bit. There is an awful lot then to do. And the great disasters in government are when people haven't thought through the whole process from the policy development right through to the end of the process and to the impact you are going to make. And I think, you know, when we talk about civil service reform at the moment, the thing that is most important is to see everything as an end-to-end process and to understand that the people at the end are critical to it. That the people who are on the receiving end of government policy need to be brought right to the heart of it because if they are not, the policy will be beautiful but people won't behave like that, you know. The number of times over the years that you sort of say, 'Well why are people behaving like that?' As though it was them who were irrational. It's us who are irrational. People behave like that because that is what people are like and there isn't enough of bringing that understanding back into the centre of policy.

They worry that any change is short-term:

We have largely hit the targets that were set for us in 1997 and 1998. Now you may say that was chance or you may say it was very, very good but rather centralized management and organization. I mean, it is difficult to deliver long-term change with the kind of approach we have adopted, which is a highly centralist and 'top down' one. And one of the things we are wrestling with now is, how you move on to a phase where those reforms are owned by the system and become part of the [system's] agenda. We put money into it, devoted money to it, we monitored performance, we zoomed in where there were weaknesses and so on. So we had a classic management model. Now you can't use that model for all reform. We have shown that in certain areas you could shift what was happening very significantly from the centre. It's clear that we can be a major influence on the system and I believe we can get a long way towards the targets through actions that we take, but it becomes more and more difficult to persuade. A lot of the job is communication, persuasion.

CONCLUSIONS

I confess to admiring the permanent secretaries. Subjected to conflicting demands from ministers and their civil service colleagues, and to the incessant clamour for change, they bring a calm insouciance to a demanding job. No one is a paragon; all would freely admit to impatience, tiredness, and frustration. They are not elitists, but they display a self-confidence that some might see as arrogance in running complex organizations. I comment on their capacity to cope, beliefs and practices, storytelling, and responsiveness.

Coping

The Permanent Secretary's schedule is hectic. His life is a non-stop series of meetings, planned and unplanned. The pace is fast and unrelenting. In all three private offices, the Private Office told me the Permanent Secretary wanted to avoid back-to-back meetings, and in every office the Permanent Secretary had them most days of most weeks. Thus, at 4 p.m., the Permanent Secretary arrives at his fifth meeting that day and cannot remember why he is there. He confesses to his lapse of memory, asks a junior colleague 'to get him up to speed', then takes over the meeting after a few minutes when he remembers. And most meetings are not about making decisions. They are about refreshing the Department's memory, updating everyone on where we have got. Thinking time, writing time, reading time, all were at a premium. So:

> When the great ones go off to their drinks and their dinner
> The Secretary stays, getting thinner and thinner
> Racking his brains to record and report
> What he thinks they think that they ought
> to have thought. (Wakeham 1993: 10)

Top civil servants can be risk averse. They are careful about facts in case they are shown to be in error later. A simple illustration will suffice. On his desk, the PPS had a red phone dedicated to monitoring the conversations of the Permanent Secretary. He kept a handwritten note of any potentially delicate or decision making call. Everyone called this phone the Bat phone, after the instrument used by the mayor of Gotham City to summon the redoubted caped crusader. Regrettably there was no spotlight projecting the departmental logo onto low-lying cloud. Even more regrettable, the Bat phone has now been replaced by a modern phone. But still calls are monitored. The world of the Department is a world where even a casual remark in a phone call can have important repercussions. Such care and caution may seem exaggerated but it is nothing compared to the maelstrom the media can unleash on the unwary.

Ministers may call for the civil service to be less risk averse. They don't mean it because it can and does unleash career-damaging headlines.

Beliefs and practices

For many academics, the Westminster narrative is an outmoded account of British government, but not for top civil servants. When Sir Robert Armstrong (1985) restates the constitutional position that: 'the duty of the individual civil servant is first and foremost to the Minister of the Crown who is in charge of the Department in which he is serving', he states a belief widely shared by top civil servants. What is the function of the Westminster story? The short answer is, to legitimate the role of the civil servant. In classic Weberian fashion, the doctrine of ministerial responsibility means that the role of civil servants is to follow orders and that of politician, to give them. So, a belief in the Westminster model is integral to the anonymity and political impartiality of civil servants. However, such beliefs are no mere convenient cloak for the self-interest of civil servants. They shape actions. Outside commentators may scoff at the effectives of the doctrine of ministerial responsibility to parliament but top civil servants behave as if it is a binding constraint.

Similarly, there is a belief in a public service ethos.[10] Sir Richard Wilson (2003: 367) defines the character of the civil service as integrity, political impartiality, merit, ability to work for successive governments, and public service. On public service he comments:

> What attracts people to the Civil Service is the wish to make a contribution to the community. We have some of the best, most challenging jobs in the economy at every level. This gives us a deeply committed workforce.

They may live in the era of new public management, but long established patterns of behaviour persist. They are still socialized into the broad notions of the Westminster tradition, such as ministerial responsibility, as well as the specific ways of doing things around here. They are 'socialized into the idea of a profession', and learn 'the framework of the acceptable' (Bevir and Rhodes 2006, ch. 7). These beliefs and practices are captured by the term 'generalist', someone who is clever, loyal, reasonable, and able to synthesize complex arguments quickly and clearly for the lay minister.

A corollary of minister accountability to parliament for the actions of civil servants is the permanent secretaries' loyalty to their ministers. It was an 'implicit contract' [FWNBs]. It shines out of my interviews. Perhaps the greatest crime in the civil service canon is to betray one's minister. Loyalty is a core belief and practice socialized into the newest recruit to the senior civil service. And that loyalty can spill over into, literally, devotion. He was 'very upset' when the Minister had to resign (see Chapter 9). And loyalty is extended not only to ministers but also to other colleagues. The corollary of trusting ministers and civil servant colleagues is that they trust you. And trust is not just a matter of personal loyalty. It is also about being trusted to get on with the job, of being kept in the loop, and of respect for one's judgement. Secrecy is defensible when dealing with 'strangers' but not in dealings between ministers and civil servants.

The beliefs and practices of the Westminster narrative are sustained by socialization into the ways of both the civil service in general and the department in particular. A new fast stream recruit will have a mentor to guide them through the early years. They will have patrons as they progress through its ranks. They will work in a private office and have a stint in either the Cabinet Office or the Treasury, perhaps both. They are taught the norms and values of the higher civil service and learn about personal behaviour, the job, and its values (see Chapter 6). Now that civil service appointments are increasingly made by open competition, there are fears the newcomers will not be socialized in the service's traditions. They will not have sat across the desk from a mentor learning the rules of the Whitehall village game. They will not have had a patron to advise them on career development. They will not have worked the rites of passage through a private office, the Treasury and the Cabinet Office. Thus, the public service ethos could be eroded. Loyalty might become conditional and contingent and formal mechanisms of management may replace the glue of trust and shared codes.

Storytelling

Top civil servants and ministers learn through the stories they hear and tell one another and such stories are a source of institutional memory, the repositories of the traditions through which practitioners filter current events. The basis for much advice is the collective memory of the Department, its departmental traditions or philosophy. It is an organized, selective retelling of the past to make sense of the present. Permanent secretaries explain past practice and events to justify recommendations for the future.

Most if not all civil servants will accept that the art of storytelling is an integral part of their work. Such phrases as 'are we telling a consistent story?' and 'what is our story?' abound. They do not necessarily use the term 'storytelling'. They talk of *'getting the story straight'* [PPS, TI]; 'getting it together' and 'we've got the story'. Some phrases were music to my ears— 'when you explain it, when you have the narrative' [FWNB]; and 'we've reached agreement on some of the main storylines' [FWNB]. Officials are explicitly invited to tell a story (see Chapter 7: p. 200). The emphasis falls on finding out what happened, analysing the situation, testing the facts, and judging how things would play publicly. Lying is a worse sin than error, accident, even incompetence. In telling the story, they are also rehearsing lines and explanations to see what they sound like. Is it plausible? They want the reactions of their colleagues so they can anticipate the reaction of a larger, external audience. However, in using the phrase storytelling I do not want to give an odd impression of what was going on. Many of the meetings I attended were not about making formal decisions. They were part of the process leading up to a decision taken around the minister's table or at the Department's Management Board. The phrase storytelling does not imply that no decisions emerged. However, it does capture the care taken in preparing for decisions.

Responsiveness

Doubts are often expressed about the capacity, even willingness, of the civil service to reform. For King (2007: 347), this 'upright pillar of the British establishment . . . has started to show signs of crumbling and decay'. The prognosis is not new. Young (1990: 12) noted, 'what we have lost and are in danger of losing forever is institutionalized scepticism'. Others bemoan the politicization of the civil service brought on by the call for greater responsiveness. Some saw the government reforms of the Government Information Service as politicization, with Alastair Campbell replacing civil servants with his preferred spin doctors (Jones 1999: ch. 3). Others saw the increase in political appointments to the No. 10 department that dare not speak its name as evidence of politicization. Some senior civil servants argued that the career cadre, or continuity of experience, sustained a code of neutrality and shared standards that external appointments would erode. My permanent secretaries see the dilemma around constitutional bureaucracy, or neutrality, and political responsiveness but have mixed feelings about it.

My view is that there is no serious politicization. That the times are changing and people's attitudes and approaches change and their behaviour have changed. Fashions have changed, management changed, political context has changed and so the civil service has adapted. I would be amazed if there were no political decisions or politicization issues under Churchill or Attlee. Under Thatcher of course there were.

The purpose of bringing more people in from outside is to weaken the strong corporate culture . . . yet it is precisely that strong culture that nurtures the great virtues of the British civil service. . . . The professionalism, the political neutrality and most especially the ethical standards and incorruptibility of the British civil service are regarded with envy throughout the world. . . . Political neutrality has not yet been lost; but we should not imagine it invulnerable.

One of the external appointments supports the view that outsiders do not understand the corporate culture:

PS: What I hadn't understood at that point and which I understand much better now, is (a) the individual [the Minister] and (b) probably the political perspective on this, which is that he is somebody who is interested in the issues of today. I don't mean the issues of today that may be of concern five years away, but the issues that are live <u>today</u>. I got my timing wrong, you know. In a sense I was looking at the issues that were live for me today, because I was new. But also trying to look at the whole picture. I was looking through an organizational pair of spectacles. He was looking through political spectacles. The views are different. And that's the bit which I've had to learn to align.

RAWR: Is that the first time you ran into this?

PS: It's the first time I ever worked with a national politician. And that's the bit that was a serious learning curve. And a bit uncomfortable. No doubt at all that at that stage my credibility was knocked with the Department because I appeared to be going in one direction and he appeared to be coming across. It looked as if management was just sort of knocked out the way by the politician, I have learned that for politicians and for this politician in particular, they do business in corridors, on sofas, talking on the phone as opposed to a more systematic fashion.

A cadre civil servant would have learnt such lessons with his mentor and first posting to a private office.

In my view, there can be little doubt that the permanent secretaries have been responsive to the demands of ministers and espoused the managerial cause. Management was integral to their career development. They speak the language of reform (see Chapter 7). They lead the departments' change programmes. Strategic management is what they do. It is the largest single task they undertake. It is a key test that will show whether the civil service can deliver for the government. All of them are frustrated by the speed of change, but they persist. The issue is not one of willingness but of dilemmas. The managerial narrative has not replaced the Westminster narrative; it supplements it. Their generalist skills are still prized. Ministers want a civil servant with keen political antennas for risk, who has the experience and judgement to advise on problems. They also want a strategic manager who can deliver services. They want a politically neutral civil service that can advise on snags and a can-do civil service committed to their policies. They call for joined-up government. So, ministers want a civil servant who is networked across Whitehall and beyond. This governance narrative compounds the problem of conflicting demands (see Chapter 8). The civil servants complain they are given no clear brief or the brief changes all too often.

The restless search for reform provided continued evidence of a floundering and directionless political class. As Richard Wilson (1999), the former Head of the Civil Service, lamented:

I would not want to claim that the manner in which we implemented all these reforms over the years was a model to emulate. There was not enough overall vision or strategic planning. Too often it was uncoordinated, with different parts of the centre of government launching similar initiatives simultaneously or at a pace which long-suffering managers in departments found difficult to handle.

No argument there then. The dilemmas posed by government policy lie at the heart of the slow pace of reform rather than inertia or subversion by permanent secretaries.

NOTES

1. The everyday life of British permanent secretaries has not been a topic of academic concern, although Barberis 1996 is a partial exception. They also write fewer memoirs than ministers, although there has been an increase over the past decade. See: Barber 2007; Cairncross 1997 and 1999; Denham 2002; Donoughue 2003 and 2005; Henderson 2001; Lewis 1997; Meyer 2005; Murray 2006; Packer 2006; Part 1990; Ponting 1985 and 1986; and Rimington 2001.
2. This finding is not unusual and common for senior executives in both the public and private sectors. See: Mintzberg 1973; Mintzberg and Bourgault 2000; and Noordegraaf 2000.
3. This section is based on my FWNBs for all three departments. All quotes in roman font are from the FWNBs. Throughout the chapter, all quotes in italics are from my transcribed interviews with ten permanent secretaries unless shown to the contrary.
4. *The Fall and Rise of Reginald Perrin* was a British sitcom first broadcast in 1976. It was well known for its catchphrases, most notably 'I didn't get where I am today without . . .' It was based on the book by David Nobbs 1975.
5. 'Note of [the Permanent Secretary's] Monday Morning Meeting with Directors General and Others' by his PS, 18 November 2002.
6. One of the truly challenging features in the British civil service is its ever changing nomenclature for the various grades of officials. Grade 5 (formerly Assistant Secretary) and above are members of the Senior Civil Service. But job titles vary between departments and members of the service, as here, continue to use old labels. A Deputy Secretary is now a Grade 2.
7. I can confirm that the performance of the course members was also patchy. In the 1970s, I specialized in central–local government relations. Some course members were reading their newspapers as I was introduced, and read them throughout. Outside of economics and statistics, it would seem they had nothing to learn.
8. Michael Heseltine was Secretary of State for Defence (1983–6), Secretary of State for the Environment (1979–83 and 1990–2), President of the Board of Trade (1992–5), and Deputy Prime Minister (1995–7).
9. Nicholas Ridley was Financial Secretary to the Treasury (1981–3), Secretary of State for Transport (1983–6), Secretary of State for the Environment (1986–9), and Secretary of State for Trade and Industry (1989–0).
10. For a summary statement of the traditional beliefs of civil servants see: Cabinet Office 1994; Jary 2008: ch. 7 and pp. 75–7; and the several speeches of Sir Richard Wilson, former Head of the Home Civil Service. See, for example: Wilson 2003.

Part III

Scenes

6

The Departmental Court

In Part II, I told a chronological story based on the engagement diary of the Minister and the Permanent Secretary. In Part III, I do not provide a chronological narrative. Instead, I have written scenes and dialogue. Scenes are story segments that I use as building blocks to develop specific themes. The scenes are always in the offices of the central secretariat, written from the viewpoint of, and sometimes in the words of, its inhabitants, and cover moments in time not days or weeks. Dialogue refers to reciprocal conversations, sometimes in the form of semi-structured interviews but also, during the observational fieldwork, they were part of my encounters at the office. There is no unfolding storyline or character development as in a narrative. In this chapter, I focus on the principal private secretary, the private secretaries, and three aspects of the everyday life of the departmental court: recruitment and training, internal management and its tensions, and internal networking. I look at the protocols, rituals and languages of the court, including the impact of managerialism, in more detail in Chapter 7; and at external networking in Chapter 8.[1]

'THE NATIVES ARE HOSPITABLE'

The private office has not attracted much attention. As Sir Nicholas Henderson (2001 [1984]: xvi) observes: 'I do not think that widespread ignorance of the role of the Private Office matters. On the contrary, I think it is better that way.' Of course everyone knows the famous quote from Richard Crossman (1975: 618) that he had not appreciated the private office's importance and 'under George Moseley it was a good solid Rover of a Private Office, under John Delafons it was a Rolls Royce'. Some, like Jock Bruce-Gardyne, employ the less flattering metaphor of 'prison warder' (1986: 33)! Most ministers over the past 50 years find a page or so in their memoirs for the private office. Most limit their observations to their principal private secretary (PPS) and their immediate private office. Patrick Gordon Walker (1970: 67) bears out Crossman's views on the importance of the private office: 'essential to proper control of a department' (see also Morrison 1984: 322–3). Geoffrey Howe (1994: 395) described his PPS as 'crucial' and the job as 'infinitely varied' requiring 'the utmost personal sensitivity and political shrewdness'. The PPS would have an 'intuitive sense' of what the minister would want yet would know 'just when he could not safely rely on his own judgement'. Ministers in less exalted departments differ but little. Michael Heseltine (2000: 189) considers 'an efficient private office . . . one of the most important steps for a new Minister to take'. Ministers under New Labour offer but minor variations on these themes. Initially, David Blunkett (2006: 17, 19, and 319) grumbled about the rapid turnover of staff, their lack of secretarial skills, their failure to be methodical with his tapes, and lapses of clarity in his diary entries. In the words of *Round the Horne*, he was a right 'gruntfuttock'.[2] But he ended describing his Department for Education and Skills (DfES) Private Office as a 'really tremendous bunch' and the Home Office as 'a first-class team', praising their commitment, hard work, and long hours.

As well as a consensus about the importance of the office, there is also much agreement about its role. It exists to organize the minister's life. According to Jary (2004: 15), it acts as a 'bridge' between the minister and the department. Or, as James (1999: 35) puts it, the private secretary must 'face both ways without seeming two-faced':

> He must explain the demands of the department to the Minister and the political needs of his Minister to other officials.

Richard Crossman's (1975: 21) claim that the private secretary's job is 'to make sure the Minister . . . doesn't let the side or himself down' rings true to this day. In pursuit of this goal, the tasks of the private office are many and varied: it keeps the diary, makes appointments, provides the papers for meetings, takes notes at the meetings, arranges visits at home and abroad and accompanies the minister on such visits. It inducts the minister into the ways of the department and continues to act as a source of information about what is going on in the department and elsewhere and an early warning system about possible snags. There is also a private secretaries network. Gordon Walker (1970: 67) praises this network because it 'facilitates and short circuits the dispatch of business'. So, the PPS can ring a ministerial colleagues' PPS to pass on his minister's 'observations'. As Henderson (2001: 157–8) observes, the network of private offices is 'one of the means by which the policies of the different Departments of State are coordinated'.

There is even a consensus about the main problem: dual loyalty. According to Bruce-Gardyne (1986: 35) the private secretary, 'in Whitehall folk-lore, owes his first allegiance to his Minister'. But folklore and practice can diverge. Some claim their primary allegiance:

is to support and execute the policies of the *Government*. If our Minister's policies are in conflict with those of the Government, then it is the Government we must back. (Bruce-Gardyne 1986: 36, emphasis in original)

The Janus-faced nature of the job comes out in other ways. Michael Heseltine (2000: 188) refused 'to see my private office as a training ground for junior civil servants'. In a similar vein, David Blunkett (2006: 82) complained 'the Private Office is a training scheme for people to dib in and out of'. In short, the subsidiary function of speaking for the department, and even lesser role of training civil servants, can supplant the primary function of serving the minister.

The Cabinet Office's Centre for Management and Policy Studies produced a handbook on working with ministers. It describes the private office as 'essential to managing the Minister's working life'; 'instrumental in maintaining good working relationships around the Minister', 'exhilarating places to work, providing an unequalled high altitude view of the work of a government department'; and 'valuable allies for any top official working around the Minister' (Jary 2004: 18).

There are various problems with these several accounts of the private office. It focuses on one position and one part of the ministerial support system. There is more to the private office than the minister's private office and his or her PPS. Commonly, it also comprises ministerial or special advisers (SpAds) who have their own private secretary; the private offices of ministers of state; the permanent secretary's private office, and some permutation of parliamentary, correspondence, and business support units. So, one Department had eight ministers and about 80 people supporting them. It would be more accurate to talk of a department's central secretariat because there are several private offices and often they have shared support units.

The permanent secretary will head the central secretariat with the principal private secretary as the number two. Under the PPS are several private secretaries (PS) and assistant private secretaries (APS). There is a diary secretary (DS) for the secretary of state and in each private office. The internal organization of the private office matches the functional silos of the department. Each PS will be responsible for several policies and problems coming up from the directors general (DGs). Each DG is a member of the department's Management Board (MB) chaired mainly by the permanent secretary and serviced by the permanent secretary's private office. Its role is to provide strategic direction and advice to ministers on allocating resources and monitoring performance. When it works as intended:

Every member of his senior management team had a corporate responsibility and made a corporate contribution and I think I said to you before that, during this period particularly from 1998 onwards, the senior management team of the Department was the *most powerful cohesive team I have ever worked with. And we got to know each other very well and we had a completely shared view of what we were trying to achieve. So what one was doing was agreeing with the corporate view of how the Department should develop and then in the way one operated in one's own Directorate with one's own team actually implementing this. [Permanent Secretary, TI]*[3]

For the civil servants who work in them, the differences in roles and processes between the various private offices are slight. The Secretary of State's Private Office is larger, more prestigious, more pressurized. One PS who had worked in both a minister's and a permanent secretary's private office commented:

In terms of ways of working, they are similar in many ways, feeding things in, feeding things back into policy. Lots of meetings. In that sense very similar, the difference being that we are involved at an early stage in the policy development. [PS, TI]

I found the Permanent Secretary's Private Office lower key and less busy. There was one other difference; the Minister's office was noisier than the Permanent Secretary's office.

Below, I describe the roles and responsibilities of the central secretariat but this focus is also potentially misleading. I will argue the central secretariat is better seen as a 'departmental court'. This phrase draws attention to the beliefs and practices of the court; to the court politics surrounding ministers and senior civil servants, to the competition between ministers, and to the tensions within the court and with the rest of the department and between civil servants and SpAds. My aim is to shift the focus from positions and offices to relationships both inside and outside the department. We already know that ministers, permanent secretaries, and their departments have to manage their relations across Whitehall, especially with central agencies such as No. 10 and the Treasury. The departmental court is central to that exercise. But existing accounts pay much less attention to the role of the court in managing relationships within the department. Most departments are complex organizations. They have two or more ministers of state and several DGs heading major units. The departmental court is a key part of the organizational glue holding the department together.

RECRUITMENT AND TRAINING

Recruitment

All discussions about recruitment to the private office focus on the PPS and the other PSs. In effect that means it focuses on the careers of fast stream civil servants; the best young talent in the department. The posting is prized because it is an understood route to the top.[4] The answer to the question what is the best job for an aspiring fast stream recruit is:

> *It's the Principal Private Secretary. I mean why do you join the civil service—lots of reasons but one of them might be to be right at the heart of the machine, to play a role in making this great thing work and that idea has never gone away. I think this is the plum job in the Department and when I got a shout at it my CV was being written within moments of seeing the advert. [PPS, TI]*

Selection is through the usual channels.

> *I had an interview in the first stage after a couple of weeks with the Permanent Secretary and the Director from the personnel mob. They will have then, I imagine, produced a shorter list and those people came to [the Minister] a week or so later for interview and [the Minister] selected the candidate. [PPS, TI]*

Michael Heseltine (2000: 189) similarly reports that his Permanent Secretary selected three or four of the best candidates in the department and he chose one.[5] On occasion, if promoted within the department, the minister gets to keep his existing staff.

The PPS plays the key role in recruiting to the rest of the court. His advice will be sought by both the permanent secretary and the minister (Henderson 2001: 191). Recruiting fast streamers to the post of junior private secretaries poses some problems. Although most see it as an attractive position and as a stepping stone to promotion, few stay more than 12 months. In one Private Office, no one had been there for more than six months. Because of my yo-yo visits, I noticed the turnover of staff with few staying beyond 18 months. The problem is of the civil service's own making. The PS posts are offered to:

> *'fast streamers', you know the graduate programme, who do a year in each job. They tend to want to move on. You do this job for say 6 or 7 months, you get used to it, you excel after that, you get really good at it, you hit the year mark, you reach 'burn out', you think, 'sod this, I am ready [for promotion] where I will earn the same money without all this overtime'. [PS, TI]*

Recruitment to junior posts in the private office can be even more difficult because the pay was never good (especially for Central London), and career expectations are much lower, even non-existent. When I asked a Diary Secretary if there was a career structure for her, the answer was *'probably not'* [DS, TI].

Training

The traditional pattern of training for fast stream civil servants is a series of postings to challenging jobs. In each posting the high-flyer has a mentor, usually informal, commonly a principal (now Grade 6 or 7, deputy director or team leader).

> *The fast stream is dead lucky because you get all this free attention from senior colleagues. They tend to get taken under the wing of a senior person every day, and that happened to me a lot.* [PPS, TI]

In Chapter 5 the permanent secretaries described their on-the-job-learning and patchy training. It has changed. Of courses, fast streamers are socialized as of yore, but now there is more formal training. One PPS was keenly aware of the challenges of blending old and new:

> *They sent me off to do an MBA at Imperial College, which was a good experience for me followed by a short stint working on HR strategy and then I got promoted to the Senior Civil Service when I led one of the reviews of the Department and then for 18 months after that I project managed the implementation programme.* [PPS, TI]

He felt the culture in which he had been socialized was:

> *much more a new public management one. Most of my more senior colleagues have been schooled through the 1980s and those people have traditionally always been through policy jobs and have ended up being the mandarins we all recognize, but I'm not a classic old-fashioned mandarin.* [PPS, TI]

He resisted any simple managerialism versus mandarin dichotomy, admitting he had some of the features of a mandarin: '*and as I get older I seem to have more*'. Nonetheless he insisted:

> *There is already an understanding that to be an effective civil servant, he's not in it just to be clever, you also have to manage the processes around the delivery of policy.* [PPS, TI]

When I summarized his account as 'twin track' training, combining manager and mandarin, he commented, '*I think it's very fair*' [PPS, TI].

This twin track training inculcates several values, including incrementalism, respect for seniority, and a sense of tradition. Socialization is not about such skills as drafting, '*it's all about judgement and stuff like that; it's those skills*' [PPS, TI].

The enthusiasm and commitment of the PPS was as obvious as it was unfeigned. So, I had to point out that some of his colleagues in other departments look back on the private office experience with mixed feelings. For them, the difficulty with the private office was juggling several balls at the same time and never getting a concrete policy job to work on. This PPS agreed, '*it would be crazy for someone to spend 30 years in a Private Office*', but in a private office you get the challenge of '*juggling all those balls and seeing the political reality of how things work*'. There is a '*dealing room flavour*' and '*it's no accident the Private Office has been open plan for a lot longer than other bits of the Department*'. Above all, and this point is made by everyone who works in the Private Office, *'there's a certain rush and a certain excitement working with the political side of things'* [PPS, TI]. But you have to be careful: 'In this job you flit from one thing to another and you have to make sure you finish each one' [FWNB].

Nonetheless, most PS looked forward to their next posting. They had clear ideas about what they preferred. The wanted a secondment outside the civil service to a big company, a *stage* in Brussels, a service delivery job in an agency, or a posting to a policy division, where, with any luck, they would be on a bill team:

> Civil servants <u>love</u> legislation, despite the fact that it's incredibly time-consuming and in most cases does not achieve a great deal. But it's seen as a high status thing to do within the civil service, one of the classic jobs, you work on a bill team, you prepare legislation, policy becomes law. [PS, TI]

So, training may be informal but it includes a clear sense of career progression.

Training for other support staff is focused. One Diary Secretary reported: *'I had never done any sort of PA, PS work.'* Nevertheless she received no training *'strictly on PA work'* although *'I have done training within the Department on various things'*; for example *'I have had all the IT training'* [DS, TI]. Learning on the job remains the main form of training:

> coming into this job I didn't have a proper induction, I didn't have a proper handover so it was basically relying on my own experience as well as the contacts that I had here. [DS, TI]

This comment also applies to a number of PSs in some departments:

> RAWR: Was there any kind of induction process for you when you arrived?
> PS: Not really, no.
> RAWR: Did you overlap with [your predecessor] for any period?
> PS: For about a couple of days. [PPS, TI]

Not everyone was happy with this informal process:

> I don't think that you get a huge amount of leeway. If you start making mistakes and people start frowning and saying, you know, 'What's going on?' And there is just so much to do here. There is just so much to do. So no I don't think I got an induction. [PPS, TI]

So, for most members of the Private Office, recruitment and training had changed but little, although there were signs of change for the posts of PS and PPS. There was to be a broader pool from which the PSs would be recruited. The new generation of fast streamers had 'twin track' training combining a formal management education with mandarin style learning from regular postings.[6]

INTERNAL MANAGEMENT

Managing the private office is the unglamorous but essential part of the task. The PPS '*has management responsibility*' for the departmental court. The extent to which its '*bits are stitched together*' varies. The court can be in separate rooms, not an open plan office, and even spread over different floors and sections of a large building. The PPS's job is to make it '*a coherent whole*' and to make sure '*all of us have got one purpose here*', which is '*to serve the Department and to serve the Minister and to act as that interface*' [PPS, TI].

The internal management task is burdensome. For example, one PPS had direct line responsibility for 16 people and signed off on another 60. Anyone who has taken the performance appraisal of staff seriously, rather than 'ticked and flicked', will recognize the demands of such numbers. To compound the difficulties of the job, the several constituent units have demanding roles. Few readers will have an interest in the Business Support Unit, essential though its financial tasks may be, but the parliamentary branch is another matter. It manages the department's link with parliament. The workload is often mundane and routine but it is always large; for example, the minister will get about 12 written parliamentary questions a night in the red box (see below). So, when I talk of the management responsibilities of the PPS and about the private office and its attendant units coordinating policy, resolving internal conflicts, and managing its external environment, I am talking about the heart of the departmental machine; about a mini-version of the central capability around the prime minister. I try to give a flavour of life in the private office by looking at the role of the permanent secretary, managing the court, and private office tensions.

The permanent secretary and the departmental court

The permanent secretary is the boss, and everybody knows it. Only the secretary of state has an equivalent aura, and that depends on the personality of the secretary of state. Not all are a commanding presence. Ministers of state know their place, and it does not include getting on the wrong side of the permanent secretary. There are exceptions; there are no invariant rules in these matters. Folklore tells you about previous ministers and permanent secretaries and their foibles and 'unfortunate' behaviour. But the incumbents are seen through rose-coloured spectacles. One PS can speak for many; 'he is just so easy to work for' [PS, FWNB]. When asked about the permanent secretary, the first response is to say they are 'nice'. One DS used the term 'nice' six times when talking about her permanent secretaries. However, when we returned to the subject, she found there were things she disliked about them: forgetful and, as she warmed to the task, she added arrogant. Other senior civil servants were not spared. They were *'gradist'* treating *'the rest of us as mere minions and scullery maids of the office'*. The Private Office *'don't give a tinker's bloody cuss what grade they are'* as long as the *'person out there can give me the information that I need'* [DS, TI].

Even the PPS can suffer intimations of rank. The PPS is described by the Permanent Secretary as *'the Minister's representative on earth'*. It is said with a smile, but like many flippant remarks it is double edged. The phrase recognizes his standing while reminding the PPS that he is the [Permanent Secretary's] subordinate. In turn, the PPS comments that the [Permanent Secretary] sometimes *'takes his frustrations with the Minister out on me'* [PPS, TI]. It is probably inevitable in a bureaucracy with a defined hierarchy that people will be reminded of their place in the scheme of things. However, life in the Private Office is mainly informal:

> *Everyone talks across the desk. It is informal. I think that's how it works out there as well [referring to the rest of the court].* [PPS, TI]

For example, everyone called the Permanent Secretary by his first name when in the Private Office. There is no formal roster of duties. They arrange cover for the Secretary of State informally between themselves [PPS, TI].

What the private office can forget is the impression they make on the rest of the department. They may be informal and relaxed around the permanent secretary or the minister but other officials are not. Some are intimidated. The surroundings are impressive. They see the permanent secretary irregularly. They sit bird-like, perched on the edge of their seat, rubbing their hands together, and expressing tension. Sometimes the private office jokes about its standing. So, one PS jokingly answers the phone with: 'Hello, we're scary; we're the Permanent Secretary's Office.' He's right, and it's no joke.

Managing the court

The permanent secretary runs the department, the PPS manages the court, and the PS manages his or her private office. Both the PPS and the PSs have to cope with the internal management tasks on top of their primary role of looking after the minister or the permanent secretary. One found the demands of being a manager frustrating and vented at some length:

> *I find [management] the most challenging bit. That's the bit that I worry about. Managing [the Private Office] out there is hugely difficult, given the volume of work. The core tasks of the job have to sit alongside your management responsibility. I know exactly what I ought to be doing to be the perfect manager. And short of sacrificing my future health, I physically can't do that; for example, finding time to*

sit down and have formal 'round the table' meetings. Or knowing there is a particular document on the [internal reform], which everybody has received a copy of, which I ought to be sitting down and talking to them about. Because of time pressures it's impossible to do that. I have to make sure that I have some kind of substitute for it, which is making sure that wherever I can, I give them feedback on how they are doing. I make sure we observe the formal processes, although to be honest, even now it is a struggle. None of them have got completed [performance appraisals] although they all have objectives. I have had to deal with the leaving process of two people and difficult recruitment processes, because there is no one interested in working here. That side is hard to do justice to. And it's a particular struggle in this office compared to other private offices in that I am the sole manager of the unit, and I am also the Private Secretary. In other private offices, the private secretary will manage two more junior people [APSs] who then manage the most junior people. And the burden of trying to make sure that [the recruits] develop as they should when they are both new to the job and need simple things explaining to them and need to know how [the Department] operates, why they're here, what the bigger picture is. I mean it just sends me spare sometimes because I spend the core day helping [the Permanent Secretary] or answering the phone or shuffling papers. If I am spending time with them then when do I do the notes of meetings, when do I do the stuff that [the Permanent Secretary] wants me to do? It's quite difficult. And the [internal reforms]! What difference does the [internal reform] make to you in your job? Trying to bring that alive to people. It's pretty impossible, to be honest. [PS, TI]

This commentary sees the permanent secretary's private office as a separate part of the court. Some PPSs had a different view.

[We should be] looking at ourselves as a team and as a management outfit and talking about how we get together. You see it is important to the way I run it, I think that the whole private office thing comes together in this office, and in many ways comes together in my seat, I think it's a bit like jazz. [PPS, TI]

His metaphor of the private office as a jazz band that must allow, even encourage, solos while remaining a coherent ensemble resonates.

There's an old-fashioned way of running a private office and I've seen it, and I've worked with principal private secretaries who've done this—you control everything. You can do that. You can do it but I think it's a suboptimal way to do it. In a modern world where you've got all these different bits of information lying around, especially when you've got a switched on Secretary of State like this one, it is desperately suboptimal. Instead what I want to say to colleagues is, 'I understand it's a bit frightening, it's a bit brinky, but there are a lot of things going on that I can't see. I'm going to sit here and I'm going to say to you "Let's all play this game together and let's jam together and what we get at the end will sound good".' You've got to trust me to be the one in the middle and if people don't trust me then it will break down. And that goes back to what I said about my skill with relationships. [PPS, TI]

However, this PPS was the only one who so described the private office and his tasks. Others had a more circumscribed view, focusing mainly on the needs of the minister or the permanent secretary, not internal management. Individual private offices become isolated: *'I move from my desk to the loo, to the kitchen, to my desk'* [PS, TI]. The PS 'sticks her head down and ignores you'. The PPS worries that 'people need to realize we are all part of the same team' (departmental induction video).

Private office tensions

Private office tensions are all too common, a case of 'so it goes'. For example:

> There is a tension between the Private Secretary, Diary Secretary half, and the clerical correspondence half [of the departmental court]. [PPS, TI]

The PS side of the court refer to the correspondence side as 'corres girls' and they are not being nice. The correct title is 'Correspondence Managers'. When I ask about allocating mail, I am told the 'corres girls' have a list of the subjects covered by each PS but *'they ask all the bloody time'*. The 'corres girls' reply *'That's not the way it's done'* [PS, TI]. But some problems are more intractable, notably the rapid turnover of the PS, and the culture of long hours.

Turnover

Most private secretaries are aware they irritate the long-stay members of the private office:

> They always have the knowledge that you are going to go and there is going to be another one comes through. So you know you are just passing through the office and they are permanent and you are not. Which I don't think is healthy and is a big barrier. [PS, TI]

If you have worked with 17 PSs while DS, irritation can mount if the PS passing through has views about how the private office really ought to work. It can prompt an intemperate comment like *'eager, maniacal, arrogant, little horrors'* [DS, TI].

One PPS was grappling with the rapid turnover of private secretaries:

> We're trying to make it longer now. There's been a policy until relatively recently of getting young, whizzy 'fast streamers' in, who have been placed here rather than through the Department's internal advertising scheme. I have moved away from that and said that we will recruit through the advertising scheme. Which apart from anything else means you can fish in a wider pool and you give opportunity to other people who might not normally think about coming into Private Office. I've

also stipulated that I want people staying here longer, so 18 months or 2 years.
[PPS, TI]

Such concern is rare. The following exchange shows the issue has low priority
for the permanent secretaries.

RAWR: They go so quickly as well, they seem to do about a year?
PS: About a year because it is a classic 'fast stream' process.
RAWR: You have just got them up to speed, they've just done a full cycle, and have got
to a point where they are really, really useful and they're gone!
PS: Yeah (laughing).
RAWR: I am just curious about it.
PS: It's (short pause), I think (short pause), I'm not sure that we would attract people
in if we said basically you're going to be here for 18 months to 2 years. We wouldn't
necessarily attract the talent in because people see it as, I hope, an interesting and
potentially exciting opportunity both for a job and to progress. But I mean there is an
issue, you are right to unbundle the issues, yeah. [Permanent Secretary, TI]

It is not simply that PSs come and go but some, during their short stay, never
fit in. I saw one PPS struggle. The mistakes seem minor to an outsider but they
undermined the rationale of the Private Office; for example, papers had gone
to the Permanent Secretary for the meeting but not to the rest of the Department's Management Board. The PPS was upset: *'whenever things go wrong*
I feel terrible not just because I like to do things right' but because *'I am thinking*
all the time about not letting him down'. I asked if that she received any
mentoring—no. There was no regular monitoring or appraisal while learning
the job. The PPS was learning the preferences of the Permanent Secretary and
trying to win his confidence. It seemed obvious to me that the PPS was not
succeeding.

The PPS commented that *'there are people who have been close to [the*
Permanent Secretary]', who are *'finding it hard to let go of that personal*
relationship', so *'they service the [Permanent Secretary] directly'.* In other
words, the DS went direct to the Permanent Secretary and ignored the PPS.
On a couple of occasions, the DS simply refused to do what the PPS asked. The
PPS was *'only just beginning to relax'* and to act on the problem; *'I have set up*
some team building events.' The PPS's confidence was shaken: *'I do have access*
to him, and I can put something in the diary if [the DS] will let me' (emphasis
added). When I asked about her successes in the job, she um-ed and ah-ed
before saying *'I guess I have established myself'.*

By this time I knew everyone in the private offices well. I sat in on one
Private Office Keep-in-Tonch (KiT). It is attended by 21 people, although
there is a lot of coming and going. The idea is to brief one another on matters
of concern, but it is disorganized. People are left out by the chair on the round

robin briefings and are visibly irritated. The conversation deteriorates into a discussion of the smells from the microwave oven. The Permanent Secretary has complained about it. It would seem he is an 'ogre'! There is grumbling over the rota for staying on. It is staccato, no one wants to speak and, frankly, the meeting is a shambles. I catch fragments of unconnected, irritable conversation within the KiT: 'that's the way it is', 'we'll revisit the issue', and he is being 'precious'. The last remark provokes a flurry of dissent. The meeting dithers to a close.

After the event, I nattered about this and that with various members of the Private Office. The phrase 'teamwork' recurs. It is the preferred, understated euphemism for the Private Office's little local difficulties. No one was prepared to criticize the PPS. And no one helped. The PPS was flailing and failing, so everyone else backed off. The body language was stiff. Much was said with glances between desks. The language was determinedly polite. The Private Office coped by keeping its distance. When the PPS asked if everyone had had a lunch break, they all said 'yes', but none had and she must have known that. At one point, I asked her why her desk faced the wall instead of the Private Office. The next day she had turned the desk to face the Private Office, and there was a deal of muttering. Distance had been breached. Now the glances between desks had to be rationed. When I returned to the office on a repeat visit, the PPS was gone. Why? She had done the usual stint in the Private Office and returned to the Department. It was a short stint and a rapid return.

Such problems can prompt drastic action. Another Private Office member commented, '*We have had two horrors*', referring to private secretaries. So,

> We call 'total honesty sessions'. You basically shut the door and it's 'no holes barred', no recrimination, no repercussion and everybody gets it off their chest. They say 'I can't stand what you do and the way you do it.' And the times we've had to do it with some of the private secretaries, it worked, and some of the people that we've done it with I am still friends with. [DS, TI]

The evil thought crossed my mind that some university deans would benefit from similar sessions.

THE CULTURE OF LONG HOURS

There is also the problem of an entrenched culture of long hours, which has repercussions for recruitment, training, and morale.[7]

> It's the culture of the office. You can't, you couldn't, it's so busy, the volume of business within the office, you couldn't work on a 9–5 basis. You just couldn't. [DS, TI]

Long hours and the related stress are harder to manage at the lower end of the departmental hierarchy:

> when I was up here before it was stressful and I remember when, just before Christmas, I went home and I was very upset because I just found it so stressful and people had been ringing me up and had been talking in this rapid way to me about things I didn't understand—it was always stressful. I was always aware that if I got something wrong it would be damaging, it would be embarrassing, people would shout. [PPS, TI]

Others suffer physical side effects

> I find I will have physiological reactions to the stress sometimes. I will have weeks where I will have awful skin and my heart rate doesn't want to go down. Yesterday it was [the Minister] being in a bad mood. And that's stressful just because the service element of the job comes in. None of us knew how to make him feel better about his day. [PS, TI]

One DS works 'say 9 a.m. to 7 p.m. I enjoy the job, I enjoy the work, I have no kids, I have a flexible husband'. There are rewards. She enjoys working with the Minister; 'I've had the good fortune of working with five secretaries of state who I have got on with and seem to be able to bear me' [DS, TI].

Ministerial attitudes vary. Edwina Currie (1989: 19) commented:

> My girls in the office are working all hours and it is not fair to them. It's all right for me. I asked for it but they didn't.

Other ministers are less sympathetic:

> People were hard working and diligent and frankly did go that extra bit. Partly because everybody knows it's not forever. You know ministers last 18 months on average. You're never going to see this again. You're in the heart of government, the excitement of it all, you know, the interchange, you're in politics and public administration, you know, you're meeting people that are well known personalities. It is exciting, I think. So the trick is to work hard for what in a lifetime is a relatively brief moment of time and get as much out of it as you can. [Minister, TI]

But the excitement wears off:

> I have done a year-and-a-half, and you get 'burn out' in the job. Meeting [the Minister] or the Chancellor or the Prime Minister has worn off, so then the hard work kicks in and sometimes you feel like 'I don't want to be in work at 8 a.m. because I will have to sit and listen to ... You know, it's a very negative attitude but the novelty has worn off. [PS, TI]

When I asked about their social life, the responses were almost identical.

> Social life? I have not lost friends, but I have friends who are exhausted with saying, 'Let's go out Wednesday' and me saying, 'Yes' and ringing them up 20 minutes

before we are to go out saying, There's absolutely no way I can make it to the cinema. Absolutely no way.' [PS, TI]

I mean that's the worst side of it, I mean you 'pack in' a social life. [PS, TI]

There is none. [PPS, TI]

For members of the private office it is hard to strike a decent work–life balance. They leave:

My partner is pregnant. We are expecting our first baby in a month and I knew that I wouldn't physically be able to do these hours and have a family. [APS, TI][8]

The clerical staff work fewer hours; *'I don't class it as a long hours culture'* [Clerical Assistant, TI]. Core hours are normally 10–12 a.m. and 2–4 p.m. They can make up the rest on flexitime. Some have part-time jobs—one was a bingo caller three nights a week. But the culture of long hours affects this group as well. An Assistant PS left home at 6.30 a.m. and did not get back until 9 p.m. He lived some way out because *'it's just too damned expensive'* to live in London [APS, TI]. One DS explained she had one early evening a week, leaving at 5 p.m. but commented *'you just can't plan anything'*. Most get the weekends free but many, including the DS, take work home [DS, TI].

So the departmental court may be an exciting place to work but it also exacting for those who struggle and for those with families. One Permanent Secretary told his Private Office, 'Go home some of you, I don't want a long hours' culture in [Rod's] book'. The remark simply confirmed its existence. And no one left.

INTERNAL NETWORKING: BROKERING AND GATEKEEPING

Networking inside and outside the department is a major part of the communications task of the departmental court.[9] It is crucial to the court's efforts at coordination and managing conflict. I describe internal networking here and external networking in Chapter 8, although in practice they overlap. I look at three sides to networking: working with the department, with ministers, and with SpAds.

Working with the department

The court is at the top of the departmental hierarchy and a nodal point in the flow of information. So, it filters that flow; it acts as a gatekeeper. It does not decide policy. It may not exercise much influence over the substance of any policy. But it does decide who has access to the permanent secretary and the minister and, often as important, when they have access. Its gatekeeping role means, therefore, that it influences priorities. So, the DGs seek to influence the PPS and PSs. The court brokers deal over access and timing.

For most PPSs and PSs:

> *This is the best job in the world. Ask anyone in private office they'll tell you that. I just like the sense of responsibility. I mean you wouldn't get this amount of responsibility at my grade anywhere else in the Department.* [PS, TI]

Being a PPS is being '*at the centre of a great and powerful web*' and '*wading through treacle*' [PPS, TI]. The attraction of working in the departmental court is:

> *You get to know all the senior people in the Department, all the senior officials, and you have all sorts of conversations with them.* [Permanent Secretary, TI]

> *It's being at the centre of things, knowing what's going on, and meeting people.* [PS, TI]

> A good thing about this job is you get to talk to lots of people you wouldn't otherwise talk to. They're always pleased to hear from you. It's because of who you are, working here, but it's still quite nice. [PS, FWNB]

Every PPS and PS freely admits that working in the Private Office gives you '*an incredible network*' [PS, TI]. It was ever thus. Today's Permanent Secretaries were the PSs and PPSs of the 1970s and 1980s. They describe their days in the private office in similar terms.

> *I suppose the job was quite boring, processing papers in and out, minuting meetings and attending meetings which the Minister chaired but you of course use that opportunity to see how the Department and the government works. So you see papers which you have never seen before—interdepartmental correspondence, the Treasury, Cabinet Committee papers. Plus, in the private office circuit, high-grade gossip, high-grade voyeurism, both political and civil service. So both politically, policy-wise, and departmental civil service-wise, a huge learning experience for a young civil servant.* [Permanent Secretary, TI]

> *At one level [it's] absolutely fascinating because you have insight into the way government works. At another level the work is <u>incredibly</u> routine and monotonous and repetitive. As Principal Private Secretary you do get the chance to delegate down to others, a bit, and the interest in the job is how you interact with your Secretary of State and whether you can win his confidence.* [Permanent Secretary, TI]

Old hands concur there is much 'sheer drudgery' (Henderson 2001: 136). Nonetheless, it is a prized posting. One Permanent Secretary observed that: '*I started using skills which I didn't know I had, and which not all civil servants had or have now*' and that is '*trying to get people to gel together, to work together, to match the machine to the requirement, what turns out later to be called "emotional intelligence"*' [Permanent Secretary, TI].

The PPS continues to occupy a nodal position in the court and in the department.

There is another dimension that you don't get out in the Department. This is where perhaps it comes together. If you're going to do well in those big jobs in the Department, the one thing that you've got to be perhaps above all else is strategic. Of course, you've got to deliver it and you've got to manage it and so on, but if you're not strategic then what on earth separates you from the people that are below? It seems to me that this phenomenon of having to deal with 30 or 40 things at once in a Private Office, it gets you in to strategic management because you see there is a much wider reality than just your little individual piece of work. [PPS, TI]

I put it to one PPS that the core skill was sifting and prioritizing what lands on the Minister's desk but:

That is not the core skill. That is one of the important skills but I think the core skill for a principal private secretary, as opposed to a private secretary, is making sure that the relationships work at the top of the shop. I spend a lot of my time trying to make sure that these big powerful brains that are our senior colleagues on the board and so on fit together seamlessly. I spend a lot of my time talking to them about whether they're happy. They sometimes get emotional and worried about particularly the Secretary of State's view of them. I do a lot of smoothing of that and quickly shifting my focus from kind of looking at them and making sure they're happy, looking at policy issues and making prioritizations, decisions you talked about, and looking at [the Minister] and [the Permanent Secretary] as my primary customers if you like, and making sure that they are happy with the way it's all working. So I have to stitch it all together. [PPS, TI]

To stitch everything together, to orchestrate the court, there are, of course, regular meetings. The PPS meets all the PSs every Friday for an hour:

They have just a couple of minutes each to say what's on their minister's mind and what are the big issues that have come in and then we try—I try anyway—to mesh them together as a team. I try to engage them on management issues and leadership issues.

Then:

On Monday morning we have a more issues-focused discussion, just me and the private secretaries in this office, when we go through [the Minister's] calendar for this week and we look at what's happening, what we can do and how.

Also:

I have a monthly session with [the Permanent Secretary] where we talk about whatever needs to be talked about, whatever is on our minds. [The Permanent Secretary] and [the Minister] have more or less a weekly meeting that I sit in on and I try to stitch together some informal agenda for that as well.

In fact, in some departments it was a weekly session. Finally:

> *[The Minister] has weekly meetings with them [other ministers] that I'm in on. I chat with them all informally.* [PPS, TI]

Similarly the Permanent Secretary has two formal meetings with the Minister every week and '*I'll see him every day and at other meetings*' [Permanent Secretary, TI]. Whatever the specific arrangements, there is a regular programme of meetings. The task is to ensure close, effective working relationships between ministers, between ministers and the DGs, and between DGs.

The internal structure of departments is often likened to silos (Blunkett 2006: 219). The departmental court is the point of coordination, although some private secretaries think '*there is no mechanism for enforcing collective work efforts*'. There are mechanisms, but they do not enforce. The private secretary is one informal mechanism. For example, the DGs will approach the PS to sound out a specific proposal before seeking a bilateral meeting.

> *The culture of the Department is very much based around the individual Director General's responsibility for their groups dealing bilaterally with the Permanent Secretary. And they always argue the case for their group. Directors-General wanted to lobby the Permanent Secretary personally and get him to take decisions which were favourable to their group.* [PS, TI]

Of course, the DGs do not necessarily get their own way. I sat in on one such bilateral and thought that, although the Permanent Secretary had been perfectly clear about what he wanted, the DG and his colleagues had not been listening. When I put the point to the PS he commented:

> *They are a bit like teenage children, they listen, they stick their bottom lips out and they argue and then they go away and think about it and then go and do it.* [PS, TI]

Although I was not present at such a meeting, the PPS and the minister can also have informal sessions supplementing the plethora of other meetings:

> *There is always a moment when all the officials have gone home, when you are there with him by yourself and he starts talking about, how we are, where we are, and what's going right and what's going wrong.* [Permanent Secretary, TI]

Working with ministers

The departmental court is the minister's cocoon, perhaps even prison. On the first day:

> *They arrange for a driver to pick you up and the whole machinery goes into place. Your private secretary meets you at the door and then the first few days are a series of meetings. There are lots of logistics like filling in security forms, you know, your*

nearest and dearest, who you can take phone calls from. It's a lot of putting those systems in place. Who is in your [constituency] office? So it's the civil service linking in to your existing life. It's like a space module locking onto your existing life. [Minister, TI]

And the module takes care of your every need and whim for as long as you are minister.

Both the Permanent Secretary and the PPS provide the Minister with regular briefings. The following meeting was typical. The Permanent Secretary had a diary meeting at 6 p.m. attended by the PPS. He discussed the developments in the change programme, arrangements for the away day, the agenda for the board meeting, and dinner with the board. It was about running the Department. There was nothing on policy, although any urgent matters would be discussed at such briefings. The aim was to survey the week ahead to make sure the Minister was briefed and any surprises spotted. The Minister made the occasional comment. The PPS took notes of anything requiring action either by himself or the Minister. This meeting was a tad regal. There was fruit tea, which I dislike almost as much as trying to eat and drink when making notes. The Minister would not let me sit at the back but beckoned me to sit next to him. I felt conspicuous, clumsy. On the way out I knocked the coffee table. 'Careful', said the Minister, 'take your tea with you.'

The role of the PPS is Janus-faced:

When I talk to others in the Department I must make [the Minister's] points. So I need to wear a number of hats, to be rather Bernardesque about this. I need to be [the Minister's] representative to the Department, I need to be the Department's representative to the Minister, and I need to make sure the whole thing links together. [PPS, TI]

The court speaks for the minister and his or her priorities. So: the Minister lets 'it be known (through the invaluable Private Secretary) that I would take no action on their item unless they jumped to it on mine' (Kaufman 1980: 45). So, to employ an analogy from a PS:

You are a loud hailer down for the Department, so whatever [the Minister] says has to be boomed loud and clear, and you are a filter coming backwards. [PS, TI]

Of course, there are dangers in this Janus-faced role for both the secretary of state's PPS and for the PS of the permanent secretary:

You're facing the Minister, you're facing the Department, you're facing the PS, and you're facing the other ministers. And you are sort of caught between these different forces, and you know that there are going to be times when you can't please everybody. That's quite difficult but that's the job . . . [PPS, TI]

Care is essential.

PPS: Because you are linked to an important person, people treat you as if you are important. And I think it's really, really important to remember that you are who you are and that you are representing somebody else and to try hard not to be superior or supercilious.

RAWR: Is there a danger when they ask you what [the Permanent Secretary] thinks, you tell them what you think?

PPS: There is a huge danger about that. A huge danger, which I watch with care. And I am sure I've slipped into it from time to time. I try not to. [PPS, TI]

Care is also essential because the political side is not monolithic. Henderson (2001: 1) describes the PPSs as 'the impresarios of Whitehall' privy to 'the dramas and friction between politics and the machine'. Regular meetings are the vehicle for managing the dramas and frictions.

The purpose of the several meetings is to scan what is going on in the Department. You have got a Secretary of State's Office and then you've got all these ministers, then you've got the Permanent Secretary then you've got a parliamentary team as well—in a sense it's a team and it's all at the top of the shop, but it's also a bit loose. They've all got their own agenda—there are a lot of egos in there doing things. [PPS, TI]

The PPS and the PS pride themselves on their ability to work with any minister put in front of them (see Chapter 5). They do not have to like them but they do:

I like about half of them, you know. I would kind of be happy to spend an evening with that half, have a few drinks and a chat about nothing. [PPS, TI]

Whatever they may think of them personally, they do have to build a good working relationship with them.

I happen to be the sort of person that it is much easier with me if I get on with someone. But it doesn't necessarily have to be a friend, it doesn't have to be a friendly relationship. It can be one of respect. But it is more important, I think it's more important that there's frankness and openness, rather than a friendliness that then results in things being 'brushed under the carpet' and not discussed. [Permanent Secretary, TI]

In fact with most ministers most of the time:

I get on well with them. I made it my business to go and see them all when I arrived. They can be a precious little bunch generally. To get on in the world of politics you do need some of that. I think they are much less precious and certainly less objectionable to many previous ministerial teams I have known which colours my approach. [PPS, TI]

Keeping in touch is important.

If I hadn't seen one of them for a few months I would go and seek them out and get the Private Secretary to set me just a 10-minute chat—'how are you doing?' And so on.

Of course they have views on ministers. The previous ministers were '*a tired bunch*'. One has a '*fiery reputation*'. Another is '*an extremely nice bloke, really competent, works like an absolute bloody dog*'. One minister '*has a history*'— code for stuffing up—but most are seen as '*nice*' (used about three). In short,

There's a bit of coldness from one group to another, and you can see the way people line up. But there's no disloyalty. [PPS, TI]

Ministers can be difficult.

[The Secretary of State] will come out and say, like you heard this morning, 'Why the hell haven't you written to Tom?' That's pissed him off. And too bloody right it has. And we all look round the Private Office going, 'the fucking Treasury should have done it'. Nothing to do with us. Why aren't Treasury talking to [The Secretary of State]? We get it done. That's stressful. And that's why [the Secretary of State] is in a bad mood when you know it is nothing to do with us. [PS, TI]

Difficulties arise for a multitude of reasons, major reasons—the civil servants spots a snag too far; and minor reasons—ministers get tired and frustrated. Other difficulties arise from questions of financial propriety, libel cases against ministers and, of course, the tabloids with their endless search for a story, especially ones involving the sexual peccadilloes or financial dealings of ministers.[10] There were no major improprieties or peccadilloes while I visited the departments. There were some minor ones on which the Permanent Secretary had to rule and for which the Private Secretary had to dig out the relevant information. For example, one Minister wrote an unpaid column in a local magazine but forgot to get formal permission to do so. Another failed to register that he was renting out some property. Issues of fiscal propriety are a 'constant backdrop' to their work. The point here is that '*the civil service takes over: [the Secretary of State's] had to stand back from the inquiry full stop and, in essence, all the decisions were taken by officials*' [PS, TI].

Working with SpAds

Political advisers are not new but their role continues to attract much attention.[11] The permanent secretaries are cautious about attributing more influence to them:

The special advisers are more powerful now than they were but it's a trend and I can look back to occasions which look similar. [Permanent Secretary, TI]

Ministers have differing views on the role of SpAds. Civil servants have different expectations. Put simply, there is choice between political advisers and expert policy advisers (Blick 2004: 194–5). In the three departments, most ministers wanted, and most civil servants expected, a variant of the political adviser:

> *He was one of the archetypal 'spin doctors' and very, very good at his job. 'Spin doctor' doesn't quite capture it but he was the communications person and that was new.* [Permanent Secretary, TI]

They wanted their SpAds to have:

> *good working relationships with the other people you've got to work with or, if you can't manage that, at least understand where the different people are coming from. That's what I expected the political advisers to do: represent me to the outside world, represent me with the Parliamentary Labour Party and its staff and all its other facets, but above all check what I'm doing with the documents that are coming across the desk and make sure that I haven't missed a point of detail.* [Minister, TI]

In a phrase, they were the Minister's 'political antennas', proffering advice on the presentation of policy to the media, and on speeches (see Chapter 7). The links with the private offices and the Press Office were close. In all three departments, they worked well with the civil servants:

> *There are now three [SpAds], very different people but wholly supportive of the civil service and mutually liked. [They] make it their business to work <u>extremely</u> constructively with the civil service. As a result the civil service responds very, very willingly and so, as we speak anyway, it's almost an ideal relationship.* [Permanent Secretary, TI, emphasis in original]

Burying SpAds in an obscure office, corridors away from the minister, is just an old joke from *Yes Minister*. Nowadays, they are seen as an asset for their communication skills:

> *The civil service was helped by having party political appointees. We need them because of the multiplicity of contacts and connections and communications that's necessary nowadays. The traditional civil service model could never have coped and ministers would have had a hopeless burden to be in contact with all the people who want to be, and <u>can</u> be now in contact with them by e-mail.* [Permanent Secretary, TI]

The main reservation concerned the *'fine but perfectly correct line between challenges and adversarial'*. The Permanent Secretary was *'strongly in favour of a sense of challenge'* but *'if you have got competing agendas, then it is a bad thing'*. *'The key thing is that everybody is in the loop'* and the SpAds do not see *'any difference between what you might call the "well-being of the Secretary of State" and the "well-being of the Department"'*. However, he claimed there had been no adversarial, competing agendas in any of his departments [Permanent Secretary, TI].

I attended two meetings between the SpAds and the Minister with the PPS. The civil servants refer to them as the Minister's 'cauldron of Spads'—their collective noun and obvious analogy to the witches of Macbeth. There is no obvious difference in dress code between SpAds and civil servants but they are younger. Above all, they are enthusiastic and committed to 'their' minister. The meetings are almost like a family. They gossip furiously about the party and rival ministers. It is relaxed. People are sprawled out on settees, feet up. It is staccato and unstructured. People talk over one another. The formality ever-present when officials attend is missing.

The expert adviser is a less common species. Page and Jenkins (2005: 117–21), in their study of middle-ranking civil servants in policy making, found that SpAds were conspicuous for their absence. That is not the case at the top of the Department; they are ever-present. Their policy role varies. There was some discussion of the merits of individual departmental policies at the meetings I attended, but it was not their main contribution. The emphasis fell on progress chasing already agreed policy, ensuring the effective presentation of the Minister and his policies, advising on broader, party political matters, and external liaison most notably with No. 10. Within any of these broad activities, they were firefighters; for example, they would issue rebuttals of any adverse stories in the press. Progress chasing and firefighting can lead to one-to-one contact with DGs and collecting information for the Minister. Such work is important but no one, least of all the SpAds, would dignify it with the label 'policy analysis'.

I encountered one exception. Michael Barber was seen as a policy expert in his own right:

> *Alongside me was Michael Barber. Michael Barber is now the Head of the Delivery Unit. He had been brought in to head the Standards and Effectiveness Unit as a sort of special adviser and for most of the parliament he remained a special adviser and not a civil servant. He had worked with the ministerial team, David Blunkett particularly in opposition, and he in a sense was the guardian of the policy. He had tremendous influence and had access to all the ministers. He wasn't a conventional special adviser, he was an expert adviser if you like, but he was also somebody who was sympathetic to the government. . . . Now as it turned out that was a stroke of luck for me because he and I hit it off, we had complementary skills. He knew everything to know there was to know about education and I knew quite a lot about how to manage the policy process.* [Permanent Secretary, TI]

Another Department divided its work into two. Each adviser had half the Department! Obviously, they *'have a role in* [the Minister's] *speeches but they are essentially policy advisers. They are not communication special advisers'* [Permanent Secretary, TI]. If so, it is hard to imagine they had much impact beyond spotting political pratfalls and knowing the Minister's mind and explaining it to civil servants. I wondered if the Minister and the Department had worked out how to make the best use of their SpAds.

It is more common for SpAds to grasshopper from one topic to another. So, in a nanosecond we move from media coverage to Iraq to internal Labour Party machinations about the euro to a possible cabinet reshuffle. The Minister tells them it may not be at cabinet level. So, they concentrate on junior ministers in other departments and backbench MPs who might be suitable recruits for the Department. It is gossip about standing in the party and in government. It is the lifeblood of such meetings. They love it. The Minister remembers I am there. He says, 'you didn't hear any of this'. They all laugh. I smile.

Beyond the impatience and odd curt word that can occur in any office, I saw little evidence of tension with the rest of the court. They lived near to the rest of the departmental court—all are members of an open plan office. One Permanent Secretary observed, 'open plan's been good. We can hear more than they think!' [Permanent Secretary, FWNB]. He was teasing. Everyone talked to everyone else continuously. On one occasion, their informality jarred with the civil servants' expectations of what is proper. One Permanent Secretary objected to their passing notes to one another in a meeting. He thought they were 'off-side' [Permanent Secretary, FWNB]. Each accepts the other plays a necessary role. If officials can be 'stick in the muds', they also have expertise and information. If the zeal of SpAds can exceed judgement, their ability to manage the party and the media are seen as an essential complement to civil service skills. In any office there are raised voices, disagreement, even quarrels. I saw nothing other than a mild irritation; 'he's our Jo Moore—all over you like a rash!' [PPS, FWNB]. Thus the PPS snapped, 'they think we are not up to the job but you'd have to be psychic to know what they want. Anyway they are too focused on spin.' Occasionally a SpAd had to be 'tamed' but from what I saw it meant only that newcomers had to get used to the way things were done [PPS, FWNB].

So, SpAds are another link in the web of coordination and conflict resolution forming the departmental court. Most had a good working relationship with the rest of the court. It is also worth remembering there will only be two, at most three, SpAds in any one department. So, they have little time, even if they have the knowledge and skills, to replicate or replace the work of officials. As Stanley (2008: 10) points out, advice from officials is more likely to be accepted if they understand the political realities facing the minister. SpAds can and do explain those realities. So, they are an important supplement but hardly a counterweight to the civil service. There is, however, one other role of key importance: their links with the SpAds at No. 10 and the influence of the latter on departmental policy. This link was a cause for concern with some ministers. Although he appointed political advisers, one Minister railed against spin:

I've got strong views about this. I've never employed a spin doctor. . . . Handling of the press goes through the press office. . . . [And] no gossip about ministers or [Labour Party] politics. We don't do that and we didn't do that. [Minister, TI]

In fact, the Minister meant he did not use his SpAds to brief against colleagues in the press. He was as great a gossip as any of his ministerial colleagues. If you can't gossip in private with your SpAd with whom can you gossip? But he is correct in suggesting that SpAds are used to brief against ministerial colleagues. As the former Permanent Secretary of the Ministry of Agriculture Fisheries and Food recounts with some bitterness, No. 10 SpAds briefed against him (see Packer 2006). I will look at the multiple (and allegedly nefarious) roles of the No. 10 SpAds in Chapter 9.

CONCLUSIONS

The departmental court may be a new name for the PPS and the private offices but its main tasks, its beliefs and practices, and its gatekeeping role are longstanding.

Coping

The key task of the departmental court is to cope. Coping is not a dramatic activity. It is surprisingly ordinary. Private offices exist to domesticate trouble, to defuse problems, and take the emotion out of a crisis. Confronting a major issue with a public corporation, the Permanent Secretary commented, 'Thank you, a good way of cheering me up'. Everyone smiled. The style of the permanent secretaries was low key. What we have in Whitehall is 'willed ordinariness'. These everyday routines are unquestioned, to a degree unrecognized. The conventional portrait of the central secretariat focused on the PPS, the private office, and the private secretaries. I have described a departmental court that acts as the fulcrum for internal coordination, conflict resolution, and networking. When viewed from this standpoint it is more than just a 'bridge'.

- It socializes high-flying civil servants as part of their career development.
- It coordinates the departmental policy process by filtering and packaging proposals from the department.
- It contains and manages conflicts between the different sections of the department.
- It acts as the keeper of administrative protocols and language (see Chapter 7).

- It acts as the gatekeeper and broker for the department's internal and external networks (see Chapter 8).

In other words, it is a complex coping mechanism at the fulcrum of both internal and external networks. It is not a strategic planning or policy unit, a politically appointed cabinet as in France, or a risk assessment unit that can provide early warnings about the crises and unintended consequences that dog all ministers' careers (Hennessy 2005: 541–2). It can be all of these things, but as circumstances dictate and minister's wish not by deliberate intent.

Beliefs and practices

The departmental court encapsulates the beliefs of the department; the Westminster operating assumptions and departmental philosophy. The core beliefs are loyalty to the minister and the department. The core practice is to maintain the cocoon in which the minister lives. The most striking feature of the court is its longevity. Most ministers since 1945 would recognize my account of work of the PPS and the private office. It is a key mechanism in handing down the beliefs and practices of the Westminster narrative. Its protocols and rituals give everyday expression to broad constitutional principles. For example, parliamentary sovereignty may be a contested, even opaque, constitutional principle (King 2007: 98–9, 129–31, and 206–7) but, to the parliamentary branch of the court, parliament is a set of entrenched protocols and its business an unquestioned priority. I describe these protocols and rituals in more detail in Chapter 7.

It is hard to overstate the dedication to making the minister's life smooth or the office's sensitivity to the minister's moods. They know the minister's mind before the minister knows what he wants. Being the centre of so much attention must be addictive. Many do not appreciate how well they are looked after until they leave office and rediscover the irritations of life as an ordinary citizen.

> The contrast is enormous. One day you have the whole of your Private Office, the press office, the Department—and the next a handful of very dedicated and committed people struggling with the expectation from me that I can carry on as though I still have a department. (Blunkett 2006: 747)

The secretary of state, like every other minister irrespective of age, race, or gender, is waited on hand and foot. Privilege goes with the turf. He has the exclusive use of his own toilet although there are two others within 20 metres. Water, coffee, tea, and sandwiches are offered and brought whenever the Minister wants them. A diary secretary controls who can and cannot see him. A member of the private office escorts him everywhere, carrying bags and files. A car sits and waits on his every movement. Although the House of Commons is a mere five minutes away, he is driven there. When he leaves his coat in the car, the driver brings it to him. I often thought the short walk to parliament and break from all the attention would be a welcome respite. I know one Permanent Secretary who insisted on a 20 minutes break at lunchtime to stretch his legs, and clear the mind, in a nearby park. I never saw a minister forgo the perks of office for anything as ordinary as a walk. The private office is just as sensitive to moods. The comment that the Minister 'is not in a good mood today', evokes the comment 'Oh bollocks' and the epithet 'friggin' PQs', meaning the Minister's impending appearance in the House of Commons to answer parliamentary questions is the cause of his bad mood.

Privilege apart, what is striking about the departmental court is the similarities between politician and administrator. Both confront unrelenting events, which they struggle to grasp with the help of a court that exists to serve. Distinctions between policy and management, politician and civil servant, are meaningless when confronted with the imperative to cope and survive. Both minister and permanent secretary are political-administrators, dependent on one another and, in many of their everyday tasks, interchangeable. It is all ordinary. And its ordinariness should not mislead. Of course, one can ask whether the minister instructed his private office to do something, but the question does not probe deeply enough. It is just as likely that the private office anticipated the minister's needs. They pride themselves on knowing what the minister wants before the minister knows he wants it. It is world in which the rules of anticipated wishes and anticipated reactions prevail. Civil servants believe ministers are different, so they treat them differently irrespective of whether they are up to the job.

Gatekeeping: the court and its networks

The central secretariat is a court because it is a microcosm of the tensions within the department. The PPSs can be bold, they can aspire. One had a plaque on her desk with a quote attributed quote to Goethe:

> What you can do, or dream you can do, begin it;
> Boldness has genius, power and magic in it.[12]

But they are embedded in internal and external networks and these webs can enchain them. One day the minister or the DG is a friend and ally, the next day he is an opponent, a bull elephant intent on his own way. It was ever thus in courts. So, coordination and conflict resolution at the top of the department are essential functions because there are many debates over policy, personal disagreements between individuals, office micro-politics within the court, strife between ministers, and tensions between ministers and civil servants.

Managing these ups and downs are the tasks of the departmental court under the guiding hand of the minister's PPS. An academic colleague commented that the PPS seemed like a 'ball bearing, caught between these different forces'. He is 'more subject than agent'. I prefer to describe him as the gatekeeper of internal and external networks. Everything of importance goes through him to the minister. Information and selective attention bestow standing.

I was also struck with the centrality of the SpAds. Their importance is recognized in the language of officials in the joking references to 'a cauldron of SpAds'. They are part of the web that links the department together but, more important as we will see in Chapter 8, links the department to No. 10. I understand why the minister wants and likes his SpAds. They are noisy, boisterous, committed—in short, fun. He also trusts them implicitly to put his interest first in both the party and the department. Officials are also trusted by most ministers most of the time but they do not operate in the party arena. The SpAds step in where officials fear to tread, covering party meetings, conferences, and all other party related matters. With civil servants, there is always at least a touch of distance, of formality. I offer no criticism. It is, and they would agree, appropriate. But I can see that the minister needs to relax in free-ranging gossip. He spends most of the day 'presenting' to others. Being a celebrity seems like privilege, but you have to meet people's expectations and behave like a celebrity. In the privacy of his own office with the SpAds, he can forget for a moment, and take off his public faces.

Bureaucracy does many things well, but how well does it function as an executive? Do its members see it as individual units or the department's executive or court? I wondered if the story of the departmental court paralleled the story of central capability at No. 10; both faced equivalent problems of coordination. I was reminded of Peter Hennessy's (1998) summary of Blair's innovations at the centre. Do we have a court that 'dare not speak its name'? Few departments plan the development of their courts or see the need to strengthen central capability. One Department saw the private offices as one unit, called it the central secretariat, and held induction sessions that spanned the full range of work. Others are probably indistinguishable from any private office of the post-war period. I never heard a conversation about the quality of policy advice, or about risk management, or about reforming the departmental court.

In sum, the private office is best seen as a bastion of the Westminster story. It lies at the crux of the conventional minister–civil servant relationship. It might seem immune to the impact of managerialism. Not so. Managerialism had an impact in two courts. In Chapter 7, I look at the changing protocols and language of the court and at the impact of managerialism. The court also lies at the hub of the governance narrative, of the web of relationships that span Whitehall and beyond. I explore that story in Chapter 8.

NOTES

1. This chapter is based on the FWNBs for DEFRA, DfES, and DTI; interviews with 20 members of three private offices; and interviews with eight ministers and ten permanent secretaries.
2. *Round the Horne* was a BBC Radio comedy programme of the 1960s fronted by Kenneth Horne. Kenneth Williams played the part of J. Peasemold Gruntfuttock, a grumpy old man with a lust for Judith Chalmers, a BBC television presenter of the period.
3. For an account of a Management Board meeting see Rhodes 2007*b*.
4. At the Treasury, Nigel Lawson's (1992: 269 and 385) PPSs included some of the most distinguished permanent secretaries to be of the next 20 years; for example John Kerr (Foreign Office), Rachel Lomax (Welsh Office, Transport), Alex Allan (PPS to John Major and Tony Blair and Permanent Secretary at Justice), and John Gieve (Home Office). On the Foreign Office see Henderson 2001; and Dickie 1992: ch. 4.
5. On recruitment see, for example: Bruce-Gardyne 1986: Denham 2002: 27; Henderson 2001: 8; Heseltine 2000: 189; and Page and Jenkins 2005: 44, 52; Kaufman 1980: 38; Lawson 1992: 385–6: 34.
6. The National School of Government now offers introductory training courses for new members of the private office and for private secretaries. See: http://www.nationalschool. gov.uk/downloads/Portfolio2009_2010/PortfolioPolicyGovernment.pdf. Last accessed 26 October 2009.
7. On the long hours culture see, for example: Blunkett 2006: 673 and 729; Bruce-Gardyne 1986: 34; Henderson 2001: 182; and Lawson 1992: 385. The problem is not peculiar to either Britain or New Labour. For example, 23 of 39 staff in the Office of the Prime Minister of Australia, Kevin Rudd, left in the first two years to claims of a gruelling workload and poor staff management. *Herald-Sun*, 17 October 2009.
8. Some senior civil servants had to make similar decisions. Gus O'Donnell current Head of the Home Civil Service turned down the opportunity to become Nigel Lawson's PPS at the Treasury for the same reason (Lawson 1992: 385).
9. On internal networks see, for example: Henderson 2001: 157–8; Page and Jenkins 2005: 115; and Walker 1970: 67.
10. This study covers the period 2001–5, so it misses the parliamentary expenses scandal of 2009. Of course, MPs' expenses were not policed by departments but by the officers of the House of Commons. This system of, in effect, self-policing has now been replaced by an independent Parliamentary Standards Authority.
11. On special advisers the best general account is Blick 2004. Useful insider accounts include: Blunkett 2006: 279, 354–5, 510, 601, 638, 677–8; Donoughue 2003; Henderson 2001: 168 and 180; Prescott 2008: 256; and Wilson 2003: 373–5.
12. On this 'very free translation' of Goethe, see: The Goethe Society of North America at http://www.goethesociety.org/pages/quotescom.html. Last accessed 6 October 2009.

7

Protocols, Rituals, and Languages

J. G. Ballard (2006) talks of 'willed madness' in modern life. What we have in Whitehall is 'willed ordinariness' and administrative protocols lie at the heart of the willed ordinariness of everyday life. They are all integral to managing the court. In memoirs, the private office can appear to run a minister's life unless he takes control (see Chapter 6). I accept that it seems like that to a harried minister. But there is another way of understanding protocols; they are the tools by which departments domesticate their everyday life in the goldfish bowl that is modern politics.[1]

The departmental court may be a forcing ground for some high-flyers, some of the time, but for most of its inhabitants, most of the time, the work is boring. The Private Secretary (PS) knows it: 'This is so boring' [PS, FWNB]. Even the permanent secretaries agree; 'the main defect of *Yes Minister* is it makes it too interesting' (Permanent Secretary, FWNB). Everyone works long hours. The minister is never unattended. Most of the work is some form of communication: mail, papers, and meetings. It is routine because the aim is to make sure everything runs as smoothly as possible. The maxim is 'no surprises'. To secure this outcome, ministers have to move seamlessly from meeting-to-meeting, engagement-to-engagement, and topic-to-topic. The pace is frenetic with barely enough time to read, let alone digest, briefings. The diversity is also breathtaking. The minister and permanent secretary have to be in the right place at the right time and with the right papers and keeping them happy is the cardinal virtue. It is the stuff of the endless jokes about bureaucratic red tape and of Sir Humphrey tying Jim Hacker up in arcane procedures.

Administrative protocols are the sedimented or codified practices of civil servants because they are formalized and written down. Such accepted codes of practices, covering procedures and etiquette, are basic tools of the trade. Some exist as videos or DVDs but the printed word remains the preferred medium of communication in the everyday life of the permanent secretary and the private office.[2] This world has been an integral part of the Westminster narrative for decades. Protocols form part of the socialization of every civil servant, no matter how junior. It is embedded in their language.

A related notion is that of departmental rituals. Rituals are habitual practices that, unlike protocols, are not written down; they are uncodified.[3] Indeed, people may not be aware of their habits until they are pointed out. They include for example 'coffee sipping amity' (Stothard 2003: 34 and 61). He also describes the messengers who deliver it as 'a source of continuity and a kind of comfort' (see also: Stewart 2004: 21–2). In my departments, it was tea more often than coffee but the quality of ritual comfort remained (Rhodes 2005). I felt I was part of the furniture when the messenger brought my tea in a mug without my asking.

Protocols are supported by a distinctive Westminster vocabulary. I explore the layers of that language. It is the language of the tradition; of the old verities. But it is under attack from managerial reforms and its associated language. In place of procedure, we have targets. In place of administration, we have management. The dilemma posed by the clash of ideas of constitutional bureaucracy, managerialism, and political responsiveness can be acute. This chapter explores the long-standing administrative protocols and rituals; the language of Westminster; managerialism, its language, and the resulting dilemmas posed for everyday life at the top.

PROTOCOLS

The private office will recognize my focus on administrative protocols:

> *I am a glorified postbox and I'm here for communication. I am just churning through the paper.* [PS, TI]

Indeed even civil servants are frustrated by procedures, by:

> *the need for discretion, the rules, the things you can't talk about. I am bored by the process and procedures, all that stuff. I am ruled by all the rules and hanging around, things I can't do here. So I am impatient. In principle I'd like much more freedom, not sure that I'd use it well. I would probably be quite cautious but I would like the idea of being able to consider doing it and I am bored being told I can't do things. I can't appoint people. I can't recruit people. I can't sack people.* [Permanent Secretary, TI]

The protocols as coping mechanisms come in many forms. I came across the following: the diary; the red box; telephone; correspondence and filing; travel and hospitality (including drivers); meetings, committees and briefings; submissions and policy advice; speeches; and secrecy.

The Diary[4]

The traditional diary secretaries (DS), sometimes nowadays called the diary manager are key players in keeping everyone happy. They regulate access to the minister and the permanent secretary. Some DSs had been in post for 20 years. Some moved with their minister and permanent secretary. They know what he wants before he wants it. The diary rules, so the DS is in a nodal position. As one PS observed:

> I've always thought, from the minute I started in private office, the diary secretary is probably <u>the</u> most important person in that office because if the diary is wrong the whole day collapses. [PS, TI]

This view is shared by the Principal Private Secretary (PPS):

> I've got a slightly old-fashioned diary secretary. I think that's an area where you don't want jazz. You do want control there and no one should touch that diary without her. [PPS, TI]

And by ministers:

> I wanted a diary secretary who was not just well organized and efficient and could plan out my day in a way that I wouldn't waste time unnecessarily moving from one thing to another across London, but also somebody who was effective and good at dealing with officials right across the Department because the job of a diary secretary is to get the material together that you need for whatever the event is that you're going to go to. [Minister, TI]

As Stanley (2008*a*, 5) observes; 'nothing in your official life will ever run sweetly again if you dare to commit the Minister without his or her written agreement—which will not be forthcoming for several weeks'.

Although nodal, the DS does not decide on engagements.

> The Secretary of State agrees everything that goes into the diary. There are certain things that have to go in, Cabinet, Budget Cabinet, all those things. There are certain things which are routine which [the Minister] expects me to get in the diary like monthly meetings with the [national interest group]. And I feel I have a reasonable amount of flexibility to adjust here and there. I am always conscious that various secretaries of state have worked in different ways and have obviously had different thoughts about the way their time is organized. I am always conscious that it's their diary and they're doing it and I always think it's a courtesy, if nothing else, to keep them in contact. You probably see me come in and out saying, 'You know, what about a phone call here?' Because [the Minister] might have a 20-minute slot in the day and might think, 'I am going to ring my parents'. [DS, TI][5]

The phrase 'keeping the diary' sounds simple enough but:

> the diary is just a nightmare and you have to be very, very flexible. Nothing is set in stone, you know. You have to be flexible and be prepared, like you know when meetings with the Prime Minister, meetings with the Secretary of State, have got to be completely rescheduled. [DS, TI]

I just think the diary is the hardest thing to work on because it's so fast moving. You have to be able to change it sometimes at the drop of a hat, especially the Minister's office with parliamentary business. [PS, TI]

There are several versions of the diary. For the minister, there is the master electronic copy kept by the diary secretary. There is the whiteboard which records the day's engagements, which changes regularly, and is visible to the whole private office. There is the long-term diary for the red box, so the minister can look ahead. Sometimes there is a meeting between the DS, PPS, and the minister to discuss the week ahead in detail and look at what is happening over the next six months [FWNB]. Most of the time, the minister pops out, the DS pops in, to schedule and reschedule the minister's activities. If the minister or the permanent secretary is out that day, then a folder of pending diary decisions is prepared to be read overnight.

And part of the job is to protect the minister and permanent secretary.

I can't stand this old-fashioned thing of being the 'lion at the gate' or the 'gatekeeper'; it sounds so archaic. But I suppose that's the way it is. But [the Assistant Diary Secretary] and I tend to have an unwritten rule that <u>we</u> are the people that make the changes to the diary. [DS, TI, emphasis in original]

So, they redirect calls to other members of the department, delay appointments pending consultation, and even fake entries on the whiteboard to discourage requests [FWNB].

Even the permanent secretary knows the rules and asks:

But if [the Permanent Secretary] comes up and he loiters, to put no better a word on it, and says, 'Is [the Minister] in?' and he's working at the desk, we'll say, 'Oh yeah pop in'. [DS, TI]

Of course, he should get his diary secretary to ring. He knows. The same protocols apply in his private office. The funny thing about protocols is they become more rigid as you move *down* the hierarchy. When a junior minister walks in asking for five minutes, it is not possible and, after he left, he is described as 'a lackey' with 'bad manners' (DS, FWNB).

Protecting the minister or the permanent secretary requires their cooperation. There are supposed rules like '*no back-to-back meetings*' [Permanent Secretary, TI] and protecting 'the paperwork period'. They are observed more in the breach. Meetings overrun and start late. I listened regularly to comments like 'not one of our finest hours in terms of organization', 'it's a bad day', and 'today is the day from hell' [FWNB]. I decided it was a form of machismo; a mark of one's virility. As one Minister confessed, '*I often had back-to-back meetings and we couldn't survive without back-to-back meetings*' [Minister, TI].

One Permanent Secretary helped to manage the Minister's diary:

*He thinks about the Secretary of State's diary as well, quite seriously because he's
not good at managing his diary and he's keen to get sight of his diary as soon as he
can. And if he thinks that he is missing things then he suggests things and they go
into his diary.* [PS, TI]

Also, the need for flexibility can be overstated. Not every private office was
frenetic. One DS had '*never*' improvised a time for the Permanent Secretary to
see the Minister and '*there isn't much need for improvisation*' [DS, TI].

The job is not limited to the diary and scheduling. She—I never met a male
DS—is also responsible for meeting folders (see below). She also smooths the
Minister's day.

*I see that as important because if [the Minister] is not happy or if it's not done the
way he wants it and it doesn't fit with him, you know, it will change. So, I will do
double the work on that sort of thing.* [DS, TI]

So the DS is the authority on ministerial preferences both minor—for example, sandwiches—and major—no more than two dinner engagements a week.
She will tell the partner whether it is black tie or lounge suit, short cocktail
or long dress. One used to pin the Permanent Secretary's medals on because
he changed into formal wear at work. As one PPS commented with some
venom, 'the [Diary Secretary] is the authority on the [Permanent Secretary]'
[PPS, FWNB].

Some have high informal standing. One DS was not managed by the PS but
reported directly to the Permanent Secretary. It is part of departmental
mythology that fast streamers are 'little upstarts' (departmental induction
video). One new PS was in left no doubt about his standing; he deferred to
the DS. Other DSs were less like the dragon at the door. They held sway, but to
a lesser extent. They know their limitations:

*There is always an office joke about, but it's a great joke, about training the PS's up.
But I don't think of myself as being that grand.* [DS, TI]

Most DSs try to help the private secretaries by:

*giving them an idea of what [the Permanent Secretary] would like and not like, and
pre-empting any problems and if they say this is the way to do it, I will say no he
won't like it that way, you know, it's best to do it this way.* [DS, TI]

Finally, the DS can be a traditional secretary and type letters about future
engagements, senior staff, top secret affairs of state, or personal matters. The
most common items are about staff management. Some diary secretaries can
take shorthand, so the minister or permanent secretary will dictate. Others use
dictaphones. Others get the PS to write a draft that they then correct and the
DS types. One DS described herself as 'Mrs Fix It' because she did odd jobs like
arranging for the permanent secretary's home phone to be repaired.

Red boxes[6]

Every day the private office prepares and collates the papers the ministers and the permanent secretary must read for the next day's meetings and the letters that need to be signed. They are collected in a rectangular, box-shaped, briefcase for the minister to take home each night. It is commonly red. It is sometimes blue. It is always battered. I never saw a new one. In the spirit of *Monty Python*, I wondered if there was an office for battering boxes. Inevitably, some ministers don't like the red box. It is seen as '*ostentatious*'; '*I like them for souvenirs but I rarely used them. [Laughter]. I love the history of all this, so I like them for that*' [Minister, TI]. He used a standard briefcase.

The red box is a focal point of office activity and governed by its own rules. Thus, at the start of the day, the PPS will write a time (say 17.15) in the top right-hand corner of the red box. Everyone now knows the box must be ready by that time because that is when the minister will leave the office. Everyone understands that it is '*best to get it all in one box. If there are two they get discouraged*' [PPS, TI]. By 4.30 p.m. the box will be the focus of a flurry of activity. All the paperwork in the private office must come together at this point. After the diary, it is a key organizing device for managing, even controlling, the minister. It is just a cardinal rule that it must be ready by the stated time.

The role of the PPS in preparing the box varies.

They [papers] come through me to check them off, just to check that they make sense. The same way that when I'm putting stuff in the box I just try and check things to make sure it looks reasonably okay. [PPS, TI]

[We used to have] some divisions that [the PPS] was first point of contact for and I have changed that because I think I can add best value by being able to look across the pitch. I see everything before [the Secretary of State] sees it whereas [my predecessor] didn't. Stuff went in and [my predecessor] saw it on the way out. I felt uncomfortable with that so I now see most things before they go in to [the Secretary of State], certainly anything of importance will be shown to me. So the trade-off with the private secretaries is they might have more divisions to look after but they know that I'm going to help them take a proper view before it goes in to [the Secretary of State]. [PPS, TI]

These quotes don't capture the process; 'it's incredibly difficult to know what's important, what will cause controversy' [PPS, FWNB]. They develop political antenna for both court and party politics:

More to the point, you become alert to things which nobody else understands. So you can use the opportunity to look through, to see nuances and things and you gained credit from alerting ministers to other things that you thought the Minister would be interested in, which would otherwise get lost in the paperwork, and when the Minister was being off message, you would then get credit from going and telling the Department this was the case. So, and this is a skill not all civil servants have, if you were alive to nuances and if your antennas were wobbling properly, then you could do an important job. And you got visibly praised and seen by both by the Permanent Secretary and by the Principal Private Secretary. [Permanent Secretary, TI]

A director general (DG) will have a quiet word to make sure his submission is in the box but the PPS will exercise judgement about what the minister needs to see. The sheer volume of material could overwhelm even the most committed minister. Jary (2004: 18) claims a 'typical' box contains: 20 letters to sign, 3 draft speeches, 4 draft replies to parliamentary questions (PQs), 10 briefings for meetings, 6 submissions for decision, 3 draft press releases, a question and answer brief for an interview and the minutes of last week's cabinet meeting. This summary is not wrong but it can err on the side of understatement. Indeed, Jary (2008: 18) adds such items as 110 pages of press cuttings and doubles the number of briefings. One of my departments estimated there were on average 12 PQs in a box. Also, most had difficulty limiting the paperwork to one box.

To help the minister, there are two folders at the top of the box: a priority folder of matters requiring immediate action, and the diary folder of engagements. In an ideal world of course the red box is returned next morning, not only with the priority folders done but also with letters signed and decisions made. For obvious reasons, many ministers will skim through much in the box. So if, for example, a letter needs his attention, it had better be flagged. Some ministers and permanent secretaries like to put their mark on letters and submissions (for example, David Blunkett). One DS announced with great glee that she had written the perfect letter; for once the Permanent Secretary had made no changes to it. Some are less assiduous:

> The first five letters have been signed, one speech and one submission has been read and agreed, one further submission has been lost behind the cooker, and the rest are untouched. (PS in Jary 2004: 18)

There is a world-weary cynicism to this quote that I did not meet. With most ministers, most of the time, most of the box was done. And the private office becomes adept at judging what it can expect from the minister and adjusting its demands. With the diary, the red box organizes the minister's day, week, and month. As well as organizing him, it can control him; it is a way of taming the unruly minister; he can be domesticated by the way things work around here.

Correspondence[7]

It might sound portentous but 'Ministerial correspondence is democratic accountability in action' (Jary 2008: 29). From the prime minister down, it is taken seriously. ministers are no exception:

There were things that always frustrated ministers, like the correspondence section.
I bet you haven't interviewed a minister who hasn't sooner or later mentioned the
correspondence sections of the department. [Minister, TI]

The volume of mail is high. One departmental court dealt with an average of 772 letters a week and, in addition, each e-mail inbox received an average of 120 e-mails a day. The Secretary of State's Private Office alone received 178 pieces of correspondence a day (excluding e-mails). It is hardly surprising, therefore, that the protocols for both snail mail and e-mail are elaborate. I will bore readers to death if I describe them in any detail. The protocols about all forms of written correspondence are so central to the life of the private office that they are written down. The civil service is all too aware that the devil is in the detail.[8]

Protocols vary from department to department. However, there is invariably a correspondence section. The court may have separate correspondence sections in each private office. In that case, a PS or an assistant private secretary (APS) can manage the correspondence team, although *'they didn't have the time to oversee what they were doing'* [PPS, TI]. Sometimes, all the staff is in one central office with its own correspondence manager. It is the team's job to sort, code, and distribute all external mail and send it to the appropriate section for action. Thus:

We record the details on our database which is a correspondence database. We record who it came from, who it was addressed to, the subject of the letter, when it was received, and when it was dated. And we keep a record of whom we sent the document to. Anything that comes in we copy it for information or provide the draft reply to the reply to that letter, and we need to keep a record of whom we send it to and when it's due to be answered. [Clerk, TI]

Inevitably the system for recording snail mail is called 'Postman Pat'.[9]

There are targets for handling mail. They vary between departments. For example, the correspondence section has 24 hours to allocate mail. The Department has 15 days to reply to ministerial correspondence. The DGs have 8 days to prepare a draft reply and the Private Office has 7 days to get the letter signed and sent. The system automatically flags any late responses. There are also cross-departmental targets for dealing with correspondence and they are taken seriously because the Cabinet Office publishes a 'league table' of departmental performance; for example, initially, the Department had 10 working days to reply to an MP. When the Secretary of State was told the Department would not meet its targets, letters were sent to those ministers who were slow to reply telling them, *'Come on, up your game'.* Even the Prime Minister gets involved:

The Prime Minister makes a big thing of correspondence. I go over to No. 10 on a regular basis, every three–six months. They have a seminar over there for all the correspondence managers around Whitehall and he always makes a point of coming to speak to us, which he doesn't have to do. [PPS, TI]

Ministers know; we're judged on how quickly we turn around correspondence, and the numbers go to No. 10 or Cabinet Office or somebody and you are benchmarked on this stuff and if you are not doing well enough . . . well! [FWNB]

No. 10 receives about a million letters a year. Departments answer many of them. As the correspondence manual notes, many of these letters 'do not seem important in the scheme of things'. But the Department must meet No. 10's deadlines, and the Secretary of State must 'clear' any drafts for No. 10. So there is even less time for the Department to process these letters because the Private Office now has 4 days to clear the reply.

Obviously, these targets create distortions The No. 10 and MPs' letters go to the top of the pile irrespective of their content. As the correspondence manual notes, correspondence with officials is 'the poor relation' to ministerial correspondence. Targets are adjusted to suit circumstances. When the 10 day target proved impossible to meet because of the volume of letters, the target was changed to 15 days, which brought the Department into line with other large Whitehall departments.

Correspondence is categorized in various ways. For example, in one Permanent Secretary's Private Office, a green folder signifies background mail (that is, the Permanent Secretary has been copied in); and purple signifies high priority mail. Letters which go out for advice, draft reply, and come back to the Private Office are in blue 'float' folders. Mail is filed by topic, in date order, topics are then organized by weekly files and kept for three to four months as temporary folders before weeding and storing in orange folders. Most private offices have a 'clear desk' policy. Files are not left lying around but locked away at close of business.

One thing is not supposed to happen. Papers do not disappear. Only they do. It invariably leads to a major search that can involve everyone in the private office. Other work just stops until the paper is found. If it is not found, there is a review of the system. The flow of paper is so central, it cannot break down. Of course, there is a second-best solution to finding the missing paper; the mistake could lie with another office sending through an incomplete file. 'Good', said the PS with great relief 'it's not our fault'. Or, as good, the Permanent Secretary has got it and not returned it. Thus, when all the memos for 19 November went missing, the Private Office thought 'he [the Permanent Secretary] must have eaten it'. Unfortunately that still left the question of why they did not know he had them. The PS was, to be frank, pissed off: 'see how much time we waste when our systems don't work' [FWNB]. In the face of this rebuke, the Private Office was silent. If Lord Butler (2004) was concerned about falling standards of record keeping at No. 10, he would be reassured by departmental procedures.

Members of the court are talking about the paperless office. One Private Office had a target of 90 per cent of all correspondence by e-mail. Beyond the dramatic reduction in the use of postage stamps and the reduced workloads of messengers, I doubt any outsider will see the difference. It may save space but the protocols will change little. Nowadays, incoming snail mail is scanned and distributed as an e-mail attachment, but it is printed out for filing. Mail for the Secretary of State is printed out for the red box. One Permanent Secretary had a personal e-mail account for staff, which was sifted by the Private Office, printed out, and given to him in a folder for weekend reading.

The main concern seems to be how to make e-mail like snail mail. The correspondence manual notes, disapprovingly, that the process for handling e-mails 'differs in each office'. Jary (2004: 31; and 2008: 31) continues to worry that civil servants will dash off replies without due reflection, with an inappropriate tone or style. The private office shares some of these worries. One PPS agreed: '*sometimes the speed of e-mail can be a bit of a problem*' and '*it is a dangerous tool to have people wield*' [PPS, TI]. Jary recommends writing the usual letter as an e-mail attachment. He is also concerned that departments do not have the relevant protocols, for example, about politeness in e-mails and avoiding replies that might be seen as abrupt.

E-mail is filed like snail mail; '*anything that comes to us we don't delete at all*'. I pressed. Did they keep all electronic correspondence? Reluctantly one clerk admitted that '*sometimes we do chuck away [advertising brochures]*'. Others were a tad less anal. They just deleted all junk e-mail and advertising. But, as with snail mail, every piece of correspondence was filed initially before weeding. So far as I could tell, electronic and snail mail were handled the same way; delete with caution. In the words of one Permanent Secretary, '*I like to see nearly everything so you must remember that, not to throw things away.*' The PS commented later, '*there are things that he doesn't see. Quite a lot that he doesn't see. I guess he just doesn't realize*' [PS, TI].

Nonetheless the arrival of e-mail is changing procedures, whether for good or ill I leave to the reader's judgement. There used to be a 'red pen culture', in which trainees had their various briefings, letters, and drafts of all kinds edited to be pithy and catch the essence of the argument (see Chapter 5). E-mails and electronic transmission have changed that. Nowadays, there may be '*a bit of red pen about*' but '*I think that's gone away a bit now*'. On occasion, '*I find myself doing a kind of a post-e-mail version*' [PPS, TI]. Indeed ministers complain about the quality of submissions (see below p. 186).

Telephone

Every time a minister or his PPS makes a telephone call, they invoke and reinforce the distribution of authority in the department and across Whitehall. Use of the telephone is governed by a strict protocol that covers all Whitehall. There is a hierarchy of ministers. When the prime minister announces his cabinet, there is a public list. That list is the official hierarchy of ministers and ministries. So, the more junior minister rings and waits to be put through to the senior minister. Senior ministers wait for no one on the phone other than the prime minister. The prime minister waits for nobody. Whenever you hear the phrase, 'Do you want to put your minister on and I'll put him through', you know the protocol hierarchy has been invoked.

The minister's and the permanent secretary's business calls are monitored. The world of the department is a world where even a casual remark in a phone call can have important repercussions. Such care and caution may seem exaggerated but it is better than the alternative of unwanted media coverage.

> *RAWR: Do you monitor [the Secretary of State's] calls?*
> *PPS: I take a note of [the Secretary of State's] calls, yes. If anything significant is to be said I would do a note of it. No one else would. Then there's an e-mail straight down, just to let you know I just took a call from Mr X.*
> *RAWR: Would you listen in?*
> *PPS: One of us would, one of two. I don't—the whole of the Department's responsibilities are split among my private secretaries and the relevant one would listen. I might listen as well, depending.* [PPS, TI]

Bruce-Gardyne (1986: 33 and n. 1) similarly reports that: 'all calls are filtered through the Private Secretaries, whose duty it is to listen and take note of what transpires'. He claims 'they are apparently trained to replace their receivers at the signal of personal endearments'. Indisputably, the minister relies heavily on the PPS's discretion.[10] But technology has struck! Nowadays, ministers can use their own mobiles for personal endearments.

It was possible to preserve privacy in the old days. At the old Department of Trade and Industry (DTI), the PPS had the red bat phone dedicated to monitoring the conversations of the Permanent Secretary. He kept a handwritten note of any potentially delicate or decision making call. But the bat phone could be circumvented. The Permanent Secretary had a private line and:

> *above the door was a great big red light and when [the Permanent Secretary] lifted the receiver on his phone the light came on, and you didn't go in. I mean death. Death would be meted out if you went in when that light was on.* [DS, TI]

However, informality spreads. In one Department, '*I listen to them all*' [PS, FWNB], but in another the PPS listened to the Permanent Secretary's calls only at his request [PPS, TI]. It varies not only between departments but also between private offices in the same department. Also, technology has struck again. I was struck by the quiet in the Private Office. I expected a maelstrom of ringing phones but there were few telephone calls. The decline of the telephone is further evidence, if it were needed, of the e-mail revolution.

There was a striking range of telephone manners. I could not listen in but I could observe the body language. I was particularly struck with the way the

PS could impose authority over the phone. One Department thought it was being left out of the loop so the PS rang. She was not lolling back in her chair. She leant forward, back straight, eyes concentrating hard on the desk in front. Her tone was always polite but unshakeable in its firmness. It was a request to which there was only one answer; the Department would now be included. She spoke with the authority of the Permanent Secretary and the listener knew it; I knew it.

Travel

I went on a number of short trips around London. The arrangements for these visits are as elaborate as any of the other protocols. The diary secretary will organize the train, the car, and the hotel for domestic visits. A PS will accompany the minister. Speeches will have been prepared (see below). There will be briefings about the purpose of the visit and the key people the minister will meet. The written briefings will be supplemented by informal conversation in the car.

The pomp and circumstance of such visits is integral to the appearance of authority but the most interesting person on these trips was the minister's driver.[11] Their role is akin to that of the tea lady; they are an everyday voice in the minister's esoteric life. The car offers some respite; the conversation is mundane, pleasant, even soothing.

My favourite driver was Jo Broadhurst who played for Charlton Athletic women's football team (known as the Addicks) and England. Signed from Doncaster Belles in 2001, she was a member of the Addicks team that won the Nationwide Women's Premier League Cup Final in March 2004, their first major trophy. They went on to win the FA Cup in 2005. I am not a football fan. I prefer rugby league. But she was fun to talk to and her elation over the Addicks recent victory was infectious. So, we chatted about football, food, and wine waiting for the Minister—Minister, what Minister! She was contemplating retirement; it was hard fitting in the training given the demands of the job. She retired in style two years later. She scored the winning goal as Charlton's women's team reserves lifted the Kent County Cup in a 3–2 victory against Millwall. I am sure she was happy with her status as 'veteran midfielder'. Given Jo's conversation with me, it was not hard to see why the Minister liked her and found the chats in the car a welcome change of pace.

The privileges of the minister extend to the driver. When we drove to the Treasury, we parked outside 70, Whitehall where there are double yellow lines. The traffic warden had a word and the driver was, to be blunt, rude. The warden having been told to piss off was pissed off. 'They know', explained the driver. I raised my eyebrows. 'It's simple', he continued. 'I have an official badge. They should just leave us alone. Most do. We don't leave the cars.' Even if a warden gets bloody-minded and issues a ticket, the driver just gives it to the diary secretary who writes a letter and the fine is waived. By now the driver is warming to his topic. 'They don't realize' this car isn't a taxi; it's security for the minister. He displays his protection badge, which means he has been trained to drive an armed police vehicle. I ask if he carrying a gun. He isn't but, when he drove for Geoff Hoon (then Secretary of State for defence), there were two armed police in the car which, in turn, was accompanied by a Range Rover with armed personnel. And I thought I was going to be bored waiting in the car. It is further evidence of the separate, even hermetically sealed, world in which ministers live.

I did not go on any overseas trips with a minister, so I cannot report first-hand on the protocols surrounding travel and hospitality. Ministers more often than permanent secretaries travel overseas, although trips to the EU Commission in Brussels make big demands on officials in some departments. I saw the itineraries for overseas visits. The engagement diary is full. The briefings intensive and to ensure there are no diplomatic gaffes they will involve the Foreign Office and the relevant British Embassy. The schedule is tight, and all the time the minister falls behind with his departmental work. No wonder secretaries of state send their ministers of state instead. The price paid in fatigue and backlog is high. As with so much of this diplomatic work, I wondered about the pay-off. The costs are obvious but what are the benefits beyond such intangibles as reputation and standing?

Committees and briefings[12]

I need to note some elementary rules. For meetings, ministers receive brief-ings. To help them make a decision, ministers receive submissions.[13] So, this section covers briefings. I discuss submissions under 'Advice'. Second, minis-ters never travel alone, not even between floors of the same building. They always have a PPS or a PS with them. It varies from permanent secretary to permanent secretary. The PS does not always see the point—'*Sometimes you just sit there a bit like a spare part and you wonder why you are there*' [PS, TI]. Each PS always has an A4 size bound notepad in which he or she records action to be taken, decisions made, calls to be made and letters to be written. The notebooks too are filed, shelved to be precise. Most PSs get through about one a month.

Committees

I attended two or three committees on every day I observed a minister or permanent secretary at work. Committees are ubiquitous and come in many forms. They are not always about making decisions. I sat in on committees with advisory, briefing, coordinating, governing, inquiry, legislative, management and administration, negotiating, scrutiny, and control functions. I provide detailed examples of these several types of committee at various points in this book. Table 7.1 summarizes these examples by type of committee.

I am sure that committees exist for a multitude of other overt purposes. Most had a clear rationale and took decisions. As one Minister explained:

> The Department would like you to have done literally 'back-to-back' meetings. I don't like that because, I like going over a meeting. I use meetings to help me make decisions. Therefore if it's 45 minutes—20 minutes is no good to me—if it's 45 minutes, I want to be able to go 50 minutes. It's no good if the next meeting starts immediately. So we basically learned to reschedule the day to give me 15 minutes in between which ended up not being spare time but it gave me time to decide. [Minister, TI]

Other meetings had covert functions and served mainly symbolic purposes; they were appointed, they met, and they parted. No more was expected and nothing was decided. As Northcote Parkinson (1965: 34) observed, a committee is a plant that 'takes root and grows, it flowers, wilts, and dies, scattering the seed from which other committees will bloom in their turn'. I saw

Table 7.1 Types of committee

Type of committee	Example	Chapter in which I describe the committee
Departmental		
Advisory	Management Board	Rhodes 2007*b* and Chapter 6: 139–140
Briefing	Departmental ministerial meeting	Chapter 4: 93–94, 99
	DGs' meeting	Chapter 5: 112–14
Coordinating	Joined-up government	Chapter 4: 96
		Chapter 8: 228
	Permanent Secretaries' Group	Chapter 8: 222–4
Governing	Cabinet and its committees	I did not have access to the cabinet
	No. 10 stocktakes	Chapter 8: 214–16
Management	Building refurbishment	Chapter 4: 94
Negotiating	Treasury and PBR	Chapter 5: 114–15
Parliamentary committees		
Inquiry	Public Administration Select Committee	Chapter 8: 232, Witness and observer PASC 2000
Scrutiny and control	Select Committee on Public Accounts	Chapter 8: 232
Legislative	Midlands Airport	Chapter 8: 231

committees that scattered, bloomed, and wilted. For example, the Minister had to attend a forum of sports representatives, which was not his normal area of responsibility but, in the era of joined-up government, his Department had to be there. He was 'dreading' this meeting because the forum exists at the instigation of a prominent sports personality, who is a friend of the Blairs. He persuaded the Prime Minister to set it up. With some venom, the Minister described the sports person as 'a lobby of one'. The Minister was the Chair because Tony Blair asked him and he did not see how he could refuse. Its terms of reference were . . . there's the rub, and the reason he describes the meeting as dreadful. They were at 'loggerheads' over them. The topic of today's meeting was sponsorship and sport. It was a good job the PPS told me, because I would never have guessed. Throughout this discussion, the Minister did a good job of appearing interested. He nodded in all the right places, looked at the speakers, and turned his papers at the right time. He did NOT shuffle and organize his papers, check his diary, read and annotate a paper, or talk to his neighbour at the table. He spoke rarely but on the few occasions when he did he stressed setting priorities, limiting their interest to a manageable number of topics, and realistic costing. If anyone was listening carefully, they would know he is criticizing them and telling them what he wants if there is to be any progress. No one is listening.

What value was added by this meeting? The most obvious output was that the Minister obliged the Prime Minister, normally a wise course of action. But for Blair's involvement, he would have sent a junior minister. A second outcome was that the Minister discharged his diplomatic function in Whitehall and beyond. The main characteristic of this meeting was that it was unnecessary. It existed as an unquestioning reaction to prime ministerial whim. It had no clear agenda and if it had outputs it had no obvious outcomes (and on pointless meetings see also Blunkett 2006: 34–5 and 99).

The usual characters attended the committees. There was the chair, commonly the minister or the permanent secretary of the lead department. There was the secretary, commonly the PPS or a PS, to record any items requiring action and note decisions. There were the interested parties, commonly officials from another department there to defend its interests, and seen, even described, as 'strangers'. However, other ministers would also attend, especially ministers of state. There was the layman, whom I saw only on the Department's Management Board, but who was regularly appointed to the Department's non-departmental public bodies. From time to time, I also saw outside experts, commonly imported from business or a university but sometimes the minister's SpAd had the relevant policy expertise.

Apart from their formal position as the member of the committee, individuals played different roles. Commonly, most people played instrumental or task-oriented roles and tried to help the meeting achieve its goals. Others had expressive or social roles and sought to foster the meeting's morale. Thus, many committees had their 'joker', who relaxed people with badinage and reduced any tension with the well judged witticism. Bales and Slater (1969: 259) also identify questioning and negative roles. Undoubtedly individuals asked questions and disagreed but I prefer to stress the representative role of some group members. They attended to represent some other interest. Ministers represented their political party in parliamentary committees. Officials engaged in bureaucratic politics to delay a decision, to deflect another department straying on to their turf, or to drive a wedge between allies. In effect, they were guerrillas in the bureaucracy, skilled at representing and protecting the interests of their departments and their minister.[14]

I have noted the variety of committees, but they have much in common despite their different functions. First, we may live in the eras of both managerialism, with its emphasis on decisive action and individual performance, and of ministerial bilaterals or sofa government, but committees remain the dominant forums for making decisions. Ministers and permanent secretaries spend much time attending, and the departmental court spends much of its time setting up meetings and preparing ministers for those meetings.

Second, there are protocols for both internal and external meetings. In both cases, who visits whom is governed by protocol. Normally, inside the department, the permanent secretary would go to the secretary of state's office, not the other way round. However, ministers of state would go to the permanent secretary. Some rile at this status hierarchy. Michael Heseltine:

> felt it appropriate that he should visit me to discuss the issue. This resulted in a compromise of which the television series *Yes Minister* would have been proud; we met in the corridor, at the top of the marble staircase. (Heseltine 2000: 189)

There is now much more informality:

> *I would suspect that one of the simple indicators is that in the good old days they would be always referred to as Permanent Secretary. Nowadays they will call you [by your first name].* [Permanent Secretary, TI]

But the old ways persist. To be frank, some secretaries of state love their standing and the phrase 'lording it' was coined for just such circumstances (see Chapter 4).

Informality is more common lower down the hierarchy when the meeting is attended only by departmental members. Strangers induce formality. Thus, inside the department, the PPS's relationship with ministers of state can be informal. The usual protocols would have their private secretaries ringing to say 'X wants a quick word. Are you free?' and the PPS would go to them. But '*Again it's quite informal*', so '*If they wanted something, and indeed this has happened on a number of occasions, I can think of three or four of them have done this, they would stroll around here*' [PPS, TI]. It would never happen between departments.

Third, for committees outside the department, the conventions about the 'lead department' still apply:

There was always some resentment being felt by major departments when a small one took the initiative. I was conscious that the high ranking the Prime Minister gave me in the Cabinet pecking order, above the Secretaries of State for the Environment, Trade and Industry and Defence, meant that officials from major departments had to come to my small department to discuss proposals. That is Whitehall protocol. (Walker 1991: 215)

Being the lead department means you get to choose who attends. The permanent secretary and the PPS will decide who attends, taking into account, of course, the minister's preferences. Normally, they will invite the lead officials for the topic under discussion. However, depending on the topic under discussion, it can also involve lawyers and someone from the Press Office. According to Stanley (2008a: 5) for meetings involving strangers, the rule is 'one official to each visitor'.

Fourth, all committee members use non-verbal communication. I am convinced committee members speak to one another through their body language (De Paulo and Friedman 1998; Goffman 1969). When the Permanent Secretary pushed his chair back, turned his outstretched legs away from the group, and stared at the ceiling, everyone knew he was bored. Similarly, when the Minister locked his hands behind his head, in the classic expression of self-confidence, and looked around at the assembled group, it was seen as a message of self-confidence and control (see McKay et al. 1995: 56–7). They were dominant in the hierarchy and in the specific committee setting. I am unclear about the extent to which body language was always used deliberately. Dominant behaviour was just a habitual operating practice, not a specific decision for that committee. I don't think they consciously decided to show their boredom. Of course, sometimes it is deliberate. Non-verbal behaviour is regulated. When the committee members lean forward, hands folded on the table or resting on knees, and make eye contact with the chair, it is the language of determined engagement and borderline aggressive. Similarly, when a committee member bangs the table, it is seen as clear evidence of withdrawal. Or, when a member drapes his legs over the arm of the chair, it is a gesture of indifference. Indeed, there can be a marked contrast between the spoken word and its codes of civility and the body language (see the discussion of politeness below). Typically the men's body language expressed self-confidence, aggression, and control. Many spoke with a polite voice and a harsh body. Others had a broader repertoire. One Minister was skilled in managing large groups, sitting on the table, not in a chair, with hands out front, and palms spread inviting comments. He then switched to hands on hips, leaning forward, determined face, throwing questions back at the audience. The shift from one to the other posture was seamless. He engaged the audience. There were few asides or drooping eyelids. As Goffman (1969: 13 and ch. 6) observed, regulating non-verbal behaviour when presenting oneself in everyday life is essential to the smooth conduct of social interactions. People set the ground rules of any social exchange with great speed. With committees, its members brought their mutually understood expectations about hierarchy, turf, and politeness to every meeting. 'The gesture is mightier than the pen' (De Paulo and Friedman 1998: 27) when it communicates such expectations.

Finally, committees pose problems for the Minister who has to pay attention. Many of us who go to committees switch off at some point. I am an endless fidget and easily bored. The Minister pays attention; a simple phrase for a hard task. He also has to keep up, switching from topic to topic. I know the Private Office is efficient because they provide the briefings for all these meetings and their multifarious agendas and he moves through them without a hitch. The Minister knows his limitations; 'I'm not as on top of this as I need to be'. But he also knows it is possible to be fully informed on only a few subjects. Without his briefings he would quickly be lost. Even with them, he can struggle. If challenged by an expert, he does not have the detailed knowledge to sustain an argument. He escapes by agreeing to 'take it back for further consideration'. That phrase could be translated as 'oops'. As the PPS observes, 'he is pretty clever. He's clear about what he wants. He's decisive quite a lot of the time. So there aren't many times when I think he's completely lost' [FWNB].

Briefings

The briefings for meetings are as essential as they endless. As ever there can be a note of self-mockery. So, civil servants talk about the *Spotlight Syndrome*. Today the minister is concerned about A so everyone grabs A and starts desperately trying to improve it. Tomorrow the minister (who has limited time and attention) is concerned about B so everyone forgets about A and makes a grab for B. The next day it will be C. Thus, nothing gets properly finished as the clever people move on to the next priority.[15]

Briefings come in the guises of oral briefings and files. The defining element of both is a succinct summary of key points so the minister or permanent secretary is up to speed for the meeting. The Private Office will commonly liaise with the appropriate person from DG to team leader. A subsidiary aim is to spot likely difficulties at the meeting; sometimes referred to as 'elephant traps'. Such traps are topics the minister does not want raised by others and matters the minister should not raise (Jary 2004: 28).

The diary secretary collates briefings. She prepares files that have:

All the paperwork from the inception of how that came about, right through. It's got all my notes, any paperwork, and it's just a way of containing that in one place. And that's where the briefing eventually goes. I hand it to the PS, the PS sorts it, decides what, flags it, into [the Secretary of State]. It's my responsibility to request briefing. There is a slight exception in the fact cabinet and cabinet committees are done on papers that come out of Cabinet Office and they are dealt with by the cabinet documents person. [DS, TI]

Flagging papers for ministers or the permanent secretary is common practice. There is far too much to read and flagging is a way of separating the wheat from the chaff. The initial sift will be done by the PS. For the secretary of state, there will be a final sift by the PPS.

The DS in the Permanent Secretary's Private Offices has an equivalent role:

Basically, in a nutshell, it is making sure the Permanent Secretary is fully briefed for all of his meetings. That he has all the support papers before the meeting and that he gets there, that he's in the right place at the right time. [DS, TI]

An experienced DS can be invaluable because *'If I need anything I know exactly where to go'* [DS, TI]:

[The Permanent Secretary's] correspondence, requests for meetings, and other things, I deal with all of that. And if something comes in that I am not particularly sure about and I have an idea that [the Permanent Secretary] won't know the answer, I usually send it out to the various officials asking for advice, whether they think this is an appropriate way for the Permanent Secretary to spend his time, or is there something he needs to do, or can it be delegated. Once I've got an answer, then I put it [the request] into [the Permanent Secretary] with the advice. [DS, TI]

To go with their knowledge of the department, some DSs have a choice vocabulary for describing their contacts ranging from *'a right royal pain in the arse'* to *'fag hag'* and the less common *'cephalopod'*. Few are spared. Security is the 'sphincter police', a feisty DG is 'Penelope Pitstop', a duo from a DG are introduced as 'French and Saunders'. [DS, FWNB][16]

The skill of the PPS and the PS is to sift the material so the minister and permanent secretary are fully briefed without being swamped; and to keep the department happy, not agitated, because they have been pushed down the list of priorities. Games are played over access to the minister. The department puts material to the minister in which he has no interest. The department is slow to respond to a request from the minister. So the minister responds, through the PPS:

As I asked for this well over a year ago . . . if I do not get a paper . . . within a month, I shall commission it outside the department. (Minister cited in Stanley 2008a: 4)

Gone are the days when the civil service had a monopoly of advice. Instead as one SpAd told me, '[the Minister] likes to take advice from anywhere, so it is seamless between politicians, advisers, and officials' [SpAd, FWNB]. And civil servants are content with this arrangement provided they know what advice is going to the minister. As one Permanent Secretary remarked with satisfaction:

I have never, never read in the Sunday Times a policy initiative that I didn't know about. Okay? That's one of the tests. So I have always been in the loop. [Permanent Secretary, TI]

Advice and submissions

A mainstay of the literature on the relationship between minister and civil servants, and of the *Yes Minister* television series, is endless jockeying for position between the two over policy. Indeed, there is much discussion and debate about policy.[17] During my stay, however, I saw little evidence of Sir Humphrey's obstruction. The PPS talks about the importance of '*incremental-ism*' and '*seniority*':

> *I am completely, completely committed to transformational stuff, but what I'm not interested in is just knocking the walls down and building something from scrap. I don't think we need to do that.* [PPS, TI]

So, advice is infused with a respect for tradition. There is no intent overtly or covertly to oppose or undermine the minister's policies. They are simply doing what civil servants are programmed to do; learning from experience and using that experience to draft feasible policies. In a phrase, they are trained to spot snags. As Douglas Wass (1984: 19 and 40), former Joint Head of the Home Civil Service, stresses, this tradition exemplifies pragmatism and muddling through. It is but a short step from spotting snags to caution and conservatism. Such beliefs and practices can feel like opposition and obstruction to ministers in a hurry to make their name. For Tony Blair it was evidence of inertia: of a civil service in thrall to its own past, 'to a time and a way and an order that had passed, a product of the last hundred years of history' (Blair 2010a: 205). One dreads to think what a prime minister would say of a civil service that did not warn of impending snags.

The PPSs are the fulcrum of advice to ministers because of their position in the flow of communication. As Henderson (2001: 163) would have it, the PPS 'in a somewhat feline fashion' picks his way between 'dangerous, criss-cross paths'. James (1999: 35–6) is more direct: 'private secretaries are not policy advisers'; rather their task is 'brokering access to the Minister'. No one denies that the PPS can overstep the mark. David Blunkett (2006: 305) complained that his PPS was 'audacious': 'they really do think that they run the show, and we Ministers are just the passing flotsam and jetsam' (see also Donoughue 2003: 358).

Ministers also receive informal briefings on policy matters. One Minister told the Private Office:

> *There are some people who energize you and there are some people who you have to work very hard with. And the office knew the energizers in that Department. 'Look', I said, 'You know if any of the "good picks" or the energizers come up after 6 p.m.,' I said, 'You know they are always welcome.' Because that fed me, that's when we developed policy to tell you the truth, you know, a cup of tea or a take-out pizza.* [Minister, TI]

Stanley (2008a: 11) similarly enjoins his colleagues to be 'innovative and enthusiastic'; 'personal impressions count heavily with Ministers'. Non-verbal communication is again important: 'remember your clothes, appearance and body language send clear messages...take care those messages are the ones that you wish to send'. In short, snag spotting is not enough.

From my conversations and the few submissions I was allowed to see, the basic rules were stick to the facts and deliver a clear message briefly.[18] Ministers sometimes complain submissions are too polished:

> *I remember Michael Rifkind*[19] *saying he felt there was too much kind of polish on submissions, where some of the challenges had taken place in the departments, on difficult issues, had been so carefully glued together that you couldn't have the argument easily. One of the other things I think civil servants need to understand better about working with good ministers is that they don't want fully baked submissions with two days to decide. A good minister would prefer to be engaged as thinking develops, and therefore put crudely, get the half-baked outline submission, kind of a month before the decision. And they then can engage with it. And sometimes I think the civil service finds that difficult because we prefer to get our own thinking straight before we put it up. I think a good minister would want to be engaged earlier on, and the department should encourage that.* [Permanent Secretary, TI]

One Minister with experience of government in the 1970s had the opposite complaint. He wanted:

> *Good skills in drafting because civil servants don't have those skills in the way they would have done...in the 1970s. Something is not quite as it used to be. Lots of things needed rewriting and correcting and I did some of it myself but the two private secretaries were meant to be able to do some of that work and take some of that load off me.* [Minister, TI]

David Blunkett (2006: 374 and 803) had exactly the same complaint and one PPS admitted the 'red pen culture' had declined (see above p. 175).

I was struck by the differences in handling submissions compared with the *Yes Minister* stereotype. Such games as hiding bad news or unwelcome advice at the bottom of the box, or trying to manipulate ministers in other ways, were seen as pointless. If anything, the attitude was 'get it over with straight away'. If you make a mistake say you are sorry. The key is building mutual trust. The PPS plays a central role. He or she will determine the priority accorded to a submission, balancing the DG's wishes against the minister's interests and preferences. If there are any games, they will be played around the PPS as DGs jockey for position. The trick is to know the minister's mind without giving the impression you are the minister. It also explains why I saw so little policy analysis. It is simply not done in the departmental court but in the Directorates General by middle-ranking officials (see Page and Jenkins 2005). The departmental court filters, packages, and processes advice produced elsewhere, mainly but not exclusively in the departments' Directorates General.

Speeches

Everybody works with the media, not just the elected politician, and most had a poor opinion. The media were variously described as 'nasty', 'a bad lot', and 'unfair'. There was almost a whine in the voice as they complained 'we're a soft target', living in a 'goldfish bowl', and 'utterly exposed'. I sympathize. As I show in Chapter 9, there is a feral quality in the media's treatment of ministers. But, ministers conspire in their own fate. The government fed the beast; for example, ministers do the rounds of TV studios courting attention. They relish the celebrity that so often bites back. Much of the time, the beast was supine, happy to be hand fed. Spin is a policy of manipulating the media to produce stories favourable to the government. The complaints simply mean that spin had not worked, but the hand feeding continued as one of the routines of government. Links with the 'trade' journals that specialized in the departments' policy areas were often amicable bordering on trusting. Most political correspondents of the tabloids and broadsheets were not trusted. Alastair Campbell's invective was invariably directed at the latter not the former. He set the tone.

Permanent Secretaries increasingly appear in public, often to explain departmental policy to stakeholders. They also present seminar papers and lectures. Such presentations usually involved the PS with assistance from the relevant DG. They did not involve the SpAds as, necessarily, there is no political gloss; the intention is to stick to the facts. The permanent secretaries recognize they have becomes the public face of their departments:

I had to learn how to speak in public . . . and . . . make, for me, big speeches to hundreds of people, which I had never done before. [Permanent Secretary, TI]

Speaking for all his colleagues, one Permanent Secretary commented:

They now find they get involved in these things in a way in which their predecessors would never have been involved. [Permanent Secretary, TI]

Some enjoy the limelight; '*I am up for talking to journalists*' [Permanent Secretary, TI].

Speech writing is part of everybody's skill set. I was naive about ministers and speeches. I have done many conference addresses for audiences large and small over the years, but I still had no idea it would be such an elaborate production number. For any event, the organization started months before when the conference organizers contacted the Private Office about a possible date. Once a date was agreed, the next step was to prepare the speech. On this occasion, preparation started two days before, although for big events, it can be much earlier. Media management and speech writing are the areas where SpAds play a regular and important role. Drafting begins at a meeting with the Minister, the Press Office, and the SpAds. The Minister asks them to draft him

'20 minutes max' and in it he wants 'some anti-Conservative stuff'. Beyond that they are casting about for a structure, bandying about ideas and examples and there are some fine examples of New Labour-speak: 'Do you want to come over as value driven?' The next day, there is a brief meeting with the Press Office to polish the speech and to identify 'nuggets' for the press release.

The SpAds and the Press Office may be prominent but officials still play an important part. The department invariably provides the basic information for a speech. The departmental court takes care of the logistics of delivering a speech; from driver to red carpet, to lecture hall and make-up, to the ubiquitous PowerPoint and subsequent reception, while taking care of security and praying there isn't a three-line whip. They also draft speeches. Stanley (2008a: 23–4) offers sensible practical advice: for example, don't write them, dictate, and don't show to senior colleagues who will spot all the split infinitives and turn it into written text (see also Jones 2008). Jary (2004: ch. 6) is a man for the written text, not the spoken colloquialism. Some officials have an aptitude in this area, and they are prized; no minister willingly turns away a mellifluous phrase.

In an ideal world, the purpose of a speech is 'to persuade or even inspire, and, above all, to entertain' (Jary 2004: 53). Maybe, but ministers and their speech writers often aim lower; they stick to the basics. Depending on mood and the political climate, the minister may settle for dull and short. It is safe territory. However, on occasion, the minister may aim higher with the political gloss and the headline catching turn of phrase coming mainly from the minister and the SpAds.

I knew ministers gave many speeches. I did not know quite how many. Nor did I realize just how much time it took to write a speech. It is hard to be dull and say nothing that can attract media criticism. I attended several speeches. The audience did want to be persuaded or inspired. They would accept being bored, provided it wasn't for too long. Given that alcohol was to hand, the audience did not want thought-provoking ideas. For preference, they wanted to be entertained. What they wanted above all else was the minister at their event.

Secrecy

It is commonplace to claim the British civil service in particular and the government in general is secretive. Hennessy (1989: 345) claims 'it is Whitehall's cardinal value and dominant characteristic'. I have left secrecy until last not because it is unimportant but because it surfaced but rarely in everyday life. I saw several specific examples. The most obvious was the straps on the Iraq war (see Chapter 4, p. 83). Also, in the discussions on new appointments to non-departmental public bodies, one nominee raised concern because of a history of association with radical groups when young. This association was known because the 'spooks'—yes, they used that term—provided a briefing.

The most obvious influence of the culture of secrecy was the caution in handling paper. Most private offices have a 'clear desk' policy. Files are not left lying around but locked away at close of business. There is a separate cabinet for secret documents. It is security vetted with a combination lock and only accredited 'Readers' have access. It is a major disciplinary offence if left open. Its presence is a constant reminder of the need for care and caution. Discarded paperwork was either torn or shredded and at the end of the working day disposed off in tied plastic bags.

There was also some caution in handling me. They would remember I was there when gossiping about senior colleagues—'you didn't hear any of that'— or sensitive policy or commercial issues, when there was a conscious decision about whether I could attend. I was not necessarily excluded but equally I could never take it for granted that I would attend. If I did attend confidential meetings, as I often did, I was also given the relevant documentation.

I remained a professional stranger. Yet they allowed me to do the fieldwork for this book and explicitly excluded me only from confidential personal appraisals and top political meetings. I cannot imagine Warren Fisher, Edward Bridges, or any head of the Home Civil Service before Robin Butler and Richard Wilson agreeing to this arrangement. I know of no equivalent case. It might be going too far to describe the departments as 'open' but it would be churlish not to recognize the spirit of openness with which they approached my research. The obvious qualification to this statement is I had no direct contact with 'the secret state'; none of my departments touched on the 'sensitive' areas of defence, security, and terrorism. I witnessed no breach of the civil service's code of loyalty to the service and to the minister. Also, I have no idea what went on 'backstage'. I saw what I was allowed to see. Virtually by definition, I do not know what I was excluded from.

RITUALS

I came across three rituals or webs of habitual practices. They were as common as they were unremarked. They surrounded politeness, gossip, and humour.

Politeness[20]

Politeness 'presupposes [the] potential for aggression as it seeks to disarm it, and makes possible communication between potentially aggressive parties' (Fox 2004: 97 quoting Brown and Levinson, 2000). Politeness governs most workplace encounters. So, most meetings start with a discussion of the weather and general enquiries about one's health, journey to work and, of course cups of tea or coffee. And as Fox (2004: 185) points out, this chit-chat includes 'the usual full complement of pleases and thank yous, appreciative murmurs from the visitors and humorously self-deprecating apologies from the host, and so on, and on'. An effective way of unearthing such language codes is to explore events where they are breached. In the civil service the code of civility or politeness is breached by anger and by swearing.

Consider the following scene. At an internal budget meeting, a DG lost his temper. His section was suffering the largest budget cuts. He wanted a strategic review of base spending and his colleagues did not. He is excited, short of breath, and he raises his voice. His body language is stiff, angular. His colleagues stare at the table and avoid eye contact. Some try to suggest compromise solutions but they all involve cuts. It is clear he is getting nowhere so he leaves the meeting. Everybody was embarrassed by this outbreak. The event was described as the Department 'at our worst'. The DG was 'OTT' and the meeting was 'hard work'. No one thinks the DG should have lost his temper. It would have been better if he had been 'disappointed'. He had breached the civility code [FWNB]. The Permanent Secretary apologised for this behaviour all the way back to his office from the meeting. It simply wasn't done. Overt aggression was discouraged by the almost mandatory conventions of polite behaviour. People do not run, they do not shout, and they do not express overt emotion. Points are made politely. There are few if any cries of 'rubbish', and even expostulations are expressed mildly. All defer to the chair. Remarks are addressed to others through the chair.

This scene prompted an extended comment from one civil servant.

> Your bit about language and part about anger/aggression and civility/politeness caused a great big light bulb to flash on over my head. 33 years in the civil service, I hadn't connected it all up. I knew, of course, that a refusal to speak the management lingo marks you as an outsider—and I've certainly annoyed an awful lot of senior people in this way over the past 20 years. But I hadn't connected that to the typical senior civil servant's awkwardness about people issues, and their fear of anger and emotion. Years ago I went to a meeting at the (then) DES at which some clot said: 'You lot really care about this, don't you?' He seemed aghast. We did—such was the leadership and the urgency and the importance of our task. As the son of a soldier (who probably should have been one himself), I'm mostly polite but have lost my temper a few times—only with senior people which I thought was OK. I realised reading your paper that this plus emotional commitment plus language differences has damaged an awful lot of my professional relationships with senior civil servants, with whom I've long had a problem. It all suddenly fell into place.[21]

This scene and the commentary illustrate two features of civil service language; understatement and distance (or lack of emotion).

Now consider the following scene. In the aftermath of Jo Moore's 9/11 gaffe, negotiations took place between Sir Richard Mottram (the Permanent

Secretary) and Martin Sixsmith (Moore's boss) about his resignation. Stephen Byers pre-empted the negotiations by prematurely announcing Sixsmith had resigned. According to *The Times*, Mottram provided one of the quotes of the year when he commented:

> We're all f****d. I'm f****d. You're f****d. The whole Department is f****d. It's the biggest cock-up ever. We're all completely f****d. (*The Times*, 28 December 2002)

This scene illustrates two points. First, it shows the influence of social class on language. Mottram was criticized because he was born in the West Midlands, had gone to a grammar school, and had not gone to Oxford or Cambridge. There was surprise, whether feigned or pained is unclear, that the administrative elite swore. Our social superiors were setting a bad example. It was seen as evidence of declining standards. The old verities were slipping away. Of course, ministers and members of the senior civil service use profanity, and the Private Office laughed at any suggestion they do not. One Permanent Secretary thought the Private Office was the only place you could swear, and then added quickly he did not swear at staff; he was just venting. Many would agree with *The Observer* (29 June 2006) that Mottram demonstrated 'not only a clear proficiency in profanity but a knack for the forgotten art of conjugation'. And the most unexpected people can be foul mouthed. One Minister who exemplified quiet, lady-like, middle-class reserve told her startled officials that it would happen 'over my dead fucking body' [Minister, FWNB]. If you believe *The Thick of It*, such behaviour is the norm.[22] It is not. Mottram was embarrassed. The Minister used swearing for an effect that would be spoilt if done often. What these scenes throw into relief is the belief in '*the proper way of doing things*' [DS, TI]. In fact, and second, the more common way of dealing with anger is to become cold. I came across variations of the phrase, '*He was one of those quietly icy men*' [DS, TI]. '*It's a kind of withdrawal and coldness*' [PPS, TI]. The following scene would be typical of my departments. The Permanent Secretary is 'mild'. It would be 'unacceptable' for him to swear. If something goes wrong, the PS will 'confess' that she lost the papers and the Permanent Secretary will 'sigh'. Then 'you know you've been ticked off' [PS, FWNB]. Anger is managed by politeness; by detachment, not swearing.

These preferences for politeness, understatement, distance, and detachment pervade the everyday phrases used by the civil service. They are examples of the way in which the civil service takes the emotion out of everyday life. They are all too well aware of their linguistic oddities. So, 'disappointment' does not 'express the view that a particular junior official is quite possibly the most incompetent person it has ever been my misfortune to come across' (Stanley 2008*b*). But it is a clear signal that performance was not up to scratch. Similar terms include 'concerned' and 'surprised'. Stanley correctly observes that were all three words to occur in the same sentence or paragraph, the effect would be 'devastating'. So, while the conventions and practices of politeness might seem amusing to outsiders, they have a serious purpose. They relax committee members before stressful encounters and diffuse potential aggression.

Gossip

Gossip is 'the process of informally communicating value-laden information about members of a social setting' (Fox 2004: 42, citing Noon and Delbridge 1993). It is the currency of exchange in a culture of secrecy. It is ever-present and practised by politician and official alike. However, the unspoken rule is that it is done discreetly behind the closed doors of Westminster and Whitehall and not in public. A minister who went public with frank comments about his colleagues would damage his own reputation. So, David Blunkett's attributed comments on his colleagues in his biography were injudicious at best. For example, Alan Milburn (DoH) had 'grown in competence and ability', Margaret Beckett (DEFRA) is 'just holding the ring', Charles Clarke (DfES) 'has not developed as expected', Patricia Hewitt (DTI) does not think strategically, and Gordon Brown (Treasury) throws his weight around (Pollard 2005: 27–8). Of course his colleagues reciprocate. John Prescott, Deputy Prime Minister, is said to hold Blunkett in a mixture of contempt and suspicion while others grit their teeth at his 'idiotic indiscretion' (*The Observer*, 12 December 2004). We have here a public example of a conversation that Westminster and Whitehall conducts all the time in private.

Gossip is not just about relative standing. It is used to advance careers. So, one junior minister felt impelled to tell me he 'was *really loyal*' to a colleague who had resigned. He claimed, '*I did not bad-mouth him at all, and in many ways he and I got on very well.*' Then came the punchline: '*although he was not good at building a team and getting the ministers working as a team, which I found frustrating*'. Then straight away: '*But I did absolutely nothing to undermine him.*' Well, not a lot anyway: '*All I did, I had a conversation with Ed Milliband* [then Gordon Brown's special adviser]. . . . *Then I had a conversation with Gordon*' [Minister, TI]. Here is an odd conception of doing 'absolutely nothing'. And, yes, he did become Secretary of State.

The comparisons are often invidious. One Minister offered some unflattering comments on his ministerial team

> *They weren't experienced, oh God no. They weren't experienced enough. If you think of the team between 1997–2001 how many have made the cabinet. Five of us made the cabinet. My 2001 team won't make the cabinet. I got [XXXX], he's a good man, it was the wrong job for him, and I wasn't to know that at the time and that's my fault. But I was given (pauses) three people who had never been ministers before and one person who was barely a politician.* [Minister, TI]

Such gossip is as pervasive as it is insidious (see Chapter 9). No one is exempt. To greater and lesser degrees, everyone is an exponent of the art. At an interdepartmental committee meeting two permanent secretaries are gossiping about the fate of an unpopular junior minister.

PERMANENT SECRETARY 1: Will he go?
PERMANENT SECRETARY 2: Will he, or do I want him to? [Laughter]
PERMANENT SECRETARY 1: I know what you want! What will he do?
PERMANENT SECRETARY 2: If he's to go, now's the time. I prefer [another junior minister].
PERMANENT SECRETARY 1: Yes he's so good and so loyal.
PERMANENT SECRETARY 2: I think there is a good chance he will go. [FWNB]

He did. This item of gossip was not confined to the Minister of State's home department. Other departments knew the junior minister might be moved. They expressed 'horror' he would come to their department. In this way reputations are left in tatters.

The other popular topic of gossip is promotions. When I was interviewing, the Prime Minister was looking for a new Cabinet Secretary. There were rumoured to be five candidates. I was interviewing one of the five.

PERMANENT SECRETARY: *I thought you were going to ask me whether I was going to be Cabinet Secretary.*
RAWR: *No, no, heavens forbid that I should be so indiscreet, especially as the gossip about this is endless.*
PERMANENT SECRETARY: *Well I won't tell you.*
RAWR: *Go on then tell me. Are you going to be the next Cabinet Secretary?*
PERMANENT SECRETARY: *I don't think so.*
RAWR: *Are you going to apply for it?*
PERMANENT SECRETARY: *Well I am 'in the frame'. In the last few weeks I have been encouraged to put my name 'into the frame' for the Cabinet Secretary's job.*
[Permanent Secretary, TI]

And we talked on for another five minutes. For sure, I was not the only person party to such a conversation. The gossip was reported in the broadsheets.

As well as the gossip of 'high politics', there is the everyday or 'low politics' office gossip. One member of the Private Office is a martial arts expert who has appeared in cage fighting on TV. His prowess is the cause of much Private Office gossip. They speculate on such matters as the likely outcome of his next fight and, veering to the lewd, his body. It provokes much hilarity; they get a kick out of his Warholian fifteen minutes of fame. And the Permanent Secretary joins in, describing him as 'a TV star'. Gossip glues the hierarchy together.

The Department also gossips about its own internal promotions. Here a Permanent Secretary reflects on earlier times.

> *RAWR: And are you looking forward to whatever the next promotion might be?*
> *PERMANENT SECRETARY: Yes and you are wondering what it is going to be.*
> *RAWR: You're discussing it furiously with all your peers?*
> *PERMANENT SECRETARY: Yeah, yeah, it happens all the time. And you know, by now I know a lot of people around the departments and there is a lot of gossip isn't there, it's like a big family.* [Permanent Secretary, TI]

Here the sharing of value-laden information acts as organizational glue. It expresses the shared interests of the departmental family.

Humour

Humour does not refer to the jokes of a stand-up comic or the monologues of a Billy Connolly but to the 'wit, irony, understatement, banter, teasing, pomposity-pricking—which are an integral part of almost all English social interactions' (Fox 2004: 179). Humour is low key but ever-present. It releases tension and stress and sustains routines. The badinage is endless:

> RAWR: What does John do?
> THIRD PARTY: On a good day, you know, when he can keep both eyes open.
> JOHN: I work normally to about 5 p.m.
> Third Party: Did you say work? [Laughter]. [FWNB]

Much humour seeks to humanize the boss:

> DS: Look at that. [pointing to the Permanent Secretary's handwriting] [Laughter from colleagues]
> DS: You may well laugh. I can't read any of it.
> PERMANENT SECRETARY: It's good so far. [calling from his office where he's reading the text already returned]
> DS: He's crawling. [FWNB]

And the Permanent Secretary plays along. His socks have become the focus of attention. The PS notes that he has his name on the socks. The Permanent Secretary takes off his shoes and shows them it's not just his name but also the meaning of his name. There are howls of laughter. 'It is my one concession to eccentricity' says the Permanent Secretary in his defence. No one is listening.

Humour is also ever-present in the ministerial team and about ministers. There is badinage about trips to Trinidad and Tobago. A junior minister is going there and he asks for a briefing. There is much raucous laughter and various suggestions about what he could do, only some of which involve sunbathing and swimming in the sea. Another is going to China during the SARS outbreak. A colleague suggests he 'take a mask'. He replies it would be better 'to send a SpAd'. Another Minister chats about her 'favourite' journalist and wonders 'if you can put poison in his breakfast for me'. The SpAds doubt he will be there because the pubs are not open. Ministers tell 'insider' stories about one another.

> Nick Brown, a man of burly bonhomie, used to work for Margaret Beckett, a woman of bird-like delicacy, when she was the frontbench spokesperson on the Treasury. They were at the Labour Party conference. Nick was in his hotel room, in the shower, shaving. The phone rings. Covered in foam, naked and grumbling, he leaves the shower to answer it.
> 'Yes, what do you want? I was just taking a shower,' says Nick
> 'It's Peter [Hyman], is Margaret there? [FWNB][23]

They also use humour to pass judgement. One Minister of State has an 'award of the week' named after him. The award goes to the 'most brown nosed crawly creep'.

I suspect I saw more of the officials. Maybe I became acclimatized to their style, but they were funnier. My favourites were all deadpan.

> You shouldn't be happy, motivated but not happy. There have been too many changes to be happy.
> There might be something in the wording that you and I, great men though we are, might miss.
> Change is like dieting. Everyone knows the rules but not everyone follows them.
> Too much comfort in this room, not enough pain.
> Ambitious, handsome, and debonair, the [Permanent Secretary] begins his meetings with a group hug to foster the corporate spirit among his reinvigorated team. (Self-mocking introduction to an imminent newspaper interview) [FWNBs]

Civil servants also love to mock themselves, inventing syndromes and circulating lists of civil service jargon. We have already met the *Courtier Syndrome* when civil servants tiptoe round and suck up to the minister (see Chapter 4: 105–6) and the *Spotlight Syndrome* when the civil servants grasshopper from one issue to the next on the whim of the minister (above p. 183). There is also the *Sat Nav Syndrome* in which civil servants sit around looking awkward, but lost. They have worked hard but ended up in entirely the wrong place. Nevertheless, somehow, everything's going to be all right because they pushed all the right buttons and followed the correct procedures. Morally they clearly feel they should be in the right place even though they patently are not! For example, on a training course held in the Department, no lunch arrived for the students. The course organizer explained several times that he had filled in all the forms so there ought to be sandwiches. But there were none. And he could go no further.[24]

Of course lists of civil service jargon are meant to be amusing—a joke. But they are only a joke to the extent this language is used by the civil service, and it is used. Two examples, courtesy of Martin Stanley's *Mandarin English* (2008*b*), will suffice.

'The Minister was grateful for your submission which he read without comment':

It definitely went in the red box and it definitely came out again. Did they look at it? Search me squire. Usually means that the submission was (a) very dull, (b) on an insignificant subject well below the Ministerial radar, or (c) both.

'Bi-Lateral':

A posh sounding meeting which involves 2 people at a time having a chat, usually involving Ministers/Perm Secs/Senior Officials in their swanky offices. But bilaterals sound so impressive that the purpose of a bilateral is never asked nor is the information often given. The fact that you have no hope of ever attending a bilateral, nor do you really need to know that these meetings ever take place, reminds you that you are not and never likely to have equivalent influence. Bringing ego is essential, otherwise entry is refused.

Most of these jokes are characterized by a political cynicism which, for the most part, I did not encounter. It is the civil service's preferred style of humour; dry and deadpan.

LANGUAGES[25]

Protocols are supported by a distinctive Westminster vocabulary that expresses their beliefs and traditions. One Minister described his Department as 'a different planet with a different language', claiming 'nobody but nobody outside understands about acronyms' (Morrison 1984). Nothing has changed. It is probably the first thing any outsider notices on arriving in a department; they talk in alphabet soup.

I can remember thinking, I am never going to learn all these abbreviations and then within about three weeks you are saying the words. We would generally ask whichever policy team or directorate to bring a note taker just because they know all the abbreviations. [PS, TI]

If you cannot talk acronym you are lost. On my first visit to the Department, I had to ask if there was a list of them because the meeting I had attended was nearly incomprehensible. I had no idea who or what they were talking about. The Diary Secretary earned my undying gratitude by producing one. It was seven pages long! Afterwards I never went to any department without asking for one. They all found one, although it was not necessarily up to date. They had to have it. Even their own kith and kin, when they came from other departments, needed help. However, they need only the acronyms for other organizations. They thought they knew about Keep-in-Touch (KiTs), usually group meetings, and '1:1s' (one-to-one meetings), usually a meeting with one other person. Unfortunately, to make matters even more confusing, there was no consistency. So, a 1:1 could be a KiT in another department!

After the names of organizations come the names of people. Kaufman (1980: 34 and 37) notes the 'strange tribal customs'. He reports that the minister calls the PPS by his first name, and may not know the surname, while the PPS calls the minister, 'Minister'. However, the permanent secretaries will use the minister's first name. In fact, the tribal customs are now much more relaxed. In the private office, most people use first names most of the time. They only slip into the Minister or Permanent Secretary mode of address when at a meeting where 'outsiders' are present. They would also wear a jacket, while they often work in shirtsleeves when back at the private office. Of course, some ministers insist on formality; on being treated as the Queen's Minister. Although I adopted the phrase 'departmental court' to stress the shifting complex of relations at the top of the department, it can seem like a court with some ministers, and the expressions 'holding court' and 'granting an audience' remain all too fitting.

Exploring the language used by the civil service is an exercise in geology. There are historical layers, with the usage of the previous era buried below present-day strata. I will distinguish between the traditional or classical Whitehall language, and managerialism. Of course, neither is monolithic and everyone uses both.

Westminster language

By their nature traditions persist. Many phrases survive from the era when civil servants were administrators, not managers, in itself a signifier of shifting beliefs. As one Permanent Secretary observed waspishly, '*they go out of their way to take pride in their secrecy or coded references and all that*' [Permanent Secretary, TI].

Traditionally permanent secretaries are from 'Oxbridge', a term that refers to the universities of Oxford and Cambridge. There is a long-standing tradition of the civil service recruiting people from fee-paying schools and Oxbridge. It is a clear marker of a middle-class upbringing. It is associated with a specific accent, variously described as plummy or BBC. Words like 'chap' resonate of Oxbridge between the wars and an age I thought long gone. In England, accents and language are always reducible to class. As George Bernard Shaw famously commented, 'it is impossible for an Englishman to open his mouth without making some other Englishman hate him or despise him'. Such stigmata may be less acute today but there are still residues of the earlier era. I was surprised to hear phrases like chaps, who are 'sound' and even echoes of a colonial heritage in 'elephant traps' and 'Sherpas'.[26] There were even references to cocktail parties. They are archaisms, and not the dominant discourse. They are trace elements of an earlier time although some of them, such as probity and 'doing the right thing', are as relevant now as they ever were. Of such older traces, the most common surround homage to the Queen's Minister who has an eye for pomp and circumstance. The minister is a celebrity if not quite royalty (see Chapter 4).

Other terms do not resonate of times gone by. So, civil servants 'clear lines' with ministers, worry about being 'off message', want to go 'with the grain', and avoid 'back-to-back meetings'. I found the best examples of this language in a video made for civil servants about working with ministers. It was made tongue-in-cheek but the key point is that everybody knew the phrases. The video presupposes familiarity with civil service beliefs about ministers. So, the mystique of ministers is impressed on officials. They are told 'to put yourself in the minister's shoes'. Or, more formally, the Cabinet Office's booklet on working with ministers advises, 'while it is helpful if ministers understand the needs of civil servants, it's essential that civil servants understand the needs of ministers' (Jary 2004: 5). You must recognize that 'we are all on the same side'. This advice is mixed up with office folklore; 'get off the phone, you'll get it quicker' and 'everybody sticks their head down and ignores you'. Some care is necessary in decoding some words. Most references to the 'mandarin-ate' had a double meaning. The term refers to the classical generalist civil servant of yore but it also refers to a style of personal behaviour that favours civility and reserve in equal measure (see Chapter 5). Enthusiasm and frankness are seen as gauche (see the earlier discussion of 'politeness'). 'Clever' is another loaded term. It is seen as an essential attribute: *'you've got to be clever, because if you're not clever, and you've got to be as clever as all of them or better, you lack credibility with the best'* [Permanent Secretary, TI]. It has the obvious meaning that someone is intelligent, but it does not refer only to academic ability; *'he is very clever, fabulously clever, in the best sense not just intelligent but clever'* [Permanent Secretary, TI]. For one Permanent Secretary it was a combination of the *'size of his brain and his judgement'* [Permanent Secretary, TI]. When a civil servant says someone is clever, they mean he brings a practical intelligence to bear on an issue when practical refers to savvy or streetwise smarts or, as in this quote, robust in managing the system.

> *He was looking for someone who was bright because he was very clever and who was robust because he was suspicious about the system and whether what he wanted to do was going to be transmitted through the system. I don't know whether my story is true, it may be apocryphal, but he thought he was a difficult person to work with. I found him charming but he was a robust character and he thought he needed somebody who was personally robust.* [Permanent Secretary, TI]

It is also common for civil servants to use indirect language to avoid conflict. So, I came across such phrases as: 'I am reluctant to support'; 'I haven't formed a view yet'; 'I am happy to discuss'; 'you might consider'; and 'you should be aware'. All signify a lack of agreement. Depending on the context, they can suggest more than a mere lack of agreement. There is also an understated vocabulary for mistakes. 'Annoying' is a useful all-purpose word for an omission. 'It must have slipped through when you weren't looking' means 'why don't you know what happened?' The meeting with the Treasury (see Chapter 5, pp. 112–13) was also a fund of under stated, ironic commentary. I have a soft spot for the Treasury's 'we would be grateful for your views', which seemed to be synonymous with 'do as you're told'! And why say 'yes' when you can say 'I'm open to this line of thinking'.

Apart from archaisms like 'chap' and 'elephant traps', I have described the language of the old verities. It is the bedrock of the recurring language games of the departments.

Managerial language

Managerial language abounds, expressing beliefs about the reforms. It is unavoidable. The most common usages include: capacity building, customer, delivery, stakeholders, mission statement, partnership, strategic, vision, and value added. Less common are: process engineering, scoped, champion, trajectories, and civic entrepreneur.[27] David Blunkett (2006: 441) happily conceded, 'They talk the language' but, to his obvious irritation, 'they don't do anything'. That is not accurate. There is much strategic planning, statements of our vision, and glossy mission statements. Here I describe one Department's efforts to embed its management reforms.

Drilling down managerialism

I attended a two-day workshop that sought to build commitment to the Department's business plan and to 'drill' (sometimes 'drive') reform down the hierarchy.[28] It was targeted at the heads of the management units. The event was divided between presentations by senior management followed by small group discussions and report backs. For senior management one of the objectives was to 'celebrate' the 'realistic overall story' of the Department's business plan. I attended the general sessions and moved among the groups with the members of the Department who attended as 'roving reporters'. I provide only a partial report on the event because I have one simple aim, to show that managerialism is both widely used and contested.

The Permanent Secretary's day has got off to a bad start. The newspaper article based around his interview (see Chapter 5, pp. 115–16) has just been published. It is critical of the Department, but not of him. It takes him a while to get over it; 'what a long road we have to travel'. He is unusually quiet amid the cheerful bustle of arrivals, morning coffee, good mornings, and other social chit-chat.

Top management took the event seriously. It was not a jamboree. Senior management had several planning meetings before the event and a lengthy debriefing session afterwards. It was seen as integral to change management in the Department. There was also a coherent message and it centred on three keywords: performance, delivery, and leadership. The documentation was built around this message. Every participant was given a conference notebook, or 'journal', and a ring-binder with all the PowerPoint slides and handouts. Much care and attention had been given to their design. For my academic conferences, the conference notebook only gets elaborate if there is a sponsor in which case we get a cover with a logo. For this event, the journal also contains the outline timetable and, for each group breakout session, it has the questions to be addressed with space for individual and group answers. So, participants are asked to record their 'stories' about positive improvements in performance over the past six to nine months. Then, the group move on to delivery. Again the groups are 'tasked' to 'build the story' and 'add to the story'. It continues in this vein for the 'ownership of operational objectives'; 'bringing the leadership model to life'; and 'managing poor performance'. It is a lexicon of managerialism.

A Minister of State has been sent to show that the political masters support the management reforms. Because it is a Minister of State, rather than the Secretary of State, I wonder if his presence sends the right message; it is a moot point. He attacks 'silos', stresses delivery, leadership, evidence-based policy, and better performance measurement. I talk to the Minister over lunch. He claims to give two types of speeches: this is what we want from you; and what do you want to hear. This morning's speech was in the latter category. So, he is on message. The Permanent Secretary has doubts about one of the DGs, but he did not need to worry. The DG tells me, 'I'm uncomfortable with some of what we are doing but I'm comfortable with what I said this morning.' So, all the key speakers give perorations for change along the right lines. They do not address the issue of how to make it happen and that is what concerns the groups.

If the speakers are on message, the groups are not. They challenge specific objectives. Senior managers are urbane in answering these challenges. Afterwards a DG snaps; 'they are challenging set objectives, they can't do that'. At the report session, the roving reporter comments that the group 'made a constructive and interesting start'. The group howls with laughter. Indisputably the group was argumentative. The group discussions turn to 'how can I change?' The abrupt answers include, 'say "no" more often'; and 'the minimum'. They talk about finding 'real resources' to support change. There is a grumbling tone to many of the group meetings. They want senior management to 'walk it not spout it'.

Through the day, the Permanent Secretary became increasingly impatient with the discussions. He lectures the facilitator for the reporting sessions about getting the groups back on message. He stands at the back and paces. When he sits still, he taps one foot on the ground continuously. His body language expresses frustration and impatience. When I talk to him he is almost vehement when he says 'we have to know how to drill it down'; and 'by the end of the year we have to know the story'. He thinks the groups were too focused on process and there was a lack of action points. Then he returns to the newspaper article, which still rankles with him; 'we volunteered it so we shot ourselves in the foot'.

On the second day, the facilitator provided a summary of where the middle-level managers had got to and off we go. I begin to spot slogans in the presentations and the discussions; 'partnership, not turf war'; 'the vision thing—it's so powerful'. The groups are more puzzled than querulous on the second day. They ask straightforward but hard questions; 'what do you want to drill down?' At the summary session for the first day's end, the facilitator said emotional intelligence would be a key topic for the second day. 'I can't wait' was my first thought. The group I attended had nothing to say on the subject. They comment, 'what you are talking about does not affect me'. Their problems are more prosaic. They are not convinced they are leaders and, if they are leaders, they don't think they have been given permission to lead. They see internal communication as the biggest problem and want top management to talk with the lower levels more often; 'staff might value you more if you represented them'. On performance measurement, they want specific suggestions about what they should do, starting with 'clear measurable objectives'.

I note the DGs are networking with one another, not with the middle-level managers. They skip group sessions to discuss performance measurement. The tough–tender divide returns over 'making space' (see Chapter 5, p. 113). There is a clear but unstated assumption that too many middle-level managers are not good enough and we need to get rid of them. The DGs are concerned that the reforms have not been drilled down anywhere near far enough. They fear they have not 'engaged' with the middle-level managers. Some of these managers agree—they have voted with their feet and left early. Those who stayed now confront the question of 'what am I going to do to push this forward?' Everyone faces a colleague and tells him or her which two things I will leave behind and which two things I will embrace. There is much hilarity but many sensible answers. So, one manager will stop thinking why things can't be done. Another will support his team and say thank you.

At the debriefing session the following day, the DGs and the Permanent Secretary agree some basic questions need to be answered such as 'what is the story?' and 'have we got the right people?' There are some pat clichés about the importance of praise and the need to be ruthless about failure. Somewhat to my bemusement there is talk of 'getting to grips with emotional intelligence'. I think they mean they need better communication with the middle-level managers. Whatever it means they are going to 'stop pussyfooting' and make 'painful decisions'. Goethe is paraphrased: 'boldness has a genius and madness to it'. They agree they have taken an important step forward; 'we are on the road'.

I attended, even ran, such away days as a university manager. I recognize they are about getting everyone on-side; about a shared understanding of what we are doing, and where we are going. It is present-day best practice in team management. And that is the point of this example. The event itself exemplifies managerialism before even considering the language. And the language is what you would expect. The keywords were delivery, performance, leadership, and a touch of emotional intelligence. Even the gap between senior- and middle-level management was entirely predictable. The most relevant point is that the middle-level managers talked the language of managerialism in criticizing the reforms. They did not reject performance measurement but asked for clear, operational objectives. They wanted better managerialism!

This message was common to all the departments. As we saw in Chapter 2, delivery was the new mantra of the Blair government in its second parliament. The message was carried forth by the Treasury (see Chapter 5, pp. 112–13). It was perhaps most prominent at DfES, which had a major service to deliver, and was the initial home of the guru of 'deliverology', Michael Barber. Performance measurement was also ubiquitous as were its problems. One Permanent Secretary remembered that '*I had targets to deliver but I had no sense that the appraisal was about that . . . my annual appraisal didn't seem to be as much about the delivery of those formal targets as it is now*' [Permanent Secretary, TI]. All three departments laid less emphasis on measuring performance than on a qualitative assessment. Targets and appraisal were part of everyday vocabulary but the practice of measurement lagged some way behind. As one Management Board observed in its comments on the Department's business plan: 'you don't have the metrics in place to measure progress'; 'detailed action plans are missing'; 'get some measures and learn as you go along'; and 'there is too much waffle, too much wooliness, it needs to be crisp, more precise'.

Or as one PPS observed:

> We've got away from inputs but we're still stuck a bit on outputs so I think that what I have seen is not so much a shift from policy to delivery, because I don't understand that language, but it is a growing awareness of the requirement for us to focus on outcomes. [PPS, TI]

Others mock managerial language. One PS talked about challenges, ventilating, and forward posture in a parody of the language. He is mocking, but he knows the language is widely used otherwise there is nothing to mock. Others are 'off message'. Some brave spirits rail against jargon but fail to understand its core functions are to demonstrate that one is an 'insider' who is 'on-side'. For example, Jary's (2004: 63–4) booklet on working with ministers, published by the Cabinet Office, lists jargon words, many of which are the everyday language of managerialism. Among the 'words and phrases to avoid' are such staples as customer, delivery, stakeholders, and partnership, to name but a few. A critical interpretation of these judgements would be to class him as an opponent of managerial reform of the civil service. A more sympathetic interpretation would note his preference for the traditional Whitehall ways of speaking. Whichever interpretation is preferred, it seems odd for the Cabinet Office to undermine management reform in this way. The British civil service has managerialism but not as the textbooks know it.

CONCLUSIONS

In this chapter, I have argued that administrative protocols of the departmental court lie at the heart of the willed ordinariness of everyday life in government departments. I have documented, probably in exhausting if not exhaustive detail, the role of such coping practices as: the diary; the red box; telephone; correspondence and filing; travel and hospitality (including drivers); meetings, committees, and briefings; submissions and policy advice; speeches; and secrecy. I have also documented the role of such rituals as politeness, gossip, and humour in coping. Such practices may flounder when dealing with a rude surprise (see Chapter 9) but for your everyday political and administrative ups and downs they are the tried and most important trusted tools. Earlier chapters also documented coping beliefs and practices. This chapter has shown how such beliefs are embedded in everyday life. I will draw together this description of coping and explore the implications for our understanding of British government in Chapter 10. Here, I want to highlight the dilemmas confronted by those running a government department when the traditional beliefs and practices of the departmental court have to adjust to the beliefs and practices of managerialism.

Beliefs, practices, and dilemmas

Dilemmas arise when a new idea stands in opposition to existing beliefs or practices. In Chapter 2, I identified three dilemmas: between the classical Westminster roles of ministers and permanent secretaries and managerialism; between constitutional bureaucracy and political responsiveness; and between the neo-liberal policy agenda and departmental philosophies. I also noted that there were three strands to managerialism: performance management, marketization, and delivery. Each set of ideas posed dilemmas for civil servants because each had unintended consequences; namely, responsiveness and performance measurement, reform and the loss of institutional memory, and delivery and indirect steering. I discussed responsiveness in Chapter 5. I will discuss the dilemmas posed by steering in Chapter 8. Here I focus on performance measurement and the loss of institutional memory. Finally, I highlight the importance of language, of being multilingual, in coping with the dilemmas of managerial reform.

Performance measurement

Donald Schon (1973: ch. 2) used the phrase dynamic conservatism to refer to the active resistance to change. Theakston (1999: 255–6) sees permanent secretaries as administrative conservers or guardians of the institutions, values, and staff of the public service. The permanent secretaries in my three departments were 'dynamic conservers'.[29] They preserved institutional memory, integrity, impartiality, and the risk-averse tradition that seeks to protect the minister. Sir Robin Butler (1995) former Head of the Home Civil Service was explicit on the point:

> We should remind ourselves there are some important elements which have not changed and should not change. In this country there remains widespread agreement on the value of maintaining a civil service based on the key principles of political impartiality, accountability through ministers to Parliament, objectivity, integrity and recruitment and promotion on merit.

So, management reforms were filtered through inherited traditions and their practices. They were adapted to local circumstances, and many struggled to implement management reforms.

Ministers and senior civil servants are still trying to rule in terms defined by the Westminster tradition and the departmental court. They also seek the alleged efficiencies of managerial rationalities. All kinds of civil servants struggle with the dilemma of combining these competing demands, often moderating even resisting the imperatives of managerialism. The new managerial rationalities only changed some office practices and the work of some senior managers. Implementation was patchy, with a gap between senior- and middle-level management with the latter feeling the reforms applied to everybody but top management.

For one PS, the absence of targets was a result of a heavy workload. She simply did not have time to conduct the performance appraisals because the work of the Minister and the Permanent Secretary always came first. Middle-level management talked the language of managerialism. They did not reject performance measurement. They knew targets were used by senior management to control them. But they did criticize its implementation; they wanted clear, relevant operational objectives or better managerialism. For one DG, targets influenced his behaviour but they formed but a small part of his appraisal. The main effect on senior management was a greater workload because they were now explicitly office managers. They devised and ran formal appraisal systems. The PPS now had twin-track training that combined manager and mandarin. He also had a dual responsibility to political management for the Minister and to the canons of the new managerialism. The unintended consequences of this combination were a culture of long hours, high staff turnover, and stress. Managerial rationalities were experienced as control, not, as is sometimes claimed, greater managerial freedom.[30]

The loss of institutional memory

Constitutional bureaucracy, or a professional, non-partisan, anonymous, permanent public service, is a core set of beliefs of the Westminster narrative. Thus, permanent civil servants have time on their side; they can remember yesterday's snags. They know what goes around comes around. But managerial reforms with its endless departmental reorganizations, recruitment from the private sector and elsewhere in the public sector, and rapid turnover of staff all erode institutional memory. For example, in 2004, outsiders accounted for 18.7 per cent of the senior civil service with 6 of 29 permanent secretaries from outside the ranks of the senior civil service (Levitt and Solesbury 2004: 19). It is little surprise that insiders and outsiders alike worried that the collective memory was:

> so short, and the departmental records are so poor, that you end up in a situation where only a handful of people ever remember what has been said or done... people deal only with the instant they are living in, rather than drawing on any kind of history or knowledge of the detail and background to a particular issue. (Blunkett 2006: 424; see also Lodge and Rogers 2006: 39)

I visited one office that had a nigh 100 per cent turnover of staff in recent months. There was one exception; the clerical officer responsible for the files. By default, she became the office's institutional memory. If anyone wanted to know what had been done before, she could find the relevant file and embellish its sparse account with her memories of who was around at the time. It was a salutary reminder of the need to preserve institutional memory and that one person's filing system is another person's maze. As is ever the case, institutional memory is most appreciated in its absence. One Minister observed that his portfolio '*did not exist before and some of the issues I'm dealing with there were no people doing that work, at ministerial or any other level [so] everybody is pretty stretched*' [Minister, TI]. There was no memory to fall back on, and it was a problem.

Language games

The problem with simple categories like the Westminster and managerial stories is they squeeze the social world into artificial boxes. I was discussing the language of the civil service with a PPS. His views were sophisticated and reminded the interviewer never to underestimate the interviewee. He said:

> *I've often thought that the sort of thing that sets senior people apart from not so senior people is their ability to use language; to always have a story for something that's happening.* [PPS, TI]

He then gave an example of such skill in language games.

> *I remember in one of my postings, stuff would happen and I wouldn't know what the hell to do about it. I would think 'Oh, bloody hell, it's a disaster. I'll go and see one of my bosses.'*
>
> *I'd say, 'It's terrible. I don't know what I'm going to do.'*
>
> *He would say to me 'Yes, yes, you're right'. And then he would come up with an anecdote. They would always end with, 'And then I realized that I was in Bulgaria and I didn't have any trousers.'*
>
> *I'd look at him and I'd think, right! But the point is that he had been to this place before in 1973. So, there is a sense in which that story is critical.*
>
> *I think the web, which I'm talking about being in the middle of, is a little bit like a language game and it only has meaning insofar as people use it and to ask for the meaning of it is to miss the point, rather ask for the use instead. We use words to go where we're going and that's what this web is. It's a web of—is it a web of words? I don't know, but it's a web of relationships.* [PPS, TI]

I consider these remarks an insightful account of much of the life of a PPS; it is a web of words embedded in a web of relationships. I have an equivalent example, this time from two retired permanent secretaries. In a discussion of the interpretive approach during a paper I presented at the Public Records Office, they commented as follows. 'Postmodernism is only a posh way of saying what Henry Ford said: history is bunk! I remember coming to this conclusion when I was the PPS at No. 10. You could not give an accurate account of 24 hours there, especially at times of crisis (that is, most days). It was a painful re-education of an Oxford educated history student.' And, more succinctly: 'It seems like chaos. We impose some order for the Minister but it is so arbitrary.' The language game is integral to imposing order.

NOTES

1. This chapter draws on all the FWNBs. Also, many protocols are written down in induction packs and equivalent internal departmental documentation. Of the publicly available sources, Jary 2004; and Martin Stanley's website 'How to be a civil servant'

at http://www.civilservant.org.uk/ are useful. Martin Stanley was the Chief Executive of the Competition Commission who joined the civil service in 1971. His advice to aspiring civil servants codifies many a protocol with a welcome leavening of humour. I last visited his website on 6 October 2009.

2. See, for example, the DVD entitled: *Just One of those Days: A Day in the Life of a Fictitious Minister*. London: National School of Government, 2009.

3. In Goodin's (1980: 167–72) terms, they are 'schematising rituals' that both construct social reality and foreclose debate on potential conflicts. See also Kertzer 1988.

4. On the diary see also, for example: Blunkett 2006: 82 and 271; and Kaufman 1980: 39; and Stanley 2008: 5.

5. Indeed Jary (2004: 6) stresses that 'Ministers are human' and urges the Private Office to be 'sympathetic to the sacrifices ministers and their families are often making'.

6. On the red box see, for example: Henderson 2001: 96–7 and 189–90; James 1999: 34–5; Jary 2004: 18; Kaufman 1980: 37 and 40–1; and Stanley 2008*a*: 5.

7. On correspondence see, for example: Blunkett 2006: 14, 41, 84, 168, 374, 455, and 803; Henderson 2001: 87–8, 105, 106, 107, and 193; James 1999: 40; Jary 2004: ch. 4; Kaufman 1980: 40 and 43–5; Page and Jenkins 2005: 86; Stanley 2008*a*: 5; and Theakston 1987: 117.

8. See, for example, *MPST Correspondence Best Practice and Desk Instructions* (DTI, 10 April 2003). Such manuals are updated regularly. See also: Jary (2004: chs 4–6) on writing letters, answering PQs, and preparing speeches. Stanley (2008) also offers general advice on correspondence and speeches. Both are civil servants writing for civil servants.

9. *Postman Pat* was an animated children's TV series of the 1980s. Pat, and his 'black and white cat' Jess, deliver the post in Greendale and help the villagers with their problems. For any parent who watched the series regularly with their children, the theme tune became particularly irritating.

10. Similarly for mail, the PPS would open a typed letter marked confidential but not a handwritten one [FWNB].

11. Donoughue 2003: 338–9 claims his shabby vehicle—'MAFF trashcan'—betokens the lack of respect for ministers and all who work in public life. I am no aficionado of automobiles—watching *Top Gear* is purgatory—but they looked like decent limousines to me, not old bangers.

12. On meetings see, for example: Blunkett 2006: 34–5 and 99; Jary 2004: ch. 3; Kaufman 1980: 46–7; and Stanley 2008*a*: 4 and 19–20.

13. Jary 2004: 21 also adds information (or updating) briefs, and question and answer briefs. He also provides advice on how to write briefings in chapter 3. See also Stanley 2008*a*.

14. For a survey of the literature on small groups see: Levine and Moreland 1998; and Burke 2003. Small group research, especially on intra-group roles, has declined since its heyday in the 1950s. Much was of marginal relevance for my work because these experimental groups are made up of strangers, commonly carrying out trivial tasks, for a short time, and in an artificial laboratory environment. The early classics in political science are probably Wheare 1955; and Barber 1996. See also Chapter 9 below on siege mentality.

15. Personal communications, 8 August 2009.

16. A cephalopod is, of course, an octopus. The Diary Secretary refused to explain why it applied to the individual. The tempting explanation is that the individual had little

control over his many, wandering arms. Penelope Pitstop is a cartoon character in *Wacky Races*, and the archetypal damsel in distress always calling for help. French and Saunders are Dawn French and Jennifer Saunders, a British comedy duo with several hit series to their credit, both together and solo.

17. On advice to ministers see: Henderson 2001: 162–3, 165, and 168; Jary 2004: ch. 3; Page and Jenkins 2005: 72–4; and Stanley 2008a: 4, 8, 9, and 16–17. Many ministers have recorded their policy disagreements with civil servants from Tony Benn, Richard Crossman, and Barbara Castle to Michael Heseltine and Margaret Thatcher. Latterly, see: Blunkett 2006: 342, 344, 354, 355–6, and 41.

18. See: Jary 2004: 13, 21, and 23. He provides a template for a submission on p. 27. See also Stanley 2008a: 5, 7, and 8, and on drafting a submission see: 17–18.

19. Malcolm Rifkind was Minister of State for Europe (1983–6); Secretary of State for Scotland (1986–90); Secretary of State for Transport (1990–2); Secretary of State for Defence (1992–5); and Foreign Secretary (1995–7).

20. The contrast between Australia and Britain is sharp and nowhere more obvious than in the behaviour of senior politicians whose public language can be summed up, at best, as 'choice'. There is a banana-shaped book of Prime Minister Paul Keating's (1992) insults in which a journalist is described as a 'cane toad', the National Party as 'putrid barnyard bullies', and the leader of the opposition as 'a mangy maggot' and, famously, as 'a shiver looking for a spine'. He appears positively mild compared with the former leader of the Labor Party, Mark Latham (2005), whose invective encompassed describing a conservative journalist as a 'skanky ho' and Prime Minister Howard's cabinet as 'a conga line of suckholes'. Such language is not deployed by parliamentarians or civil servants in Britain.

21. Personal communication, 8 August 2009.

22. *The Thick of It* (2005) is a BBC comedy series seen by some as a successor to *Yes Minister*. The focus is on the work of the spin doctors and political advisers and the struggles between them and civil servants and between the departments and No. 10. The central character is Malcolm Tucker, who is short tempered and foulmouthed. He is a caricature of Alastair Campbell. The series was aired after I completed the fieldwork so it was not part of the Whitehall lexicon during my fieldwork.

23. Peter Hyman was a personal friend of Peter Mandelson, speech writer for Tony Blair, and former Head of Communications at No. 10.

24. Personal communication, 9 August 2009.

25. On the languages of Whitehall see, for example: Blunkett 2006: 153, 210, 441, and 519; Denham 2002: 208; Henderson 2001: 161; and Kaufman 1980: 34–5, 37, and 44. Although I focus on the Westminster and managerial languages, they are not the only ones. The civil service employs several professional groups with their own technical language and the territorial offices of Scotland, Wales, and Northern Ireland also have their own variations.

26. Sherpas are civil servants who go ahead of a summit meeting to prepare the ground. The work covers the logistics of any meeting, the agenda, and supporting documentation.

27. There are also genuine oddities like 'grazing with the private sector'. I had to be careful to distinguish managerial language from today's buzzwords. For example, 'challenge' kept cropping up and I wondered if it too had managerial connotations. I decide not. It was just today's buzzword like 'nurdish', which was used regularly at one committee meeting about anyone who raised a detailed point. It was never so used again. Challenge also disappeared.

28. This section is based on my FWNB and the workshop documentation.
29. Successive heads of the Home Civil Service explicitly saw conservation as part of their leadership role. For examples, see: Cabinet office 1994 and 1999c; Butler 1993; and Wilson 2003.
30. For general critiques of managerialism as a tool for measuring and controlling performance see: Dean 2007: ch. 2; Miller and Rose 2008: ch. 3; Power 1994; and Travers 2007: ch. 7.

8

Networks and Governance

So far, I have focused on the traditional Westminster story about British government and the challenge from managerial and market reforms of the past two decades. In this chapter, I focus on the governance story; on the horizontal and vertical networks that criss-cross Westminster, Whitehall, and beyond. The core argument is that interdependence adds yet another dilemma to be managed by ministers and civil servants. This time the dilemma is between the departmental way of doing business, and its associated departmental philosophy, and network governance, or working with and through a multiplicity of other actors who deliver services. Ministers and civil servants understand this shift to working with and through networks. For example, when asked what he understood by the term 'governance', David Blunkett replied that it meant 'the plurality of different agencies and public delivery mechanisms that have changed the way that particular aspects of our life are dealt with'.[1] So, governance is not just an example of academic analysis. Every department is part of a web of links encompassing: the central agencies (the Treasury, No. 10, and the Cabinet Office); other functional departments; parliament and the political parties; and broader links beyond Westminster and Whitehall. Individuals know they are part of a web and deliberately build links, play games, and otherwise manage their dependence on one another.

CENTRAL AGENCIES

I sat in on five meetings between the departments, No. 10, and the Treasury.[2] The Treasury commanded the meetings it attended. The departments rehearsed their answers for anticipated Treasury questions. They waited in nervous anticipation. No. 10 was received politely and in a much more relaxed atmosphere. It is too sharp a distinction to say the Treasury had levers of control and could command, while No. 10 had mainly the power to persuade, but it captures an important difference. The Cabinet Office was the junior partner in the central troika. For all these central agencies, contacts focused on the secretary of state and his top officials (see also Chapter 4: p. 80 and Chapter 5: pp. 114–15).

The Treasury

The Treasury was seen as '*a very controlling department, and more so than I remembered it from the 1970s*' [Minister, TI]. It was said to have '*a laddish culture*' [Minister, TI]. And the relationship was often adversarial:

> *Daggers drawn, it's a thoroughly unpleasant exercise, bullying, there was no meeting of minds at all. So I just used to stand our corner but the trouble was when I got there, the spending round had been decided.* [Minister, TI]

The Treasury's view sometimes prompted much mirth. When the Chief Secretary told a meeting, 'We are the Treasury and we are here to help you', his remarks were greeted with gales of laughter [FWNB], although a more common reaction was irritation. One Permanent Secretary complained to the Treasury about a 50-page paper that was littered with mistakes. The Treasury sent it five days before the meeting, which was 'too little notice' and 'made us negative and defensive' [FWNB].

Ministers of state were involved only on occasions; as one confessed, he was '*below the radar screen*' [Minister, TI]. Another commented '*most secretaries of state keep fairly tight hold*' on dealings with the Treasury [Minister, TI]. Another correctly observed there wasn't '*a great deal of traffic directly between me and the Treasury*'. Rather, '*most of it goes through officials*' [Minister, TI].

Departmental officials spend much time and effort preparing for their contacts. Depending on the topic, there were mock 'question and answer' sessions to rehearse presentations [FWNB]. One Principal Private Secretary (PPS) was critical of the caricature that the Treasury is clever, humourless, and arrogant. He insisted there '*are very good one-on-one relationships in lots of areas*'. He talked to the Treasury's PPS and he felt:

> *comfortable talking to special advisers. The special advisers at the Treasury are very powerful. In a sense they're more like junior ministers, but I would talk to them, and we have.*

Also part of the problem was with the Department:

> *The problem with the Treasury is they sit around and they have a chat in the Chancellor's room like this and they say 'Well, issue X is important.' A day later they've got like a hit squad that's out there and they're all over it. They're all over it, you know, whereas we spend months ruminating about these bloody things, you know, before we decide to put it to paper. We've got to be quicker and we've been looking at that, about moving to projects, about getting ourselves so we can respond*

much more quickly than we used to. But I would like to see the Treasury versus other's walls completely broken down. [PPS, TI]

There were constraints on the relationship. So, *'some fixed political relationships are difficult to cha*nge'; an allusion to the Blair–Brown divide and attendant 'TeeBee-GeeBees'. Also:

The nature of the purse strings [means] departments tend to be a little bit more structured in their relations with the Treasury. So our finance people lead on the relationship because we don't want every Tom, Dick, and Harry talking to someone at the Treasury about how good it would be if we had a bit more money. That would be a disaster. [PPS, TI]

I attended one session at which the Permanent Secretary and a Treasury spokesperson were negotiating Public Service Agreement (PSA) targets [FWNB]. The Permanent Secretary wanted to review his department's existing targets. He thought they were 'aspirational' and he wanted 'management' targets. Also the cross-cutting targets, which covered more than one unit, 'didn't work' and some of the cost data were 'bizarre'. The reply from the Treasury spokesperson is 'give us an overall strategy and we can free up controls'. He also reminds the Permanent Secretary that they have 'held money back' from departments that were not up to the mark. The Permanent Secretary is not put off. He wants broad cash ceilings and he argues against detailed ring fenced allocations. It is a vigorous to and fro. 'It's all paper, paper, paper' says the Permanent Secretary. The process is 'directive, detailed, bureaucratic'. I think, 'where have I heard that before?' It was said at the last meeting with the Treasury I attended with a different Permanent Secretary. The Treasury replies that no one is specifying, but 'trying to identify blocks that you can use'. I see little signs of progress. 'Look upon it as customer feedback', says the Permanent Secretary. 'Useful' replies the Treasury spokesperson, as he leaves. When he has gone, the Permanent Secretary says to me, 'What was that about?' I have no idea. It looked to me like the gaming that surrounds most systems of performance indicators; another round in the game. I know the Treasury will win. So does the Permanent Secretary, but he might get some concessions if he persists. He persisted. He was not pleased at the outcome: 'we are bruised and furious'.

There is ambivalence running through these snatches of dialogue and scenes. The PPS started out criticizing the Treasury's image. But at various junctures he admits the Treasury needs *'to address what signals they want to send'* and confesses *'we are on the back foot, timid, slow, lambs to the slaughter very often'*. For all that he insists, betraying his business school training, that the relationship must change: *'you cannot have a networked organisation where you have those sorts of dynamics. You've got to fix that'* [PPS, TI].

Others were less reticent about the Treasury.

There were moments that are unbeatable, you know, when something goes right. I can remember the last rows with the Treasury. I love the [Chancellor] and [the Secretary of State] on the phone to one another. You get to listen in and you hear [the Secretary of State] 'kick-ass' with him. And [the Secretary of State] comes out and goes, 'Right get those words over to him. You send them over.' And the great thing is the PSs go into theatrical mode. So [the PS] over at the Treasury, he is then the Chancellor, and I am then [the Secretary of State]. You have these phone conversations and you are horrible to each other in this diplomatic way. It hones your skills. You know you have to do the diplomatic thing and there is a real thrill to it. There is a real absolute thrill. [PS, TI]

One Permanent Secretary acidly observed the Treasury had religion but the trouble was the religion kept changing and they believed the new one as fervently as the old one. As one Diary Secretary observed of her Permanent Secretary:

The only time I have ever heard [the Permanent Secretary] swear and use the 'f' word was when the Treasury tried to screw us on something. [DS, TI]

For most, however, the emphasis falls on cultivating an informal relationship:

The team leader in the Treasury on this Department used to work with me in the [Cabinet Office]. So we have an informal line where we just chat about things and I have quarterly get-togethers with him and his boss. Every three months or so, not looking at the kind of usual day-to-day discussion of the Treasury, but standing back and having an hour on how the Department is going, what I see as the priority issues, and what it looks like for them, and that is useful. [Permanent Secretary, TI]

So, the relationship with the Treasury is adversarial and networked, formal and informal, cooperative and competitive, trusting and fearful. Much hinges on the politics of the day. The departments' stances are streaked with ambivalence.

No. 10

I did not attend a meeting at No. 10 Downing Street, although I attended several meetings where No. 10 special advisers (SpAds) were present. They were 'selling' the delivery agenda even when they were not from the Delivery Unit. Without exception they presented themselves as the authority on what the Prime Minister—invariably, 'Tony'—wanted: 'we are learning'. A good PPS would avoid appearing so ministerial. Phrases like, 'it is an opportunity to tell the PM what you need him to do' were common. One declaimed the visit was 'not just a threat'. I could see no evidence that the assembled officials saw him as such. Some SpAds were too impressed with themselves (and see Blunkett 2006: 275). The counter was some sardonic wit; 'a brilliant delivery strategy, but there's no policy' [FWNB].

The links with No. 10 were frequent and demanding. Whether a minister has regular direct contact with No. 10 depends on his or her personal standing, the priority accorded the department's policy, and current political circumstances. On occasion there is a breakdown of trust; *'the Prime Minister probably didn't fully trust the Department'* [Permanent Secretary, TI]. Beyond the prime minister losing interest and your minister slipping down the pecking order, which matters greatly to him, there did not seem to be many costs attached to a loss of favour. All too often, the costs arose when No. 10 was interested. It often meant that something had gone wrong; firefighting was, and remains, a way of life for them. I revisit firefighting in Chapter 9. There were more routine contacts. One of the striking innovations was the policy stocktake.

Stocktakes

As I described in Chapter 2 (pp. 27–9), the Prime Minister had four priority policy areas in the second term: crime, education, health, and transport. Each department had a regular stocktaking session roughly every two months with the Prime Minister to explain the progress made towards their targets. It was a major event and the departmental team would be led by the secretary of state.

> We'd be absolutely clear which bits we were leading on. So [the Secretary of State] would say, 'You have the main bit for that.' At stocktakes [the Secretary of State] took much more control. He wasn't that great at letting you get a word in at stocktakes. [Minister, TI]

I attended departmental briefing and debriefing sessions for a stocktake. They had prepared carefully. Before the meeting, the Secretary of State wrote the Prime Minister a stocktaking letter identifying the issues to be discussed. The small departmental team comprised the Secretary of State, the relevant Minister of State, the Permanent Secretary, and the relevant director general (DG). The Prime Minister was supported by Andrew Adonis (Policy Directorate), Michael Barber (Delivery Unit), and Andrew Turnbull (Cabinet Secretary). The meetings lasted about an hour. Each side made a five-minute presentation (Barber 2007: 91–6).

The discussion was not a chat or a briefing. The Prime Minister had committed himself publicly to improvements. He wanted hard evidence that there were improvements. If it could not be provided, then the Delivery Unit would be despatched to the Department. The Permanent Secretary was content with the DG's presentation, but Michael Barber's data showed that performance had not improved greatly. The Prime Minister was 'engaged' and 'nice' but concerned. He gave them a lecture on 'taking a grip'; he was 'focused and stone faced'. His team raised other issues, about reducing bureaucracy (Adonis) and leadership (Barber), but discussion was desultory.

The stocktakes were taken seriously in the departments. Permanent secretaries received delivery reports that ranked their performance. Barber (2007: 118) records that some permanent secretaries were 'edgy' and felt he had been 'too negative', while ministers were 'nervous about the Delivery Unit and indeed about No. 10 as a whole'. Nonetheless, they were ready 'to engage with the process'. There were follow-up meetings with Barber to identify the lessons to be learnt. The Permanent Secretary agrees:

> *the Delivery Unit and all that is a big part of my life, you know, the actual delivery of the four priorities that the Prime Minister has given us, the reviews of the Prime Minister every six weeks, and all that stuff is very, very real and I need to be very focused.* [Permanent Secretary, TI]

The departmental debriefing also confirmed Barber's views. The Permanent Secretary reported, 'we survived', 'we got away with it', although the data showed little improvement. He was 'uncomfortable' with this result; 'I don't want to be here again'. He insisted, 'we must return to this issue regularly'. It was an 'implementation issue' and we must focus on the weak links; for example, the weaker schools and replacing their heads if necessary. In an exasperated tone, he posed the rhetorical question, 'who knows the names of these schools and if they have a plan?' No one knew the schools' names. They all knew the schools did not have plans. With heavy emphasis he tells his team, 'we'll only get one more shot'. The key task is to persuade Andrew Adonis and Wendy Thompson (OPSR), otherwise 'the PM won't believe us'. Although everyone is 'disappointed', the debriefing is upbeat, relaxed, and chatty. They feared worse. The Permanent Secretary does not rant or upbraid his colleagues. He is just clear and firm; 'failing schools must be targeted'.

To this professional stranger, the stocktake was notable for several reasons. It clearly demonstrated the Prime Minister's commitment to these four policy areas (see Blair 2010a: 338–9). To find time in his diary for an hourly meeting with each department every two months was a major commitment of prime ministerial time. It concentrated the minds of the departments wonderfully. As the Iraq war came to dominate the political agenda, the stocktakes went ahead without the Prime Minister or, if he came, he had not read the brief and appeared distracted (Barber 2007: 205 and 243–4). But for a time, they were an effective way of showing a department they were on the Prime Minister's radar. They kept a department focused on prime ministerial priorities, and helped it to sort problems with the Prime Minister's support (and see Blunkett 2006: 292). Stocktakes highlighted the central role of No. 10's SpAds. Both Michael Barber and Andrew Adonis were enmeshed in departmental policy and its implementation. Finally, the effectiveness of the links depended on the degree of trust. Michael Barber was respected in the Department for Education and Skills (DfES). When he spoke, the Department listened. I sat in on one meeting with him separate from the stocktake on measuring the performance of schools. It was a meeting of old colleagues, swapping stories and ideas on diverse topics from the A-level crisis (see Chapter 9) to removing ineffective school heads and measuring transformational leadership. Andrew Adonis did not command the same degree of trust or attention in the Department (see Chapter 9).

No. 10's SpAds

For many ministers, No. 10 was seen as an *'incestuous place'* revolving around *'Tony's inner circle'* [Minister, TI]. With the proliferation of special units and increasing numbers of SpAds, it was called a 'department' by the departments [FWNB]. For most departments, No. 10's SpAds were the most conspicuous members of the prime ministerial department or court. They played a prominent role in linking departments to No. 10 and the Treasury. They attracted criticism. John Prescott[3] 'railed' against No. 10's special advisers; he called them 'teeny-boppers' (*The Times*, 8 July 1999) and the 'beautiful people'. With obvious irritation, he records:

> They used to ring up and say 'Number Ten here', and I would say, 'No you're not, you're just Jo Bloggs. Tony's Number Ten'. Then I'd hang up. (Prescott 2008: 256)

Other ministers were more accommodating and officials had little choice; what No. 10 wants, No. 10 gets.

It is a matter of public record that Andrew Adonis and Michael Barber had close links with, and much influence on policy at, DfES (see Barber 2007: 54)

PERMANENT SECRETARY: No. 10 are very powerful in education policy and the special adviser there, Andrew Adonis, is a significant influence and you will, we will often consult him. Clearing policy isn't quite, doesn't always work like that but there is a quite a lot of exchange with him about policies we are thinking about and so on, so it's a two-way thing, it's a lot of things coming from him on behalf of the Prime Minister. The working relationship is close.
RAWR: Who would contact Adonis to check that he was 'on-side' or discuss with him?
PERMANENT SECRETARY: Well.
RAWR: Would you do it?
PERMANENT SECRETARY: I might, I used to, as Head of Schools Directorate, have a monthly discussion, a regular monthly discussion with Andrew Adonis where we reviewed the whole area of policy. But the main contacts would be Michael Barber on the schools policy, a major conduit, and probably Connor Ryan on sort of presentational type issues. Lots of contacts between ministers and junior ministers and Andrew Adonis. But yes there was, we used to have, I mean officials met Andrew and meet Andrew still. Quite a bit of the policy was developed around a table with a mixture of special advisers and civil servants. The Teachers' Green Paper was all done that way. Andrew Adonis was at that table for the Teachers' Green Paper and Estelle chaired the meetings, and she, and I were there and Michael Barber and some of our teachers group officials and Andrew

Adonis.[4] *And together we were developing the policy, it was a good example of, that was perhaps the best example of, us working out the policy with all the relevant people around the table.*

RAWR: Now my understanding is that it is relatively new, relatively unusual, for No. 10 to be treated as a stakeholder in policy in that way?

PERMANENT SECRETARY: I think that is probably a bit beyond anything that has been, that has happened before. I can think of examples of that happening under the Conservatives but it happens much more often, it's a more normal part of the process. It's changed again since the election because, we, in a sense, they have merged the old Private Office of No. 10 with the Policy Unit, so that Andrew Adonis and his colleagues play both roles now, they are both the Private Office contact, in the sense, the Prime Minister's office contact for the conduct of business and they are the policy adviser at No. 10 as well. They are doing both of those roles. Whereas often those roles, in the past, have been split, there were civil servants who managed the progress of business, and there were policy advisers, special advisers, who were inputting into the policy process at various points. And that was easy for the civil service because there were people you deal with who were civil servants. Now it's muddled up so, it's you know, there is, and that's a No. 10 change, so there is a, a merging of roles and therefore that means that civil servants need to deal with people at No. 10 who are special advisers because they are also managing the process of business. [Permanent Secretary, TI]

In this extract from the transcript, I have left out the hesitations by the Permanent Secretary to make the text more readable. However, when reviewing the transcript, the Permanent Secretary agreed with me that these hesitations showed he was reluctant to concede too great a role to No. 10.

Not everybody wanted to play the SpAds game:

RAWR: So it is you talking direct to the special adviser over there?

MINISTER: It is, although it may be through our special advisers as well.

RAWR: A number of people have told me that in fact it is quite common practice now to clear policy initiatives and especially publicity for policy informally by talking to somebody at No.10. Do you do that?

MINISTER: I don't normally, no. [Minister, TI]

For this Minister, it was no big deal. He talked to them if he judged it necessary, but that wasn't often. Other ministers had a stronger aversion:

RAWR: Is there any informal contact in terms of picking up the telephone and talking to anyone at No. 10?

MINISTER: No. Wouldn't do that.

RAWR: Why do you say you wouldn't do? Because I know other people do.

MINISTER: It's not my style. Not secure enough to do it. Don't think you should. Not quite secure. Know [the Permanent Secretary] does it any way so why do they need the two. What can I say? Why am I ringing them? If I am asking a question it wasn't often

that they could answer it for me. I'd ring Michael Barber constantly, constantly. I'd occasionally ring Andrew. But not much. I didn't need to. That's the way my job was. [Telephone rings]
RAWR: I understand. Just forgive me for pressing slightly. Certainly some colleagues would see their job as to manage their political reputation.
MINISTER: Well I was bad at that.
RAWR: And being in good standing with people they saw as key figures would be something they would make a point of?
MINISTER: I desperately wanted to be in good standing. I've never thought you'd do it by phoning them. I think you do it by delivering the goods. Simple as that. I have seen people crawl round phoning and talking to people. [Telephone ringing again] I am not at ease doing that. That will stop in a minute [nods towards telephone]. I have never done that. I think the difference is that it means you come to their attention later but I hope it means that when you do come to their attention it's because of what you've done. [Minister, TI]

The permanent secretaries, the PPS and some private secretaries (PSs) knew who to ring at No. 10 and rang regularly if not often. Such discussions were not limited to the Prime Minister's priority policy areas. They encompassed any issue of the moment. For the PPS, the links with No. 10 and the Treasury are important:

Conversations with the key people in No. 10. There aren't many. There's only one or two. There are good links that exist between the senior officials, the special advisers, this office and the Secretary of State, so that does work quite well. [PPS, TI]

However, the contacts will go down to a Grade 5 and the team with the most expertise. Of course, the danger is that senior colleagues will be left out of the loop: '*it's one of the things that if I am the jazz meister I need to keep an eye on, isn't it?*' But the PPS's involvement calls for judgement:

Sometimes it is my judgement not to record a conversation that I know is happening but sometimes I do not join in the conversations because I don't wish to face the question of whether or not I should record it. One of the reasons why I need to have a close relationship with DGs in particular is so that they can perhaps feel relatively comfortable that I'm not going to let them get shafted. [PPS, TI]

Opinions may differ about the relative influence on departments of the Treasury and No. 10 but one conclusion seems clear. Tony Blair believed the idea that SpAds made policy 'would not be recognized by any Cabinet Minister, even if you were talking to them off the record in private' (cited in Blick 2004: 276). Ministers agree. Some sarcastically comment that Michael Barber believes he appointed David Blunkett in Education, not the other way round, as a way of belittling him. Others deliberately broke the link with No. 10; for example, Charles Clarke closed the Standards and Effectiveness Unit in DfES to curtail the influence of the

Delivery Unit in No. 10, with few if any adverse consequences. Nonetheless, both No. 10 and the Treasury intervened often even if they did not necessarily control the departments. Their interventions were not coordinated (Barber 2007: 114 and 308). At times they conflicted, seemingly by intent, an epiphenomenon of the Blair–Brown struggle. But whether using the financial levers of the PSA, or political persuasion in stocktakes, these central agencies spread their tentacles into the departments as never before.

Cabinet Office

As the Treasury and No. 10 competed, the Cabinet Office looked to carve out a coordinating role so the central agencies could speak with one voice from the same hymn sheet. It was not a new challenge; the search for 'central capability' has a long history (see Lee et al. 1998). Members of the departmental courts talked to me often about the Treasury and No. 10. They volunteered information and stories. The Cabinet Office cropped up much less frequently. More often than not I had to ask direct questions about its work. Members of the departmental court were more likely to talk about the Cabinet Secretaries, Sir Richard Wilson or Sir Andrew Turnbull, than of the Cabinet Office.

Part of the problem is the amorphous nature of the Cabinet Office. It is hard to get '*the right degree of strategic oversight, stretch and so on, as opposed to micro-managing*'. One Permanent Secretary remembered, '*when I was in the centre*', we had many discussions about '*the "unit-itis" within the Cabinet Office*'. He thought the problem had '*clearly got more complicated since the 2001 election*'. He talked of '*the elusive prize*' of a corporate centre that was '*relatively coherent, unified, real value added and provides the right degree of stretch without micro-management*' [Permanent Secretary, TI].

Another Permanent Secretary set his sights appreciably lower. He inclined to the traditional view that the Cabinet Office reflected the style of the incumbent Prime Minister, and Tony Blair favoured sofa chats to system and committees.

PERMANENT SECRETARY: [The job] wasn't as good as all that. The fun of it was the voyeurism and being close to Brown and Blair as they sorted things out. They thought it worked. It was pretty unsatisfactory because [the Cabinet Secretary] was watching his prized system of cabinet committees being ignored and torn up. I was meant *to be in charge of all these cabinet committees. I didn't want to be particularly. I had no allegiance to them but I was working for a bloke who thought his whole pack of cards was being torn down. I had no sympathy for this because I had never seen the pack cards. [RAWR laughs] So if you don't see the cards, you can't worry. I was quite happy with all the informal gatherings. We saw the Prime Minister every Monday and Thursday mornings. We had a chat around local issues. Rather than have a cabinet committee they sort of asked me to try to sort it.*

RAWR: So you were firefighting?
PERMANENT SECRETARY: Yes I am. Thinking back [exhales puff of air] I think
most of us were firefighting. I do firefighting exactly when Blair or the centre feels
that something is going wrong. To [the Cabinet Secretary's] horror they wouldn't
have a cabinet committee meeting. They would ask the Cabinet Office chap to try
and sort it. I saw a lot of the Policy Unit at that time. I made it my business to get
close. [The Cabinet Secretary] liked a clear divide. He often talked about cabinet
committees and structures. I didn't support [the Cabinet Secretary's] line which
created an unnecessary war. He was so obviously <u>wrong</u> that it would have been a
foolish person to have obeyed. I was keen to make a difference [to] the relationship
between the Policy Unit and the Cabinet Office. Not that I made much of an
impression because the war is still going on now. [Permanent Secretary, TI]

So, the Cabinet Office struggled with the new style of government. To make
matters worse, the Prime Minister did not know what he wanted in place of
the traditional ways of coordinating the centre.

It was <u>fairly</u> obvious that the Blair centre didn't know what they wanted. They just
didn't know. I knew it didn't, and it still doesn't understand departments, or what
it was like to be in a department, what it was like to be an interdepartmental
minister, an intergovernmental policy unit person. It didn't know quite what it had
to do. [Permanent Secretary, TI]

Efforts to reform the Cabinet Office were further confounded by the structure
of the department.

It is quite difficult to lead a change programme for a thousand people, if 250 of
them don't owe you any allegiance. It's just intrinsically difficult. [The Cabinet
Secretary] supported what we were doing, what I was doing, but clearly he had a
million other things to do. So there was that challenge and the other issue is simply
the structure of the centre. I mean, what was the corporate centre? Was it the
Cabinet Office? Was it No. 10? Was it the Treasury? And the other interesting
challenge was the role of Cabinet Office ministers, who may or may not agree 100
per cent with the No. 10 view of things. So managing all of that was an interesting
set of challenges but inherently not entirely satisfying, as you can imagine.
[Permanent Secretary, TI]

The extent of the problem should not be overstated. None of this is new. Prime
ministers have fidgeted with the Cabinet Office for decades without any
fundamental long-lasting reform. As the Cabinet Office's Capability Review
concluded: the Cabinet Office lacked a 'a clear operating framework running
across the complex and varied business of the Department', which 'seriously
weakened . . . its impact in delivering change', especially as departments faced
'a series of unprioritised, or sometimes competing, central civil service initiatives' (Cabinet Office 2006*a*: 22; see also Barber 2007: 287). Or as the House

of Lords Select Committee on the Constitution (2009) put it, 'the Cabinet Office is presently struggling to come to terms with its own identity'.

Beneath the flurry of 'reform' activity and despite its identity crisis, the Cabinet Office continued to carry out its traditional work. Like their predecessors, ministers attended cabinet sub-committees, which grew in numbers through the life of Blair's second parliament. Some ministers devoted much of their time to such work, most notably Margaret Beckett and John Prescott. They sorted business not just in the committees but also 'in the margins of cabinet'. Officials serviced the system. The Cabinet Office's secretariats also continued with their usual coordinating work. One former Permanent Secretary in the Cabinet Office identified three stimuli for coordination:

> *When someone 'gave themselves up'; you've got a department that says, 'here is this big proposal coming up, we know that it raises issues for a number of departments, we need coordination'. The second is what I call 'copper's nose'; we knew from looking at something that it needed some coordination activity. And the third was what I called 'tip off', where somebody else said, 'Yeah this is going on and it needs to be coordinated.'*

The trick for the secretariats is *'getting the balance right'*. If a secretariat is *'proactive when it's not necessary, then you put departments' backs up'* [Permanent Secretary, TI].

The permanent secretaries differ in the extent to which they are involved with the Cabinet Office and the corporate management of the civil service, but all are involved to some degree.

> *Looking back at the personal objectives I wrote over the summer last year, I did have one about wanting to play an active role on corporate civil service issues. It was partly genuine interest from my Cabinet Office job, and partly because I think it is right that the head of department should spend some time on these issues.* [Permanent Secretary, TI]

And the centre goes out to the departments. For example, the Head of the Home Civil Service came to a Department's DGs meeting to discuss the future of the civil service. There was a draft document, which they talked through. The Permanent Secretary thought there was too much about vision and values and not enough about outputs, delivery, and citizens. They discussed the department's change programme. There was no conclusion to the meeting. The Permanent Secretary told his team after the Cabinet Secretary left, 'there is something there but I am not sure what it is; there's nothing there for us'. Comments on the Department's change programme were seen by some as 'interference', an 'irritant'. The Permanent Secretary stressed 'the importance of allies in the Cabinet Office' to avoid such interference [FWNBs].

Permanent Secretaries Group

Also known as both the Wednesday Morning meeting and 'Perm Secs', this meeting is one of the long-standing examples of the corporate, coordinating work of the Cabinet Office.[5] It involves most permanent secretaries most of the time. I attended two meetings in the Board Room of Admiralty House.[6] History is never far away in Whitehall. Tradition lurks in every room. Completed in 1726, Admiralty House was the first purpose-built office block in Britain. It is a complex of five buildings, including three ministerial flats, two of which are occupied by Margaret Beckett and John Prescott. Alexander Pope thought it rather dull. He never listened to a discourse on comprehensive performance assessments (CPAs) for local and regional government; the main topic of today's meeting.[7]

The Audit Commission produced CPAs. It reported 'how well a council was performing overall compared to other councils in England' by drawing together several performance indicators covering, for example, local service delivery. The lead department is the Office of the Deputy Prime Minister (ODPM). There are 15 permanent secretaries at the meeting with a representative of the Local Government Association and staff from the Office for Public Service Reform (OPSR).

The atmosphere of the meeting was relaxed. Jackets were removed. There was much chatter, side remarks, and banter. It rapidly emerged there is a 'dialogue of the deaf' between central and local government because central performance measurement conflicted with local priorities and the need for flexibility in service delivery. Interestingly, this view was shared by some central departments. Some permanent secretaries agreed that 'CPAs may not reflect key objectives and we have a joint interest in not focusing too narrowly on the measures in CPAs'. One Permanent Secretary invited ODPM to take the lead, volunteering, 'we are right behind you'. There were howls of laughter and asides to one's immediate neighbour. I sat by the wall, not at the table, so I could not hear the remarks. I just know someone added, 'a long way behind'. The meeting greeted the suggestion that CPAs should combine 'freedom with flexibilities' with much scepticism. The Chair opined there are 'a lot of issues to take away with us' and suggested the way forward was to focus on the ten worst local authorities. There was a lot of muttered dissent in the sidelines of the meeting. One corner of the table was in open if polite rebellion. The corner wanted to know what value was added by this exercise. They had no interest in which ten local authorities had the worst 'number of missed collections per 100,000 collections of household waste'. OPSR was defensive. When the conversation switched to regional government, the Home Office protested that it 'was never discussed with them'. The rebellious corner expostulated with an audible, 'God!'

In effect, this meeting of Perm Secs was a large Keep-in-Touch (KiT). There was an explanation of what was happening and a sharing of concerns. Although the ostensible topic was central–local government relations, there was a strong undercurrent of permanent secretaries resisting intervention by central agencies. Targets and performance indicators were seen as clumsy, inflexible, and out of sync with other policy developments, whether in local government or central departments. They were worried about such controls, more for their departments than for local government. There was no clear, let alone agreed, outcome to the meeting.

As the meeting broke up, there was much chatter. Permanent secretaries were doing business in the fringes of the meeting but I was button-holed by the Head of the Home Civil Service, so I only overheard some of what was going on.

PERMANENT SECRETARY 1: If he writes the book of rules I couldn't bear it.
PERMANENT SECRETARY 2: Don't worry. It'll take three years and you'll head the department by then.
PERMANENT SECRETARY 3: We have shamed them into serving wine.
PERMANENT SECRETARY 4: The [Secretary of State] has not been invited.
PERMANENT SECRETARY 5: That's what she has been told. It's extra piquancy.
PERMANENT SECRETARY 4: Do you think there will be a fudge?
PERMANENT SECRETARY 5: Yes, and if that's what they want, we'll do it.
PERMANENT SECRETARY 3: It won't be comfortable for the government. [FWNB]

I noted these overlapping conversations, although I had no idea what they were about most of the time. It was gossip about one another, their ministers, and the issues of the day. As one Permanent Secretary said to me later:

They are a support group which I enjoy. A, it's good voyeurism; B, it's a mutual support group, you can discuss a mutual problem; and C, it's an early warning of other things.

However, there was a feeling it could do more.

There is much more scope [for] more visible and collective management leadership in terms of the civil service, which would have helped us. [Permanent Secretary, TI]

And some did not find it much of a support group. One Permanent Secretary explained the current difficulties of his Secretary of State to the meeting and was disappointed at their response:

PERMANENT SECRETARY: No—I had very, very little support from my colleagues in this period.
RAWR: Would you expect to get support from them?
PERMANENT SECRETARY: Well obviously not. [Joint laughter].

One of his colleagues told me it was not a permanent secretary's job to protect his secretary of state. The affected Permanent Secretary both disliked and disagreed with this stance [FWNB].

Some permanent secretaries saw the meeting as a club and did not see themselves as members.

> *I see them on Wednesday mornings [expels air]. I am not clubbable in that way, I mean several of them are clubbable, I just don't, don't mix easily in that club. The Wednesday morning club is rather influential. But for some reason or another I have just never [been part of it].* [Permanent Secretary, TI]

Others see it as a peripheral activity and do not attend regularly.

> *I am a fairly poor attendee on Wednesday mornings. I do the odd thing with other departments, I go and talk at the Civil Service College or with the 'fast streamers' to discharge my corporate duty, but I feel I've got a big department and frankly, you know, that is where my major focus of attention needs to be.* [Permanent Secretary, TI]

Permanent secretaries come in many guises ranging from charming to reticent, from sartorial to the invisible grey suit; from BBC tones to regional origins. They tell jokes against one another and their political masters. The Wednesday morning meeting may be a club that excludes some but for this professional stranger it communicated their individuality; it was a loose amalgamation not a cohesive group. I was intrigued by the different personalities, which gave colour to Butler's (1993: 404) fear that departments would become 'unconnected elements in the overall public sector, with ... no real working mechanisms for policy coordination'. This part of the core executive was collegial, not hierarchical, able to steer by consent but not direct.

OTHER DEPARTMENTS

Ministers are members of the ubiquitous interdepartmental committees:

> *You could get allocated to things like that where it's a matter of taking a general interest in what the government was doing across the board. And occasionally there might be a departmental matter come up, but often it wasn't but you were there to engage in a political and policy discussion with your colleagues across Whitehall, across the government.* [Minister, TI]

> *The big feature of a lot of what we do is interdepartmental working. I think we've got good working with DCMS [Department for Culture, Media and Sport] on digital TV. We have to work closely with DEFRA [Department for Environment, Food and Rural Affairs] on a whole host of things on energy. We also have a close relationship with another bit of DEFRA, Rural Affairs, and on broadband, also on*

post offices. We have a joint team, so it's quite a big feature of what we do. [Minister, TI]

The working relationship can be close. One Minister commented with some pride on the response of a Department of Trade and Industry (DTI) official to interdepartmental working:

> *'I prefer to describe myself as leading the joint DTI/DEFRA team'. I thought that was quite generous, and it may sound trivial, but the body language with which that was said, said something to a room full of people, that it was quite important about the relationship between [us].* [Minister TI]

Similarly, permanent secretaries attended interdepartmental committees regularly. In interview, most could give me a list off the top of their heads. Invariably, it was '*a handful of areas of mutual interest*' and often focused; '*there are two departments in particular where we have a lot of overlapping interest*' [Permanent Secretary, TI]. These areas were specific, not general (see below). His PS told me there were marked knock-on benefits for the Private Office; they now had good contacts with the PSs at ODPM, Transport, and DTI [FWNB].

Working in the departmental court gives the PPS and the PS valuable networks across Westminster and Whitehall.[8] One PS put the point succinctly:

> *I have got good relationships with all the private offices and all the rest of Whitehall. I know how Whitehall works, I know how parliament works, a good knowledge base.* [PS, TI]

Most members of the private office work more to other departments than to No. 10 and the Treasury:

> *My problem with No. 10, the Treasury, the hugely high-level bit is that I find it hard to follow because if you are not in on all those meetings all the time and you don't operate at permanent secretary level all the time, you don't know half the time what they are talking about. And it's all allusions as well, it's never direct. He [No. 10 SpAd] chews up his words a lot. He is difficult to understand on the telephone.* [PS, TI]

Over the course of their career, deliberately, they build up personal networks with other departments across Whitehall. They know that winning friends and influencing people requires a network of contacts. They even *arrange* 'informal' contacts.

> *We were too busy just to say stop in the corridor and have a cup of tea. But there were arranged informal contacts because, you know, we'd have dinner from time to time. The Secretary of State always believed [it] was important. [It] involved the top management of the department and the ministerial team. We also had away days regularly. And so there were opportunities for informal contact there.* [Minister, TI]

Such work-based networks were complemented by internal and external *social* networks; '*the private offices up here, we all try to go out together every two or three months*' [PS, TI]. Not everyone went. Some lived a long way out but would have gone if they lived in London. They also met PSs from elsewhere, usually the ones with whom they dealt regularly. The Christmas party was a favoured venue.

These informal networks grow into formal networks.

> *RAWR: Now mistakenly perhaps, I had understood you to be saying that initially you had a lot of contacts within the DoE [Department of Education] and the odd contact outside with the Treasury or when something required you to, you had adventurously built up contacts with the local authority associations and equivalent, now you seem to be getting an extensive network around Whitehall.*
>
> *PERMANENT SECRETARY: Yes. [sounds of crockery] Network isn't quite right, before that it was a, it was a voluntary achieved network of mates. Now I am chairing and leading a team of disagreeing colleagues and it's my job to get them together as UK Ltd. So it's a bit different. So before it was spontaneous and informal, but this is definitely the opposite. This is a UK Ltd meeting where hopefully you have cleared the lines back at the ranch first. We were disciplined British government.*

Networking can make links with other departments sound amicable. They can be. But 'turf' warfare is never far away: 'they are in major territorial mode' [FWNB]. Or, more memorably:

> *The Minister stands over my desk and says, 'I want you ring up [the PPS]', and said, 'I want you to pass a message to [your Minister] which is get your tanks off my lawn.' So I pick up the phone and I said, with [my Minister] standing there, 'Are you going to stand there?' And he said, 'Yes. I want you to pass that message on.' So I pick up the phone and I get [the PPS] and I said, 'I am going to give you a message to pass on to your Secretary of State and you have to pass it on without any elaboration. And just to be clear, my Secretary of State is standing beside me as I give you this message and it is from my Secretary of State to your Minister, "get your tanks off my lawn".'* [Permanent Secretary, TI; see also Lodge and Rogers 2006: 44–5]

Links can be complicated by personal matters. One Minister observed of a colleague that '*the fact he didn't get a promotion*' made '*the relations between the departments difficult*' [Minister, TI].

It is easy to overstate the extent of networking. When asked about the balance of work inside and outside the Department, one PPS believes:

> *It is quite departmental, so my main contacts are very much, in terms of the network thing, people I talk to in the Department. Other departments, less so. I mean the Treasury, we have a pretty regular sort of flow of correspondence with, but there aren't any other departments I regularly talk to.* [PPS, TI]

Joined-up government

He who says bureaucracy says division of labour and specialization. They are the organizational expression of bureaucratic expertise. However, the flip side of this coin is tunnel vision; people do not see beyond the boundaries of their area of specialization. In other words, departments and sections of departments become silos or drainpipes. Thus, a former Permanent Secretary at DTI commented on the merged Trade and Industry: 'you know, of course, they still operate as silos' [FWNB]. David Blunkett (2006: 217 and 219) talks about 'interdepartmental reservation', or the reluctance of departments to share information; and about 'the Balkanisation of government', or 'the breakdown of departments into tiny units'. The comment that '*we were excessively hierarchical, excessively silo-like, and insufficiently enabling*' captures the push for joining-up [Minister, TI]. To compound the difficulties posed by specialization, the silos do not match the problems that confront government; wicked issues like poverty do not fit the silos but need a multi-agency response.[9]

The response to silos and wicked issues, the way to improve interdepartmental working, was joined-up government. Tony Blair (2004*a*) was clear: 'It means working not in traditional departmental silos. It means working naturally with partners outside of government.' He stated the aims succinctly: 'joined-up problems need joined-up solutions' (*The Observer*, 31 May 1998) and this theme runs through the *Modernising Government* White Paper (Cabinet Office 1999*c*) with its frequent references to 'joined-up' government and 'holistic governance'.[10] The term covers both horizontal joining-up between central departments and vertical joining-up between all the agencies involved in delivering services. ODPM was an enthusiastic proponent, prompting one Secretary of State to observe 'it has got religion' [Minister, FWNB].

The policy of joining-up did affect the way many people saw their roles. One Minister at DEFRA can speak for them all. He saw his job as going out and asking: '*How can we work with you on the design of your policies?*' He saw:

> *Developing the right relationships and developing partnerships is not an added extra, it is of the essence. Given that I think that most things at a local level will increasingly in the future depend on local partnerships, developing a government department that understands partnerships is no bad thing.*

He saw DEFRA as a '*network organization*' and his job was the '*building of networks, working through networks, trying to find out where the resources are and getting them to the right people*' [Minister, TI]. I attended three interdepartmental events that were equally explicit exercises in joined-up government.[11] For example, the PowerPoint slides at one meeting included a schematic representation of the 'network' involved. It was seen as 'fundamental' and included other government departments, users, research councils, and regional bodies.

I described the Perm Secs meeting as a KiT and that description may underestimate its impact. A few days later, there was a 'joined-up' response to that discussion. The Permanent Secretary who was most vocal in his concern about CPAs and flexibility arranged a 'set piece' meeting between the relevant people. He admitted he had a 'bee in his bonnet'. He had spoken to ODPM in the margins of cabinet to get informal agreement on the way forward. He wanted to see the departments 'engaged with one another' and to set up joint working arrangements. He was clear that 'this is joined-up government in action'. For example, he wanted a broader discussion of waste management than just collection; landfill cannot be the only form of disposal. Similarly, he failed to see how you can discuss air quality without taking traffic plans into account. He saw the specific performance indicators of CPAs as obstacles to such broader discussion. Also, the Treasury was not part of the discussion yet, and there can be no serious planning for flood management without them because the scale of capital spending is potentially enormous.

The meeting was amiable. 'Is it true you had a Sustainable Communities Unit on Delivery—SCUD—and had to change its name?' ODPM claim the story is apocryphal. The Permanent Secretary posed a core question for the meeting, 'How do we press the right buttons to take the policy forward?' To begin, they discussed probable areas of cooperation. For example, they agreed they needed to do something on air quality and flood management but not on anti-social behaviour. The policy agenda was limited to functions where the departments already had overlapping responsibilities. They found it easy to agree on the areas needing joint action. They then discussed names: 'I can send my Grade 7 to talk to yours'. In effect, the meeting became an exercise in identifying the particular individuals who could take the lead on specific issues like air quality and traffic. They knew what they wanted. The task was to make sure the Level 7s were talking to one another. As with management reform, the emphasis was on 'drilling down'.

ODPM was pleased with the progress made. They agreed on joint activities with the names of the people to take them forward. The assembled senior management agreed 'we talk a good talk', but they were laughing at one another. They knew they had only made a start.

As with all meetings they broke up with general chit-chat. In universities, the conversation in the margins of meetings is as likely to be about cricket or soccer as it is about work related matters. Of course, professors are more than happy to character assassinate a dean but for many colleagues deans are deeply uninteresting people; some even play golf. Whitehall is genuinely interested in the comings and goings of its political masters. It is standard end of meeting gossip. The Permanent Secretary gossips about the future of various junior ministers as he takes his guests down in the lift. As we ascend back to his office, my Permanent Secretary has a momentary tinge of fatalism; 'what's the point, does anybody believe?' His remark is not addressed to me. I am not sure he is aware he said it out loud. To me, it sounds like weariness; another meeting, another attempt to galvanize people into action, another uncertain outcome, and another meeting in the offing.

PARLIAMENT AND THE POLITICAL PARTIES

The departmental court is also part of both the parliamentary network and the party network.

Parliament

The impact of parliament on the departmental court, and the ministers in particular, is massive in time and energy if in nothing else. Whether through oral parliamentary questions (PQs), ministerial statements, debates, divisions, passing legislation with its various committee stages and amendments, or simply party management in the Commons tea room, parliament is seen as a major imposition by many a minister. Thus, Blunkett (2006) complains about the demands of parliament on his time and its role in contributing to his 'crazy life' with its late sittings and elaborate procedures.[12] It also makes major demands on the departmental court.

Commonly, there is a parliamentary section and its parliamentary clerks provide the link between the private office, the Whip's Office, and parliament. It organizes PQs, provides briefings for debates, ministerial statements, and appearances before select committees, and organizes amendments to bills. The workload is often routine, always considerable, and all too regularly frenetic. The section has its stresses and strains, its own pet hates. On one visit, there was much mirth at the expense of the Stationery Office, which posted the wrong version of the Department's bill. This 'absolute howler' led to invective about parliamentary draughtsmen. Normally, comments by civil servants are funny, waspish, tinged with an acid humour, but still funny. On this occasion, the clerks were aggressive beyond the point of unpleasant; fully paid-up members of the Alastair Campbell School of Invective. It was not for my benefit. Mistakes and delays are the bane of the clerks' lives.[13]

For ministers and permanent secretaries there is no escape. When parliament calls, they must obey. Both believe in that hoary old chestnut of the constitution, ministerial accountability. The PPS was succinct: '*we're the executive and we answer to parliament*' [PPS, TI]. The Minister said the same thing:

It was my decision. I did it, but you wouldn't have to say that to parliament every day. I mean that's the assumption—that we are. The decision's mine and you've got to be able to explain that to parliament and do it truthfully. [Minister, TI]

Of course, they may tell parliament little but that little must be accurate and must not deliberately mislead.

Parliament is a source of stress and irritation for ministers. Every minister complained about the demands on their time, the unpredictability of votes, the rush and disruption, the late hours, and the lousy working conditions. They are right. No self-respecting chief executive of a blue-chip company, and certainly no university vice-chancellor, would put up with the working conditions in the House of Commons. I have already described both the disruptions to the ministerial timetable caused by the division bell and the discomfort of working in the House (see Chapter 4: 94–97). So, a few more examples will suffice.

The workload is probably the biggest downside. It's better now since the reform of the hours in the House of Commons.[14] *That was getting hard when we were here every night until well after 10 and had to be back here first thing in the morning.* [Minister, TI]

I'd been trying to sleep on the two person couch in my disgusting House of Commons office. I couldn't, so I shoved some cushions on the floor, covered myself up with my coat, turned the light out, a catnap, because I can catnap, just falling asleep, 3 a.m. the bell goes. So I get up and twist my knee, so I am in agony. I am 50, I am not a fucking student sleeping on somebody's floor. People think it's a glamorous life and we swan about with our noses in somebody's trough. So here I am 'ahhh', you know. Jesus Christ, drove me up the wall, drove me up the wall. [Minister, TI]

Or more succinctly: 'the House is like a morgue' [Minister, FWNB]. The Minister was referring to both the empty chamber and the liveliness of its few denizens. It was also the case for ministers in the House of Lords: '*the need to be here as lobby fodder, would keep me from my bed and going off and going home*' [Minister, TI].

As a final example, during the interview with a Minister of State, we went back and forth to the House of Commons three times in an hour and a half. I conducted the interview in his office, in the car, and in the courtyard of the House of Commons. We then ended the interview and resumed an hour later at 7 p.m. back in his office. It was bizarre, but not atypical of the fragmented ministerial lifestyle [Minister, TI].

Ministerial involvement with the House takes many forms. I attended the adjournment debate on regional broadcasting in the East Midlands; a session of the Public Administration Select Committee (PASC); the debate on the UK Olympics bid; and various meetings with constituents and colleagues from both the Commons and the Lords. There is, of course neither rhyme nor reason to this list. Each event occurred simply because I was with that minister on that day. I give a flavour of these various scenes.

As well as in the main chamber, the House of Commons also sits in Westminster Hall (or the Grand Committee Room). On Tuesdays and Wednesdays, there are a series of private members' adjournment debates. They are general debates on topical subjects with the relevant minister of state attending, or in this case, standing in for a colleague. I attended an adjournment debate on regional broadcasting occasioned by the decision of ITV to close its Nottingham studio and move to Birmingham. The Labour MP from Mansfield led a debate on whether the move violated the company's charter, which requires it to cover regional and sub-regional news. With other MPs from the East Midlands, he also objected to the slight to their regional identity. They bandied around words such as 'furious', 'major anger', and 'disquiet'. OfCom was pilloried for its 'indifference'.[15] The Minister was placatory, understanding that the region needed its own voice but, equally, the company had the right to decide how to organize to survive in a competitive world. 'Balance' became the keyword. The Minister was interrupted by members rising and gave way. The speakers repeated the point about the charter. The Minister replied that the company's targets for regional news remained the same. Moreover, news gathering would remain in the East Midlands. Only news presentation would move to Birmingham. So, the Minister believed the company would meet its targets and refused to intervene (*Hansard*, 30 March 2004: Col. 411WH–419WH).

The debate was an example of the House providing an opportunity for MPs to air their constituents' concerns. It also showed the skill of the Minister in rapidly mastering a brief, reading it while having a cup of soup for lunch. Yet the Minister controlled the debate though the topic did not fall within her area of expertise, or frankly, interest. The MPs achieved nothing beyond venting their feelings.

Another scene, and a different set of skills. The Minister was meeting some constituents in the central lobby of the House. It was a meet and greet, there was no agenda, no complaints. It was a retired couple on holiday and they were thrilled to meet 'their' Minister (and MP). The Speaker's Procession passed through the Lobby and the Minister explained what was happening. The procession was the prelude to the House's sitting. The procession included the Doorkeeper, the Serjeant-at-Arms, the Speaker, a train-bearer, the Chaplain, and the Speaker's Private Secretary. The Speaker wore a black court suit and black robe with a train. Not only ministers are surrounded by pomp and circumstance. Here parades the authority of the House of Commons. There was silence as they passed. Heels clicked with military precision.

The Minister was at ease. The constituents were also relaxed if starry-eyed. They told the Minister when they last saw him—in the local library at a meeting about the closure of local post offices. They had been ill and they heaped praise on the NHS. The Minister went through the day's order paper with them. He explained that the Home Secretary, David Blunkett, was leading a debate on immigration. The Minister went off to get their daily pass for the public gallery where they will watch the debate. The couple talked to me; 'he's sweet'. He was. The lobby was a swirling mix of constituents, MPs, tourists, and heavily armed guards. The Minister returned and escorted them to the gallery while I waited in the central lobby.

Another change of scene—select committees, which come in many shapes and sizes. I appeared before the PASC (PASC 2000). It was pleasant, polite, and urbane. It had the qualities of an academic seminar. I felt at home. Not so for the Permanent Secretary who appeared before the Public Accounts Committee (PAC):

> *RAWR: How intensive were your briefings when you appeared before the CPA?*
> *PERMANENT SECRETARY: The PAC, before the PAC, hours and hours and hours. I've got one next week and I have already had seven hours of briefing.*
> *RAWR: Is it just the PAC or is that true for select committee as well?*
> *PERMANENT SECRETARY: Less, I am much less bothered with select committees.*
> *RAWR: Because?*
> *PERMANENT SECRETARY: The questions are usually more general and one can just sort of get through it whereas PAC is the opposite to general, it's very, very specific.*
> [Permanent Secretary, TI]

Most ministers and permanent secretaries 'get through' an appearance before a select committee. It tended to provoke only weary cynicism; 'it could have been worse'; and 'I've been more depressed by this committee'. Or as one Minister put it, appearing before a select committee was 'to suffer for the cause' [FWNBs]. He did not mean it was a forensic, intimidating experience. He meant it was tedious, with long-winded, boring questions from people who did not understand the issues and could not be bothered to master their brief. Perhaps I do not quite capture the force of his complaint.

There is a danger in weary cynicism. A minister's standing in the party hinges to a degree on his performances in the House. It would be an error of judgement not to take the House and its committees seriously. Similarly the Permanent Secretary who believed he can 'get through' might not. Sir John Kerr, Permanent Secretary at the Foreign Office, was subject to 'somewhat choleric evidence sessions' (Select Committee on Foreign Affairs 1999: para. 101) over his refusal to provide access to telegrams and despatches and to answer questions.[16] The final report pointed to errors by senior officials and concluded the Permanent Secretary 'failed in his duty to ministers' (Select Committee on Foreign Affairs 1999: paras 68–71). The House of Commons might be dwarfed by an over-mighty executive, but it remains a theatre of action that can tarnish or destroy reputations.

The party network

The party network refers to the Labour Party in all its manifestations: annual conference, the Parliamentary Labour Party, and the constituency party.

Parliament does not sit regularly on a Friday as it is the minister's, and everybody else's, constituency day. They were remarkably assiduous in cultivating their constituency, although two of my ministers had safe seats. Despite their heavy schedules as ministers, they were regular attendees of constituency events. The constituency office had a regular link with the private office through the diary secretary, and they liaised over the minister's travel and schedule:

> [The constituency] organizes his Fridays. But if I need [the Secretary of State] for a Friday, or something comes up for a Friday, or if there's a trip overseas, it's up to me to keep in touch with [the constituency]. [The Secretary of State] doesn't want to be bothered with that. He expects [the constituency] and I to work in tandem. I'm aware that [the constituency] needs [the Secretary of State] in the constituency for things. He's got to have his constituency time. And I will work round that. [DS, TI]

However, the diary secretary did not organize travel; that is party business and done by the constituency officer. That is one example of the dividing line between departmental and party business. The SpAds step in where officials fear to tread, covering party meetings, conferences, and all other party related matters. With the diary secretary, they police the boundary between two networks (and see Chapter 4: p. 80).

The extent of a minister's party duties varies, but none can ignore the demands of the party. I expected speeches to party conferences and other high visibility activities but party management also takes more mundane forms. After a long day in the department, the minister had an evening meeting with the North-West Parliamentary Labour Party (NWPLP), a grouping of Labour MPs from Manchester and the surrounding region. It took place in a House of Commons' committee room. The room was filled with northern voices, Lancashire rather than Yorkshire but a welcome reminder of home. There were 11 people, excluding the Minister and, unusually, the PS. The group was formally constituted. It has a chair, a secretary, and keeps minutes. The first item was constituency business covering such topics as pension funds and brewing. To be clear, it was about matters affecting the constituency as region, not the MPs' constituents. The latter were taken care of in local surgeries. The Whip's Office then addressed the group. There was a big vote in the Commons. Many MPs were on holiday, so he wanted people to 'stick around, it's serious'. Also the local elections were coming up, so would everyone get their bids in for a pairing as soon as possible.

The Minister provided a briefing on the work of the Department relevant to the north-west. It was a pep talk for the MPs. He gave examples of policies and of public spending in the region. They listened respectfully. He also affirmed his support for both Tony Blair and Gordon Brown, a statement probably only necessary because of Iraq and turbulent times in the PLP. His talk was followed by a question and answer session that ranged widely—for example, the merger of the University of Manchester and University of Manchester Institute of Science and Technology, the effects of the euro, the television rights for Premier League football. He explained the government's position and where necessary he agreed to take a question back to the Department or talk to another cabinet colleague. The PS kept a note of all matters requiring action. At times, the Minister skated over topics. On the euro, he presented the cabinet line that no decision would be made until Britain passed the economic tests. He did not mention his doubts or argue the political case for joining; a small example of collective responsibility in action.

For the Minister, it was an exercise in party management, and a pleasant one. For the NWPLP it was a way of keeping the Minister in touch with the 'real world' of the party and the constituency. The Minister behaved as if parliament matters. It may not force ministers to resign but it can harm reputations and reputation is an integral to any minister's standing in the pecking order.

Ministers also had one-to one-meetings with colleagues in both Houses. On one occasion we met a Labour Lord in the Guest Bar of the House of Lords. They had been colleagues since 1976. He wanted to talk to the Minister about unemployment and industry closures in his old Welsh constituency. The Minister explained about EU rules on subsidies to industry but promised to explore long-term funding for economic regeneration. They then reminisced; he was a sheep farmer by background and his wife wanted him to leave the Lords and return to farming. The Minister was sympathetic and patient. In the car afterwards, he explained such meetings not only give him background information about what concerns fellow party members, but it also defused possible 'trouble-making'; that is, a speech in the Lords about the state of the Welsh economy. The interesting piece of information for the Minister was the Lord's possible retirement. The Department thought he was staying on. He was 'useful'. The Permanent Secretary and the PPS will know first thing tomorrow [FWNB].

In sum, for the departmental court, parliament and the party are two more networks to be serviced, more demands to be managed, and more conflicts to be reconciled.

BEYOND WESTMINSTER AND WHITEHALL

The notion of policy networks refers to the sets of formal institutional and informal linkages between governmental and other actors structured around shared, if endlessly negotiated, beliefs and interests in public policy making and implementation.[17] These actors are interdependent and policy emerges from the interactions between them (Rhodes 2006). I studied policy networks for over 15 years. When studying life at the top, I expected to find much more evidence of engagement with policy networks than turned out to be the case. All too slowly I realized that permanent secretaries, ministers, and the departmental court were intermittently the fulcrum of policy networks. Mainly, it was always the section of the department that specialized in the policy area. Of course, the top brass emerged for public events or when there was a specific problem needing their talents. Like so much of the work in the departmental court, policy networks and their concerns were but one of the several balls that had to be juggled. They surfaced as a priority intermittently, but the main focuses were links inside the department and with the rest of Westminster and Whitehall.

Of course, the departmental court knew external links were important:

There's another slightly more amorphous group which is our [client group] circles, where I don't think any departmental official could operate properly at any level of seniority without having some sensible contacts with people outside the civil service. So I maintain contact for historical or this job reasons with a number of people from various sectors. [PPS, TI]

This quote is important for two reasons. It acknowledges the importance of policy networks but does not see such links as a priority for a PPS. He keeps the links pending his return to a policy job in the department. For the DGs and the functional silos in the department links with their stakeholders were important: 'the emotional commitment some officials have to particular sectors is incredible' (Lodge and Rogers 2006: 38). Farmers and teachers remain classic examples of such commitment.

Ministers were also as aware of their department's client groups and they cultivated them; 'we must mobilize these networks' [Minister, FWNB]. It is part of their job to represent the department to the outside world. So, one Minister asked the Department to compile a list of their 'top 50' clients. The Department took way too long and, when he tried to jolly them along, he realized '*the department did not know who it had relationships with or needed to have relationships with*'. So, he got his SpAd to organize the dinners. The Minister thought the dinners were '*really useful*' but they became a slog:

When I think of all the bloody dinners I have eaten. More of those fucking captains of industry not thinking we're going on the right track, but anyway I have to eat some more. But I do a lot of that. I do a lot of awards dinners, that kind of thing. God forbid. Some of them are painful. [Said under breath.] Some of them are seriously painful, but I do them anyway. [Minister, TI]

Ministers also cultivated a few, privileged peak associations:

> *I'd work at the relationship with the [peak association]. You know we are on the phone*
> *to each other, and there are occasions when I practically drafted his press releases. He*
> *will ring me and say, 'Look are you free? I need you to do this.' I'll say, 'Fine, I will do it*
> *because I know you won't ask unless it's important.' So that's terribly important. It*
> *doesn't mean he'll always support what we do, but it does mean he will never criticize*
> *me personally, and he'll warn me when things are getting difficult and I can ask him for*
> *favours and he can ask me. Very important that relationship.* [Minister, TI]

The departments also have a miscellany of agencies and non-departmental
public bodies (NDPBs). They comprise another network to be managed. On
one visit, the Department had arranged an elaborate seminar and reception
for all its NDBPs: 51 people attended and they were addressed, briefly, by
the Minister on the problems posed by the new spending round. They were
being told to absorb the efficiency saving and inflation within existing
budget ceilings. The Secretary of State answered a few questions before
handing over to a Minister of State. He had to go to a cabinet sub-commit-
tee. The Minister of State's manner was aggressive. Rather than answering
questions, he asked them. He wanted to know in specific terms what they
were going to do to make the savings. They replied they will benchmark,
measure performance, and look at the economic pay-offs from their spending. Neither minister used this language. Obviously managerialism spread
beyond the department. Like all seminars with a large audience, the discussion was all over the place. Two key points were flagged: economize and
look elsewhere for funding. In fact, the meeting's atmosphere was jaunty,
not down, and the St Émilion and canapés helped matters along nicely. The
Minister jokes they used an outside caterer because, if left to the PPS, we
would have got crisps.

It was another one of those networking mingles. For all their prosaic, taken
for granted quality, such mingles are important. As Vickers (1968: 27) argued,
a key element of decision making is maintaining a complex pattern of relationships over time. The civil service have embedded this notion in the KiT, which
permanent secretaries and the PPS practice every day of their working lives.
They do not deliver services; they regulate other organizations delivering
the services. So, maintaining relations inside and outside Westminster and
Whitehall—mingling—is an important part of their decision making.

CONCLUSIONS

In Chapter 2, I described British government as a planetary system with three
rings. The networks described in this chapter bridge those rings. If bureaucracy

gives formal hierarchical expression to the authority of government, then networks are the informal authority supplementing hierarchy. They work in the shadow of that hierarchy but they are not necessarily controlled by it. Control is an aspiration, not an assumption. Its extent is a matter to be determined, not taken for granted. So, what does this network governance narrative add to our understanding of life at the top? What are its distinctive beliefs and practices?

Beliefs and practices

Network governance encompasses a family of beliefs and practices about networks and networking, and the shift from hierarchy to markets to networks. It also has its characteristic dilemma encapsulated in the term 'metagovernance'.

Networks and networking

I have discussed the common beliefs about networks elsewhere and often (see, for example: Rhodes 1988, 1997a, and 2006), so I will be brief. In this book, networks are not a set of institutions and their interactions. Instead I talk of networking to draw attention to an activity infused with beliefs, not a monolithic phenomenon. Networks are fluid, constantly being contested and remade. Nonetheless this fluid activity has some family resemblances around trust, reciprocity, and diplomacy. Networks have a network of similarities, not all of which will be found in any one network.

Trust

Networks are different from markets and hierarchies because trust is 'the most important attribute of network operations'. It is the central coordinating mechanism of networks in the same way that commands and price competition are the key mechanisms for bureaucracies and markets respectively (Frances et al. 1991: 15). Shared values and norms are the glue which holds the complex set of relationships together; trust is essential for cooperative behaviour and, therefore, the existence of the network. It is central to the loyalty between ministers and their top-level civil servants and to the standing of any 'outsiders'. Its everyday manifestation is KiTs, a prime vehicle for the never-ending task of keeping in touch with one another.

Reciprocity

Networks involve friendship, loyalty, even altruism (Thompson 1993: 54–8) but above all network culture is characterized by reciprocity. As Powell (1991: 272–3) comments the anthropologists conception of reciprocity emphasizes 'the normative standards that sustain exchange', especially indebtedness, obligation, and a long-term perspective. So, a lack of equivalence creates a moral sanction, bonds which keep the parties in touch with one another; the books are balanced eventually. It is also a symbolic relationship and 'in the constant ritual of exchange, deep obligations and duties are established, symbolic statuses confirmed, metaphorical social references invoked' (Thompson 1993: 58). In this way, networks become stabilized. So, the minister helps to draft the press releases of a leading peak association.

Diplomacy

The idea of diplomacy is not new, but it has been misplaced. For example, Nicholson (1950: 15 and 116) defines diplomacy as management by negotiation, identifies the diplomatic virtues such as truthfulness, calm, and good temper, and advises the budding diplomat 'above everything do not allow yourself to become excited about your work'. Even earlier, François de Callierès (1963 [1716]: 103) advised the Prince, 'the more often he puts himself in the position of others, the more subtle and effective will his arguments be'. For all their slightly old-fashioned, even quaint, language, their emphases on sitting where the other people sit and helping them to realize their objectives are at the heart of networking. I noted in Chapter 2 that it was a central part of the toolkit of both ministers and permanent secretaries. The same point was made by Douglas Wass, former Head of the Home Civil Service: 'finesse and diplomacy are essential ingredients in public service' (cited in Hennessy 1989: 150; see also Keeling 1972: ch. 5; and Part 1990: 66 and 69). In short, they mingle.

From hierarchy to markets to networks

The reforms of the New Right and New Labour have brought about a shift from hierarchy to markets to networks. This shift might not be found in patterns of rule in other times or countries but it offers a compelling picture of the British state. Indeed, Marsh (2008b: 738) is concerned it 'may be becoming the new orthodoxy' (see also Kerr and Kettell 2006: 13). So, network governance highlights these features of the British polity.

My focus on 'situated agency', on individuals using local reasoning to modify inherited beliefs and practices, suggests that the notion of a monolithic state in control of itself and civil society was always a myth. Westminster, managerialism, and network governance are not given sets of characteristics. They are the stories people use to construct, convey, and explain traditions, dilemmas, beliefs, and practices. The myth of the centralized executive, and leaders who know best, obscured the reality of diverse state practices that escaped the control of the centre because they arose from the contingent beliefs and actions of diverse actors at the boundary of state and civil society. The state is never monolithic and it always negotiates with others. Policy always arises from interactions within networks of organizations and individuals. Patterns of rule always traverse the public, private, and voluntary sectors. The boundaries between state and civil society are always blurred.

Elites understand this story. They know that policy is constantly remade, negotiated, and contested by many agencies in widely different ways within widely varying everyday practices. Their problem is the governance story conflicts with Westminster hierarchy. The departments have to convince themselves that they do not know best and defer to others. They struggle with the dilemmas.

Dilemmas and metagovernance

Network governance encounters some recurrent dilemmas; the problem of many hands, the holy grail of coordination, and it's the mix that matters. Metagovernance is the response to them.

The problem of many hands

The spread of networks undermines accountability. Bovens (1998: 46 and 229) identifies the 'problem of many hands' where responsibility for policy in complex organizations is shared and it is correspondingly difficult to find out who is responsible. He also notes that fragmentation, marketization, and the resulting networks create 'new forms of the problem of many hands'. As Mulgan (2003: 211–14) argues, buck-passing is much more likely in networks because responsibility is divided and the reach of political leaders is much reduced.

The holy grail of coordination

The spread of networks also undermines coordination. The search for coordination lies at the heart of New Labour's reforms in the UK. The government seek to coordinate departments and other agencies—whether of the centre or local government, whether public or private—by imposing a new style of management on other agencies. The Blair government was explicit. Although the government does 'not want to run local services from the centre', it 'is not afraid to take action where standards slip'—an obvious instance of a command operating code (Cabinet Office 1999c: 37). Such a code, no matter how well disguised, runs the ever-present risk of recalcitrance from key actors and a loss of flexibility in dealing with localized problems. Gentle pressure relentlessly applied is still a command operating code in a velvet glove. When you are sitting at the top of a pyramid and you cannot see the bottom, implementation or control deficits are an ever-present unintended consequence.

Networks make the goal of central coordination ever more elusive. As Peters (1998: 302) argues, 'strong vertical linkages between social groups and public organizations make effective coordination and horizontal linkages within government more difficult'. Once agreement is reached in the network, 'the latitude for negotiation by public organizations at the top of the network is limited'. However, networks do provide their own, informal, messy, decentralized version. Lindblom (1965) argues that coordination refers to 'a set of interdependent decisions' that is 'coordinated if each decision is adapted to the others in such a way that for each adjusted decision, the adjustment is thought to be better than no adjustment in the eyes of one decision maker'. Mutual adjustment occurs when a decision maker either simply adapts to decisions around him or seeks to induce changes in other decision makers. The methods by which a decision maker can induce such adjustments include bargaining, reciprocity, manipulation, and compensation (see Chisholm 1989; Davis 1995; Peters 1998; and Wildavsky 1979: 131–3). The overlap with the idea of diplomacy is both obvious and inescapable.

Metagovernance

The language of metagovernance refers to the response to the dilemmas posed by the spread of networks. Marketization and privatization challenged the departmental way of doing things, fragmented service delivery systems, and undermined bureaucratic hierarchies. It multiplied networks, or the packages of organizations that now delivered public services. It fostered unintended consequences for accountability, coordination, and implementation. Metagovernance brings the state back in to resolve these dilemmas. Metagovernance, or 'the governance of government and governance' (Jessop 2000: 23, and 2007), is the umbrella concept used to describe the role of the state and its characteristic policy instruments in network governance. Given that governing is distributed among various private, voluntary, and public actors, and that power and authority are more decentralized and fragmented among a plurality of networks, the role of the state has shifted from rowing, or hands-on commands, to the more diverse toolkit of indirect informal modes of steering (Rhodes 1997b) through other agencies and non-departmental public bodies.

This chapter provides three examples of metagovernance. The first example is 'joined-up' government as the Blair government sought to devise policy instruments that integrated both horizontally across central government departments and vertically between central and local government and the voluntary sector. The second example is the Treasury's use of the financial levers of the PSA to spread their tentacles into the departments as never before (see also James 2004). It sought to become a policy department. Finally, as Fawcett (2009: ch. 4) argues, the reforms at No. 10 'increased the Prime Minister's capacity to achieve effective metagovernance over the rest of Whitehall; for example, the Delivery Unit's stocktakes' (Richards and Smith 2006: 341). Fawcett also quotes a senior No. 10 official arguing you have to 'strategically manage the landscape' by 'rethinking how government can keep control of those things they need to control'. That is not to say such steering was successful. As one official commented, 'the relatively subtle changes which have taken place in the reform agenda between 1999 and now don't seem worthy of close analysis from our end of the telescope' (Bovaird and Russell 2007: 319). Or, more bluntly: 'they see another piece of paper from the centre and say stuff that' [DG, FWNB].

It's the mix that matters

The network governance narrative and the metagovernance response draw attention to a third dilemma. All three stories—Westminster, managerial-ism, and network governance—are incommensurable; they mix like oil and water (Rhodes 1997*b*). Bevir and Rhodes (2006: ch. 9) show that, for the police, the shift from hierarchy to markets to networks poses specific dilem-mas. They know how to rewrite the rulebook, manage a contract, or work with Neighbourhood Watch but they struggle to reconcile these ways of working, believing they conflict and undermine one another. For doctors, the equivalent shift poses different dilemmas: the key issue is how to preserve the medical model of health and medical autonomy from managerial reforms that stress hierarchy and financial control (Bevir and Rhodes 2006, ch. 8). For ministers, the network governance story conflicts with the Westminster story's beliefs in hierarchy and leaders who know best. So, remaking policy is seen as a control deficit; a failure of implementation. The solution is better service delivery through joining-up and by velvet drainpipes that dress rules and command in diplomatic clothing. For top civil servants, the issue is how to combine the generalist tradition of coping with the uncertainties of ministerial life with 'can-do' managerialism that wants better service delivery.

I have shown ministers and top civil servants coping with everyday life. I have identified the dilemmas of responsiveness and metagovernance posed when the Westminster story confronts managerialism and network govern-ance. I have shown how they respond to those dilemmas by twin-tracking, joining-up, and indirect steering. But I have not shown what happens when the system of protocols and rituals, of shared meanings, confronts rude surprises. I turn to that task in Chapter 9.

NOTES

1. David Blunkett, former Secretary of State for Education, interview by Helen Mathers and Dave Richards, 19 January 2007. Cited with permission.
2. This section is based on FWNBs for all three departments.
3. John Prescott was Secretary of State for the Environment, Transport and the Regions (1997–2001); Deputy Prime Minister (1997–2007); and First Secretary of State (2001–7).
4. See also Barber 2007: 38.
5. I attended the meetings on 20 November 2002 and 2 April 2003. I report on the latter. Latterly, under Sir Gus O'Donnell as Cabinet Secretary, it has mutated into the Permanent Secretaries' Management Group with a Steering Group that meets more regularly.
6. For a brief history and photographs see: http://www.british-history.ac.uk/report. aspx?compid=68108. The room has a fine fireplace with wind-dial. Last accessed 19 October 2009.
7. See: http://www.audit-commission.gov.uk/localgov/audit/cpa/pages/default.aspx. Last accessed 19 October 2009.
8. On external networks see, for example: Blunkett 2006: 601 and 638; Henderson 2001: 157, 158, and 159–60; and Prescott 2008: 256.
9. See, for example: Perri 6 1997; and Perri 6 et al. 2002. This work emerged from Demos, a New Labour think-tank, and several of its personnel were subsequently SpAds in No. 10 and the Treasury (see Bevir 2005: 30–1).
10. On joined-up government see: Bevir 2005: 48–51; Bogdanor 2005; Ling 2002; MAC 2004; Pollitt 2003; Rhodes 2000*a*; and Richards 2008: 106–8 and 114–15.
11. The joined-up policy areas were sustainable communities; innovation in the knowledge economy; and CPAs. I had access to the supporting committee papers.
12. On the various forms of engagement with parliament see: Blunkett 2006: 12, 13, 80, 124, 152, 165, 191–2, 193, 501–2, 508–9, 576, and 600.
13. For advice to civil servants on how to draft answers to PQs see Jary 2004. I add one more piece of advice to Jary's eminently sensible list—if there is any political doubt, consult the SpAd.
14. See: Sear 2002; and House of Commons Information Office 2009. Although all-night sittings became less common, they did not disappear. On 10 March 2005, the sitting on the Prevention of Terrorism Bill lasted for 32 hours and 22 minutes. Also the House adopted September sittings in October 2002. It remains a hard task-master for ministers.
15. The Office of Communications (or OfCom) is the regulatory body with responsibility for television, radio, telecommunications, and wireless communications services. Its duties include: ensuring a wide range of TV and radio services of high quality and wide appeal; ensuring there are several providers; and protecting audiences against offensive or harmful material, unfairness, or the infringement of privacy. See: http://www.ofcom.org.uk/about/. Last accessed 21 October 2009.
16. Sandline International was a private military company—the polite term for mercenaries—that provided arms to the Sierra Leone government of President Ahmed Kabbah. The issue was whether the British government knew.

17. Networks other than the ones described below include, for DEFRA, the networks based on its regional offices and the devolved governments of Scotland and Wales; and for DEFRA and DTI, the European Union. Several interviewees commented on the importance of the EU at earlier stages of their career. I know there is a 'Euro-village' based around the European Secretariat of the Cabinet Office [Permanent Secretary, TI], but no one in any of the departmental courts had anything but the most fleeting contact with either that network or the EU while I was observing.

9

The Resignation

In Chapters 6–8, I explored in some detail the coping behaviour of ministers and civil servants. I assumed they lived in a media goldfish bowl punctuated by crises big and small but I have not described any specific crisis. In this chapter, I tell the story of Estelle Morris' resignation, describe the impact of stress and life in the goldfish bowl on personal lives before reflecting on why they do it. I return to the narrative form. These events took place between July and October 2002.[1] As ever, my focus is the Department view of events; my aim is to understand how members of the Department for Education and Skills (DfEs) coped with a rude surprise. It will become clear that others held different views. I note these differences. Given the sensitivities, legal and otherwise, I must make it clear that I write my construction of their construction of what happened. The interpretation is mine and mine alone. In my stories about protocols and rituals, I introduced a touch of humour. In telling this story, the tone is sombre with a hint of tragedy.

There is a problem with the label crisis. Top civil servants resisted my suggestion that they regularly confronted crises and insisted they coped 'because one is able to control and shape the timetable and the decision making processes'. They preferred to dismiss their several crises as 'a one-off'. When I was shadowing, every department had a crisis; for example, foot-and-mouth disease in the Department of Environment, Food and Rural Affairs (DEFRA), the collapse of British Energy in the Department of Trade and Industry (DTI), and the Criminal Records Board in DfES (see below). If a crisis necessarily involves a perceived, serious 'threat to the basic structures or the fundamental values and norms of a system, which under time pressure and highly uncertain circumstances necessitates making vital decisions' (Boin et al. 2005: 2), then the departments had crises but they were not an everyday event. Everyone told me of their recent crises. Everyone told me it was exceptional—'it's not like this normally'. Maybe, but compared to universities, or local government—two other types of organizations with which I am also familiar—life in a government department is more demanding because they live in a media goldfish bowl which can take any problem and make it a crisis.

If the label crisis is reserved for threatening and urgent events, I need a label for the disruptive events that abound in everyday life. Conventionally, uncertainty is defined as a risk that cannot be measured or randomness with an unknown probability (Emery 1969; Knight 1921). I use the term to refer to the contingent unintended consequences of other people's beliefs and actions. Uncertainty is a fact of political-administrative life but how do you manage it when you do not know when, where, how, or why it will happen? Protocols and rituals are the tools of political-administrators for managing uncertainty and for ensuring there are no surprises. But when they get a 'rude surprise' (Boin et al. 2005: 139), they struggle to cope using their existing repertoire of tools. For political-administrators, it is important not to create a crisis by so labelling an event. The resignation of a minister may not be a crisis, therefore, but it is a rude surprise because they must cope with high levels of uncertainty. Whether a rude surprise becomes a crisis depends on whether the actors so define it. A crisis is in the eyes of the several beholders.

THE RESIGNATION

The headlines of the day tell the unfolding drama:[2]

'CLASS WAR. The deliberate marking down of A-level results shames our education system' (*The Sun*, 19 September 2002)

'The great betrayal' (*Daily Mail*, 19 September 2002)

'. . . but her legs show the strain' (*The Times*, 20 September 2002)

'ESTELLE FIGHTS FOR SURVIVAL. She caves in and orders exam probe' (*The Sun*, 20 September 2002)

'Fall of the cabinet golden girl who refused to play the political game' (*The Guardian*, 24 October 2002)

'Estelle: I'm not up to job' (*The Sun*, 24 October 2002)

Uncertainty invites stories to make sense of what is happening. I am telling a story about other people's stories. So, the first question is whose story? There are at least two stories; by the DfES and its Minister; and by No. 10. The DfES story is about demonstrating ministerial and departmental competence. The No. 10 story is about promoting the choice agenda in education. The stories intersect but they have distinct storylines.

The 15th of August was the day on which A-level results were released. As ever, there were wild allegations about dumbing down because there had been an increase in the number of students passing. The press and opposition backbench politicians treated the increase as evidence of falling standards, not better student performance. The usual feeding frenzy had an extra frisson in 2002. On 1 September, *The Observer* claimed that grades had been fixed to suppress grade inflation. The awarding bodies, and the peak associations speaking for head teachers, also expressed concern that the regulatory body, the Qualifications and Curriculum Authority (QCA), had put undue pressure on the awarding bodies to prevent grade inflation.[3]

The Department's story

The DfES storyline is about ministerial and departmental competence. In so saying, I am not suggesting that anyone was incompetent. I suggest only that the Minister and the Department saw competence as the main storyline. Their task was complicated by recent bungles and rumblings.

The Criminal Records Bureau (CRB) runs criminal records checks on, for example, staff who work with children. After the murder of two schoolgirls by a school caretaker, the CRB was asked to check school staff more thoroughly. It could not cope with the extra work, schools were left short of a staff, and Estelle Morris had to apologise and return to the old system. In 1999, Gordon Brown announced the Individual Learning Accounts (ILA) scheme. It provided tax incentives and cash payments for employers to improve, for example, the IT skills of their employees. By late 2001, it was clear the scheme was in trouble. It was not Estelle Morris' policy but she carried the can for it, and it was a mess. In October 2002, the National Audit Office (NAO) reported there had been £97 million of fraud and abuse, mainly because there was no effective regulation of the scheme. Then along came the QCA and as Seldon (2007: 110) observes: 'Number 10 had already begun to have doubts about her leadership . . . but it was her handling of the A-level crisis that sapped confidence in her.'

How was it handled?

I attended many meetings with the Permanent Secretary and the Minister both separately and together. I could not be in two places at once, so I missed several meetings that, in an ideal world, I would have attended. Also, as events unfolded, the number of meetings multiplied. On several occasions, the Minister and the Permanent Secretary, together and apart, were in meetings on this issue for five or more hours during the day. It is impossible to describe all these encounters in a single chapter. So, I have selected those meetings that best illustrate how events unfolded.

Monday 16 September 8.45 a.m.

The Permanent Secretary is 'disappointed'. The Oxford, Cambridge and RSA Examinations (OCR) is one of the three awarding bodies setting exams, marking, and awarding grades.[4] It refused to answer questions from the press about the marking down of A-level results. However, he has several other meetings this morning so cannot pay much attention to the matter, although it is discussed in the margins of these meetings. Most of the time, it is just general office chit-chat but there is one significant encounter. He discusses developments with the Minister's political adviser. They agree 'we should stay well away' because 'it is blowing up into a storm'. The point of agencies is they are distanced from the Department. So, the Department should point out that it has no involvement in marking but the QCA is conducting an investigation. It is the early stance. It does not last.

Most of the morning is taken up with a Keep-in-Touch of directors general (DGs) that focuses on internal performance and promotions; it is business as usual. At the end of the meeting the Minister's Principal Private Secretary (PPS) joins them. He tells them the Minister is 'concerned, not worried but concerned' and wants to know what the Department knew and when. They are trying to get the story straight to answer this question. They believe that, on 12 March 2002, Sir William Stubbs (Chair of the QCA since 1997)[5] at one of the regular meetings between the awarding bodies and the QCA, told the awarding bodies to pay attention to the proportion of A-grades in the first year of the new A-level. On 25 March, the Chair of the Management Committee of the Joint Council for General Qualifications (JCGQ), Kathleen Tattershall, wrote to the QCA to clarify the situation. Sir William replied on 19 April saying:

> I do expect last year's A-level results to provide a very strong guide to this year's outcomes.[6]

This sentence bears two interpretations. To Sir William's critics, he was saying the proportion of students passing this year should be the same as last year irrespective of their performance. Sir William insisted he was saying only that standards had to be maintained and be consistent year on year; that was his job.[7]

There was substance to the complaints about lowering marks. The OCR 'felt pressurised by the QCA to suppress grade inflation' (ESC 2003: 22) and 'tightened up on the marking of A-level course work' but it was 'an example of the sort of adjustment which awarding bodies make every year to secure consistent standards'. DfES decided to issue a statement that 'Ministers and officials have had no influence over the awarding process'. They stick to the theory that agencies are at arm's length from the Department. Indeed, the Minister went further, believing the responsibility for examinations should 'never' rest with ministers. The Permanent Secretary also wanted more discussions with the Minister. He uses storytelling language: 'what is our story?' and 'is it convincing?' The Minister has to agree the story is internally consistent and a plausible version of events.

By mid-afternoon, the Department's stance begins to change. There are a series of short meetings between other engagements, some in the Permanent Secretary's office and some in the Minister's. As the media warm to their task, the QCA is 'rattled' by the headlines. It had not taken the complaints 'as seriously as it should'. Ken Boston, who had just become Chief Executive of the QCA, and Sir William Stubbs will begin the round of media with an appearance on the BBC's *Today* programme. The Permanent Secretary shows increasing concern and pushes for stronger action; he is seen as 'the boss'. He is concerned that the QCA's account will not be seen as plausible compared with the counter-claims of the head teachers of independent schools. He wants a report by Wednesday morning and is told there will be an interim report by tonight. He is mollified but now believes the Minister 'can't stay out if it affects young people's careers'. Sob stories about pupils failing to get the required grades for university abound in all the media. Again, he asks for the facts and 'the most accurate story'. The Department has to be 'upfront and transparent' otherwise the press will say the Minister can't run education.

There is an inner circle around the Minister. Its core is the communications group that meet weekly: the Permanent Secretary, the PPS, the Ministerial Adviser, and the Press Officer. They are joined by other officials, commonly from the Schools DG as needed, and later by friends and supporters of Estelle Morris. They provide not only advice on handling the A-level problem but also strong personal support.[8] They agree their immediate aim is to 'make sure the system is credible'. They feel they are hampered by the QCA, which seems slow to respond and defensive. The Permanent Secretary concludes 'she is not going to set the agenda this week'.

Everyday business ends just after 5 p.m. and the Permanent Secretary shows me the interim paper on the QCA and marking. It sets out the known facts and the procedures being followed. The Press Office reports that the QCA has sprung into action and done the rounds of all the major evening news programmes on radio and television. Also, they are not being defensive; they are telling the audience what they are doing; not justifying what happened.

Tuesday 17 September 10 a.m.

The Private Office provides newspaper cuttings every morning and the Minister and the Permanent Secretary go through them. The Permanent Secretary announces 'we survived'. Not everyone is so confident. Andrew Adonis asks: 'This A-level business, it's all right isn't it?' The Minister replies 'No it isn't.' She has been stung by *The Times* leader which indeed claims she can't run education. The Minister is no longer concerned; she is worried, because she has been sucked into events and believes it is now about the credibility of the examination system. She talks about the headlines. However, for both of them, the morning is taken up with the Department's spending review, so the Private Office is told to keep an eye on things, as if they wouldn't! The Permanent Secretary has also told his office that he is 'on call' for the Minister, so his other appointments may be subject to cancellation.

The Minister is on edge. She does not lose her temper or otherwise express anger. The Permanent Secretary thinks he's one of the few who notices when she is in a temper. He is relaxed and good at defusing situations. His response is 'let's step back and look at this'. One Minister [TI] described him as '*understated*'.

The Minister meets Ken Boston and Sir William Stubbs. Sir William invited himself to the meeting and the Minister is irritated. The Press Office is also there but not the Permanent Secretary. He paces and fidgets with the blind in his office until he is called in. The meeting tends to go round and around. They have no agreed account of what happened and why. It is not hard to understand why. There isn't a shared understanding of the issues. The Minister wonders whether Sir William did steer the awarding bodies not to increase the proportion of candidates passing. Sir William believes he was maintaining standards. They want to end the press speculation but are unsure how. Events are unfolding around them. The Permanent Secretary says 'we are 48 hours behind the game' but they still agree there will be no account of what happened before Friday. Also, they agree that the Press Office and Special Adviser (SpAd) must not initiate stories. There have been accusations of 'freelancing' and, if there is any truth in them, they must stop. They are to be reined in. Whether their off-the-record briefings are reined in becomes a bone of contention.

Wednesday 18 September 9 a.m.

The PPS hurries into the Permanent Secretary's office from the loading bay where he has just despatched the Minister in her car to a meeting elsewhere. The Minister is in 'a strop'. *The Times* will be gratified by the frequency with which it is consulted—'The Thunderer' lives.[9] It led with the headline 'Board [OCR] admits moving A-level goal posts'. Also Edward Gould, Chair of the Headmasters' and Headmistresses' Conference (HMC), which represents the heads of some 250 private schools, claims the QCA has been 'coordinating' the move to mark down some students, and the HMC calls for a regrading of papers and an independent inquiry.[10] The Minister demands something 'dramatic', suggesting an independent inquiry headed by Boston. The Permanent Secretary must talk to Boston now. The Department must be seen to be addressing the issues. 'She knew she was being over the top', says the PPS but 'she wants a meeting at 1p.m.' 'Let's pause', says the Permanent Secretary, 'I'll discuss with Boston and come back for 1p.m'. 'She'll only get one shot at it', says the Press Office, 'no drip, drip response'. 'We can't wait for Friday', says the PPS. Events are gathering pace.

The Permanent Secretary is worried. Although the concerns of the private schools were known already, the HMC's intervention makes the story credible. He sees it as a turning point, but has to go to the weekly meeting of Perm Secs. The SpAd asks to see him for five minutes but he says no. He chats as he heads off. There have been too many crises—ILAs, CRB, and now A-levels. It is important to have success and dealing with 'crises' (his word) helps. 'She's not a big hitter', so she's worried about her future. He thinks the inquiry is a 'barmy idea' and he does not approach Boston. He gets the PPS to ring and brief him. The Minister was 'unnerved' by the press reports. Although the OCR's admission was correct, the presentation was appalling. He agrees they need to take decisive action but it's a big issue and they must have the facts first. He believes the grades were adjusted, as they were each year, to maintain standards.[11] He is unsure whether there was pressure to contain grade inflation.

The Minister is 'seriously rattled'. No. 10 in the guise of Andrew Adonis wants to know why the Minister isn't doing the rounds of the media. He wants her to go public and 'take a grip'. No. 10 remains in regular touch.[12] The Minister is also cross. At the 1 p.m. meeting the Permanent Secretary argues her out of an inquiry. What will it inquire into? We still don't know what we are dealing with. There are two issues; today's problem about marking standards and the long-term credibility of the system. The Permanent Secretary persuades her to let Boston report on the standards issue. The inquiry, if there is to be one, can look at the long-term credibility of the system, and that decision can wait until we know what has happened.

They are now in limbo. The Permanent Secretary cannot settle. One submission is 'too boring to read'. The Private Office is 'keeping stuff from me' and he needs 'more distractions'. Boston rings and the Permanent Secretary briefs him on the 1 p.m. meeting. Boston agrees to the two-step approach. They then discuss the situation more generally. The Minister 'wants to fill the vacuum' and 'she feels she can't go on another 48 hours without saying something'. Boston insists he needs time to collect the data from the schools. His report won't be ready before Friday. However, the Minister believes the QCA's inquiry is too narrow, looking only at the technical issue of grade boundaries. The intervention of the HMC broadened the issue to one of trust in the credibility of the system. So, they discuss the possible head of an independent inquiry. They agree Mike Tomlinson is 'reliable'.

The centre of the story now shifts to the role of the Chair of the QCA. As events unfolded, the Permanent Secretary and the Minister became increasingly concerned about how he is being portrayed in the media. He might have said that the 'Minister and officials behaved impeccably', but they worry about his continuing reactions. They were not to worry for long.

Sir William rings the Permanent Secretary. After a few preliminaries about when the report will be released, they turn to the main business; Sir William proposes to release his letter of 19 April to Kathleen Tattershall to the media. He believes his letter is about maintaining standards and that teachers 'seriously misdirected themselves'. He denies, and continues to deny, that any letter from the QCA said there should not be a rise in the pass rate (see also

ESC 2003: 99). The Permanent Secretary believes the offending phrase bears more than one interpretation. It could refer to the consistent standards year on year (as Sir William claimed) or to 'no grade inflation' as others claimed. He thinks releasing the letter 'won't help but it won't hinder', provided teachers are not blamed. Rather, he is more concerned the QCA and departmental press offices speak with one voice.

The Minister has decided she must make a statement and is drafting a speech. She feels she can wait no longer for two reasons. First, she was convinced that 'something had gone wrong in at least some parts of the marking system', so 'it was right to check the system'. Second, it was necessary 'to restore public confidence in the system as soon as possible'. The problem with going public with a broader inquiry is that the media want blood and will call for resignations; Sir William's, if not hers. She calls in her inner circle. She will speak at 11.30 a.m. tomorrow and announce a broad inquiry into standards, not just grade boundaries. It will be chaired by Mike Tomlinson. She is much happier now a decision has been taken. Her improved spirits will not last.

Thursday 19 September 8 a.m.

No. 10 has turned up the heat overnight. Andrew Adonis paged the Permanent Secretary in his car on the way home. He was worried about the headlines on the 10 p.m. news. He made it clear that the inquiry must investigate the QCA, not just the specific allegations. The Prime Minister has said 'contain this' and 'widen the inquiry'.

The early morning meeting in the Minister's office is low-key, business-like. There are no smiles, no jokes. The Minister is sat leaning forward, poised, strong body language. She will announce an inquiry, with Ken Boston by her side. It will inquire into the QCA: 'I promise you we are not about to throw the QCA or Bill to the wolves.' The Permanent Secretary is less sanguine. As he heads back to his office he says, 'I must speak to Bill', who has no idea that there will be a broad ranging investigation; 'he will be upset but I have to persuade him'. And it is the beginning of the end, and not just for Sir William.

The Diary Secretary tries to get Sir William on the line but 'he won't speak to me'. Why becomes clear. He has faxed a letter, which calls for an inquiry into the allegations against the QCA by the HMC.[13] The Diary Secretary gets through to Ken Boston who agrees to attend the press conference. They have yet to decide whether to put him on the platform. It may lead to questions he is not yet able to answer. They also want to stop Sir William doing interviews so the momentum lies with the Minister. The Press Office doubts it can be done.

Thursday 19 September 11 a.m.

The Minister started work on her speech yesterday. She worked on it, off and on, with the Permanent Secretary, the SpAds, and the Press Office until late last night. Even at this late stage, Alastair Campbell is dictating passages to her over the phone. She will deliver the speech from handwritten notes. It is typed as she speaks. The atmosphere in the office is fraught as the press conference looms. The coverage will have a marked effect on her reputation and standing. The Minister is composing her thoughts and trying to anticipate questions and follow-ups. The Permanent Secretary wonders if he should go: 'I don't normally go to press conferences'. He decides not: 'it may be seen as indicating just how serious it all is'. Jokingly, he comments 'I have nothing to do now. What shall I do?' The Private Office hands him a file on a programme called Sure Start. He comes to the press conference anyway and stands at the back, unseen and unremarked.

The conference room on the fifth floor is like any university seminar room except there is more equipment, newer equipment, more expensive equipment. The Private Secretary (PS) who accompanies the Minister's party observes, 'this is fun, not every week is like this'. It may be a break in his routine. I doubt the Minister thinks it is fun. The room is packed; 'they're queuing at the door, what for, the royal handshake?' This sarcastic remark from a journalist sets the tone for what is to follow. It is a thoroughly unpleasant event and a disaster for the Minister.

The Minister stands at the lectern and reads the text (Morris 2002*a*). She is nervous and stumbles over it. Her voice is clear and firm but the act is not convincing. She looks besieged. She explains the Department has no role in marking papers but she is responsible for the integrity of the system so there will be an inquiry by Mike Tomlinson to report within a week. She sits down at the desk for questions. Someone has committed a gaffe. Normally a table has a cloth draped over it that goes down to the floor. Not today. The Minister's legs are in full view and she keeps twining her legs around each other. In answering questions, her style is 'help me to reassure parents and children'. She is convincing when she bluntly asserts, 'I'm not in this job to fiddle marks'.

It would seem obvious the press conference should have covered what happened and why. Also, the Minister should explain what was to be done about the students with lowered grades. These were the substantive issues. The Minister had cogent answers. There is one small problem. The overwhelming majority of journalists had no interest in her answers. Indeed, the specialist journalists who could understand the subject were outnumbered by the political correspondents who had no interest in education. They talked among themselves and then complained 'she's making it more confused'. Call me naive but I was amazed by their cavalier behaviour. I thought they were ill-informed and impolite. Their comments ranged from 'it will dissipate the pressure, temporarily', to 'pretty textbook' and 'Stubbs should go'. And that last comment is the nub. The game was called 'gotcha'; they wanted a resignation. It did not matter who. It was all summed up by *The Times* next day under the headline ' . . . but her legs show the strain'. The paper printed a picture of the Minister's entwined legs while Laura Peek wrote of her tortured posture, white knuckles, and angry flush. The reference to self-touching as a source of confidence in infancy was equally mean-spirited. None of it was germane to the question of what to do about the kids who had lost university places. Perhaps standards at 'The Thunderer' have also been lowered.

The Minister had no time for reflection. Immediately after the press conference she had television interviews. There is only time to adjust hair and make-up before delivering crisp, clear sound bites: 'I know the rules; the government does not mark papers'. She knows what she wants to say and says it almost irrespective of the question asked; 'I don't think that is the issue, we need to focus on . . . ' I hear all the interviews and the same phrases recur: 'there are complaints every year'; 'no one has been downgraded'; 'we can put it right'; 'we will review the grades'; 'for most students and most subjects there is no problem'; 'I am proud of the students'. When she stops for a cup of tea, the producer for *News at One* flaps; 'we need her back now, where is she, where is she?' She walks in grinning, 'OK, OK'. She assumes the same body position, same crisp, clear tone of voice, same message. She does 14 interviews.

Back in the office the Permanent Secretary thinks 'we are ahead on points'. He believes the Sunday papers will be the key. He is still worried they don't know the full story. But that task now belongs to Tomlinson and he discusses with Human Resources the staff, office space, equipment, and records for the Tomlinson inquiry. There is little time. The PPS sticks his head around the door: 'are we happy?' 'It will be mixed but not bad' is the reply. 'Estelle is happy with her performance', says the PPS and disappears. 'Every week we are thrown off course by something', sighs the Permanent Secretary. It is not over yet.

Friday 20 September 9 a.m.

Friday opens with a problem. Sir William is centre stage again. He believes the Press Office and the SpAd are out to get him. He accuses the Minister of 'panicking'. In fact, relations between Sir William and the Department have a chequered history. They think his accusation is groundless; as one DG observes, they don't need to brief against him because the press already dislike him. QCA has a press conference at 2 p.m. covering what happened, at which Sir William will make a statement. They fear that no one will believe his story that there was no manipulation, particularly if his tone is complacent or defensive.

To compound the problem, the 7 p.m. news yesterday was awful: 'it's not a storm in a teacup'. *The Sun* talks of the Minister 'caving in' when the Department wanted the paper to say the Minister 'takes control'. The Permanent Secretary 'choked on his breakfast' when he heard the teacup phrase. It had been used regularly by Sir William in meetings and he now thinks Sir William is briefing the BBC.

Sir William rings. It starts off in a friendly manner with jokes about chiropractors. This mood does not last. He repeats his complaint about the Department briefing against him. He names the Press Officer. The Permanent Secretary replies, 'we can only go on assuring you we are not briefing against you'. The Permanent Secretary points out there are 'plenty of people out there critical of you'. They turn to the main issue: the press conference. The Permanent Secretary does not want Sir William or anyone else at QCA to blame teachers; 'are you certain you did not?' 'The phrase "storm in a teacup" is your phrase so we thought you'd briefed somebody at the BBC.' 'We are lost if you say the same thing at the press conference.' Sir William reassures him: 'I'm relieved you are not going to.' 'I'm glad we've had this conversation.'

But Sir William is not finished. He reads the Permanent Secretary his proposed statement. He wants to challenge the independent schools to prove their case.

'That's coming out fighting,' says the Permanent Secretary. 'Are you sure you've got the correct information? Is there any doubt it's a few schools, and a few subjects? I'm not clearing this on the phone.'

The Permanent Secretary is being patient: 'I don't mind you feeling angry.' He does not think there is evidence yet that only a few schools are affected but he needs Sir William on-side and this conversation is the means for getting there. So his voice is patient but his body is taut. He is drumming his fingers on the desk. He picks up his rubber stress car and squeezes it. 'Let's keep in touch. It's a changing scene.'

Now it's off to the conference room for no other reason than the Permanent Secretary wants a change of scene. He summons the Press Office, the SpAd, and the PPS. They agree the tabloid coverage is 'nasty' but 'it could have been worse'. The SpAd tells them the Sunday papers 'will not be pretty'. However, No. 10 is happy for some reason. They discuss the Minister's performance and agree she needs to project more self-confidence. The most damaging development is that 'the story is now Estelle'.

The Permanent Secretary gives a frank report on his conversation with Sir William. He tells them, 'there's no gain in him going down, at least not at the moment'. He does not know what they have said, if anything, off the record but still he fires a warning shot.

He is also concerned again that he is not getting the full story. The DG has told him that there is a letter on file from Kathleen Tattershall received at the end of July. On 26 July, there was a meeting between the QCA and the awarding bodies about the early A-level results. There was an increase in the pass rate. Reportedly Sir William expressed his displeasure. Tattershall's letter expressed her concern about this pressure. The Permanent Secretary expresses his displeasure that the letter has only just come to light: 'You should have found it earlier.' 'How many letters were there?' 'Are we on record anywhere?' He issues a clear instruction to go back through all the files: 'I must have *all* the relevant correspondence.' He knows the correspondence establishes a direct link with the Department. It means 'nobody out there will believe us', although there were no meetings and he knows they had nothing to do with lowering the marks. For the first time his head goes down.

He needs and takes a short break. He recovers quickly. He turns his attention to the terms of reference of the Tomlinson inquiry. No. 10 has been on the telephone to the Minister. They agree there should be an inquiry and insist Tomlinson is given full access and all the resources he wants to conduct it. 'There must be no stakeholders', which is No. 10 code for teachers. The Permanent Secretary has few problems with any of this. He trusts Tomlinson and is happy to leave such matters as publishing the documentary evidence or public hearings to his discretion.

Sir William's draft statement is faxed to the Department; it is '150 per cent better than the version on the phone'. The Permanent Secretary makes some detailed amendments to the draft, taking out the combative elements. He then rings Sir William and reads out the revised statement. I do not see or hear a discernible response.

Friday 20 September, midday

With any rude surprise, there are blips. One minute you seem to be on top of events. The next minute, events are on top of you. Yesterday, Chris Wood-head, the head of Ofsted, said: 'you only need a nod and wink' to get your message across and anyway 'there's enough correspondence'. The Press Officer was in a 'rage'. Estelle was in 'complete despair'. Today, it is literally yesterday's news. There's a new blip, courtesy of advance notice from *The Observer* of their Sunday story that Estelle knew some ten weeks ago, never told anyone, and did nothing.

PERMANENT SECRETARY: It may get worse.
PPS: Oh, it will get worse.
PERMANENT SECRETARY: It will be said we knew and did nothing. We are losing this.
PPS: I can't see the endgame.

There is no time to brood. The Minister is back from a school visit; 'I've been better'. Alastair Campbell rings; 'it's serious but not a disaster'. The QCA report arrives. They have been full of foreboding. They need the QCA press conference to go well but fear the report will be a dry as dust factual document. It is (QCA 2002). Even worse, in the Permanent Secretary's opinion, it is unclear on whether there is a problem. The report is too technical. It will take too long to read and understand. It will get buried by other stories. They should be so lucky.

They all gather around the TV to watch the press conference on Sky. A PS takes notes. I muse; it is still a writing culture. Why not video it? But they don't. The press conference is flat, detailed, and technical. The response is not. Damian Green, opposition spokesperson on education, talks of 'Examgate' and points out that the report does not address the issue of pressure to lower grades. Indeed it does not. It explicitly excludes the subject because they do not admit there was any pressure! John Claire, *Daily Telegraph*, calls it a 'fiasco'. On Sky News, Martin Bright, *The Observer*'s education correspondent, calls it a 'whitewash', and a 'disgrace'. The attempt to blame the press and teachers is met with derision: 'it is an insult to the intelligence of teachers. Something went wrong. Someone moved the goal posts.' The QCA is accused of 'trying to blind us with science, with meaningless statistics'. The Permanent Secretary knows 'the QCA have blown it'. They focused on narrow technical issues like grade boundaries and ignored the larger issue of confidence in the system. Throughout the day, there have been lows, moment of doubt. There is now a deep depression. There are meetings to attend, briefs to read, but the Permanent Secretary's batteries are flat. He is low key, still.

As we leave at the end a hectic week, he reflects:

> They don't want to know the facts. They want someone to blame. I tried to persuade the Secretary of State to wait because we didn't know the facts but the story ran so fast, the facts didn't matter.

And the newspaper headlines bear out his worst fears. The unkindest cut probably came from *The Sun* which, under the banner headline 'She has so much to learn', claimed that 'Estelle Morris inspires as much confidence as a domestic science teacher whose souffle won't rise'. Of course, 'soufflé' was spelt wrongly.

The Tomlinson inquiry and the sacking of Sir William, 27 September

I did not shadow either the Minister or the Permanent Secretary during the week beginning 23 September and the rest of this story is based on my interviews, newspaper accounts, and memoirs. Events in the second week focused on the Tomlinson inquiry, although it was not without its tumultuous blips. Fully capable of reading the political runes, Sir William knew he was a sacrificial lamb in waiting. He fired a warning shot, accusing the Minister of improperly intervening by ordering the regrading of A-levels before Tomlinson reported.[14] He was interviewed on the BBC's *News at Ten*. When asked if there was a whispering campaign against him, Sir William again repeated his view that the DfES was briefing against him: 'there probably is, we know the way in which government departments work in modern society. It would not surprise me if that was going on.' The Minister was 'personally offended' and responded with her own media round. She admitted officials had spoken to the awarding bodies so that they were 'as ready as they can be' to implement the inquiry's recommendations. She denied categorically she had ordered the remarking of papers and refused to comment on whether Sir William would remain in his job: 'I am not even thinking about that. I have to concentrate on what matters.'

Others were thinking about it: 'She can't run her Department if she is at war with the people that implement her policies.'

Protestations such as: 'this is not about personalities, this is about the substance of an issue, which is how it affects students' could only come from an official. These blips kept the Minister in the headlines and, therefore, a target. She was the issue for the opposition. The Conservative Party leader, Iain Duncan Smith adopted the expected posture: 'her position is untenable. She should either be sacked or resign.' The endgame was increasingly clear.

Tomlinson responded briskly to Sir William's remarks: 'Whatever happened late yesterday afternoon . . . has, in my considered view, had no impact on my inquiry, nor will I allow it do so. . . . I am completely satisfied that my inquiry remains independent.' Sir William accepted his assurance. This flurry was the beginning of the end. The rude surprise had acquired new characteristics. It was not only about A-level standards but also about resignations. The issue was how many.[15]

The Tomlinson report (2002) provided the story the Permanent Secretary had been seeking, and it was a story of misunderstandings. There were two key ambiguities. First, the report concludes there was no clear or consistent view about the standards required at the AS-level (para. 14) and a lack of consistency in the practices of the examining boards (para. 36). In other words, there was no common standard for grading papers. Second, the report distinguishes between students passing because of lower examining standards and because of improved performance. The issue then was what Sir William had said. He insisted his concern was to maintain standards year on year and the report confirms that this role was 'wholly proper' (para. 46). The awarding bodies begged to differ. They were convinced they had been told to limit the number passing to the same level as last year with the 'threat' of an inquiry if there was an increase in numbers (para. 47). Confronted with these divergent stories, Tomlinson concludes: 'I am unable to fully resolve the clear differences in perception of what was said at the meeting' (para. 49). The report exonerates the DfES from exerting any pressure or guidance on grading (para. 51). The report tellingly concludes:

> At the root of this is a longstanding misunderstanding of the difference between maintaining a standard and the proportion of candidates meeting that standard and hence deserving to be awarded a GCE A-level. This misunderstanding appears to exist at almost all levels of the system, and in society at large.

At the press briefing Tomlinson said it was 'an accident waiting to happen'. The report recommended regrading some units as well as better training and guidance on standards.

Sir William issued a statement that he was pleased the inquiry had 'confirmed that I acted properly, and within my powers, as a regulator should'. However, he went on: 'you have informed me that you believe that there has been a breakdown of trust between me and the awarding bodies'. So, 'I formally offer you my resignation.' It would seem he had done the decent thing and fallen on his sword. Not quite.

Back at the DfES, the inner group already knew that Sir William would have to go after releasing the Tomlinson report. His outburst accusing the Minister of improper interference made his departure inevitable.

> *Bill did me a favour that night, little did he know, because he made it far easier to say, 'He's got to go.' He couldn't stay after that. I couldn't work with him after that. He clearly had no confidence in me and I couldn't find a good working relationship with him. Simple as that.* [Minister, TI]

The breakdown of trust was not confined to the awarding bodies. In her statement, the Minister focused on the steps that would be taken immediately to protect students before turning to the question of standards. Consistency:

> will be achieved through new leadership at the top of the QCA. We have only recently appointed a new chief executive and I would like the changes recommended by Mike Tomlinson to be achieved with the QCA led by a new chairman. I have removed Sir William Stubbs from his post as Chairman so that we start that process now. After I told him of my decision, Sir William formally offered his resignation. (Morris 2002*b*)

In her letter of 27 September to Sir William, the Minister gave four reasons for his dismissal: the perception of pressure by the awarding bodies; the Tomlinson report's criticisms of the performance of the QCA; the loss of confidence in the QCA by the wider education community; and Sir William's public criticism of the Minister and the resulting 'irretrievable breakdown' in trust.[16] So, he did not fall, he was pushed. He did not go quietly.

Doorstepped at his London home, Sir William suggested 'Estelle Morris must consider her own position. She was minister for schools when this matter arose.'[17] He remained convinced there was no crisis and the media coverage caused panic in the Department (see ESC 2003: 95, 101, and 106). His daughter was vigorous in his defence; 'I will not rest until I have seen Estelle Morris go down. My father is a man of honour and Estelle Morris should go down if she has a conscience.'[18] The Minister left for the Labour Party's Annual Conference in Blackpool until 2 October.

The Minister's resignation 22 and 23 October

The first three weeks of October were supposed to be business as usual but there were more surprises. On 10 October, the Minister overruled an independent appeals panel but did not have the legal authority to do so. Much more important, however, was the ruckus over the key targets for primary schools; they were not being met. On Tuesday 22 October, *The Guardian*, among others, reported that she 'was accused of lying to parliament . . . after it emerged that she had reneged on a commitment to resign over the government's failure to achieve literacy and numeracy targets.' She had mistakenly denied making that commitment (*Hansard*, 2 March 1999: Col. 948). It was the last straw. She felt her integrity had been impugned. Taken with A-levels, CRB, ILA, and the rest, it was a cocktail that undermined both the Minister's self-confidence and the confidence of No. 10 in the Minister (Seldon 2007: 110). She saw Tony Blair for an hour on Wednesday night and slept on it. She refused to take telephone calls from David Blunkett: '*she wouldn't answer my phone calls in the 24 hours before she signed that wretched letter and resigned because she knew I would try and persuade her* [to stay]' [Minister, TI]. She resigned two days before the debate in the House on primary school targets.

In her letter of resignation, which Alastair Campbell helped her draft, she admitted:

> I am good at dealing with the issues and in communicating to the teaching profession. I am less good at strategic management of a huge department and I am not good at dealing with the modern media.

She felt 'I have not been as effective as I should be' and 'I was not enjoying the job'. She concluded, 'I don't think this is for me' (*The Guardian*, 24 October 2002; and Seldon 2007: 110). When I interviewed her she was convinced that she had dealt with the A-level issue:

> *I always thought I could be judged on how well I dealt with the 'A-level' problem. And I think I dealt with it well. Well, put it this way, my successor has not changed it. Policy has not changed.*

She recognized that she took a risk.

> The politically astute thing might have been to close the issue down as quickly as you could, rush the reports and narrow the inquiry as much as possible. To some extent we did the opposite.... We gave Mike Tomlinson as much time as he needed and encouraged him to report in two stages which gave more focus to the issue.
>
> Given there was a major problem with the credibility of the exam system I think to have examined all the concerns, been able to reassure all candidates, make proposals for improvements to the system and set out the beginning of what became a national debate on the 14–19 agenda in about six weeks wasn't bad! [Personal correspondence]

The problem was that 'politically, it left too many gaps which the media filled'.

However, it was not the rude surprise around the A-level results that precipitated her resignation. It was '*the literacy and numeracy stuff, that's when I decided to resign*'. She felt that '*my going "lanced the boil"*' and '*gave the Department a period of stability*'. She resented the media and the distress they caused:

Getting home Sunday night and the press had been on to friends wanting to know who you lived with, why you split up, things like that. At that time I needed my privacy.

Perhaps even worse: '*I thought the press had rewritten me as a politician and I would forever be nice but incompetent and not strong enough for the job.*'

At the time and afterwards, there was much gossip that she had been undermined by No. 10 in the guise of Andrew Adonis (*The Guardian*, 27 October 2002). Estelle Morris conceded that she '*never socialized with the No. 10 political network*':

The political network I didn't manage well. I'd never managed it. I didn't know about it. I wasn't skilled at it and I was conceited enough to think I didn't have to do it. Naive. A mixture of naive and conceit. [Minister, TI]

When asked outright about the role of No. 10, she denied it had a role.

RAWR: Did No. 10 interfere in this at all?
MINISTER: No.
RAWR: Why is there gossip that Adonis decided you needed to go?
MINISTER: I don't believe that. No I don't believe that. Andrew is not my politics and I disagree with Andrew a great deal on a lot of education. I have no evidence to believe that that's the case. I don't actually believe that it's true.
RAWR: Can I rephrase the same question. I listen to gossip, and I know it's gossip, and all you can do when you hear gossip is just ask and see whether anybody bears it out or not. Was there a sense in which No. 10 collectively thought 'she's got to go because, to use your language, we have got to lance this boil'?
MINISTER: I didn't think so at the time.
RAWR: Were they briefing against you, which they have been known to do?
MINISTER: They weren't doing enough to support. I didn't think this at the time, this is all afterwards. I don't think they were briefing against me, but I don't think they were briefing for me. I think they could have come in behind.
RAWR: They were letting you sink or swim depending on how the wind blew.
MINISTER: Yeah.
RAWR: Did Tony Blair speak to you at all about it?
MINISTER: He must have phoned me over the difficulties about four times. No complaints of that. He phoned me, and he called me in after the statement. He said, 'Very, very good yesterday'. I also had a meeting with him during that period as well.

I leave the last word with the Permanent Secretary who lost a friend, not just a Minister. He stressed their informal conversations and dropping in to see the Minister two or three times a day during the crisis: '*it is a part of the job, not in the job description, it's sort of a pastoral care and support role and that's what you are there for and you would do it—and do—for other ministers in a crisis as well.*'

He considered his good relationship with Estelle Morris a '*stroke of luck*':

We had worked together for several years before she became Secretary of State so we had a lot of shared understandings. We have also been through some really difficult things together and we have stood together. She has an almost unique ability to connect with her audience; that is something quite special about her. She is somebody who listens intently to others and to civil servants and respects her advisers, all of them. And she is someone who trusts people and enters genuinely into a debate.

The Diary Secretary spoke for everyone from the Permanent Secretary to DGs to clerical officers when she said everyone was upset over the Minister's resignation. Senior officials told me this degree of universal regret was unique in their experience. The Minister was relieved it was over; the job was not for her.

Why did the Minister resign?

The classic account of ministerial responsibility suggests that ministers resign when 'the minister is yielding, his [*sic*] prime minister unbending, and his [*sic*] party is out for blood' (Finer 1956: 383; Woodhouse 2004).[19] Estelle Morris had the support of her party and the Prime Minister but she did yield. Many accepted the Minister's statement. David Blunkett (2006: 404) thought 'she got in a panic':

> None of these (crises) added up to a bag of beans and all were perfectly manageable, and with decent advisers and a decent press office all of it could have been handled perfectly well. The worst thing is that she just declared herself as not being up to the job.

With many others, he saw her as:

> the heroine of the moment—the honest politician, the person who says 'I'm not up to it', the person who says, 'I liked my previous job but I don't have the strategic approach to manage this department.'

Above all he felt sorry for her:

> how can your heart not go out to her and want to support her, as some of us have tried to do for the last two months, desperately trying to bolster her and having more confidence in her than she has in herself. (Blunkett 2006: 404)

Several people bought into the story that she was brought down by the evil media.

> Morris's resignation was traumatic for everyone, especially of course for her. She was loved wherever she went and was a wonderful performer—so genuine—on the media and at teacher conferences. . . . I had worked with her closely for five

years by 2002, and hated seeing the media destroy her career by chipping away at confidence in her, especially her own confidence in herself. (Barber 2007: 185)

The Department considered the behaviour of the media 'sickening'. One senior official commented:

Three months ago, a colleague said the press are looking for another Byers. They tried Blunkett but he's a big beast, so they looked for the weakest member of the pack. I was not sure I believed it at the time. But that's what it feels like now. The press is unscrupulous. It makes you wonder why you live in this world. [DG, FWNB]

Woodhouse (2004: 17) concludes 'the key factors in the resignations . . . were the media and the minister'. This consensus downplays the role of No. 10.

No. 10's story

In a nutshell, No. 10 didn't care one way or the other about the issue or the Minister. They just wanted either a speedy resolution, or the resignation, or both. Although portrayed as the golden girl by the media, she was not because she was not seen as on-side.

Andrew Adonis was education adviser to the Prime Minister and subsequently Head of the Policy Unit.

His school boffin appearance belies an underlying steeliness that has seen him rise to senior positions in three professions: academia, journalism and politics. . . . Although Andrew is personable and rarely confrontational, his influence is renowned, as is his habit of bombarding Ministers with '10 ideas a day, of which about one sticks'. (*The Observer,* 27 October 2002 cited in Blick 2004: 275)

He is absent from other accounts of Estelle Morris' resignation but he lies at the heart of the No. 10 story.

John Prescott calls Andrew Adonis the 'Mekon'[20] (Blunkett 2006: 659) and Beckett and Hencke (2004: 202–8) subscribe to this view. They argue that 'the extent to which he [Blair] and Adonis sidelined and humiliated his education secretary was unprecedented'; and they allege Blunkett (2006: 204) complained 'someone's got to decide who's running this thing'. They cite as evidence of No. 10's influence: the reappointment of Chris Woodhead as Head of Ofsted; retaining selective schools; the attack on the 'bog standard comprehensive'; introducing foundation or specialist schools; and city academies funded by the private sector (see Chapter 3: pp. 63–4). Blunkett concedes that Adonis helped with firefighting and the presentation of policy but *not* with policy development (Blunkett 2006: 184–5, 212, and 214). He blocked the introduction of the new A-level plus and top-up fees for universities. He also points out that much of the policy had been decided before

Adonis was appointed. The wellspring was the bilaterals between Blunkett and Blair, not a newly arrived special adviser:

> *Andrew wasn't as painful as he later got after the last election. Andrew had just been appointed as Chief Policy Adviser a year before the general election so he was still finding his feet. So we were in charge, we were in control. It was a good time.*
> [Minister, TI]

Also, Blunkett believed in keeping possible opponents close: '*I've always been a great believer in hugging people, you know, it's much more difficult for them to stab you in the back when you've got your arms around them.*' Also, it '*made it impossible for him to go back and say that we weren't forward thinking, we weren't on the ball, we weren't visionary, because we clearly were, and it was very important to demonstrate that*' [Minister, TI]. It was not a black-and-white world of friends and enemies; he admired Adonis' drive but felt able to resist his ideas.

But that was before 2001. There is much evidence that Adonis sought to influence education policy during the second term. Tony Blair 'brought on Andrew Adonis, who more than any other person helped to formulate his domestic policy agenda' (Seldon 2007: xi). He said of Adonis: he 'thinks fundamentally the same as me. He reaches the same conclusions before I do. He's brilliant' (Seldon 2007: 40 citing private interview). Adonis' views 'chimed with the Prime Minister's instincts. They thought the same. Andrew gave him a lot of his ideas' (Seldon 2007: 108 citing private interview). Adonis' relationship with Blair, 'blossomed in the second term' and 'was key to establishing the new agenda' (Seldon 2007: 108 citing private interview). He was 'the prime influence on Blair's radical thinking on the public services' (Seldon 2007: 221–2; see also Barber 2007: 103, 207, and 219; Blair 2010a: 487; Campbell 2007: 558–9). To put it simply, Adonis and Blair wanted autonomous schools everywhere with greater choice for parents (Seldon 2007: 108, 420, and 506).

However, the Prime Minister was not convinced the DfES was 'equipped to push [his radical agenda] through' because it had a 'real timidity in taking big policy changers on board' (Seldon 2007: 115 citing a Blair memo dated August 2002). The Secretary of State for Education 'was not an easy position with policy effectively being driven from Number 10' (Seldon 2007: 111). Indeed, No. 10 expected her to be 'cautious with a big C'. Estelle Morris 'was uncomfortable with the introduction of variable tuition fees for universities', a policy advocated by Adonis (*The Observer*, 27 October 2002 cited in Blick 2004: 276). She was caught between No. 10 which wanted differential fees and the Treasury which wanted neither top-up nor differential fees. Everything was frozen: 'I can't resolve this until they resolve it between them' (Estelle Morris cited in Rawnsley 2010: 231; see also Blair 2010a: 483). So, she was seen as 'unable to make up her mind: Number 10 thought her "aimless" at this time'.

Relations between Adonis in No. 10 and Morris in the DfES 'were often strained. She felt she was being harried: Number 10 felt she was ponderous; "she was not on the same page"' (Seldon 2007: 108). The Minister instituted two weekly meetings to build a more effective working relationship, but the policy differences were hard to negotiate. The Minister told me 'she had not signed up' and her PPS admitted they were looking for options. The Minister did not look forward with any relish to the battle with the party over fees [Minister, FWNB]. So, Andrew Adonis was seen as *'painful'* but he was *'never publicly criticised'* [Minister, TI]. He interfered. He spoke for the Prime Minister. But success lies in persuasion and cooperation. It was a trick he did not pull off in education. Rather, the Minister 'believed she had been through the mill on a whole host of issues' and, although she supported raising fees in higher education, 'she felt she could not fight off Andrew on the issue of differential fees' (*The Observer,* 27 October 2002 quoting a DfES official source). No. 10 conceded their 'personalities clashed'. The Minister felt the issue of university fees was 'overplayed by the media; it was never as big an issue as they said'. Subsequently, the government settled for top-up fees, not differential fees, and the Minister supported this compromise.

Similarly, various commentators claimed few officials in DfES 'were committed to Adonis's agenda'. Indeed, No. 10 thought that Morris 'was going native and absorbing the DfES mindset' (Seldon 2007: 429). Michael Barber claimed the 'only true believers on education were Andrew [Adonis], the Prime Minister and me'. Officials at DfES were:

> 'hostile because they feared the argument with local authorities, unions and the left-wing education establishment'. From the Permanent Secretary, David Normington, downwards, the department's strategy was 'not really in tune' with Number 10. (Seldon 2007: 289 citing private interviews with Michael Barber and others)

The Department disputes this interpretation. There is evidence that Estelle Morris was unhappy with parts of the choice agenda such as city academies (Blair 2010*a*: 578; Rawnsley 2010: 353) and she did not drive the agenda forward with the vigour No. 10 sought. To that extent she was off-side and Blair, although he expressed mild public regrets, was 'privately glad' she resigned because it provided an opportunity to appoint a more committed minister (Rawnsley 2010: 231). It is a moot point whether her successor, Charles Clarke, was indeed committed to the choice agenda. What is not at issue is that No. 10 did little to save her and as Seldon (2007: 249) concludes 'her departure [was] prompted in part by her misgivings over the direction of higher education reform' and by No. 10's 'doubts about her leadership' (Seldon 2007: 110). They believed that 'Estelle Morris on her own admission [was] struggling to stamp her authority on the department' (Barber 2007: 133). Of course No. 10 played down its doubts. Rather it stressed her self-doubt.

She was clearly stressed, fiddling aggressively with her hands, her neck bright red, and at times she seemed closer to tears. It seemed to me that deep down she maybe felt she wasn't up to it.

She said to me that she was just not capable of coping with the nasty personal stuff in the media, like her nieces at school being approached, or a boyfriend of fifteen years ago being looked into. The growing sense I had was of someone who was looking around for reasons to go, but didn't want to say that actually she was just finding it very difficult. (Campbell 2007: 645–6)

According to Campbell, Blair 'didn't "think she should go, but that only she could know if she was really up for it"' (cited in Seldon 2007: 111). It is probably as accurate to say 'he didn't think she should stay unless she knew she was up to the choice agenda'. Estelle Morris may not believe No. 10 briefed against her, but she is correct is supposing she got only long distance support.

The aftermath

Many a movie ends with little résumés of what happened to the various characters afterwards.

DfES

The DfES set up the Working Group on 14–19 Year Reform, again chaired by Mike Tomlinson, which reported in 2004. In 2007, it became the Department for Children, Schools and Families. It also had three new ministers over the next five years: Charles Clarke (2002–4), Ruth Kelly (2004–6), and Alan Johnson (2006–7). As David Blunkett observed, ministerial turnover coupled with a Prime Minister diverted by the Iraq war *allowed the department to revert back, and it did* [Minister, TI]. Some other things also did not change. The A-level results are still released in early August.

Estelle Morris

Estelle Morris remains convinced she took the right decisions. There was the clear and present danger of a national breakdown in confidence in the examination system. Her action restored confidence in the system. No one questioned the validity of the reports she commissioned or thought she had avoided the real issues. All the major complainants, including HMC and the Secondary Heads Association (SHA), felt she had done a good job in dealing with the substantive issue.

She returned to government in April 2003 as the Minister of State for the Arts in the Department for Culture, Media and Sport. She stood down as MP for Birmingham Yardley in the 2005 General Election. In May 2005, she became Baroness Morris of Yardley and joined the Labour benches in the House of Lords. According to David Blunkett, she is still angry with herself for allowing Alistair Campbell to write that '*wretched letter*', which downplayed her significant achievements [Minister, TI].

Sir William Stubbs

Sir William expressed his regret at Estelle Morris' resignation. On 31 October, Sir William announced he would seek a public apology and compensation. If not forthcoming, he would take legal action for unfair dismissal. He continued to insist there was no major problem: 'it is only in OCR and only in a minority of subjects' (ESC 2003: 97). The Education and Skills Select Committee agreed and its Chair said Sir William should never have been sacked. DfES did not agree. Sir William also continued to insist that DfES had briefed against him (ESC 2003: 101 and 104). The DfES said his remarks were 'untrue' (ESC 2003: 141). On 5 February 2003, 'without accepting liability' the DfES paid him £95,000 compensation for unfair dismissal. The (then) Secretary of State, Charles Clarke, called the matter 'regrettable' and agreed that Sir William had 'acted in good faith'.[21]

No. 10

Andrew Adonis prospered, becoming Baron Adonis and Parliamentary Under-Secretary of State responsible for schools in the Department for Children, Schools and Families, eventually rising to Secretary of State for Transport under Prime Minister Gordon Brown.

The students

The Education and Skills Select Committee (2003) concluded there was no grade fixing but there was some confusion over standards because the new system had been introduced without trials. The grades were reviewed for 18 units affecting 733 candidates for the AS-level and 1,220 for A-levels (out of 1,079,566 AS-level candidates and 783,878 A-level candidates). The Education and Skills Select Committee (2003: 22) concluded:

> The exaggerated, almost hysterical, way in which the A-Level debate was reported was extremely unhelpful and was consistently more damaging to the system than the problems with the grading, which ultimately resulted in some minor changes to the allocation of a minority of grade boundaries.

In other words, there was a minor problem with grade boundaries but a more important problem of public confidence in the system fed by a hysterical media.

STRESS AND PERSONAL LIVES

I turn now from this specific rude surprise to the general issues that it raises, in particular to the stress that is ever present in ministers' lives.[22] As I looked at the unrelenting diary, I wondered how anybody can keep up this pace and remain at the top of their game. I think I know the answer. They cannot, at least not indefinitely. Of course, stress can enhance performance. It can lead ministers to focus; it motivates them. It goes with the adrenalin surge that many miss when leaving office. Some ministers are also good at putting the various bits of their life into little boxes. So, stress is compartmentalized and thus managed. Ministers differ in their capacity to absorb, compartmentalize, and use stress. But everyone has their limit and it is commonly reached when the stress is unrelenting and the minister is seen as underperforming. Ministers have so many good intentions, so much to do, but they also have finite energy and enthusiasm which can be sapped in a long-running crisis. So, there is irritability and anger, mistakes, defensive and short-term behaviour, and a sense of frustration (and on the physiological and psychological symptoms of stress see Roberts 1988: ch. 9).

Similarly, senior civil servants must cope with stress as part of their everyday lives. Obviously, as with the resignation, they have to cope with the exigencies of the minister's life. More generally, however, they also have sources of stress specific to their job as a manager. For many, implementing management reform was a challenge.

PERMANENT SECRETARY: The management of [change] is difficult and my box of tissues is on my desk for people bursting into tears in my office, which happens a lot.
RAWR: How did you cope?
PERMANENT SECRETARY: I handed them a tissue.
RAWR: On nothing like the same scale I hasten to add, I have been in the same position in the university, and I hated it.
PERMANENT SECRETARY: Quite a lot of these people I have known for years and years and years and therefore it can get to you. I think probably you come out of it a bit hardened.
RAWR: That was okay during the day when I was doing it, the problem was when I went home, I couldn't sleep it off.
PERMANENT SECRETARY: Yeah, that is true and sometimes when it was coming up the next day, you would have a completely sleepless night because there were points at which I <u>knew</u> I had to persuade somebody, I had grown up with, to take early retirement. In fact, usually, just at the point where you thought you were going to have to tell them to go, they went. It's surprising how often, if you, you know, they get the messages before you tell them.

RAWR: So what was the atmosphere like?
PERMANENT SECRETARY: [Short pause] The Department was very turned in on itself. Very fraught and anxious and stressed.

All the permanent secretaries reported equivalent periods of stress. As one concluded:

I think that it gets to you. I just think it is likely after five years to wear you down and I think you probably have to try to recognize that. I mean that was [my predecessor's] strength. He recognized it and he decided he had had enough. He had the confidence to draw the line and go and do something else. We just all hope we have that confidence I think. [Permanent Secretary, TI]

Yet Sir Richard Mottram is described by Wikipedia as 'the multi-purpose Permanent Secretary' because he served as the head of five departments over a period of 15 years. Resilience must be numbered among his virtues.

Both ministers and civil servants are aware of the effects of stress—how could they not be? Some struggle.

I wasn't sleeping at that point. I couldn't sleep. I am a very good sleeper but at that point I was taking [pause] I remember going to have a health check because I can remember saying you know, 'I don't fall asleep as easily now and I wake up early.' So I was probably sleeping, I probably wasn't sleeping till 1 a.m. or just gone 1 a.m. even though I had been in bed since 11.40 p.m., which is very, very unusual for me. I didn't sleep in at the weekends because I didn't want to get used to sleeping in. Ratty, not with the staff with whom I worked, I hope. But I would get ratty. I think what happens is if something doesn't quite work out, your ability to adapt to it, if logistics don't quite work out, your ability to adapt to it becomes less. I think I am about to explode about this which is pathetic because it's not a big issue. But that's how it is, I'm ratty when the system doesn't go absolutely smoothly. [Minister, TI]

I sometimes do get exhausted. I mean sometimes the days are too long and the number of things I am being asked to do are too many. You know this constant tussle to take charge of your day and your diary, the arriving home exhausted, the day-to-day frustrations are all there. [Permanent Secretary, TI]

I think probably the workload is probably the biggest downside. I've had a fairly gruelling weekend so today I'm wilting a bit. Last week, having most of the week off, I was feeling in great shape, so it varies a bit. [Minister, TI]

I find that very, very stressful. I have had to do that more here than ever before, put myself above the parapet much more, putting my name and energy behind a particular [initiative]. Naturally what I am proposing is not perfect but you have to deal with individuals and that's been very, very difficult and the civil service doesn't help because you can't get rid of anybody and so they maximize the stress. Even now as we speak, there are about five or six senior individuals who are neither in their current jobs and they don't have anywhere particular to go. So that is indeed very stressful. [Permanent Secretary, TI]

In theory, there is one shared coping mechanism—the diary. However, it tends to organize the pressure, not reduce it. Ministers would need to say 'no' more often, the departmental court would need to be more ruthless in its protection, for the diary to be a barrier to stress. Everyone, ministers and departmental court, see blank spaces in the diary as slots to be filled, not protected.

So most people develop their own, different coping mechanisms. Some find consolation at home:

> She [his wife] keeps my feet on the ground. She has a good appreciation of the opinion of the 'man on the Clapham omnibus', and combines this with a healthy disrespect for anyone who gets too obsessed with their work. She's also fairly fed up by the fact that the career I've chosen is one often denigrated by ministers and the press. And one where the relative pay has got lower and lower. She also regards it—fairly—as her role to make sure that what you might call the extra-marital relationship I have with my job doesn't get out of hand.
>
> I was struck during [the recent crisis] about the pressure partners are under, something I hadn't thought about. I would leave home at 7 a.m. and return around 10 at night, and while I was away the media would be dealing pretty constantly with the cock-up my organization was allegedly making. As I say, this put her under a stress I hadn't thought about.
>
> Essentially, she knows me and the sort of person I am, and helps ensure that I keep a sense of proportion. [Permanent Secretary, personal correspondence]

Others combine family and leisure activities.

> *I mean there are two things that I try to do and one is to create time for seeing my grandchildren which is, my wife says, the only time I relax. And the other thing is walking; it is my great love.* [Minister, TI]

Others prefer a sharp divide between work and home: '*I talk a bit about generalities of work but not that much. I try not to bring it home too much*' [Permanent Secretary, TI]. Instead they divide their week between central London and a house in the Home Counties. They have a London social circle.

> *I have mates in London, some of whom are civil servants and some of whom aren't, so during the week I arrive in London and might ring them up sometime. So I go with friends or I will go to a Greek restaurant and chat around, you know, but I don't count that as work. I mean it's work related, it's part of letting off steam about that, you know we would gossip about each other's successor but that's not work is it?* [Permanent Secretary, TI]

In this managerial era, others employ a professional mentor who:

> *Permanent Secretary: Advises me on my own performance in these things and is helping, but it's not you know, not a hundred per cent.*
> *RAWR: What I am trying to get at is, was it just the simple fact that you do have somebody?*
> *PERMANENT SECRETARY: I do.*

RAWR: That you can talk to in confidence all the time is actually good?
PERMANENT SECRETARY: It is good.
RAWR: Because clearly to some extent you can't talk to some of your colleagues.
PERMANENT SECRETARY: No I can't. That was completely true here when I first started when, half the ones knew I wanted to get rid of them. So, it was particularly difficult, that's why I needed somebody else to [talk to]. You put your finger on it, the help they give is being there to talk to. Unfortunately they haven't got the golden key which I thought they might have! [Permanent Secretary, TI]

Some have just adjusted to the stress:

I tend to worry out things rather than worry about things. I think one of the advantages of being through the mill a bit, you know, and I have had that in previous roles, is that you tend to not get overexcited about the pressure. It is knowing when to worry about things and when not to. [Minister, TI]

For some, being in control is the key to managing stress. One PPS, who admitted to stress earlier in his career, offered a couple of reasons for his current ability to cope. First, *'It's probably . . . something to do with me being a bit older and a bit more confident'*. Second, he has *'more clout. I mean nobody messes with me now.'* As a result, *'If you ask my wife how do I seem she would say that I seem completely relaxed. I sleep well and everything is fine'* [PPS, TI]. Ministers agree. They think stress is worse for subordinates because *'they're not the masters of their own destiny'* [Minister, TI; and see Chapter 6: pp.150–1 on stress lower down the hierarchy].

Not everyone agreed it was stressy:

MINISTER: You shouldn't do these jobs if you haven't got stamina, I would say. I mean part of being involved in politics or at the top of big companies, is that you do have quite a lot of reserves of energy. And I think it does actually divide—to use an old-fashioned expression—the men from the boys.
RAWR: OK.
MINISTER: And, you know, you can get away with having some other failings but you can't get away with not having stamina.
RAWR: OK, right. Did you find that the longer it went on, the easier it got?
MINISTER: Yes, definitely.
RAWR: Easier meaning that there was less pressure or that you just got much more used to working at that pace?
MINISTER: Ah, both. [Minister, TI]

For all the variations in the amount of stress and in ministerial capacity to absorb it, I am in no doubt it is a problem. I am no medical doctor but, over several months, I saw one Permanent Secretary display obvious signs of stress—white pallor, a greyness of flesh tone, taut skin around the eyes, and an absence of humour previously ever-present. Decision making under stress may be an 'adrenalin high' but they pay a price in health and in their personal lives. It prompts doubts about the quality of advice and decision making under such conditions.

WHY DO THEY DO IT?

Observing the harried lives of ministers, I wondered why they do it. I was reminded of Samuel Beckett (1996: 89): 'Ever tried. Ever failed. No matter. Try again. Fail again. Fail better.' Many ministers were incorrigible optimists. 'Fail better' was not an option. They were convinced they could make a difference.

It was the most common reason given to me: '*If I'm going to be here I'm going to damn well make a difference*' (see also Blunkett 2006: 201; Paxman 2002: 207). The Minister continues:

> *I am amazed at the number of ministers who can't do that. I am amazed at the number of ministers who can't get their heads above grumbling about the amount of travel, or focusing on their office decor or whatever it is that gives them a sense of deep satisfaction. That is in fact displacement, just blatantly, desperately casting around for a role because they don't quite grasp what they have got to do. And that's the difference between a good and a bad minister.* [Minister, TI]

In the same vein, another Minister said:

> *There's nothing more exciting than to move from that horrible position* [of being in opposition for 18 years] *to suddenly having the ability to make some decisions and try to make a difference—that excited me.* [Minister, TI]

Many ministers itemized a specific policy initiative they were proud of; for example, rural proofing, which meant identifying and coordinating—that is, joining-up—policy initiatives that affected rural communities, grabbed few if any headlines but was important for the affected communities. The other departments had similar examples in their initiatives on school standards and small business.

The phrase 'making a difference' has distinct but related meanings. Obviously it refers to legislation and policy that changes the lives of citizens. It also refers to the minister's standing in the pecking order of the governing party. Ministers seek to be 'on-side' with the Prime Minister and the Chancellor and look, first, to survive in the cabinet and, second, move to one of the great departments of state such as the Treasury or the Home Office. They can become preoccupied with firefighting to keep their reputation untarnished. Of course, such behaviour can be dismissed as an egotistical search for a place in the history books. Such a judgement may be true of some. Others believe, sincerely in my view, they can make life better; for children, for small business, for rural communities, or for whichever section of society they govern.

Of course, there are other reasons. One Minister was *'excited by the intellectual content of the job'*. It required *'an ability to get to the centre of things. It meant a need to be able to be analytical and to get a brief, absorb it quickly and then discard it when you had to do something different'* [Minister, TI]. They are also aware of their importance; *'to be honest the thing which I probably most like is knowing what's going on'* [Minister, TI]. This sense of being at the centre of things is shared with many others at the top of the department. Several say simply that they *'just enjoy the work'* and confess to being *'an adrenalin junkie, but I am not a workaholic. It's an adrenalin high. I love doing it, yes'* [Minister, TI]. Or, at its simplest, *'there is a buzz'* [Permanent Secretary, TI].

Some things are even more important than making a difference. David Blunkett, who has been blind since birth, provides a good example:

> The greatest thing I've ever done wasn't transforming our educational system, or dealing with the aftermath of 9/11, but contributing towards changing attitudes to disability. [Minister, TI]

Ministers are a mixed bag and as Jary (2004: 6) insists 'Ministers are human' and 'most have husbands, wives, partners and children'. It is a brutal fact but sympathy for their lot is not their due.

CONCLUSIONS: STORIES ABOUT RUDE SURPRISES

My experience of universities and other organizations leads me to describe the workload of permanent secretaries and ministers as punishing. The idea popularized by Anthony Trollope that departments are rest homes for the idle and incompetent has been embraced by political parties and tabloid newspapers ever since. It is palpable nonsense. Indeed, the fieldwork prompted the opposite reflections. It made me acutely aware of the limits to human ability; of the fragility of the webs of meaning and action that we weave. As crises unfolded, it was tiring simply watching people cope, and I was not emotionally engaged with the events.[23]

The rude surprise that confronted the DfES prompts five general observations about coping. I organize my remarks under the headings of: storytelling; protocols and rituals; siege mentality; performing; and the media.

Storytelling

So far, I have treated dilemmas as recurrent but they do not have to be so. A rude surprise is a dilemma. It arises from the random unintended consequences of other people's actions and, potentially, it is a challenge to existing beliefs and practices. The Department faced a dilemma over the resignation. Loyalty to the Minister is axiomatic but the Department has to conduct business as usual. They sought to resolve the dilemma by storytelling

Everyone looked for the story that would frame the rude surprise. There was a marked preference for the story that downplayed the rude surprise by denying it, or invoking secrecy. Storytelling is a prime skill because rude surprises 'are the domain of multiple realities and conflicting cognitions. By whom, how and why an event is perceived as a crisis is a key empirical issue' ('t Hart 1993: 46). Moreover, as Boin et al. (2009: 83) argue, winning the contest to frame any crisis is crucial for political leaders. It is important to get your version of the story out there and accepted. By naming, departments and their ministers aim to tame.

Storytelling by both the Department and No. 10 was made up of three interlinked games: the language game of identifying and constructing the storyline; the performing game of telling that story internally to No. 10 and externally to the media, parents, and students; and the managing game of getting on with business as usual.

The Department's storyline evolved. It began with the idea that the QCA was an arm's length agency that would insulate the Department from the problem. It became clear quickly that the effects on students meant the Minister could not stay out. So, the department had to find out what had happened and why, but it did not have the time. Pressure from the media and the competing stories meant the story evolved into the Minister's competence, the integrity of the system, and whether she should stay in office. Sir William claimed there was never a major problem; it was one awarding body, a few subjects, and adjustments to grade boundaries. For the Minister, it was about restoring public confidence in the examination system. For No. 10, the main story was their choice agenda. It should not be compromised by the A-level side issue. So, they pressed for a speedy resolution and, when it did not happen, focused on the Minister's self-doubts.

The Department spent much time and energy on managing the media and networking with No. 10 informally. It established an inner circle to manage the problem and when it could not be contained internally, it set up an official inquiry. Both responses are classics of crisis management. Sir William and the QCA supplement this account with claims the department panicked and allowed itself to be media driven. No. 10 kept a low profile but intervened informally to advise and draft a press statement. Significantly, it did not directly manage the crisis, as it did with the foot-and-mouth outbreak. Hands-on intervention was never an option. For the DfES it was a public performance. For No. 10 it was private audiences.

The aim of the inquiry was to return to business as usual. No. 10 also saw it in these terms and urged a speedy wide-ranging report. When that did not work, the Minister realized her resignation would lance the boil and give the Department a period of stability. So did No. 10. They were both correct.

Protocols and rituals

Rude surprises proliferate meetings; 'the days are stacked with back-to-back meetings':

> I'd say worryingly it's probably ten to fifteen hours a week, which is quite a lot. Maybe that's a harsh week. Ten would be standard I'd say. I'm just thinking of Friday, at least five hours were spent in meetings and that's horrendous really. (Wilkinson 2009: 7)

Or, to make the same point in more dramatic fashion:

> I've received a meeting request that probably deserves a mention in the *Guinness Book of Records*. It is for something called the 'People Action Team' (don't ask) and it is scheduled to last for a staggering seven hours. . . . Truly there is no God. (Wilkinson 2009: 7)

Wilkinson is describing the response of DEFRA to the foot-and-mouth disease crisis in cattle but she could just as well be talking about DfES. In effect, the Permanent Secretary cancelled his diary, was on call, and spent hours in back-to-back meetings on managing the A-level problem.

Everyday protocols continued to be invoked; for example, the Permanent Secretary wanted the complete paper trail of correspondence. But everyday life also changes. Time is of the essence. Reports were produced quicker, protocols skipped, and rules bent.

> We didn't have any faffing, you focused on the issues and *solved them* and *got on with it.* (Wilkinson 2009: 10)
>   Outbreak management is very different from peace time work. In an outbreak, it's a very, very flat structure, work is produced at extremely high pace and papers for meetings are one page, one to two pages. . . . You don't want to *waste your time* writing things up. (Wilkinson 2009: 10)

Time is at a premium. Lack of time frustrates. An important effect of the press frenzy is to deny the Department time. The Permanent Secretary is not convinced they have the full story but never has the time to find out in the rush to kill the headlines.

There are also rituals specific to rude surprises and crisis. The classic ritual in this case was the official inquiry (Boin et al. 2005: 86), which is the mechanism for reasserting control over events. It is usually described as 'independent' and judges or other elderly experts are the preferred chair. For once, age is a virtue. Presumably youth is perceived as lacking experience and maturity of judgement. It also holds out the prospect of finding who and what is to blame. In politics, as in soccer, everyone knows the manager is in trouble when the club chair calls a press conference to tell the journalists he has every faith in the manager. Similarly, prime ministers express confidence in their ministers. Neither announcement affects the departure of the incumbent. It is just a stage in any unfolding resignation; a necessary ritual, even blessing, before being thrown to the wolves.

One coping mechanism simply did not work. Agencies are based on the distinction between responsibility (for management), which can be delegated to agency chief executives, and accountability (for policy), which remains with the minister. The arrangement is supposed to protect the minister from implementation gaffs. The minister takes the credit when the policy goes well but can blame the chief executive when things go wrong. This separation is supposed to be 'advantageous to those on the policy side, and disadvantageous to managers' (Davies and Willman 1991: 34). Maybe. This 'deliberate or accidental ambiguity' (Jordan 1992: 13) means there is no clear dividing line between policy and operations that helps ministers avoid blame, as Estelle Morris discovered to her cost. The media politicized the A-level implementation problems by dramatizing human interest stories, which the Minister and her Department could not ignore. The agency defence was mounted early on, but soon abandoned, as the issue became public confidence in the system.

Siege mentality

Whenever possible, the rude surprise is confined to the specific unit and the rest of the Department is insulated from its effects: 'people are united in their stress and in their share of the extra workload' (Wilkinson 2009). The effect of the rude surprise is to create a siege mentality; a tight team with a sense of purpose, even mission, that becomes cohesive to the point of being inward looking and stereotyping outsiders.[24] The most obvious pressure for looking inward was the pressure from the media, which was intense and created a sense of us versus them. The most obvious example of stereotyping outsiders was the inner group's views about the QCA. Some believed the QCA was complacent. Others thought its tone and manner intimidating. In fact, the scale of the problem was much smaller than they believed at the time. The claim that the problem was limited to one awarding body and to a few subjects was essentially accurate. Nonetheless, with the media, the QCA became the

stereotypical baddie. Peter Hennessy has long argued that ministerial over-
load, or long hours and stress, adversely affected the quality of decision
making.[25] It is not just that Ministers get tired—they do. It is more that the
combination of tiredness, stress, and external threats lead to short-termism,
stereotyping, and inward looking processes of decision making. It creates a
variant of Samuel Beckett's theatre of the absurd in which the actors seem like
puppets menaced by outside forces, which they seek to control but barely
understand.

Performing

A rude surprise is a drama with its performances and symbolic acts, such as
press conferences and TV interviews, which send important messages to the
public and stakeholders, and not always the intended message (e.g. *The Times*
photograph of Estelle Morris; see also Hajer 2009). The media has to be
managed, so officials must keep the Press Office and the Minister informed.
David Blunkett felt that Estelle Morris had been let down by her political
advisers but conceded that the bull elephant style was not an option for her:
'*Yes, we were like bull elephants, because if you didn't stand up to [colleagues],
they just held you in total contempt really*' [Minister, TI]. As 't Hart (1993: 47)
argues:

> One of the crucial functions of the symbolic perspective is to look behind 'official'
> actions and rationales and to probe deeper into issues of authority, legitimacy and
> power.

This frenzy of activity is about the appearance of government in that, no
matter what specific actions are taken, an ever-present underlying objective is
always to sustain the legitimacy of the government; to reassure the populace
and reassert control. The Department had to market its competence; to
manage the appearance of rule.

The media

The media reports the performance and tells the story. It does not necessarily
tell either the department's or the government's story. Indeed, it may be laced
with inaccuracies, exaggeration, and lamentable logic. In this case, the Minister, who to the best of my knowledge had made no mistake, was hounded by
the press. They were not interested in the facts of the case. They wanted blood
in the guise of a resignation. I saw a Minister taut with worry trying to fend off
the pack. The voice gave facts. The body spoke tension. The press treated the
Minister as an object, not a person. It was an example of 'gotcha' journalism in

action. As one Private Secretary observed, the media 'live in a parallel universe' [PS, FWNB].

In Tony Blair's view, 'today's media, more than ever before, hunts in a pack...it is like a feral beast, just tearing people and reputations to bits' (Speech, 12 June 2007). Such views may be widely shared but they are potentially misleading. There are two other features that need attention. One of the most important effects of the media is 'white noise'; it distracts attention away from the substantive issue. The Permanent Secretary knew the Department did not have the complete story but the media denied him the time to gather the needed information. No one was prepared to cede ground to the critics; it is a counterpunch culture. Ministers and civil servants want to be ahead of the game so, in effect, they conspire with the media to create the trench warfare that breeds a siege mentality. One consequence is that the press imposes its short span of attention on the government.

No matter how good the department's storytelling skills or how attractive and convincing the minister's performance, in a world where your political future can depend on random events and the whims of the media, luck plays a part. Like Harry Callahan in *Dirty Harry*, the minister must ask whether he or she feels lucky. Even bull elephants are cut down. Everybody's luck runs out. The tragedy lies not in the fate of one minister but in the ineluctable quality of that fate for all politicians:

> All political lives, unless they are cut off in midstream at a happy juncture, end in failure, because that is the nature of politics and of human affairs. (Powell 1977: 151)

NOTES

1. This account is based on my FWNBs and interviews with the main participants, newspaper coverage at the time, the published accounts of contemporaries, and the minutes of evidence of the Education and Skills Committee (ESC 2003). There is a brief account of Morris' resignation in Woodhouse 2004. This story is not anonymous. The Minister and Permanent Secretary read and commented on the draft chapter. Quotes are attributed with permission.
2. For a further selection of headlines and commentary on the press coverage of this issue, see: Masterman 2003.
3. The Advanced Level General Certificate in Education or A-level is normally taken by 16–18 year olds to complete their secondary education and is the conventional passport to university. The Advanced Supplementary level or AS-level was introduced in 1987 with a view to giving students a broader education. It is equivalent to half an A-level.
4. The other awarding bodies are the Assessment and Qualifications Alliance (AQA) and Edexcel. Kathleen Tattershall chaired AQA, the largest body, as well as the JCGQ.
5. I knew Sir William when he was plain Bill Stubbs and Assistant Director of Education for Cumbria County Council. I was a lecturer at the Institute of Local Government

Studies at the University of Birmingham organizing training courses for Cumbria County Council.

6. For the full text of the letter see ESC 2003: 140.

7. Although the belief persisted that there was pressure to contain grade inflation from the QCA, in her evidence to the ESC (2003: paras 112–15) Ms Tattershall insisted that the QCA and the awarding bodies 'were all talking the same language; . . . we were talking about judging the evidence on the basis of what candidates actually did in the examination'. She prompted the observation from the committee that 'Sir William ought to be in the job still?' At the time, it was not clear everyone was talking the same language.

8. They numbered David Puttnam, the film producer, David Blunkett, Home Secretary, Jack Straw, Foreign Secretary, and Hilary Armstrong, Chief Whip.

9. 'The Thunderer' was the satirical nickname given to *The Times* in the nineteenth century for its pompous pronouncements on the issues of the day.

10. The HMC's stance was also supported by the Secondary Heads Association and the Girls' School Association.

11. The A-level process is complex, detailed, and technical. Examiners award marks. The awarding bodies assign grades to those marks. Strictly speaking, the awarding bodies adjusted grade boundaries, not the marks of the examiners; that is, they decided what mark is necessary to get a grade A, a grade B, etc. For a schematic outline of the process see ESC 2003: 9.

12. During the week, the Minister had booked telephone calls with Andrew Adonis (2), Alastair Campbell (2), Sally Morgan (4), and the Prime Minister (1 plus a 1:1 meeting). Sally Morgan was the Director of Government Relations at No. 10 and one of a small circle of Blair's confidantes. Her role was that of gatekeeper, security blanket, and go-between on confidential matters.

13. The letter is reproduced in ESC 2002: 106.

14. Ken Boston, Chief Executive of the QCA, did not agree with Sir William's decision to protest, although he thought the DfES should have consulted the QCA. Sir William's temporary successor, Beverly Evans, a civil servant on secondment from DfES, commented to the Education and Skills Committee (2003: para. 264) that 'it was inappropriate that the discussions were had with the awarding bodies and not with ourselves'. Some might see the Department's reluctance to consult the QCA as an indication of its views about Sir William.

15. The quotations in this section are from *the Daily Mail*, 26 September 2002; *The Guardian*, 28 September 2002; and *BBC News Education* at: http://news.bbc.co.uk/2/hi/uk_news/education/default.stm. Last accessed 25 November 2009.

16. The full text of the letter is reproduced in ESC 2003: 141.

17. In fact Sir William was mistaken. All examinations from GCSE upwards were the responsibility of the Minister of State for Further and Higher Education while David Blunkett was the Secretary of State.

18. The quotations in this section are from *The Guardian*, 28 September 2002; *The Scotsman*, 28 September 2008; and *BBC News Education* (see note 15).

19. For a general review of the hiring and firing of ministers see Dowding and Dumont 2009. Berlinski et al. (2009) suggests that ministers with troubled histories lose the support of the prime minister; and that ministers who have been subject to repeated calls to resign are more likely to resign. Berlinski et al. (2007) conclude that ministerial

tenure is greater for the Oxbridge educated, newly appointed, high ranking, female ministers and lower for older and more experienced ministers.

20. The Mekon was the green, dome-headed ruler of the Treens of Northern Venus. He was genetically engineered with a disproportionately large head and small body so he had to move around on the equivalent of a levitating skateboard. He was the baddie in the comic strip series 'Dan Dare, Pilot of the Future' published in the *Eagle* in the 1950s. As a young boy, I looked forward to the weekly trip to the newsagent to get my *Eagle* comic. If only I had kept them. They would have been a prime investment. The reference is an unkind allusion to Adonis' impressive brain power but less impressive physique and baldness.

21. Letter from the Secretary State, Charles Clarke, to Sir William Stubbs dated 5 February 2003.

22. This section is not about the Minister's resignation but about stress generally, so I draw on all my interviews with ministers and permanent secretaries.

23. On crises and crisis management, I found Edelman 1964; Hajer 2009; and 't Hart 1993, with their emphasis on performance, symbols, and drama of most use. This perspective is submerged by the modernist-empiricist stance of the more comprehensive Boin et al. 2005, but see their ch. 4.

24. The expression 'siege mentality' is known to ministers and public servants alike. In the academic world the common term is 'group think'. The theoretical debate about group think is not germane to my story but the core notions that a group under stress becomes cohesive and insulated valuing unanimity over a realistic assessment of the available options warrants consideration when looking at crisis decision making in British government. Such characteristics of bad decision making as stereotyping others, rationalizing past behaviour, and belief in one's own correctness have been observed before, nowhere more obviously than in the decisions about whether Iraq had weapons of mass destruction. On 'group think' see: Boin et al., 2005: 45–51; Esser 2003; Janis 1982; and Roberts 1988: 143–52. 't Hart 1990; 't Hart et al. 1997;

25. It is a recurrent theme discussed at greatest length in Hennessy 1995: 161–78. See also Roberts 1988: ch. 9.

10

Willed Ordinariness, Being There, and Myths

A government department is not a native village no matter how useful the metaphor. I worked with and talked to the powerful in a country where I lived, not villagers in a foreign land that I will leave. I doubt the Balinese participants in Clifford Geertz's (1973: ch. 15) famous cockfighting tale got to comment on his English language manuscript before publication. Also, no organization can be reduced to a single narrative. As Laws (1994: 263) observes, outsiders studying an organization 'are no more able to offer a single and coherent account of the way in which it orders itself' than its managers. So, just as civil servants seek to domesticate the everyday life of their minister, I seek to domesticate the many competing beliefs and practices of the departments. Just as the civil service aspires to willed ordinariness, I aspire to a willed simplicity by juxtaposing the more prevalent narratives.

After reading a draft of one chapter, a colleague commented, 'fun stuff, but at the end of the day, so what?' He has a point. So, first, I answer the 'so what?' question by drawing together my distinct and distinctive findings, using the Westminster, public management, and network governance stories. I summarize the beliefs, practices, traditions, and dilemmas that characterize everyday life at the top with the protocols, rituals, and languages used to sustain willed ordinariness in the face of rude surprises. Second, I discuss the advantages of political anthropology; of 'being there', for studying British government. Finally, I report the views of the observed on my research. Both author and reader can learn from the critical reflections of ministers and permanent secretaries on my version of their story. Of course, I have the last word!

When I settled on my overarching theme for this chapter, it came as a surprise to me. As I watched ministers and civil servants enact their everyday stories, I saw them re-enacting the nineteenth-century constitution. Perhaps the best recent account of the British constitution is A. H. Birch, *Representative and Responsible Government* (1964). He describes the several *languages* of the constitution (see also Loughlin 1992; and Rees 1977). The Liberal language talks of: 'the sovereignty of Parliament, the dominance of the Commons within Parliament, and the responsibility of the executive to Parliament' (Birch 1964: 72). He also identifies a second, Whitehall language, which talks of 'the responsibility of Her Majesty's Government for the administration of the country, the importance of protecting civil servants from political interference, of Parliament's function as a debating chamber in which public opinion is aired' (Birch 1964: 165). The two languages are not rival accounts of the British constitution; rather, 'the two complement each other' (Birch 1964: 238). Finally, Birch (1964: 241–5) identifies a third coexisting tradition of responsible government. Its sedimented beliefs and practices include strong leadership, and a 'politically neutral', 'anonymous', and discreet civil service. The government 'should be given all the powers it needs to carry out policy' and it should not be 'deterred from pursuing policies it thinks right by the fact they are unpopular'.

Even today, the debate about constitutional questions is conducted in an inherited Liberal language:

> Not everybody accepts the Liberal view as either accurate or desirable, but even those who take a different view tend to use the Liberal terminology when discussing the nature of political responsibility. To a large extent, the Liberal view has provided the language in which this aspect of the constitution is debated; the mythology of the constitution as a whole undoubtedly bears a Liberal stamp. (Birch 1964: 237; see also Gamble 1990)

Since 1988, I have criticized the Westminster narrative of British government and contrasted it with my preferred version of network governance in the differentiated polity. But even today, ministers and civil servants act as if the Liberal constitution sets the rules of the political game. American federalism is often compared to a marble or layer cake to capture the ways in which the various eras of federalism interweave with one another. The British constitution is similarly marbled or layered. I am reminded of geological strata, a metaphor which better captures the longevity of the beliefs and practices.

I do not want to suggest that nothing has changed; obviously there have been marked changes. Much has changed, but much remains. Managerialism and network governance have not replaced earlier beliefs and practices; rather, they coexist with the inherited Westminster tradition, which itself is a composite of Liberal and Whitehall strands. Ministers and civil servants are fluent in all these languages, yet they continue to act as if earlier constitutional beliefs and practices are reliable guides for present-day behaviour. So, my big surprise was that British government was riven with incommensurable traditions and their stories. There was no agreed standard for comparing the stories. Even within a government department, let alone across central government, there was no shared story of how British government worked. Yesterday's story remained an important guide to today's practice. So, the managerial story (in its various forms) and the governance stories have not replaced the Westminster central operating code. Rather they have been grafted on to it with all the attendant dilemmas.[1]

So, what do we know from my stories that we don't know from *Yes Minister* and the existing academic literature? My account of life at the top differs in five ways from other accounts. First, there is much agreement in the academic literature that the constitution is in disarray (see, for example: Bogdanor 2003 and 2009; Johnson 1977 and 2004; and King 2007). There is much to agree with in these several critiques of the constitution and constitutional reform but ministers and civil servants act *as if* the old verities are constant; for example, they believe they are accountable to parliament and act accordingly. Such behaviour is a fine example of the Thomas theorem (Thomas and Thomas 1928: 572) that, 'if men define situations as real, they are real in their consequences' (see also Merton 1957: ch. 11). I take the constitutional beliefs of elite actors 'as real' and explore the consequences.

Second, I do not privilege any one tradition but treat them all as *living* traditions. No one account is comprehensive. Each web of inherited beliefs and practices shapes some ministerial and civil servant actions. Each explains some actions by some people some of the time.

Third, I explore how these broad traditions are translated into specific protocols and routines and embedded in everyday life. In other words, I do not see protocols and routines as boring red tape but as the means by which constitutional ideas and reform are brought to life. I explore how these several protocols and rituals are re-enacted in everyday life, and change as divergent ideas bump into one another.

Fourth, I explore the dilemmas posed by the diverse traditions to show how new ideas produce not only reform but also resistance. To twist a familiar saying, 'you can change if you want but this practice is not for changing'. Indeed, it is the embedding of yesterday's beliefs in today's protocols and rituals that makes change such a hazardous enterprise.

Finally, I look at ministers, permanent secretaries, and departmental courts from an unusual angle. I do not adopt the usual focus on institutions, events, personalities, and policies. It is not about the merits or effectiveness of any reforms. It was never my intention to criticize any specific policy. I have not sought to evaluate the impact of any policy. My focus is on understanding how civil servants and ministers understand and practise policy making. I look at the everyday *processes* which individuals use to cope with events, other people, and policies. This angle of vision influences what I see. I focus on the social construction of practices through the ability of individuals to create, and act on, meanings. I unpack practices as the disparate and contingent beliefs and actions of individuals.

ON WILLED ORDINARINESS

This focus on the micro-level of individual beliefs and practices means I can highlight often overlooked features of governing. Table 10.1 provides a

Table 10.1 The family resemblances of the Westminster, managerial, and network governance narratives

Traditions	WESTMINSTER	MANAGERIAL	NETWORK GOVERNANCE
Beliefs	Strong cabinet government Ministerial accountability	Managerialism Marketization: contracts and privatization	Policy networks: trust, reciprocity, and diplomacy
	Constitutional bureaucracy Parliamentary sovereignty	Delivery	
Practices	Hierarchy	Performance measurement	Steering not rowing
	Rules and commands Coping: protocols, rituals, and siege mentality Storytelling: institutional memory and language games	Strategic planning[2]	Joining-up SpAds
Dilemmas	Westminster	Constitutional bureaucracy	Neo-liberalism and networks
	vs.	vs.	vs.
	managerialism	responsiveness	metagovernance

summary of the beliefs, practices, traditions, and dilemmas described in the fieldwork. I unpack the table using the organizing ideas outlined in Chapter 1: beliefs and practices; traditions and dilemmas; Westminster rule; managerialism; and network governance.

Governing as beliefs and practices

The beliefs in Table 10.1 are also summarized in the conclusions to Chapters 4–9. To summarize them again would be to take redundancy to excessive lengths. Perhaps the most important point is that there were three contending sets of beliefs. It is accurate to report that the civil service believe in Westminster constitutional beliefs because they protect their anonymity and party political neutrality. It is also accurate to say that ministers act as if parliamentary accountability could lead to their resignation even though they know it is a constitutional fiction; a myth. These beliefs are not parroted by self-interested individuals using them as a cloak to mask their actions. They shape everyday actions and there can be no better illustration than the time and staff resources devoted to managing the links between ministers, departments, and parliament. However Westminster beliefs are also inaccurate because they are incomplete. Ministers and permanent secretaries also believe in better management and the importance of working with and through other people inside and beyond Whitehall. So, no actor was associated with only one narrative. Ministers and permanent secretaries subscribed to core beliefs from every narrative both in interview and in their observed behaviour.

The second important point to note is how ordinary it all is. Everyday practices are ordinary. The lifestyle is prosaic. It is so familiar we can overlook it. It is made up of meetings, paper pushing, and staring at desktop screens. But, because it is routine and made up of trifles, it does not follow that it is unimportant. As Sherlock Holmes observed: 'it is, of course, a trifle but there is nothing so important as trifles' (Conan Doyle 1979: 379)

Finally, although Westminster beliefs are often written off by academics as out of date and an inaccurate account of how British government works, nonetheless they remain core beliefs for *both* ministers and permanent secretaries and help to shape their actions.

Governing as traditions and dilemmas

These stories about how British government works are incommensurable. They do not fit together, producing three recurring dilemmas: between the classical Westminster roles of ministers and permanent secretaries and managerialism; between constitutional bureaucracy and political responsiveness; and between the unintended consequences of the neo-liberal policy agenda and metagovernance. Everyone confronted each dilemma. Individuals differed in how they changed, or did not change, their beliefs and practices to meet these dilemmas, but they all recognized and responded to the challenges. They live in a shared world. They are all political-administrators. Only reformers have the luxury of choosing which challenge they will respond to. Ministers and permanent secretaries have to juggle the contradictory demands posed by recurring dilemmas.

Each narrative produced its own unintended consequences. For example, during the twentieth century civil servants were 'socialized into the idea of a profession'. Now that civil service appointments are increasingly made by open competition, there are fears the newcomers will not be socialized in the service's traditions and organizational glue will be eroded. Loyalty might become conditional and contingent and formal mechanisms of coordination may replace the glue of trust and shared codes. Protocols and rituals are tools for managing uncertainty. To erode the effectiveness of such tools for the 'uncertain' gains of private sector 'management expertise' is at best unwise and at worst dangerous. Newcomers confront a 'serious learning curve' in grasping the political perspective and learning to work with a national politician (see Chapter 5: p. 132). Or, to move down the organizational hierarchy, what will be lost when messengers go? Originally, as their name implies, they delivered mail. But e-mail has decimated that task and the coffee machine, the out-sourced delivery of food, and the microwave oven eat at their remaining overt tasks. Their covert role as office glue will be lost. Every cup of tea signals the meeting of a generic London accent with middle-class vowels to discuss the weather, TV, a new baby, or how you are—to which the answer is 'well, thank you'; any itemizing of complaints would be well out of order. It breaks tension. Perhaps it is the music of our cribs but the clatter of cups and saucer, the sound of a teaspoon on china, is wondrously reassuring. Few see the demise of the messenger as an example of work being depersonalized, but that is one consequence. If there were a clearer understanding of the willed ordinariness sustained by elaborate protocols and rituals, then it would be possible to avoid the side effects of reforms.

Civil service reform is not, therefore, a matter of solving specific problems but of managing unfolding dilemmas and their inevitable unintended con-sequences. There is no solution but a succession of solutions to problems which are contested and redefined as they are 'solved'.[3] I return to these dilemmas at several points below.

Governing as Westminster rule

I unpack the Westminster narrative by building on the conclusions of earlier chapters. So I focus on: coping, the appearance of rule, and storytelling.

Coping

Ministers and permanent secretaries cope by using the practices embedded in protocols and rituals. Chapters 6 and 7 describe the office protocols and the ever-present, time-consuming committee meetings where the ever-present danger is boredom. The rituals of gossip, humour, and politeness sustain these routines. Of course, bureaucratic rules are a staple of the political science literature. Rules (or red tape) underpin the standardization of service delivery. But that is not their sole or even main function in my departments. They are a way of making a complex and often anarchic world seem manageable. They are an exercise in willed ordinariness.

The workload for both permanent secretaries and ministers is heavy and diverse. The pace of events is relentless and endless. They live in a goldfish bowl created by the mass media and they are cocooned by their rule-driven departments. Civil servants are socialized into the kinds of gossip, humour, and politeness that sustain this everyday world. It is not taught in business school MBAs, so outsiders have no way of becoming socialized into the expectations of departments. Yet the British government recruits outsiders. Ministers strive to reduce risk and uncertainty while calling for less risk-averse behaviour by civil servants. Do they mean that civil servants should increase the uncertainties in the minister's life, because it is him they seek to protect? They know not what they ask, preferring the allure of 'modernization' and 'results-driven government' to the certainties and safety offered to their otherwise chaotic and dangerous existence by the routines of the 'bureaucracy' they are expected to criticize in public.

Given the frequent rude surprises and the routines for managing them, it is no surprise that a key maxim is 'no surprises'. This can refer to the private office making sure the minister and permanent secretary are in the right place at the right time and with the right papers. It can also refer to the frightening extent to which they live in the media eye and need to be adaptable, to cope with the many uncertainties. Private offices exist to domesticate trouble, to defuse problems, and to take the emotion out of a crisis. Permanent secretaries exist to point out the hole to the minister before he falls in, to pull him out of the hole afterwards, and then to argue that he never fell in. Protocols are the key to managing this pressurized existence. Everyday routines are unquestioned and unrecognized.

The toolkit for managing rude surprises may include the press conference, questions in parliament, and the television interview but it is also about chats, meetings, tea, a drink after work, and the everyday routines that domesticate the unexpected. Gossip, humour, and the code of civility all smooth the unexpected. The committee remains the mechanism for bringing people together and transmitting information within and between departments. E-communication has not replaced the committee; it just means the minutes are produced more quickly. Even to an Englishman it all seems 'very English', and that is an observation not a criticism.

This world of protocols is also a closed world; a cocoon. David Blunkett (2006: 424) thought civil servants should do the advice surgeries in his constituency because 'they're completely cocooned; they're isolated and protected from it all'. So are many ministers. Decisions are made by small groups of elite actors. Willed ordinariness should not mislead. These everyday routines can make the exceptional ordinary, but they can also create a siege mentality in which the unacceptable becomes acceptable. Loyalty in a closed world of routines leads to . . . Samarkand (Murray 2006: 11–12). Everyday life may be ordinary but in elite groups with embedded routines sustained by long-standing socialization practices, domesticity can have significant consequences.

The cocoon is further strengthened when a rude surprise creates a siege mentality. Within the cocoon, there is not just a rule of anticipated reactions but there is also the rule of anticipated wishes. Ministers do not have to instruct their civil servants because they know what is expected before it is spoken. This closed world is supportive and can even seem cosy. But do not break its rules. Loyalty is non-negotiable. To break the code is to invite severe punishments; consider the fate of insiders, such as Clive Ponting and David

Kelly, who go public. Permanent secretaries and ministers live in a small, at times claustrophobic, world. There are few people they can talk to other than one another. So, caution becomes habit that can all too easily spill over into secrecy. Often there are good reasons. For example, I sat in on three discussions during my short stays that I could have used for personal profit through insider trading. This combination of a genuine need for confidentiality, a siege mentality, and habitual caution can make secrecy seem like cardinal value and reinforce the walls of a closed world impervious both to diverse opinions and the consequences of its own actions as the process takes over from the people (see Chapter 7: 188–9; Keane 2009: 24–5).

The appearance of rule

The Westminster narrative includes the belief in a strong executive. Ministers see themselves as policy makers. Civil servants expect a strong steer from the minister. It can seem like a world of decision, of action. Maybe. The world-view of many ministers and senior civil servants has a tinge of fatalism. Senior officials, with their knack for giving the interviewer a clever *aperçu*, would observe that 'The great thing about being a pessimist is how often you are gratified' [Head of Secretariat, Cabinet Office]. No matter how well or badly a policy fares, no matter events conspire to undermine confidence, ministers and permanent secretaries continue to perform on both public and private stages. Ruling encompasses not only making policy but also performing.

The appearance of rule is a mixed set of rituals. It embodies constitutive rituals, or ceremonies that reinforce the minister's authority, and representational rituals that, in constructing the minister's world, reflect and reinforce social integration (Goodin 1980: 166 and 175). So, when a member of the elite swears in public or is caught in corrupt or immoral behaviour, the event is not only about law and morals but also about undermining authority and social integration. When a minister goes on a visit or gives a speech, he affirms his authority and is a symbol of the polity's continuing presence. There are good grounds for valuing transparency in government but such changes come at a price; openness exposes the myth and undermines the appearance of rule.

I suggested earlier (Chapter 4, pp. 105–6) that ministers are a combination of royalty and celebrity. To greater and lesser degrees, they have the aura of the Queen's Minister. Ministers are also actors on public stages with the ability to wear the many masks their role demands. They are not alone. Even the more invisible top officials who operate in mundane, routine administrative worlds, still 'perform'. Performing is not only about public, visible, and even exciting performances, but it is also about the ordinary, everyday performances of not-so public figures. So, all ministers have a departmental court and courtiers but only some play the lord. All civil servants recognize that ministers are different but only some suffer from the Courtier Syndrome and suck up to them. All ministers have public engagements but only some get their kicks from deference, the chauffeur driven car, red carpets, and international junkets. Everyone is a performer.

Storytelling

There is a growing literature on the 'interpretive turn' in policy analysis, public administration, and organization theory.[4] Rather than seeking to predict the best policy option or the outcomes of organizational change, this approach focuses on the looser idea of telling stories or provisional narratives about possible futures. A shared starting point is the idea that any organization 'always hinges on the creation of shared meaning and shared understandings' with metaphors exercising a 'formative impact' on the construction of meaning (Morgan 1993: 11 and 276–80; see also Weick 1995: ch. 8). Stories spell out the shared meaning and shared understandings. Of course, stories come in many versions and often have no clear beginning and no ending. They are provisional and unfolding. In telling the stories I freeze them at one point in time. They can appear set in stone. So, I insist:

> Stories . . . are . . . always open ended, inconclusive and ambiguous, subject to multiple interpretations. Some are big; others are little. Some take on heroic, folk tale proportions in the cultural lives of group members; others are tragic; and all too few are comic. Some break fast and run to rapid conclusions. Most slowly unwind and twist back on themselves. (Denzin 1989: 81)

The departmental philosophy unwinds slowly as the storehouse of many stories. It is a form of folk psychology. It provides the everyday theory and shared languages for storytelling. It is the collective memory of the department; a retelling of yesterday to make sense of today. Institutional memory resides in the stories people tell one another:

> Stories are to the storytelling system what precedent cases are to the judicial system. Just as in the courtroom, stories are performed among stakeholders to make sense of an equivocal situation. . . . Bits and pieces of organization experience are recounted socially throughout the firm to formulate recognizable, cogent, defensible and seemingly rational collective accounts that will serve as precedents for individual assumption, decision and action. (Boje 1991: 106)

Storytelling could be dismissed as another putative intellectual fashion but it has its feet firmly on the ground. In both public and private organizations, managers use stories not only to gain and pass on information and to inspire involvement but also as the repository of the organization's institutional memory. Most if not all civil servants will accept that the art of storytelling is an integral part of their work. Such phrases as: 'Have we got our story straight?', 'Are we telling a consistent story?', and 'What is our story?' abound. Civil servants and ministers learn and filter current events through the stories they hear and tell one another. So, my focus on storytelling is not an example of academic whimsy. It is an integral part of the everyday practice of civil servants. Stories explain past practice and events and justify recommendations for the future.

As I described in Chapter 9, storytelling had three characteristics: a language game, performing game, and management game. The language game identified and constructed the storyline, answering the questions of what happened and why. The resulting story had to be reliable, defensible, accurate, and consistent with the department's traditions. Lying was seen as a worse sin than error, accident, even incompetence. The performing game told the story to a wider audience, inside and outside the department. Officials tested the facts and rehearsed the storyline in official meetings to see how their colleagues responded. They had to adapt the story to suit the minister, and both ministers and officials had to judge how the story would play publicly. They then performed that agreed story on a public stage to the media, parliament, and the general public. Finally, there was the management game, which both implemented any policy changes and perhaps even more important let them get on with 'business as usual' as quickly as possible.

Stories come in many forms. Some stories are short. They are told in a single sentence. When you belong to the same organization, the listener can unpack these stories. They do not need to be recounted in full. The shortest example is 'you know' as in you know the story already. Slightly more informative is the claim that 'there is a bit of mystique around ministers and they make you feel inferior'. This story invokes the idea of hierarchy and the subordinate role of civil servants, and the ceremonial side of being the Queen's Minister. Its meaning is clear: obey. Gossip is another form of storytelling; personalized with a variable regard for accuracy. Submissions and briefs are stories by another name and recognized as such by the civil servants who tell them. The rude surprise of the Minister's resignation was my story of how the civil servants constructed their story of the A-level crisis.

Stories are performed on a public stage, but who are the directors of this performance? Rather like the domestic cat, the media can turn and sink its claws into you for no immediately apparent reason. As Ballard (2006: 100) suggests, we live in an age of:

> Fleeting impressions, an illusion of meaning floating over a sea of undefined emotions. We're talking about a virtual politics unconnected to any reality; one which redefines reality as itself.

I incline to Boorstin's (1962: 253) image of the 'age of contrivance' because it captures the active construction of events and news. The media 'do not just mirror political life, but generate a "political reality" that is tailored to their own requirements' (Meyer 2002: viii). Indeed Meyer (2002: xi and 71) argues that politicians 'conform most strictly to the codes of mainstream media', and 'feel themselves to be under ceaseless pressure to stage manage in order to get access to the media stage'. The desire of ministers and civil servants to be ahead of the game, and their acceptance of a counterpunch media culture, gives credence to this view. However, governments also manage and manipulate the media.

The media is not habitually feral. It can also be lazy to the point of supine, spoon fed by government. The age of spin and spin doctors conspires with the media encouraging its failure to find its own news stories. Hennessy (2005: 354) sees the lobby system of confidential government briefings for accredited journalists, or parliamentary lobby correspondents, as essentially 'corrupt'. Keane (2009) is scathing about 'churnalism':

> the new phenomenon of cost- and profit-conscious red-blooded journalism, which hunts in packs, its eyes on bad news, horned on by newsroom rules that include eye-catching titillation, reliance on official sources ('avoiding the electric fence'), 'give-'em-what-they want/what-they-want-to-believe', 'if we can sell it, we'll tell it' stories, and by the excessive concentration on personalities, rather than stories and analyses that are sensitive to time- and space-bound contexts. (Keane 2009: 22)

Ministers, departments, and the media meet on a battleground, but like all wars there are bouts of boredom where little happens. The general debate about the implications of the media for democracy will rage, but this book can point to specific consequences of media influence. The media creates 'white noise' that distracts attention from the substance of issues for human interest stories. It shortens the time available for making decisions. Everybody makes mistakes. By personalizing decision making and responsibility for those decisions, the media directs attention away from any serious consideration of the reasons for mistakes and the causes of a problem. It helps to create a siege mentality, which fosters short-termism, stereotyping, and inward-looking processes of decision making. No organization under this pressure will learn from its mistakes. The self-evaluating organization, by openly admitting and seeking to correct its mistakes, courts the danger of becoming a sacrificial victim, pilloried on all sides by cries of 'gotcha' (Wildavsky 1979: ch. 9).

Languages

One minister described his department as a different planet with a different language. It was a rare example of political understatement. There is no longer a single language; Whitehall is polyglot. There are several languages each with their own dialect. Stories are no longer told only in the Westminster language. Westminster itself has the classic Liberal terminology streaked with the colonialism and class languages of yesteryear such as chaps and sherpas. There is the ever-present gobbledygook of acronyms. Managerialism has three main dialects: performance management, marketization, and delivery. Also, civil servants no longer have a monopoly on advice, so outsiders import new languages. Think-tanks, management consultants, and professional experts (inside and outside the civil service) provide specialist advice in their preferred professional language. Special advisers (SpAds) provide the party political language. Top civil servants are multi-lingual, combining Westminster, managerial, professional, political, and networking languages. The choice of language is not incidental or neutral. Each encodes a bias; a different premise on which to base a decision. Westminster inclines to incremental agreement. Managerialism looks for explicit goals with measurable targets. Professional languages look to the science for the answer. Party political language looks for party advantage, often electoral advantage. Networking involves standing in the other person's shoes and using their language. Such premises are often incommensurable. Whoever chooses the language plays a decisive part. The Principal Private Secretary (PPS) is a key player in this web of words and she has to be multi-lingual. It is a steep learning curve. One PPS claimed not to understand the language of delivery, preferring to talk of outcomes, but became fluent quickly. Speaking in, if not with, many tongues is an essential skill, and now it extends to the language of networks, even metagovernance.

Governing as management

Managerial beliefs are widely held among top civil servants, and many ministers can talk the talk. The civil service has been responsive. There are targets. Performance is managed. There is organizational change with its accoutrements of business plans and mission statements. The pace of change may seem slow to some. It frustrates both ministers and permanent secretaries. But the starting point of any discussion has to be that the civil service responded to the call for better performance management.

Responsiveness

The civil service introduced performance measurement but it had variable effect. People tend to be moved rather than fired for poor performance and permanent secretaries were frustrated by the slow pace of change. Also, individual actors reconstructed managerialism even as government elites sought to introduce it. Game playing with performance indicators is a well-known unintended consequence of such reforms. The civil service is no exception. The cumulative effect of continuous, minor adjustments by actors throughout the hierarchy can be great. Indeed, it is precisely these endless minor adaptations that characterize living traditions. Managerialism is not monolithic because of the everyday actions of customers, employees, and managers and because it has unintended consequences that, in turn, foster further adjustments (Bevir and Rhodes 2010: ch. 9).

Reform was also a case of everybody but us. Top management used targets as an instrument of control both over other organizations such as local authorities and for lower levels of management in their department's hierarchy. But for the permanent secretaries 'internal performance scrutiny is not taken too seriously'; they write letters to themselves (Lodge and Rogers 2006: 48). The permanent secretaries freely admitted that targets were not a significant part of their appraisal (Chapter 7, p. 202).

Some ministers railed against this perceived lack of accountability:

> The most fundamental problem with the civil service is that it is not accountable to anybody. It is certainly not accountable to ministers. (Minister in Lodge and Rogers 2006: ix)

One minister claimed 'there is simply no price for failure in Whitehall' (cited in Lodge and Rogers 2006: 47) but it is ministers who cause this problem. They are in office for only a short period of time and this rapid turnover means they are unable to monitor either individual performance or reforms. They do not set their permanent secretaries clear objectives and then, to ensure no system of performance assessment could ever work, they intervene regularly in implementation before leaving.

Ministers are not managers. It is not why they went into politics. A minority of secretaries of state take an interest, even fewer ministers of state. These brute facts undermine reform. The civil service exists to give ministers what they want and most do not want anything to do with management reform. At best, it is not a priority. At worst, it is not even on the radar. Critics of the civil service for the slow pace of change should look instead to ministers as the main wellspring of change in British government to explain the slow pace of change. The Blair government never had a sustained interest in, let alone coherent view about reforming, the civil service. Criticizing the classical Westminster official coupled with episodic managerial initiatives do not a policy make.

In the eyes of both ministers and senior civil servants, the job of ministers had not been transformed by managerialism. They did not see themselves as progress chasers for prime ministerial priorities. They saw the department as the heart of policy making in their particular neck of the woods. As envisaged in the Westminster narrative, Britain still had ministerial government, albeit with a centre that sought to extend its influence. But the description 'seeks to extend' does not equate to 'central control'. The centre was bifurcated for much of the period under study, and then distracted by the Iraq war. Most ministers believed they had much scope most of the time to pursue their own and departmental agendas.

So, managerialism confronted and confronts the blurred accountability that happens when both ministers and top civil servants are political-administrators dependent on one another if they are to succeed:

> Accountability is the central issue but it is difficult. The current arrangements are fraught with ambiguities—and remember this suits both sides. The accountability fudge we have now protects ministers and officials. Ministers can say 'not me guv', while officials hide behind them. (Senior official in Lodge and Rogers 2006: ix)

The debate about accountability and responsiveness all too often collapses several ideas into one notion. It is best to pick out the several dimensions (Mulgan 2003), and three recur in the fieldwork: civil service accountability to ministers, ministerial accountability to parliament, and the loss of accountability in the interstices of networks. Civil service reform reduces accountability to civil service accountability to ministers. But at the heart of management reform is the relationship between ministers and their top civil servants *and* of both to parliament:

> I would say that clarifying the role of ministers and officials is the major unresolved constitutional question. It is a question that has been deliberately left untouched—the Pandora's Box that now needs opening. (Permanent Secretary in Lodge and Rogers 2006: 63)

Both live in a closed world of overlapping roles and responsibilities, and ministers want it to be so. Thus the Treasury (2005: 5) report on the corporate governance of central departments simply reiterated the constitutional conventions on accountability to parliament.

The problem of accountability for performance is further compounded if performance is taken to mean delivering a service. Ministers do not seem to have noticed that the civil service does not deliver such services as education or health. They are delivered, as is much else, by other organizations so civil servants are being held to account for services over which they have, at best, indirect controls. For example, the Department of Trade and Industry (DTI) seeks to create 'the conditions for business success' but has few if any levers to achieve that objective. Government is but one of the many conditions that fuel success (and see Chapter 3, p. 68).

There is yet one more complication in measuring performance. Conventional notions of accountability do not fit when authority for service delivery is dispersed among a network of agencies. Performance indicators are commonly particular to one organization. They may not be irrelevant where services are jointly delivered by several organizations, but they are an incomplete measure. Yet, joint or inter-organizational indicators are rare.

The unintended consequences of change—the loss of institutional memory

For three decades, management reform has been an ever-present feature of British central government. Its unintended consequences were a source of dilemmas for the beliefs of the Westminster narrative. One key unintended consequence was the loss of institutional memory. Pollitt (2007: 173) gives his recipe for losing institutional memory: rotate staff rapidly, change the IT system frequently, restructure every two years, reward management over other skills, and adopt each new management fad. All three departments under study met most of these criteria. In Chapter 7, I reported poor record keeping, the annual postings of fast streamers, and high staff turnover. Add internal reorganizations, managerial reform, especially the successive waves of the delivery agenda, and it can be no surprise that ministers complained about the loss of memory. And ministers come and go, rarely lasting more than two years. From her observational fieldwork in the Department of the Environment, Food and Rural Affairs, Wilkinson (2009: 14) concluded:

> Without this memory . . . policy makers lose the knowledge of their constitutional context, departmental history, and awareness of which policies have succeeded and failed in the past. . . . This corporate memory—understanding procedures, history, context—is maintained by bureaucracy.

There are clear grounds for concern, and it matters. There are important knock-on effects (see Pollitt 2007: ch. 7). Of prime importance for my analysis, the lack of institutional memory erodes the ability of civil servants to tell reliable stories. The taken for granted quality of protocols and rituals means they are not accorded the protection that is their due. They embed institutional memory. They are the skeletal structure of the departmental philosophy; its expression in everyday beliefs and practices. I cannot resist the thought that the next bout of reforms could explore ways to preserve and enhance institutional memory.

So, managerialism is beset with contradiction, mainly because there is much confusion over the roles and responsibilities of both ministers and civil servants. Both have a vested interest in this confusion. Both see management reform as a secondary concern. Commonly, would-be reformers want to clarify the constitutional relationship between ministers and civil servants. They want to spell out roles and relationships. I agree that effective performance measurement needs more clarity if performance management is what matters. My problem is that, when I imagine myself in a minister's or permanent secretary's shoes, performance management does not seem to matter that much. Useful, but not where the real action is. The pace of change is slow, not because civil servants are ill-trained, stupid, or venal, but because such private sector techniques do not fit the political context and can be neutered by both bureaucratic and party political games. Such internal politics are compounded by the demands of political accountability and the media spotlight, which picks up relatively trivial problems of implementation and threatens the minister's career. Finally, the call for clear roles and responsibilities, for objectives and targets, is an idealized rational model of policy making largely removed from the messy reality of public policy making. Politics, value clashes, interests, cultures, symbolic imperatives, processes, and accountability requirements all make the rational actor model untenable in public policy decision making. These limits have been spelt out so often, they need no repetition here.[5]

Governing as network governance

Network governance encompasses a family of beliefs and practices about trust, reciprocity, diplomacy, and the shift to networks. It poses dilemmas around accountability, coordination, and implementation. It seeks to resolve these dilemmas through, for example, indirect steering. Networks and networking are ubiquitous within and beyond Whitehall, visible in established mechanisms of formal coordination such as departmental courts, in new initiatives such as joined-up government, and in the work of SpAds.

Coordination

For all the talk about joining-up and the extended role for SpAds, there was one coordination mechanism pre-eminent above all others; the committee, both within and between departments. Committees joined-up the functional silos in departments and the departmental silos that comprise federal Whitehall long before the advent of joined-up government. Keep-in-Touchs, 1:1s, cabinet sub-committees, and formal interdepartmental committees for ministers and civil servants litter the landscape of the Whitehall village. Joined-up government was the new kid on the block and, again, the civil service was responsive to prime ministerial wishes (see Chapter 8, pp. 227–9). SpAds oiled this new machinery; they were the eyes and ears of the Prime Minister in Whitehall.

Despite the innovations, several problems recurred. Most ministers are in post for 18–24 months and err on the side of short-termism. How do you get ministers to buy into interdepartmental coordination? The short answer is reluctantly. They need quick results; they want to make a name for themselves, not their colleagues. Departments are competing silos. The rewards of departmentalism are known and obvious. For interdepartmental coordination, it is the costs that are known and obvious! Coordination costs time, money, and staff. Departmental silos and associated departmental philosophy are resilient and supported by, for example, the budgetary process. Existing management systems undermine joining-up, for example, targets skew performance because they are internal to the department. Joined-up-government is a side-show for most managers.

Coordination is *for* central departments. The initiative for joined-up government comes from No. 10, with its own priorities and timescale. It serves their priorities, not those necessarily of the departments. There is a tension between managerialism, which seeks to decentralize decision making, and the call for better coordination, which seeks to centralize it. Central coordination presupposes agreement with the priorities of central agencies when it is the lack of such agreement that created many of the problems—a genuine catch-22.

Responsibility is diffused between sections of departments, between agencies, and across the public sector. Many bodies outside central government prized their autonomy and resisted the central imposition of objectives, preferring to own the initiative. Most corrosive of all, formal coordination was undermined by the rivalry between Blair and Brown and their respective courts. They had different agendas, held different views on best practice, and were determined to display their differences. The tension between central coordination and ministerial departments has been a perennial feature of British government for as long as I have studied it, and remains an acute and unresolved dilemma.

The two most common forms of informal coordination were the departmental court and SpAds; both played boundary spanning roles outside any formal interdepartmental machinery for coordination. The role of the departmental court has only recently been recognized because of the unduly narrow focus on the minister's private office. It is the nodal point of internal coordination and external coordination across Whitehall. It was not only the department's executive but played a boundary spanning role before the phrase had been dreamt of. Similarly SpAds have been seen more as the political antenna of ministers rather than boundary spanners linking the department to central agencies, especially No. 10 and the Treasury. Yet this role was often important, especially in the Prime Minister's priority policy areas like education.

Informal coordination or mutual adjustment is effective but messy. As Chisholm (1989: 195) shows, only some coordination can take place by central direction and so 'personal trust developed through informal relationships acts as a lubricant for mutual adjustment' (see also Lindblom 1965). There are also limits to its effectiveness. It tends to occur in specific networks. It is intermittent, selective, improvised, reactive, and issue specific (adapted from Wright and Hayward 2000: 33). It is not strategic. In sum, whether we are talking of formal or informal coordination, it is the 'philosopher's stone' of modern government, ever sought, but always just beyond reach, all too often because it assumes both agreement on goals and an effective central coordinator (Seidman 1975: 190).

Metagovernance

The neo-liberal reform agenda begat the marketization of public services. With marketization came fragmentation, which begat network governance with its packages of organizations delivering services. But as markets and networks multiplied, the government confronted the problem of many hands, weak coordination, and implementation deficits. So, network governance begat metagovernance or indirect steering; the state governs the organizations that govern civil society. This second wave of governance focused on the governance of governance.

There are several ways in which the state can steer the other actors involved in governance (see, for example, Jessop 2000: 23–4, and 2007). First, the state can set *the rules of the game* for other actors and then leave them to do what they will within those rules; they work 'in the shadow of hierarchy'. So, it can redesign markets, reregulate policy sectors, or introduce constitutional change, Second, the state can try to steer other actors using *storytelling*. It can organize dialogues, foster meanings, beliefs, and identities among the relevant actors, and influence what actors think and do. Third, the state can steer by the way in which it distributes *resources* such as money and authority. It can play a boundary spanning role; alter the balance between actors in a network; act as a court of appeal when conflict arises; rebalance the mix of governing structures; and step in when network governance fails. There are several examples of metagovernance in Chapter 8; joining-up, interdepartmental working, the problems of hands-off steering, and the difficulties of combining hands-on and hands-off control systems.

Metagovernance is a response to the dilemmas posed by fragmentation both within and beyond Whitehall (see Bevir and Rhodes 2010: ch. 5). It is an instructive idea when applied to the changing roles of the Treasury and No. 10. The Treasury, No. 10, and the Cabinet Office sought to increase their capacity for metagovernance over the rest of Whitehall. Officials forswear line management and speak the language of metagovernance; they strategically manage the landscape with indirect controls (see Chapter 8, p. 240–1). But it is a response to fragmentation, not a solution. As civil servants are aware, there are limits to such hands-off strategies. One Permanent Secretary observed that the shift to hands-off controls needed a major cultural change and he opined that no one had attempted cultural change on this scale before. His remarks were not streaked with much optimism. Others simply say 'stuff that' (see Chapter 8, p. 241). Dilemmas confront existing beliefs and practices but they do not necessarily change them. Metagovernance had unintended consequences.

The fundamental defect of the attempt to strengthen the centre was the conflict at the centre. There was no unified centre able to steer Whitehall, only the contending agendas of the Blair and Brown courts. Their different agendas for metagovernance fuelled conflict and confused departments. Any sustained effort at metagovernance was further hampered by the short life of central units. Their life cycle was short, barely the life of any parliament. In 2006, it was plausible to claim that the Delivery Unit institutionalized central capacity as never before (Richards and Smith 2006: 341). But it was a capacity to monitor and remind, not deliver. I have shown there were clear limits to its influence and that influence did not long survive the departure of Barber in mid-2005. Prime ministers come and go. Delivery Units are relocated. Even its founder believes that the prime minister's central capability remains limited. It would be more accurate to say we had an experiment in metagovernance and that the search for an effective central capability continues.

In sum, I have told a story of willed ordinariness sustained by elaborate protocols and rituals. I have suggested the distinctions between policy and management, politician and civil servant, are meaningless when confronted by the imperative to cope and survive. I have described the world of 'political-administrators' dependent on one another to carry out their respective roles, each role one side of the same coin. Every rude surprise demonstrates their mutual dependence. Of course, the obvious retort to these comments is that we knew it already. That is an ever-present danger for all who are doing political research. But this portrait of a storytelling political-administrative elite with beliefs and practices rooted in the Westminster model that uses protocols and rituals to domesticate rude surprises and recurrent dilemmas is not the conventional portrait.

ON BEING THERE

The 'so what?' question reflects the bias of mainstream political science to 'hard' evidence. I find it odd that I am expected to answer the question because the answer is obvious. Such methods are common in anthropology, organization theory, and sociology. It would seem that only political science has a problem. In this section I discuss the benefits of observational field research under the headings: thick descriptions; decentring; beneath the surface; surprises; symbolic politics; and reflexivity.

Thick descriptions

'Thick descriptions' in particular, and case studies in general, are well-established tools in the social sciences, valuable both in their own right and as a corrective to approaches that read off beliefs from social structure. It is as foolish to dismiss thick descriptions as survey methods. As Agar (1996: 27) comments, 'no understanding of a world is valid without representation of those members' voices'. Similarly, knowledge of one's own organization is not the same as evidence about the beliefs and practices of another organization. No one would dream of mistaking one's own organization for the universe of organizations. We study organizations to identify both the common and the unique. Before I did the fieldwork, the idea of a departmental court with its elaborate protocols and rituals had never occurred to me, or anyone else, as a way of describing British government departments. It is the result of observation. So, I seek to show that the ethnographic toolkit has manifold uses for research in political science and to counter the mainstream bias to ostensibly 'hard' evidence.

Decentring

An ethnographic research strategy, when allied to an interpretive approach resolves the theoretical difficulties that beset more positivist versions of government. An interpretive approach uses ethnographic methods to decentre institutions. To decentre is to focus on the social construction of a practice through the ability of individuals to create, and act on, meanings. It is to unpack a practice as the disparate and contingent beliefs and actions of individuals. It avoids the unacceptable suggestion that they fix the behaviour of individuals in them rather than being products of that behaviour. My observations of how ministers and civil servants play their parts in the daily dramas of departmental life show that their overall roles are laid out for them by their place in the Westminster system. However, it is individuals' understandings of these roles, shaped by their personalities and experiences, which breathes life into the system, and determines the nature and quality of the collaboration between politicians and bureaucrats. Only one Minister saw his role as managing the department and worked with the Permanent Secretary to design and implement a major reform. Other ministers had classic Westminster notions of the role of minister.

Marsh et al. (2001: ch. 6) identify four generic ministerial roles: policy, political, managerial, and public relations. They argue there has been a shift to a more proactive role in policy making. Most ministers carry out some permutation of these roles, but not in any conscious way. They do not divide their days or their beliefs and practices into these categories. They do not think about their role set but about making a difference, of maintaining their standing in the party and the government, and firefighting so their reputation is untarnished. They have immediate priorities, pressing problems, but not strategic agendas that portion their time among roles. So, I reject such catch-all phrases such as 'path-dependency' and 'context' for an analysis of stability and change rooted in the beliefs and practices of individual actors as they struggle to renegotiate established policies and practices in the face of changing circumstances. The Department for Education and Skills (DfES) policy agenda was negotiated between the Department and No. 10 and it changed several times in response to specific events and changing personalities.

Beneath the surface

Van Maanen (1978: 345–6) observed the police at work and described his relationship as 'a cop buff, a writer of books, an intruder, a student, a survey researcher, a management specialist, a friend, an ally, an asshole, a historian, a recruit and so on'. He was 'part spy, part voyeur, part fan and part member'. In one or other of these several roles, I was able to get below and behind the surface of official accounts by providing texture, depth, and nuance. My stories have richness as well as context. Also, observation lets people explain the meaning of their actions, providing an authenticity that can only come from the main characters involved in the story. Chapter 7 illustrates this point many times. The diary secretary may play a relatively lowly role in the court, but she is an important gatekeeper. Individually, the various protocols and rituals may seem trivial but as a set of tools for coping they are essential if the minister's cocoon is to be effective. The PPS may juggle balls and determine priorities but more importantly the job is to help senior colleagues to work together and think strategically. Gossip and humour could be seen as a way of alleviating boredom in the office. In fact, they are the oil that helps the bits work together. Gossip isn't just amusing; it is a way of conveying sensitive information without provoking serious conflict. Politeness reduces conflict. Such outcomes are not trivial.

Surprises

The ethnographic approach admits of surprises, of moments of epiphany, which can open new research agendas. It accepts serendipity and happenstance. It is fruitful, progressive, and open. Some interviewees exemplified Mark Twain's famous phrase, 'How can you know what you think until you open your mouth and hear what you say?' I was staggered when the PPS talked about language in use and language games while musing on whether he was embedded in a web of words or a web of relationships. Tea sipping amity and the organizational glue of tea ladies is obvious after you have found it, not before. Although I focus on elites, ethnography opens a wide range of new areas and styles of research about the beliefs, preferences, and practices of any political actor—from prime minister to individual citizens—as they preserve and modify traditions and practices. Observation is a congenial tool for exploring meaning, beliefs, and practices and finding the unexpected.

Symbolic politics

The ethnographic approach helps me to see and analyse the symbolic dimensions of political action. Most political behaviour has a strong symbolic dimension. Indeed, symbols are the bedrock of everyday political life with even our most basic political concepts such as the 'state', 'nation', 'government', and 'the people' constructed through symbols. Symbols do not simply 'represent' or reflect political 'reality', they actively constitute that reality (Edelman 1985). By drawing out the negotiated, symbolic, and ritual elements of political life, ethnographic analysis draws attention to deeper principles of organization that are not visible to empiricist or positivist approaches. Although the minister was absent most of the time, everybody talked about the minister's wishes, weaknesses, and prestige all the time. When the minister was ill, 'everybody' knew about it straight away. There was an ever-present fear of damage to the minister's standing in the government and with the electorate at large. The department's routines and practices remained the same but whenever the minister was around there was a marked change of atmosphere, in the pace of work, with a quantum leap in the sense of urgency and stress. This reaction was not to the person. Indeed, officials made negative, critical comments about the individual. It is a reaction to the *office*, a symbol of authority. I had expected ministers to be conscious of their standing and to 'lord' it. I did not expect the appearance of rule to be such a central feature of their everyday life.

Reflexivity

The ethnographic approach confronts researchers with the challenges of their research roles and the limits of their data. The usual methodological qualifications found in standard modernist-empiricist accounts can seem insignificant. In effect, I had to observe the observer. I sought detachment and distance by trying to make the familiar strange and the strange familiar. I turned a critical eye not only on my material but also on myself as I wrote my part in the story. I also had to beware of 'secondary ethnocentrism'; that is, I could not accept that my informants gave me a higher order of truth or accuracy. Rather, I had to think why people said and did the things they do. I had to twist and turn the data as I interrogated my fieldwork.

In this book I chose to present mainly a confessional and impressionist narrative streaked with both comedy and tragedy. The world I present is complex, episodic, ambivalent, and contingent. I am present throughout. While interrogating the fieldwork, I had to decide the extent to which I should be present in their story. Laurel Richardson (1997: 2) argues:

> We are restrained and limited by the kinds of cultural stories available to us. Academics are given the 'storyline' that the 'I' should be suppressed in their writing, that they should accept homogenization and adopt the all-knowing, all-powerful voice of the academy. But contemporary philosophical thought

raises problems that . . . undermine that academic story. We are always present in
our texts, no matter how we try to suppress ourselves.

I have not suppressed the 'I' for the impersonal 'all-knowing, all-powerful
voice of the academy'. I was always going to be present in the text, no matter
how hard I tried to suppress myself. The challenge was to incorporate the
narrator as an observer both of myself and of the inhabitants. It was hard to
strike the balance in deciding how much personal reflection to include if any.
I had to tread warily between the 'diary disease' (Geertz 1988: 90) and 'the
doctrine of immaculate perception' (Van Maanen 1988: 74). Too little reflection and there is no point. The main advantage of including me in the story is
that I make it clear it is my account of the elite's story. The reader is
continuously aware of the 'uneasy combination of involvement and detachment' that is ethnography. The reader is also always aware that it is my story
and that I have made choices about the form in which I tell my stories and
about the language with which I tell them.

In sum, 'thick descriptions' add texture, depth, nuance, authenticity, and
surprise to our accounts of government elites. The focus on everyday practices
provided the detailed evidence about, for example, protocols and networks that
is the bedrock of my interpretation of their interpretation of what is going on.
The only way to collect that evidence was by interviewing civil servants and
ministers *and* observing them at work. I was able to tell my stories because
I focused on the beliefs and practices of civil servants and politicians and listened
to their reasons for doing what they did or did not do. Studying elite actors up
close and personal, using observation as the key method for recovering their
beliefs and practices, is essential to an interpretive political science.[6]

THINKING ON

The metaphor of a 'village' is a useful description of Whitehall, but the parallels
with anthropology stop there. As Shore and Nugent (2002: 11) observe, 'Anthropology, by definition, is the study of the powerless "Others".' But in studying
elites, 'the research participants are more powerful than the researchers'. Ministers and permanent secretaries are powerful men and women. They can refuse
interviews, deny access to the organization, declare documents secret, and insist
on anonymity. All my interviews and periods of observation took place with
informed consent. Nonetheless, it was with some trepidation that I sent a draft to
all the relevant permanent secretaries and ministers for comment.

Barley (1988: 135) asks:

How . . . do you capture the essence of an alien way of life? Anthropologists do
not even agree among themselves what sort of quarry they are hunting—whether

it is to be found in people's heads, in the concrete facts of external reality, in both or in neither. Others would view most anthropological 'knowledge' as a fiction created somewhere between the observer and the observed and dependent on the unequal relations of power between the two.

My response is that objectivity is a product of 'local reasoning'; that is; it arises from the critical comparison of narratives within an academic community, reconfirmed in encounters with practitioners. Objectivity lies in the intersubjective agreement built from comparing the different narratives. Ideas and stories are refined and redefined by academic debates; and by practitioners when we ask them if our ideas and stories make sense. So, the observed get the last word, almost. I do not argue with their comments or seek to score points. Rather, I use their reflections to underscore differences of interpretation. I seek to tell my story of their story of everyday life. It is incumbent on me, therefore, to report where the stories differ and to explain the differences where possible.

I established a good rapport with many of the village inhabitants. They supported my research. I became the butt of good-natured humour:

One Minister overheard me speaking against gambling.

'You are a Methodist', he pronounced.

'I was raised as one', I confessed.

'Of course', but he then added, 'maybe it's because you're a Tyke. Always were a tight arsed lot.'

Of course, I had to work to establish such rapport, and it was easily lost. For example, I irritated one Permanent Secretary by sending him a confidential draft for comment as, so I thought, we had agreed. He protested that I had not kept my promise of anonymity. I was placatory. I agreed to all his requested changes, but I was puzzled. Why was he irate? Eventually I worked out what had happened. In my letter seeking access, I defined 'anonymity' as 'for citation but not for attribution without agreement'. Clearly, I could not seek agreement without first writing the text and identifying the quotes. My mistake was to assume the Permanent Secretary would remember the initial letter. What I should have done in my covering letter was to repeat the terms on which he had agreed to access. I did not, and he understood 'anonymity' too literally. He thought I had attributed quotes to him when I was asking what I could and could not attribute. The lesson is obvious—always explain what you are doing and why, never assume. I should also add that, although firm, the Permanent Secretary's tone was always civil. In response to my apology for souring our relationship, his last words on our lengthy exchange were magnanimous: 'I personally don't feel at all sour and I hope that your publication is very well received, as it deserves to be.' The code of civility extends beyond the department.

Overall the comments by ministers' and permanent secretaries' were broadly supportive:

I have no problems with the text you sent. It is all suitably anonymized, so causes no problems. Interesting six years on to wonder whether anything is changing. I think PPSs stay a bit longer (2 years is more common). It is increasingly difficult to persuade some of our 'high-fliers' to regard Private Office as an essential part of their education. This is partly because of the reputation for long and unsocial hours; but partly because there are so many attractions—fast streamers these days get the chance to have a secondment to another department and/or voluntary body. And promotion offers come quickly. Otherwise I think there is much truth in the portrait, except that it is inevitably very influenced by personality—on both the PPS and the ministerial sides.

So much for the good news. It will be more instructive to concentrate on the differences. Some comments were just unhelpful. Consider the following letter from a Minister:

I am afraid I was completely dismayed to read your draft. You assured me—and my Permanent Secretary—that this was a serious piece of research and that the participants would not be identified or identifiable. In fact, both I and the Department are clearly recognisable and as a result, I believe that many of your quotations and observations will inevitably be used in a way that neither of us intended, or believed you intended, when we agreed to participate. The result, I am afraid, is extremely unfair to our departmental colleagues. I am therefore not prepared to give my permission either for my name to be used or for the quotes to be attributed.

This quote tells us something about the cast of mind elites adopt when reading comments on their beliefs and practices by outsiders. A degree of self-serving defensiveness creeps in. Politicians know they are public figures, comparable to celebrities. They act to defend that public image irrespective of whether the comments are accurate. To be fair, the private office staff can be even worse, defending their boss come hell or high water. Ethnographic studies of elites hold up a particularly acute mirror to them. It shows not just their strutting on-stage but also their 'backstage' behaviour. It echoes their ways of 'making sense'. It would be naive to think that they are invariably delighted to look into such a mirror.[7] To be fair, after reading the penultimate draft, the Minister conceded 'I'm glad to say that I found it much more interesting and substantial than I'd expected.'

Others were not convinced by my version of their story.

There is no attempt to locate the scenes in wider contexts of managerial and societal change; no comparison with equally challenging pressures on senior people in equivalent positions in the private sector, other parts of the public sector, or big charities; no discussion of the external drivers of change, e.g. text messages and emails, greater openness, the web, 24-hour news, developing management theories and styles; indeed the whole flavour is that those observed are in their own, separate, world with its own, separate, pressures. I don't think that is right, and I suspect that similar observation of leaders in other sectors would throw up some very similar conclusions.

These remarks are accurate. I set out to show how the civil service and ministers cope with these changes, not to document the changes, and the way departments cope is with their long-standing routines and rituals of village life. The Westminster and managerialism narratives are sets of beliefs held by members of the Whitehall village. The previous quote displays the managerial cast of mind. Others were of a Westminster cast of mind:

> It's interesting re-reading this several years on, after doing another Permanent Secretary job and a year after retirement from the civil service. It captures the sense of 'village' at the top of Departments. It inevitably presents a snapshot, and rather different themes could have come out if the fieldwork in any one Department had been done at a different time; but that doesn't invalidate it, and the overall impression seems to me fair. At the risk of stating the obvious, the atmosphere in this village depends crucially on the personalities of the key players, and the degree of trust between them. What has changed since the fieldwork was done? There's more emphasis now on the corporate (i.e. civil service-wide) role of Permanent Secretaries, with aspects of this featuring in the performance objectives they agree with the Cabinet Secretary. And it's harder to attract high-fliers into Private Office jobs.

I am describing these two sets of beliefs. I have no preferences. I make no judgements. I seek to show that the dilemmas that beset British government are not academic abstractions. The beliefs I describe shape the everyday actions of the inhabitants. They also pervade their reactions to my construction of their constructions of what they were doing.

Finally, the ministers wondered if I had too much contact with the civil service: 'I think you were in far more meetings with civil servants than with me and I think my comments just add a bit of balance.' Of course, ministers agreed 'that civil servants and politicians worked very well together, a point which does come over'. But, there was some concern that I had not given sufficient attention to the political realities; to the tension 'between taking action that is politically right and action that you think actually solves the problem'. It is accurate to observe that I had more contact with civil servants than ministers but I hope I have been sympathetic to the political pressures on ministers. Certainly, I became keenly aware of the frustrations of their job. All too often, 'we weren't responsible for what happened but we would...be judged by how we solved the problem...yet we were not judged in that way'.

CONCLUSION: THE WORLD WE ARE LOSING

Question—If you hear the expression 'the Westminster model', what does that mean to you?

Answer—Absolutely nothing. (David Blunkett, former British Home Secretary, interview 19 January 2007)

The phrase 'Westminster model' is, of course, a synonym for the British constitution and most ministers and civil servants believe in that. It is integral to the anonymity and political impartiality of civil servants and to the minister's understanding of his or her relationship to parliament and the cabinet. They believe in a public service ethos, and its values of integrity, honesty, impartiality, objectivity, and loyalty to the minister. They stick fast to the Westminster model's constitutional conventions. Ministerial responsibility may be a fiction in that ministers do not resign when their departments are at fault. But ministers and civil servants act as if ministerial responsibility is a brute fact of life. In other words, core beliefs and practices of British government resemble myths. Wood (1997) may be talking about John Wayne but his comments have a wider relevance:

> A myth does not take hold without expressing many truths—misleading truths, usually, but important ones: truth for one thing, to the needs of those who elaborate and accept the myth; truth to the demand for some control over complex realities; truth to the recognition of shared values (however shakily grounded those values may be in themselves). Even the myths that simplify are not, in themselves, simple. (Wood 1997)

As Orwell (1970 [1944]: 6) suggests, 'myths which are believed in tend to become true'.

Rhodes et al. (2009: ch. 9) identify several uses of the Westminster myth in their comparison of five systems of Westminster parliamentary government and three of the usages are relevant here.

- Westminster as inheritance—elite actors' shared governmental narrative understood as both precedents and nostalgia.
- Westminster as legitimizing tradition—it provides legitimacy and a context for elite actions, serving as a point of reference to navigate this uncertain world.
- Westminster as political tool—the expedient cloak worn by governments and politicians to defend themselves and criticize opponents.

The ministers, permanent secretaries, and departmental courts in this study all inherited Westminster beliefs and practices, which legitimized their actions and, at times, was used to defend them. Of course these beliefs and practices are part of the daily grind of politics. Inevitably, meanings will be contested. Beliefs will serve many purposes. There are many interpretations. We can, and do, argue at length over the viability of accountability to parliament or the effectiveness of cabinet government. Such arguments do not mean that the term Westminster (or the British constitution) has no meaning. To the contrary, it has several. No one argues that the constituent terms are not useful, even if they are in dispute, or that they should be discarded because of the lack of agreement. Westminster is useful because it serves several purposes and has no given, essential meaning. It survives and sometimes thrives because at the core it means something to those who use it and hear it. It is just that those interpretations are not precise. If we insist on one definite, unchallenged, and agreed meaning, the debate soon disintegrates into meaningless nick-picking. We benefit only when we use the concepts of Westminster flexibly as a family of ideas. Westminster lives because people believe in it.

Although I focus on the mythic qualities of Westminster because it remains the dominant narrative among ministers and civil servants, I do not doubt for a moment that the managerial and governance narratives have their mythic properties. For example, the managerial narrative extols the virtues of private sector management, ignoring irresponsible and illegal actions by private sector companies, the failures of private companies, and the important differences between the public and private sectors. One of the more recent managerial fads gives us the new myth of public servants as Platonic guardians of the public interest who create public value (see Rhodes and Wanna 2009). Network governance has a benign view of networks with its stress on trust, reciprocity, and diplomacy, ignoring the dark networks associated with crime and drugs, the arms trade, and terrorism (Raab and Milward 2003). Networks can also limit participation in the policy process by excluding some actors from the network and privileging others, focusing on a limited range of issues, and setting the rules of the game. In short, they can substitute private government for public accountability (Rhodes 1997*a*: ch. 1). Trust and reciprocity have mythic properties; they are accorded to the privileged few.

I am not a would-be reformer. In this book, I have not sought to draw lessons. My main aim in the fieldwork and in writing this book was to open the everyday beliefs and practices of Britain's political-administrative elite to a wider audience. After two years of fieldwork and interviewing and too many years of reflection, I am convinced that observation is an underused but vital part of the political scientist's toolkit. It 'leads to a thoroughgoing revision of our understanding of what it is to open . . . the consciousness of one group of people to . . . the life-form of another' (Geertz 1988: 143). Developing political ethnography with observation at its methodological core is also about 'edification'—a way of finding 'new, better, more interesting, more fruitful ways of speaking about' politics and government (Rorty 1980: 360). I believe the summary in this chapter provides a new and better way of speaking about British government. It involves 'enabling conversation' and enlarging 'the possibility of intelligible discourse between people quite different from one another in interest, outlook, wealth and power' (Geertz 1988: 147). That was my ambition when decentring British government departments and being there to identify the beliefs and everyday practices of government elites. Others will judge whether I succeed. Finally, that conversation should not only look at where we want to go but also where we are coming from.

I have described a bureaucracy at work. It all may seem very predictable and boring. There are times when I think we forget that bureaucracy is a clever invention. It has many uses and it does several things, not everything, well. If there are lessons for reformers in my research, it would be to ask what are we losing and at what cost? The ceaseless reforms of the public service are narrow, grounded in a poor understanding of everyday life at the top. Civil service reform cannot be reduced to managerial reform or service delivery. Inevitably, it is about political reform; about the role of ministers and the accountability of the executive. Reforms need to recognize the continuing virtues of the generalist political-administrator tradition and of the role of living myths in sustaining effective government.

NOTES

1. Although my research did not explore whether there were shared stories with local government, other sub-national agencies and devolved government, it is clear from my earlier work on the differentiated polity that such understandings are rare (see Rhodes 1988). It is a common complaint in local government that the centre simply does not understand how things work locally.
2. This table summarizes only *observed* beliefs and practices. In different departments, or in the same departments on different days, I could also have seen other managerial belief and practices. The most obvious omission is contract management with its practices of negotiations, haggling, and adjudication.
3. In place of specific institutional changes, or new management practices, reform could focus on creating the learning organization that can reform itself as it confronts unfolding dilemmas. On the learning, self-evaluating organization, see: Argyris and Schon 1978 and 1996; and Wildavsky 1979: ch. 9.
4. This book is not about policy analysis so I do not discuss the interpretive turn in policy analysis generally or the art of storytelling in particular but see: Fay 1975; Fischer 2003; Fischer and Forester 1993; Hajer and Wagenaar 2003; Healy 1986; Hummel 1991; Moran et al. 2006; Morgan 1993; Rein and Schon 1994; Roe 1994; Schram 1993; Van Eeten et al. 1996; Weick 1995; and Yanow 1999.
5. For critiques of the rational model see: Braybrooke and Lindblom 1963; Lindblom 1965 and 1988; and Wildavsky 1979. For proof that it is alive and well in British government see the capability reviews. For example, DfES was advised that 'The Board and ministerial team need to establish clear, strategic goals for the department' (Cabinet Office 2006*d*: 21).
6. To enumerate the benefits of observation does not mean I am not keenly aware of the limits; it can seem like 'studying snow in the middle of an avalanche' (Agar 1996

[1980]: 11). However, I am not writing a book on research methods. I have reflected on the problems of observational research at length elsewhere. The interested reader can consult Rhodes et al. 2007: ch. 9.

7. This experience is not specific to studying government elites; for example, 'horror stories' from the field abound in sociology. See Bell and Newby 1977; Burns 1977: ix–xviii; Punch 1986: ch. 3 and p. 77.

Bibliography

Adler, P. A. and Adler, P. 1987. *Membership Roles in Field Research*. Newbury Park, CA: Sage.

Agar, M. 1996 [1980]. *The Professional Stranger*. 2nd edn. San Diego: Academic Press.

Allen, G. 2002. *The Last Prime Minister: Being Honest about the UK Presidency*. London: Politico's.

Allison, G. 1971. *Essence of Decision*. Boston, MA: Little, Brown.

Althaus, C., Bridgman, P., and Davis, G. 2007 [1998]. *The Australian Policy Handbook*. 4th edn. Crows Nest, NSW: Allen & Unwin.

Alvermann, D. E. 2000. 'Narrative approaches'. In M. L. Kamil, P. B. Mosenthal, P. D. Pearson, and R. Barr (eds), *Handbook of Reading Research. Volume III*. Mahwah, NJ: Lawrence Erlbaum: 123–39.

Alvesson, M. 1996. *Communication, Power and Organization*. Berlin: De Gruyter.

Anderson, A. 2006. 'Spinning the rural agenda: the Countryside Alliance, fox hunting and social policy', *Social policy & Administration* 40 (6): 722–38.

Anderson Inquiry 2002. *Foot and Mouth Disease 2001: Lessons to be Learned Inquiry Report* (Anderson). HC 888. London: Stationery Office.

Annesley, C. and Gains, F. 2010. 'The core executive: gender, power and change', *Political Studies* 58: 909–29.

Argyris, C. and Schon, D. 1978. *Organizational Learning: A Theory of Action Perspective*. Reading, MA: Addison-Wesley.

Argyris, C. and Schon, D. 1996. *Organizational Learning II: A Theory of Action Perspective*. Reading, MA: Addison-Wesley.

Argyrous, G. 2009. *Evidence for Policy and Decision Making: A Practical Guide*. Sydney: UNSW Press.

Armstrong, Sir Robert 1985. *The Duties and Responsibilities of Civil Servants in Relation to Ministers. Note by the Head of the Civil Service*. London: Cabinet Office, 25 February. Available at: http://www.civilservant.org.uk/armstrong.shtml (accessed 15 November 2010).

Auden, W. H. 1994. *Collected Poems of W. H. Auden*, London: Faber and Faber.

Baker, A. 2000. *Prime Ministers and the Rule Book*. London: Politico's.

Bales, R. F. and Slater, P. E. 1969. 'Role differentiation in small decision-making groups'. In C. A. Gibb (ed.), *Leadership*. Harmondsworth: Penguin: 255–83.

Ballard, J. G. 2006. *Kingdom Come*. London: Fourth Estate.

Bang, H. P. and Sørensen, E. 1999. 'The everyday maker: a new challenge to democratic governance', *Administrative Theory and Praxis* 21 (3): 325–41.

Barber, J. D. 1966. *Power in Committees: An Experiment in the Governmental Process*. Chicago: Rand McNally.

Barber, M. 2007. *Instruction to Deliver. Tony Blair, Public Services and the Challenge of Targets*. London: Politico's.

Barberis, P. 1996. *The Elite of the Elite*. Aldershot: Dartmouth.

Barley, N. 1988. *Not a Hazardous Sport*. New York: Henry Holt.

Barthes, R. 1993 [1966]. 'An introduction to the structural analysis of narrative'. In S. Sontag (ed.), *A Roland Barthes Reader.* London: Vintage: 251–95.

Beckett, F. and Hencke, D. 2004. *The Blairs and Their Court.* London: Aurum Press.

Beckett, S. 1996. *Worstward Ho.* In *NoHow On: Three Novels by Samuel Beckett.* New York: Grove Press.

Beech, M. and Lee, S. (eds) 2008. *Ten Years of New Labour.* Houndmills, Basingstoke: Palgrave-Macmillan.

Bell, C. and Newby, H. (eds) 1977. *Doing Sociological Research.* London: Allen & Unwin.

Beloff, M. 1975. 'The Whitehall factor: the role of the higher civil service 1919–39'. In G. Peele and C. Cook (eds), *The Politics of Reappraisal 1918–1939.* London: Macmillan: 209–31.

Benn, T. 1988. *Out of the Wilderness. Diaries 1963–67.* London: Arrow.

Benn, T. 1989. *Office Without Power. Diaries 1968–72.* London: Arrow.

Benn, T. 1990. *Against the Tide. Diaries 1973–76.* London: Arrow.

Benn, T. 1991. *Conflicts of Interest: Diaries 1977–1980.* London: Jonathan Cape.

Berger, P. and Luckman, T. 1971. *The Social Construction of Reality: A Treatise in the Sociology of Knowledge.* Harmondsworth: Penguin.

Berlinski, S., Dewan, T., and Dowding, K. 2007. 'The length of ministerial tenure in the UK, 1945–1997', *British Journal of Political Science* 37 (2): 245–62.

Berlinski, S., Dewan, T., and Dowding, K. 2009. 'Individual and collective performance and the tenure of British ministers, 1945–97'. Working paper available at: http://polsc.anu.edu.au/staff/dowding/workingpapers.htm (accessed 12 March 2010).

Berman, S. 2001. 'Ideas, norms and culture in political analysis', *Comparative Politics* 33 (2): 231–50.

Bernstein, R. 1976. *The Restructuring of Social and Political Theory.* Philadelphia: University of Pennsylvania Press.

Bevir, M. 1994. 'Objectivity in history', *History and Theory* 33 (3): 328–44.

Bevir, M. 1999. *The Logic of the History of Ideas.* Cambridge: Cambridge University Press.

Bevir, M. 2000. 'Historical explanation, folk psychology, and narrative', *Philosophical Explorations.* 2 (May): 152–68.

Bevir, M. 2005. *New Labour: A Critique.* London: Routledge.

Bevir, M. 2006. 'How narratives explain'. In D. Yanow and P. Schwartz-Shea (eds), *Interpretation and Method: Empirical Research Methods and the Interpretive Turn.* Armonk, NY: M.E. Sharpe: 281–90.

Bevir, M. and Rhodes, R. A. W. 2003. *Interpreting British Governance.* London: Routledge.

Bevir, M. and Rhodes, R. A. W. 2005. 'Interpretation and its others', *Australian Journal of Political Science* 40 (2): 169–87.

Bevir, M. and Rhodes, R. A. W. 2006. *Governance Stories.* Abingdon, Oxon: Routledge.

Bevir, M. and Rhodes, R. A. W. 2008. 'The differentiated polity as narrative', *British Journal of Politics and International Relations* 10 (4): 729–34.

Bevir, M. and Rhodes, R. A. W. 2010. *The State as Cultural Practice.* Oxford: Oxford University Press.

Beynon, H. 1975. *Working for Ford.* Wakefield: EP Publishing.

Birch, A. H. 1964. *Representative and Responsible Government.* London: Allen & Unwin.

Blair, C. 2008. *Speaking for Myself. The Autobiography.* London: Little, Brown.

Blair, T. 1996. *New Britain. My Vision of a Young Country.* London: Fourth Estate.

Blair, T. 1998. Civil Service Conference speech, 13 October. See Tony Blair archive: http://www.number10.gov.uk/Page5283 (accessed 6 October 2009).

Blair, T. 2004*a*. Speech on modernisation of the civil service. 24 February. See Tony Blair archive: http://www.number10.gov.uk/Page5399 (accessed 6 October 2009).

Blair, T. 2004*b*. *Tony Blair: In His Own Words*, ed. Paul Richards. London: Politico's.

Blair, T. 2007. Lecture on 'public life' at Reuters, Canary Wharf, London, Tuesday 12 June. Available at: http://image.guardian.co.uk/sys-files/Politics/documents/2007/06/12/BlairReustersSpeech.pdf (accessed 6 October 2009).

Blair, T. 2010*a*. *A Journey.* London: Hutchinson.

Blair, T. 2010*b*. 'Oral evidence' to the Iraq Inquiry (Chair, Sir John Chilcot), Friday 29 January. Available at: http://www.iraqinquiry.org.uk/transcripts.aspx (accessed 8 March 2010).

Blick, A. 2004. *People who Live in the Dark: The Special Adviser in British Politics.* London: Politico's.

Blick, A. and Jones, G. W. 2010. *Premiership. The Development, Nature and Power of the Office of the British Prime Minister.* Exeter: Imprint Academic.

Blunkett, D. 2006. *The Blunket Tapes. My Life in the Bear Pit.* London: Bloomsbury.

Bobrow, D. B. and Dryzek, J. S. 1987. *Policy Analysis by Design.* Pittsburgh, PA: Pittsburgh University Press.

Bogdanor, V. (ed.) 2003. *The British Constitution in the Twentieth Century.* Oxford: Oxford University Press for the British Academy.

Bogdanor, V. (ed.) 2005. *Joined-Up Government.* Oxford: Oxford University Press.

Bogdanor, V. 2009. *The New British Constitution* Oxford: Hart.

Boin, A., 't Hart, P., and McConnell, A. 2009. 'Crisis exploitation: political and policy impacts of framing contests', *Journal of European Public Policy* 16 (1): 81–106.

Boin, A., 't Hart, P., Stern, E., and Sundelius, B. 2005. *The Politics of Crisis Management. Public Leadership Under Pressure.* Cambridge: Cambridge University Press.

Boje, D. 1991. 'The storytelling organization: a story of story performance in an office-supply form', *Administrative Science Quarterly* 36 (1): 106–26.

Boorstin, D. 1962. *The Image or What Happened to the American Dream.* London: Weidenfeld and Nicolson.

Bovaird, T. and Russell, K. 2007. 'Civil service reform in the UK, 1999–2005: revolutionary failure of evolutionary success?' *Public Administration* 85 (2): 301–28.

Bovens, M. 1998. *The Quest for Responsibility: Accountability and Citizenship in Complex Organizations.* Cambridge: Cambridge University Press.

Bower, T. 2007. *Gordon Brown.* Updated edn. London: HarperCollins

Braybrooke, D. and Lindblom, C. E. 1963. *A Strategy of Decision.* New York: Free Press.

Bridges, Sir Edward 1971 [1950]. 'Portrait of a profession'. In R. A. Chapman and A. Dunsire (eds), *Style in Administration.* London: Allen & Unwin: 44–60.

Bridges, Sir Edward 1956. 'Administration: What is it and how can it be learnt?' In A. Dunsire (ed.), *The Making of an Administrator.* Manchester: Manchester University Press: 1–23.

Brown, C. 2005. *Prescott. The Biography.* Rev. edn. London: Simon & Schuster.

Brown, G. 1999. 'Modernising the British economy: the new mission for the Treasury', speech, Institute of Fiscal Studies, London, 27 May. Available at: http://www.hm-treasury.gov.uk/newsroom_and_speeches/speeches/chancellorexchequer/speech_chex_270599.cfm (accessed 6 October 2009).

Brown, P. and Levinson, S. C. 2000. *Politeness: Some Universals in Language Use*. Cambridge: Cambridge University Press.

Bruce-Gardyne, J. 1986. *Ministers and Mandarins*. London: Macmillan, George Allen and Unwin.

BSE Inquiry Report (The Phillips Report) 2000. *Volume 1: Findings and Conclusions*. London: Stationery Office. Available at: http://www.bseinquiry.gov.uk/ (accessed 6 October 2009).

Bullock, H., Mountford, J., and Stanley, R. 2001. *Better Policy Making*. London: Centre for Management and Policy Studies.

Burch, M. and Holliday, I. 1996. *The British Cabinet System*. Hemel Hempstead: Prentice Hall, Harvester Wheatsheaf.

Burke, P. J. 2003. 'Interaction in small groups'. In J. Delamater (ed.), *Handbook of Social Psychology*. New York: Kluwer Academic: 363–87.

Burnham, P., Gilland, K., Grant, W., and Layton-Henry, Z. 2004. *Research Methods in Politics*. Houndmills, Basingstoke: Palgrave-Macmillan.

Burns, T. 1977. *The BBC. Public Institution and Private World*. London: Macmillan.

Butler, Sir Robin 1992. 'Managing the new public services: towards a new framework?' *Public Policy and Management* 7 (3): 1–14. The published version of the Frank Stacey Memorial Lecture, University of York.

Butler, Sir Robin 1993. 'The evolution of the civil service', *Public Administration* 71 (3): 395–406.

Butler, Sir Robin 1995. 'Management in government: the future', speech delivered to the Management in Government: The Future Conference, at the Queen Elizabeth II Conference Centre, London, 17 November.

Butler of Brockwell, Lord 2004. *Review of Intelligence on Weapons of Mass Destruction. Report of a Committee of Privy Counsellors* (HC 898). London: Stationery Office, 14 July.

Cabinet Office 1994. *The Civil Service. Continuity and Change* (Cm. 2627). London: Stationery Office.

Cabinet Office 1995. *The Civil Service. Taking Forward Continuity and Change* (Cm. 2748). London: Stationery Office.

Cabinet Office 1999a. *The Civil Service Code*. London: Propriety and Ethics Team, Cabinet Office, 13 May.

Cabinet Office 1999b. *Civil Service Reform. Report to the Prime Minister from Sir Richard Wilson, Head of the Home Civil Service*. London: Cabinet Office.

Cabinet Office 1999c. *Modernising Government* (Cm. 4310). London: Stationery Office.

Cabinet Office 1999d. *Professional Policy Making for the Twenty-First Century*. London: Cabinet Office.

Cabinet Office 2000. *Wiring It Up*. London: Stationery Office.

Cabinet Office 2001a. *Better Policy Making*. London: Cabinet Office.

Cabinet Office 2001b. *Ministerial Code. A Code of Conduct and Guidance on Procedures for Ministers*. London: Cabinet Office, July.

Cabinet Office 2002. 'The second phase of public sector reform: the move to delivery'. Available at: http://archive.cabinetoffice.gov.uk/eeg/secondphase.htm (accessed 6 October 2009).

Cabinet Office 2005. *Transformational Government—Enabled by Technology* (Cm. 6970). London: Stationery Office.

Cabinet Office 2006*a*. *Capability Review of the Cabinet Office*. London: Capability Reviews Team, Delivery and Transformation Group, Cabinet Office.

Cabinet Office 2006*b*. *Capability Reviews Tranche 2: Common Themes and Summaries*. London: Capability Reviews Team, Delivery and Transformation Group, Cabinet Office.

Cabinet Office 2006*c*. *Capability Review of the Department of Trade and Industry*. London: Capability Reviews Team, Delivery and Transformation Group, Cabinet Office.

Cabinet Office 2006*d*. *Capability Review of the Department for Education and Skills*. London: Capability Reviews Team, Prime Minister's Delivery Unit, Cabinet Office.

Cabinet Office 2007. *Capability Review of the Department for Environment, Food and Rural Affairs*. London: Capability Reviews Team, Delivery and Transformation Group, Cabinet Office.

Cairncross, A. 1997. *The Wilson Years: A Treasury Diary, 1964–1966*. London: THP.

Cairncross, A. 1999. *Living with the Century*. Fife: Lynx.

Campbell, A. 2007. *The Blair Years. Extracts from the Alastair Campbell Diaries*. London: Hutchinson.

Campbell, C. and Wilson, G. K. 1995. *The End of Whitehall*. Oxford: Blackwell.

Campbell, J. 2001. *Margaret Thatcher*. Vol. 1: *The Grocer's Daughter*. London: Pimlico.

Carnegie, D. 1984. *How to Win Friends and Influence People*. Rev. edn. Sydney: Angus & Robertson.

Castle, B. 1973. 'Mandarin power', *Sunday Times*, 10 June.

Castle, B. 1984. *The Castle Diaries 1964–70*. London: Weidenfeld & Nicolson.

Chabal, P. M. 2003. 'Do ministers matter? The individual style of ministers in programmed policy change', *International Review of Administrative Science* 69 (1): 29–49.

Chapman, R. 1988. *Ethics in the British Civil Service*. London: Routledge.

Chapman, R. and Dunsire, A. 1971. 'The style of British administration'. In R. A. Chapman and A. Dunsire (eds), *Style in Administration. Readings in British Public Administration*. London: Allen & Unwin for the Royal Institute of Public Administration: 13–17.

Chapman, R. A. and Greenaway, J. R. 1980. *The Dynamics of Administrative Reform*. London: Croom Helm.

Chapman, R. and O'Toole, B. J. 1995. 'The role of the civil service: a traditional view in a period of change', *Public Policy and Administration* 10 (2): 3–20.

Chisholm, D. 1989. *Coordination without Hierarchy. Informal structures in Multi-Organizational Systems*. Berkeley: University of California Press.

Clark, Alan 1993. *Diaries*. London: Weidenfeld & Nicholson.

Clifford, J. 1983. 'On ethnographic authority', *Representations* 2 (Spring): 118–46.

Clifford, J. and Marcus, G. E. (eds) 1984. *Writing Culture. The Poetics and Politics of Ethnography*. Berkeley: University of California Press.

Coates, D. and Lawler, P. (eds) 2000. *New Labour in Power*, Manchester: Manchester University Press.

Collini, S. 2001. 'Postscript: disciplines, canons, and publics; the history of "the history of political thought" in comparative perspective'. In D. Castiglione and I. Hampshire-Monk (eds), *The History of Political Thought in National Context*. Cambridge: Cambridge University Press: 280–302.

Committee an Standards in Public Life 2000. *Sixth Report: Reinforcing Standards* (Cm. 4557). London: Stationery Office.

Committee an Standards in Public Life 2003. *Ninth Report: Defining the Boundaries within the Executive: Ministers, Special Advisers and the Permanent Civil Service* (Cm. 5775). London: Stationery Office.

Conan Doyle, Sir Arthur 1979. 'The man with the twisted lip'. In *The Annotated Sherlock Holmes. Vol. 1*. Ed. with an introduction, notes, and bibliography by W. S. Baring-Gould. London: John Murray: 368–97.

Cook, R. 2003. *The Point of Departure*. London: Simon & Schuster.

Cowley, P. 2005. *The Rebels: How Blair Mislaid his Majority*. London: Politico's.

Cowley, P. and Stuart, M. 2005. 'Parliament'. In A. Seldon and D. Kavanagh (eds), *The Blair Effect 2001–5*. Cambridge: Cambridge University Press: 20–42.

Crafts, N. 2007. 'Industrial policy'. In A. Seldon (ed.), *Blair's Britain 1997–2007*. Cambridge: Cambridge University Press: 273–87.

Crossman, R. H. S. 1975. *The Diaries of a Cabinet Minister. Vol. 1: Minister of Housing*. London: Jonathan Cape.

Currie, E. 1989. *Life Lines*. London: Sidgwick & Jackson.

Czarniawska, B. 1998. *A Narrative Approach to Organizational Studies*. London: Sage.

Dale, I. and Fawkes, G. (eds) 2006. *The Little Red Book of New Labour Sleaze*: Tunbridge Wells, Kent: Politico's.

Dargie, C. 1998. 'The role of public sector chief executives', *Public Administration* 76 (1): 161–78.

Davies, A. and Willman, J. 1991. *What Next? Agencies, Departments and the Civil Service*. London: Institute for Public Policy Research.

Davies, H. T. O., Nutley, S. M., and Smith, P. C. 2000. *What Works? Evidence-Based Policy and Practice in Public Services*. Bristol: Policy Press.

Davis, G. 1995. *A Government of Routines*. Melbourne: Macmillan Education.

Davis, G. and Rhodes, R. A. W. 2000. 'From hierarchy to contracts and back again: reforming the Australian public service'. In M. Keating, J. Wanna, and P. Weller (eds), *Institutions on the Edge? Capacity for Governance*. Sydney: Allen & Unwin: 74–98.

De Callierès, F. 1963 [1716]. *On the Manner of Negotiating with Princes*. Washington, DC: University of America Press.

De Paulo, B. M. and Friedman, H. S. 1998. 'Non-verbal communication'. In D. T. Gilbert, S. A. T. Fiske, and G. Lindzey (eds), *The Handbook of Social Psychology. Volume 2*, 4th edn. New York: Oxford University Press: 3–40.

Dean, M. 2007. *Governing Societies*. Berkshire: Open University Press.

Denham, R. 2002. *The Mandarin's Tale*. London: Politico's.

Denzin, N. K. 1989. *Interpretive Biography*. London: Sage.

Denzin, N. K. and Lincoln, Y. S. (eds). 2005. *Handbook of Qualitative Research*. Thousand Oaks, CA: Sage.

Department for Environment Food and Rural Affairs and the Forestry Commission (DEFRA) 2004. *Departmental Report 2004* (Cm. 6219). London: Stationery Office.

Department of Trade and Industry (DTI) 2004. *Departmental Report 2004* (Cm. 6216). London: Stationery Office.

Dexter, L. 1970. *Elite and Specialized Interviewing.* Evanston, IL: North Western University Press.

Dicey, A. V. 1914. *Lectures on the Relations between Law and Public Opinion during the Nineteenth Century,* 2nd edn. London: Macmillan.

Dickie, J. 1992. *Inside the Foreign Office.* New edn. London: Chapmans.

Donoughue, B. 2003. *The Heat of the Kitchen.* London: Politico's.

Donoughue, B. 2005. *Downing Street Diary. With Harold Wilson in No. 10.* London: Cape.

Dowding, K. 2004. 'Interpretation, truth and investigation', *British Journal of Politics and International Relations* 6 (2): 136–42.

Dowding, K. and Dumont, P. (eds) 2009. *The Selection of Ministers in Europe. Hiring and Firing.* London: Routledge.

Dowding, K. and Won-Taek Kang 1998. 'Ministerial resignations 1945–97', *Public Administration* 76 (3): 411–29.

Dryzek, J. S. 1993. 'Policy analysis and planning: from science to argument'. In F. Fischer and J. Forester (eds), *The Argumentative Turn in Policy Analysis and Planning.* Durham, NC: Duke University: 213–30.

Eckstein, H. 1974. 'Case study and theory in political science'. In F. I. Greenstein and N. Polsby (eds), *Handbook of Political Science.* Vol. 7: *Strategies of Inquiry.* Reading, MA: Addison-Wesley: 79–137.

Eckstein, H. 1975. 'Case study and theory in political science'. In F. I. Greenstein and N. Polsby (eds), *Handbook of Political Science.* Vol. 4: *Strategies of Inquiry.* Reading, MA: Addison-Wesley: 79–137.

Edelman, M. 1985 [1964]. *The Symbolic Uses of Politics.* Paperback edn with a new afterword. Urbana: University of Illinois Press.

Education and Skills Committee (ESC) 2003. *A Level Standards. Report, Together with Proceedings of the Committee, Minutes of Evidence and Appendices.* Third Report. Session 2002–3 (HC 153). London: Stationery Office.

Emerson, R. M. Fretz, R. I., and Shaw L. L. 1995. *Writing Ethnographic Fieldnotes.* Chicago: University of Chicago Press.

Emery, F. E. (ed.) 1969. *Systems Thinking.* Harmondsworth: Penguin.

Environment, Food and Rural Affairs Select Committee 2002. *The Role of DEFRA.* 10th Report, Session 2001–2 (HC 991). London: Stationery Office.

Esser, J. K. 2003. 'Alive and well after 25 years: a review of groupthink research'. In M. A. Hogg (ed.), *Social Psychology* Vol. 3: *People in Groups.* Thousand Oaks, CA: Sage: 354–83.

Faucher-King, F. 2005. *Changing Parties: An Anthropology of British Political Conferences.* Houndmills, Basingstoke: Palgrave-Macmillan.

Fawcett, P. 2009. Government, governance and metagovernance in the British core executive. PhD thesis. University of Birmingham (UK).

Fawcett, P. and Rhodes, R. A. W. 2007. 'Central government'. In A. Seldon (ed.), *Blair's Britain, 1997–2007.* Cambridge: Cambridge University Press: 79–103.

Fay, B. 1975. *Social Theory and Political Practice.* London: George Allen & Unwin.

Fenno, R. E. 1990. *Watching Politicians: Essays on Participant Observation.* Berkeley: Institute of Governmental Studies, University of California.

Ferlie, E., Lynn, L. E., and Pollitt, C. 2005. *The Oxford Handbook of Public Management*. Oxford: Oxford University Press.

Finer, S. E. 1956. 'The individual responsibility of ministers', *Public Administration* 34 (4): 377–96.

Fischer, F. 2003. *Reframing Public Policy*. Oxford: Oxford University Press.

Fischer, F. and Forester, J. (eds) 1993. *The Argumentative Turn in Policy Analysis and Planning*. Durham, NC: Duke University Press.

Flaubert, G. 2008 [1879]. *Correspondance V: janvier 1876–mai 1880*, ed. Jean Bruneau and Yvan Leclerc. Paris: Gallimard.

Flyvbjerg, B. 2006. 'Five misunderstandings about case studies', *Qualitative Inquiry* 12 (2): 219–45.

Foley, M. 2000. *The British Presidency*. Manchester: Manchester University Press.

Foley, M. 2004. 'Presidential attribution as an agency of prime ministerial critique in a parliamentary democracy: the case of Tony Blair', *British Journal of Politics and International Relations* 6 (3): 292–311.

Foster, C. 2005. *British Government in Crisis*. Oxford: Hart.

Fowler, N. 1991. *Ministers Decide*. London: Chapmans.

Fox, K. 2004. *Watching the English. The Hidden Rules of English Behaviour*. London: Hodder & Stoughton.

Frances, J., Levačić, R., Mitchell, J., and Thompson, G. 1991. 'Introduction'. In G. Thompson, J. Frances, R. Levačić, and J. Mitchell (eds), *Markets, Hierarchies and Networks: The Co-ordination of Social Life*. London: Sage: 1–23.

Fulton Committee Report 1968. *The Civil Service*. Vol. 1: *Report of the Committee 1966–68* (Cmnd 3638). London: Stationery Office.

Gamble, A. 1990. 'Theories of British politics', *Political Studies* 38 (3): 404–20.

Gamble, A. 1994. 'Political memoirs', *Politics* 14 (1): 35–42.

Gamble, A. 2006. 'Two faces of neoliberalism'. In R. Robison (ed.), *The Neoliberal Revolution: Forging the Market State*. Houndmills, Basingstoke: Palgrave-Macmillan: 20–35.

Gay, O. 2007a. *The Ministerial Code*. House of Commons Library, Parliament and Constitution Centre, Standard Note: SN/PC/03750. Updated: 4 December.

Gay, O. 2007b. *Special Advisers*. House of Commons Library, Parliament and Constitution Centre, Standard Note: SN/PC/03813. Dated: 26 November.

Geertz, C. 1973. *The Interpretation of Cultures*. New York: Basic Books.

Geertz, C. 1983. *Local Knowledge*. New York: Basic Books.

Geertz, C. 1988. *Works and Lives: The Anthropologist as Author*. Stanford: Stanford University Press.

Geertz, C. 2000. *Available Light. Anthropological Reflections on Philosophical Topics*. Princeton, NJ: Princeton University Press.

George, A. L. and Bennett, A. 2005. *Case Studies and Theory Development*. Cambridge, MA: MIT Press.

Gershon, P. 2004. *Releasing Resources for the Front-Line: Independent Review of Public Sector Efficiency*. London: Stationery Office.

Giddens, A. 1990. *The Consequences of Modernity*. Cambridge: Polity Press.

Giddens, A. 1993. *New Rules of Sociological Method*. 2nd rev. edn. Cambridge: Polity Press.

Goffman, E. 1969. *The Presentation of Self in Everyday Life*. London: Allen Lane.

Goodin, R. E. 1980. *Manipulatory Politics*. New Haven: Yale University Press.

Grant, W. 2005. 'Agricultural policy'. In P. Dorey (ed.), *Developments in British Public Policy*. London: Sage: 7–23.

Gray, A. and Jenkins, W. I. 1985. *Administrative Politics in British Government*. Brighton, Sussex: Wheatsheaf Books

Green, S. 1979. *Rachman*. London: Michael Joseph.

Greenleaf, W. H. 1983. *The British Political Tradition*. Vol. 1: *The Rise of Collectivism*. London: Methuen.

Greer, A. 2003. 'Countryside issues: a creeping crisis', *Parliamentary Affairs* 56 (3): 523–42.

Hajer, M. A. 2009. *Authoritative Governance*. Oxford: Oxford University Press.

Hajer, M. A. and Wagenaar, H. (eds) 2003. *Deliberative Policy Analysis: Understanding Governance in the Network Society*. Cambridge: Cambridge University Press.

Hall, C., Scott, C., and Hood, C. 2000. *Telecommunications Regulation: Culture, Chaos and Interdependence Inside the Regulatory Process*. London: Routledge.

Hammersley, M. 1991. *Reading Ethnographic Research. A Critical Guide*. Harlow, Essex: Longman.

Hammersley, M. 2000. *Taking Sides in Social Science Research: Essays on Partisanship and Bias*. London: Routledge.

Hammersley, M. 2008. *Questioning Qualitative Research*. London: Sage.

Hammersley, M. and Atkinson, P. 1983. *Ethnography: Principles in Practice*. London: Routledge.

Hammersley, M. and Atkinson, P. 1995. *Ethnography: Principles in Practice*. 2nd edn. London: Routledge.

Hammersley, M. and Atkinson, P. 2007. *Ethnography: Principles in Practice*. 3rd edn. London: Routledge.

Hampton, P. 2005. *Reducing Administrative Burdens: Effective Inspection and Enforcement*. London: Stationery Office.

Harris, J. 1990. 'Society and state in twentieth century Britain'. In F. M. L. Thompson (ed.), *The Cambridge Social History of Britain 1750–1950*. Vol. 3: *Social Agencies and Institutions*. Cambridge: Cambridge University Press: 63–117.

Haskins, C. 2003. *Rural Delivery Review. A Report on the Delivery of Government Policies in Rural England*. London: DEFRA.

Hay, C. 2000 *Political Analysis*. Houndmills, Basingstoke: Palgrave-Macmillan.

Heady, B. 1974. *British Cabinet Ministers*. London: Allen & Unwin.

Healy, P. 1986. 'Interpretive policy inquiry: a response to the limitations of the received view', *Policy Sciences* 19 (4): 381–96.

Heclo, H. and Wildavsky, A. 1974. *The Private Government of Public Money*. London: Macmillan.

Henderson, Sir Nicholas 2001 [1984]. *The Private Office*. London: Profile Books.

Hennessy, P. 1986. *Cabinet*. Oxford: Blackwell.

Hennessy, P. 1989. *Whitehall*. London: Secker & Warburg.

Hennessy, P. 1995. *The Hidden Wiring. Unearthing the British Constitution*. London: Gollancz.

Hennessy, P. 1998. 'The Blair style of government', *Government and Opposition* 33 (1): 3–20.

Hennessy, P. 2000*a*. 'The Blair style and the requirements of twenty-first century premiership', *Political Quarterly* 71: 386–95.

Hennessy, P. 2000*b*. *The Prime Ministers*. London: Allen Lane.

Hennessy, P. 2000*c*. *The Blair Revolution in Government*. Leeds: University of Leeds, Institute for Politics and International Studies.

Hennessy, P. 2002. 'The Blair government in historical perspective: an analysis of the power relationships within New Labour', *History Today* 52 (1): 21–3.

Hennessy, P. 2005. 'Rulers and servants of the state: the Blair style of government 1997–2004', *Parliamentary Affairs* 58 (1): 6–16.

Heseltine, M. 1990 [1987]. *Where There's a Will*. London: Arrow.

Heseltine, M. 2000. *Life in the Jungle. My Autobiography*. London: Hodder & Stoughton.

Hodgson, L., Farrell, C. M., and Connolly, M. 2007. 'Improving UK public services: a review of the evidence', *Public Administration* 85: 355–82.

Hood, C. C. 1991. 'A public management for all seasons?' *Public Administration* 69 (1): 3–19.

House of Commons Information Office 2009. *Sittings of the House*. London: House of Commons, Fact Sheet P4, Procedure Series, revised March 2009.

Howe, Sir Geoffrey 1994. *Conflict of Loyalty*. London: Macmillan.

Huizinga, J. 1955. *Homo Ludens: A Study of the Play Element in Culture*. Boston, MA: Beacon Press.

Hummel, R. P. 1991. 'Stories managers tell: why they are as valid as science', *Public Administration Review* 51 (1): 31–41.

Hutton, Lord 2004. *Report of the Inquiry into the Circumstances Surrounding the Death of Dr David Kelly* (HC 247). London: Stationery Office, 28 January.

Hyman, P. 2005. *1 Out of 10*. London: Vintage.

James, O. 2004. 'The UK core executive's use of public service agreements as a tool of governance', *Public Administration* 82 (2): 397–419.

James, S. 1992. *British Cabinet Government*. London: Routledge.

James, S. 1999. *British Cabinet Government*. 2nd edn. London: Routledge.

Janis, I. L. 1982. *Groupthink*. Boston, MA: Houghton Mifflin.

Jary, C. 2004. *Working with Ministers*. 1st edn. London: Cabinet Office, CMPS.

Jary, C. 2008. *Working with Ministers*. 4th edn. Sunningdale, Ascot: National School of Government.

Jenkins, R. 1975 [1971]. 'On being a minister'. In V. Herman and J. E. Alt (eds), *Cabinet Studies: A Reader*. London: Macmillan: 210–20. Reprinted from *the Sunday Times*, 17 January 1971.

Jenkins, R. 1991. *A Life at the Centre*. London: Macmillan.

Jennings, B. 1987. 'Interpretation and the practice of policy analysis'. In F. Fischer and J. Forester (eds), *Confronting Values in Policy Analysis*. Newbury Park, CA: Sage: 128–52.

Jessop, B. 2000. 'Governance failure'. In G. Stoker (ed.), *The New Politics of British Local Governance*. Houndmills, Basingstoke: Macmillan: 11–32.

Jessop, B. 2007. 'Governance and metagovernance: on reflexivity, requisite variety, and requisite irony'. In M. Bevir (ed.), *Public Governance*. Vol. 1: *Theories of Governance*. London: Sage: 230–45.

Johnson, N. 1977. *In Search of the Constitution*. Oxford: Pergamon.

Johnson, N. 2004. *Reshaping the British Constitution. Essays in Political Interpretation.* Houndmills, Basingstoke: Palgrave-Macmillan.

Jones, N. 1999. *Sultans of Spin*. London: Gollancz.

Jones, S. 2008. *Speechmaking. The Easy Guide to Writing and Giving Speeches.* Rev. edn. Sunningdale, Ascot: National School of Government.

Jordan, G. 1992. *Next Steps Agencies: From Managing by Command to Managing by Contract.* Aberdeen Papers in Accountancy and Finance, W6. Aberdeen: University of Aberdeen.

Jordan, G. 1994. 'From next steps to market testing: administrative reform and improvisation', *Public Policy and Administration* 9 (2): 21–35.

Kampfner, J. 2004. *Blair's Wars.* New York: Free Press.

Kass, H. and Catron, B. (eds) 1990. *Images and Identities in Public Administration*, London: Sage.

Kaufman, G. 1980. *How to be a Minister*. London: Sidgwick & Jackson.

Kavanagh, D. and Seldon, A. 2000. *The Powers Behind the Prime Minister.* London: HarperCollins.

Keane, J. 2009. 'Media decadence and democracy'. Senate Occasional Lecture, Parliament House, Canberra, 28 August 2009.

Keating, P. 1992. *Paul Keating's Book of Insults.* Melbourne: Bookman Press.

Keegan, W. 2003. *The Prudence of Mr. Gordon Brown.* Chichester, West Sussex: Wiley.

Keeling, D. 1972. *Management in Government.* London: Allen & Unwin.

Kerr, P. and Kettell, S. 2006. 'In defence of British politics: the past, present and future of the discipline', *Journal of British Politics* 1 (1): 3–25.

Kertzer, D. I. 1988. *Ritual, Politics, and Power.* New Haven: Yale University Press.

King, A. 2007. *The British Constitution.* Oxford: Oxford University Press.

King, G., Keohane, R. O., and Verba, S. 1994. *Designing Social Inquiry: Scientific Inference in Qualitative Research.* Princeton, NJ: Princeton University Press.

Knight, F. H. 1921. *Risk, Uncertainty, and Profit.* Boston, MA: Houghton Mifflin Company.

Kuhn, R. 2005. 'Media management'. In A. Seldon and D. Kavanagh (eds), *The Blair Effect 2001–5.* Cambridge: Cambridge University Press: 94–111.

Kuhn, R. 2007. 'Media management'. In A. Seldon (ed.), *Blair's Britain 1997–2007.* Cambridge: Cambridge University Press: 123–42.

Langdon, J. 2001. *Mo Mowlam. The Biography.* London: Warner Brooks.

Latham, M. 2005. *The Latham Diaries.* Melbourne: Melbourne University Press.

Laws, J. 1994. 'Organization, narrative and strategy'. In J. Hassard and M. Parker (eds), *Towards a New Theory of Organizations.* London: Routledge: 248–68.

Lawson, N. 1992. *The View from No. 11.* London: Bantam Press.

Lee, J. M., Jones, G. W., and Burnham, J. 1998. *At the Centre of Whitehall.* Houndmills, Basingstoke: Macmillan.

Lee, M. 1995. 'The ethos of the Cabinet Office: a comment on the testimony of officials'. In R. A. W. Rhodes and P. Dunleavy (eds), *Prime Minister, Cabinet and Core Executive.* London: Macmillan: 149–57.

Levine, J. M. and Moreland, R. L. 1998. 'Small groups'. In D. T. Gilbert, S. A. T Fiske, and G. Lindzey (eds), *The Handbook of Social Psychology. Volume 2*, 4th edn. New York: Oxford University Press: 415–69.

Levi-Strauss, C. 1966. *The Savage Mind*. London: Weidenfeld and Nicolson.

Levitt, R. and Solesbury, W. 2004. *Evidence-Informed Policy: What Difference Do Outsiders in Whitehall Make?* ESRC UK Centre for Evidence Based Policy and Practice, Working Paper Number 23. London: King's College. Available at: http://evidencenetwork.org (accessed 14 December 2009).

Levy, Lord Michael 2008. *A Question of Honour*. London: Simon & Schuster.

Lewis, D. 1997. *Hidden Agendas. Politics, Law and Disorder*. London: Hamish Hamilton.

Lindblom, C. E. 1965. *The Intelligence of Democracy*. New York: Free Press.

Lindblom, C. E. 1988. *Democracy and Market System*. Oslo: Norwegian University Press.

Ling, T. 2002. 'Delivering joined-up government in the UK: dimensions, issues and problems', *Public Administration* 80 (4): 615–42.

Lipsey, D. 2001. *The Secret Treasury*. Harmondsworth: Viking/Penguin.

Llosa, M. V. 2002. *Feast of the Goat*. London: Faber & Faber.

Lodge, G. and Rogers, B. 2006. *Whitehall's Black Box: Accountability and Performance in the Senior Civil Service*. London: Institute for Public Policy Research.

Loughlin, M. 1992. *Public Law and Political Theory*. Oxford: Clarendon Press.

Lowe, R. and Rollings, N. 2000. 'Modernising Britain, 1957–64: a classic case of centralisation and fragmentation?' In R. A. W. Rhodes (ed.), *Transforming British Government*. Vol. 1: *Changing Institutions*. London: Macmillan: 99–118.

Ludlam, S. and Smith M. J. (eds) 2002. *New Labour in Government*. Houndmills, Basingstoke: Palgrave-Macmillan.

Lynn, J. and Jay, A. 1984. *The Complete 'Yes Minister': The Diaries of a Cabinet Minister*. London: BBC Books.

Lyons, M. 2004. *Well Placed to Deliver? Shaping the Pattern of Government Service: Independent Review of Public Sector Relocation*. London: Stationery Office.

McConnell, A. and Stark, A. 2002. 'Foot-and-Mouth 2001. The politics of crisis management', *Parliamentary Affairs* 55 (4): 664–81.

MacIntyre, A. 1996. 'The virtues, the unity of human life and the concept of a tradition', ch. 15 of *After Virtue* (Notre Dame, IN: University of Notre Dame Press, 1984). Reprinted in L. Cahoone (ed.), *From Modernism to Postmodernism An Anthology*. Oxford: Blackwell, 1996: 534–55.

McKay, M., Davis, M., and Fanning, P. 1995 [1983]. *Messages: The Communication Skills Book*. 2nd edn. Oakland, CA: New Harbinger Publications.

McPherson, A. and Raab, C. 1988. *Governing Education*. Edinburgh: Edinburgh University Press.

Management Advisory Committee (MAC) 2004. *Connecting Government—Whole of Government Response to Australia's Priority Challenges*. Canberra: Australian Public Service Commission.

Mandelson, P. and Liddle, R. 1996. *The Blair Revolution. Can New Labour Deliver?* London: Faber & Faber.

Marcus, G. E. 1995. 'Ethnography in/of the world system: the emergence of multi-sited ethnography', *Annual Review in Anthropology* 24: 95–117.

Marsh, D. 2008a. 'Understanding British government: analysing competing models', *British Journal of Politics and International Relations* 10 (2): 251–68.

Marsh, D. 2008b. 'What is at stake? A response to Bevir and Rhodes', *British Journal of Politics and International Relations* 10 (4): 735–9.

Marsh, D., Richards, D., and Smith, M. J. 2001, *Changing Patterns of Governance in the United Kingdom*. Houndmills, Basingstoke: Palgrave.

Marshall, G. 1986. *Constitutional Conventions: The Rules and Forms of Political Accountability*. Oxford: Clarendon Press. Rev. paperback edn.

Martin, J. 1992. *Cultures in Organizations: Three Perspectives*. New York: Oxford University Press.

Masterman, L. 2003. 'How the paper saw it: press coverage of the A-level controversy (up to the publication of the Tomlinson Inquiry)'. In Education and Skills Select Committee. *A Level Standards. Appendices to the Minutes of Evidence*. Third Report. Session 2002–3 (HC 153). London: Stationery Office: Appendix 1, 127–8.

Maynard-Moody, S. and Musheno, M. 2003. *Cops, Teachers, Counsellors: Stories From the Front Lines of Public Service*. Ann Arbor, MI: University of Michigan Press.

Merton, R. K. 1957. *Social Theory and Social Structure*. Rev. edn. New York: Free Press of Glencoe.

Meyer, C. 2005. *DC Confidential. The Controversial Memoirs of Britain's Ambassador to the U.S. at the Time of 9/11 and the Iraq War*. London: Weidenfeld & Nicolson.

Meyer, T. 2002. *Media Democracy. How the Media Colonizes Politics*. Cambridge: Polity.

Mill, J. S. 1969 [1840] 'Coleridge'. In *The Collected Works of John Stuart Mill*. Vol. 10: *Essays in Ethics, Religion and Society*, ed. J. M. Robson. Toronto: University of Toronto Press: 119–63.

Miller, P. and Rose, N. 2008. *Governing the Present: Administering Economic, Social and Personal Life*. Cambridge: Polity.

Mills, C. Wright 1970. *The Sociological Imagination*. Harmondsworth: Penguin.

Ministry of Justice 2007. *The Governance of Britain* (Cm. 7170). London: Stationery Office.

Ministry of Justice 2008. *The Governance of Britain—Constitutional Revewal* (Cm. 7342–I). London: Stationery Office.

Mintzberg, H. 1973. *The Nature of Managerial Work*. New York: Harper & Row.

Mintzberg, H. and Bourgault, J. 2000. *Managing Publicly*. Toronto: Institute of Public Administration of Canada.

Mitchell, W. 1993. 'The shape of public choice to come: some predictions and advice', *Public Choice* 77 (1): 133–44.

Moran, M., Rein, M., and Goodin R. E. (eds) 2006. *The Oxford Handbook of Public Policy*. Oxford: Oxford University Press.

Morgan, G. 1993. *Imaginization*. London: Sage.

Morris, E. 2002*a*. *Statement by the Rt. Hon. Estelle Morris MP*. London: Department for Education and Skills, 19 September.

Morris, E. 2002*b*. *Statement by the Rt. Hon. Estelle Morris MP*. London: Department for Education and Skills, 27 September.

Morrison, P. 1984. 'What I expect of civil servants'. Speech delivered at the Department of Employment, 22 November.

Morton, T. 1991. *Going Home—The Runrig Story*. Edinburgh: Mainstream Publishing.

Mowlam, M. 2002. *Momentum: The Struggle for Peace, Politics and the People*. London: Hodder & Stoughton.

Mughan, A. 2000. *Media and the Presidentialization of Parliamentary Elections.* Houndmills, Basingstoke: Palgrave.

Mulgan, G. 2001. Speech to the Conference on Joined-Up Government, British Academy, London, 30 October.

Mulgan, R. 2003. *Holding Power to Account: Accountability in Modern Democracies,* Houndmills, Basingstoke: Palgrave-Macmillan.

Murray, C. 2006. *Murder in Samarkand. A British Ambassador's Controversial Defiance of Tyranny in the War on Terror.* Edinburgh: Mainstream.

National Audit Office 2002. *Individual Learning Accounts.* London: Stationery Office.

Naughtie, J. 2002. *The Rivals. The Intimate Story of a Political Marriage.* Rev. edn. London: Fourth Estate.

Neruda, P. 2003. *The Poetry of Pablo Neruda.* Ed. with an introduction by Ilan Stavans. New York: Farrar Straus and Giroux.

Nicholson, H. 1950. *Diplomacy.* Oxford: Oxford University Press.

Nobbs, D. 1975. *The Death of Reginald Perrin: A Novel.* London: Gollanz. Reissued thereafter as *The Fall and Rise of Reginald Perrin.*

Noon, M. and Delbridge, R. 1993. 'News from behind my hand: gossip in organizations', *Organization Studies* 14 (1): 23–36.

Noordegraaf, M. 2000. *Attention! Work and Behaviour of Public Managers amidst Ambiguity.* Delft: Eburon.

Norton, P. 1981. *The Commons in Perspective.* Oxford: Martin Robertson.

Norton, P. 2000. 'Barons in a shrinking kingdom: senior ministers in British government'. In R. A. W. Rhodes (ed.), *Transforming British Government.* Vol. 2: *Changing Roles and Relationships.* London: Macmillan: 101–24.

Norton, P. 2003. 'The presidentialisation of British politics', *Government and Opposition* 38 (2): 274–8.

Norton, P. 2005. *Parliament in British Politics.* Houndmills, Basingstoke: Palgrave-Macmillan.

Oakeshott, M. 1991 [1962]. *Rationalism in Politics and Other Essays,* new and expanded edn. Indianapolis: Liberty Press [originally London: Methuen]. References are to the 1962 edn.

Oakeshott, M. 1996. *The Politics of Faith and the Politics of Scepticism,* ed. T. Fuller. New Haven: Yale University Press.

Oborne, P. and Walters, S. 2004. *Alastair Campbell.* London: Aurum Press.

Office of Public Services Reform (OPSR) 2002. *Reforming our Public Services—Principles into Practice.* London: Cabinet Office.

Office of Public Services Reform (OPSR) 2005. *Putting People at the Heart of Public Services.* London: Cabinet Office.

O'Halpin, E. 1989. *Head of the Civil Service. A Study of Sir Warren Fisher.* London: Routledge.

Orwell, G. 1968 [1944]. 'Benefit of Clergy: Some Notes On Salvador Dali'. In *The Collected Essays, Journalism and Letters of George Orwell.* Vol. 3: *As I Please 1943–1945,* ed. S. Orwell and I. Argus London: Secker & Warburg: 156–65.

Orwell, G. 1970 [1944]. 'The English People'. In *The Collected Essays, Journalism and Letters of George Orwell.* Vol. 3: *As I Please 1943–1945.* Edited by S. Orwell and I. Angus. London: Secker & Warburg: 1–38.

Packer, R. 2006. *The Politics of BSE*. Houndmills, Basingstoke: Palgrave-Macmillan.

Page, E. C. and Jenkins, W. I. 2005. *Policy Bureaucracy. Government with a Cast of Thousands*. Oxford: Oxford University Press.

Parkinson, C. Northcote 1965. *Parkinson's Law, or the Pursuit of Progress*. Harmondsworth: Penguin.

Parris, H. 1969. *Constitutional Bureaucracy*. London: Allen & Unwin.

Part, A. 1990. *The Making of a Mandarin*. London: Deutsch.

Paxman, J. 2002. *The Political Animal*. London: Michael Joseph.

Perez-Diaz, V. M. 1993. *The Return of Civil Society*. Cambridge, MA: Harvard University Press.

Perri 6 1997. *Holistic Governance*. London: Demos.

Perri 6, Leat, D., Seltzer, K., and Stoker, G. 2002. *Towards Holistic Governance. The New Reform Agenda*. Houndmills, Basingstoke: Palgrave-Macmillan.

Peston, R. 2005. *Brown's Britain*. London: Short Books.

Peters, B. G. 1998. 'Managing horizontal government: the politics of coordination', *Public Administration* 76 (2): 295–311.

Phillis, B. 2004. *An Independent Review of Government Communications*. London Cabinet Office. Available at: http://archive.cabinetoffice.gov.uk/gcreview/News/Final-Report.pdf (accessed 6 October 2009).

Plowden, W. 1994. *Ministers and Mandarins*. London: Institute for Public Policy Research.

Poguntke, T. and Webb, P. (eds) 2005. *The Presidentialization of Politics: A Comparative Study of Modern Democracies*. Oxford: Oxford University Press.

Policy Commission on the Future of Farming and Food (The Curry Report) 2002. *Farming and Food: A Sustainable Future*. London: Stationery Office at: http://archive.cabinetoffice.gov.uk/farming/pdf/PC%20Report2.pdf (accessed 6 October 2009).

Pollard, S. 2005. *David Blunkett*. London: Hodder & Stoughton.

Pollitt, C. 1993. *Managerialism and the Public Services*. 2nd edn. Oxford: Blackwell.

Pollitt, C. 2003. 'Joined-up government: a survey', *Political Studies Review* 1 (1): 34–49.

Pollitt, C. 2007. *Time, Policy, Management. Governing with the Past*. Oxford: Oxford University Press.

Ponting, C. 1985. *The Right to Know: The Inside Story of the Belgrano Affair*. London: Sphere Books.

Ponting, C. 1986. *Whitehall—Tragedy and Farce*. London: Hamish Hamilton,

Powell, E. 1977. *Joseph Chamberlain*. London: Thames & Hudson.

Powell, J. 2010. 'Oral evidence' to the Iraq Inquiry (Chair, Sir John Chilcot), Friday 18 January. Available at: http://www.iraqinquiry.org.uk/transcripts.aspx (accessed 8 March 2010).

Powell, W. 1991. 'Neither market nor hierarchy: network forms of organisation'. In G. Thompson, J. Frances, R. Levačić, and J. Mitchell (eds), *Markets, Hierarchies and Networks: The Co-ordination of Social Life*. London: Sage: 265–76.

Power, M. 1994. *The Audit Explosion*. London: Demos.

Prescott, J. 2008. *Prezza. My Story: Pulling no Punches*. London: Headline Review.

Price, L. 2005. *The Spin Doctor's Diary: Inside Number 10 with New Labour*. London: Hodder & Stoughton.

Prime Minister's Strategy Unit 2006. *The UK Government's Approach to Public Service Reform—A Discussion Paper*. London: Cabinet Office.

Prime Minister's Strategy Unit 2007. *Building on Progress: Public Services*. London: Cabinet Office.

Public Administration Select Committee (PASC) 2000. 'Minutes of evidence Wednesday 14 June 2000. Professor C. Pollitt and Professor R. Rhodes', *Making Government Work* (HC 238-v). Session 1999–2000. London: Stationery Office.

Public Administration Select Committee (PASC) 2001*a*. *Making Government Work: The Emerging Issues* (HC 94). Session 2000–1. London: Stationery Office.

Public Administration Select Committee (PASC) 2001*b*. *Special Advisers: Boon or Bane?* HC 293 Session 2000–1. London: Stationery Office.

Public Administration Select Committee (PASC) 2002. *'These Unfortunate Events': Lessons of Recent Events at the Former DTLR*. HC 303 Session 2001–2. London: Stationery Office.

Public Administration Select Committee (PASC) 2005. *Choice, Voice and Public Services*. HC 49-I Session 2004–5. London: Stationery Office.

Public Administration Select Committee (PASC) 2007. *Governing the Future*. HC 123-I Session 2006–7. London: Stationery Office.

Punch, M. 1986. *The Politics and Ethics of Fieldwork*. Newbury Park, CA: Sage.

Qualifications and Curriculum Authority (QCA) 2002. *Preliminary Investigation of the Summer 2002 OCR A-level Awards*. London: QCA, 20 September.

Raab, J. and Milward, H. Brinton 2003. 'Dark networks as problems', *Journal of Public Administration Research and Theory* 13 (October): 413–39.

Ranson, S. 2008. 'The changing governance of education', *Educational Management Administration and Leadership* 36 (2): 201–19.

Rawnsley, A. 2001. *Servants of the People. The Inside Story of New Labour*. Rev. edn. London: Penguin.

Rawnsley, A. 2010. *The End of the Party. The Rise and Fall of New Labour*. London: Viking.

Rees, J. C. 1977. 'Interpreting the constitution'. In P. King (ed.), *The Study of Politics*. London: Frank Cass: 97–117.

Rein, M. 1976. *Social Science and Public Policy*. Harmondsworth: Penguin.

Rein, M. and Schon, D. 1994. *Frame Reflection: Toward the Resolution of Intractable Policy Controversies*. New York: Basic Books.

Rentoul, J. 2001 *Tony Blair: Prime Minister*. London: Little, Brown.

Rhodes, R. A. W. (ed.) 1977. *Training in the Civil Service*. London: Joint University Council for Social and Public Administration.

Rhodes, R. A. W. 1988. *Beyond Westminster and Whitehall*. London: Allen & Unwin.

Rhodes, R. A. W. 1993. 'State-building without bureaucracy'. In I. Budge and D. McKay (eds), *Developing Democracy: Research in Honour of Jean Blondel*. London: Sage: 165–78.

Rhodes, R. A. W. 1995. 'From prime ministerial power to core executive'. In R. A. W. Rhodes and P. Dunleavy (eds), *Prime Minister, Cabinet and Core Executive*. London: Macmillan: 11–37.

Rhodes, R. A. W. 1997*a*. *Understanding Governance*. Buckingham and Philadelphia: Open University Press.

Rhodes, R. A. W. 1997*b*. 'It's the mix that matters: from marketisation to diplomacy', *Australian Journal of Public Administration* 56 (2): 40–53.

Rhodes, R. A. W. 2000*a*. 'New Labour's civil service: summing up joining up', *Political Quarterly* 71 (2): 151–66.

Rhodes, R. A. W. (ed.) 2000*b*. *Transforming British Government*. Vol. 1: *Changing Institutions*. Vol. 2: *Changing Roles and Relationships*. London: Macmillan.

Rhodes, R. A. W. 2001. 'Departmental secretaries in the UK, 1970–99'. In R. A. W. Rhodes and P. Weller (eds), *Mandarins or Valets? The Changing World of Top Officials*. Buckingham: Open University Press: 111–51.

Rhodes, R. A. W. 2002. 'Putting the people back into networks', *Australian Journal of Political Science* 37 (3): 399–415.

Rhodes, R. A. W. 2005. 'Everyday life in a ministry: public administration as anthropology', *American Review of Public Administration* 35 (1): 3–26.

Rhodes, R. A. W. 2006. 'Policy network analysis'. In M. Moran, M. Rein, and R. E. Goodin (eds), *The Oxford Handbook of Public Policy*. Oxford: Oxford University Press: 423–45.

Rhodes, R. A. W. 2007*a*. 'Understanding governance revisited', *Organization Studies* 28 (8): 1243–64.

Rhodes, R. A. W. 2007*b*. 'The everyday life of a minister: a confessional and impressionist tale'. In R. A. W. Rhodes, Paul 't Hart, and M. Noordegraaf (eds), *Observing Government Elites: Up Close and Personal*. Houndmills, Basingstoke: Palgrave-Macmillan: 21–50.

Rhodes, R. A. W. and Dunleavy, P. (eds) 1995. *Prime Minister, Cabinet and Core Executive*. London: Macmillan.

Rhodes, R. A. W. and Wanna, J. 2009. 'Bringing the politics back in', *Public Administration* 87 (2) 2009: 161–83.

Rhodes, R. A. W. and Weller, P. (eds) 2001. *Mandarins or Valets? The Changing World of Top Officials*. Buckingham: Open University Press.

Rhodes, R. A. W. and Weller, P. 2005. 'Westminster transplanted and Westminster implanted: explanations for political change'. In J. Wanna and P. Weller (eds), *Westminster Legacies: Democracy and Responsible Government in Asia, Australasia and the Pacific*. Sydney: University of New South Wales Press: 1–12.

Rhodes, R. A. W., 't Hart, P., and Noordegraaf, M. (eds) 2007. *Observing Government Elites: Up Close and Personal*. Houndmills, Basingstoke: Palgrave-Macmillan.

Rhodes, R. A. W., Wanna, J., and Weller, P. 2009. *Comparing Westminster*. Oxford: Oxford University Press.

Richards, D. 1996. 'Elite interviewing: approaches and pitfalls', *Politics* 16 (3): 199–204.

Richards, D. 1997. *The Civil Service under Thatcher*. Brighton: Sussex University Press.

Richards, D. 2008. *New Labour and the Civil Service: Reconstituting the Westminster Model*. Houndmills, Basingstoke: Palgrave-Macmillan.

Richards, D. and Smith, M. J. 2002. *Governance and Public Policy in the UK*. Oxford: Oxford University Press.

Richards, D. and Smith, M. J. 2004. 'Interpreting the world of political elites', *Public Administration* 82 (4): 777–800.

Richards, D. and Smith, M. J. 2006. 'Central control and policy implementation in the UK: a case study of the Prime Minister's Delivery Unit'. *Journal of Comparative Policy Analysis* 8 (4): 325–46.

Richardson, L. 1997. *Fields of Play. Reconstructing an Academic Life.* New Brunswick, NJ: Rutgers University Press.

Ricoeur, P. 1981. *Hermeneutics and the Human Sciences: Essays on Language, Action and Interpretation*, ed., tr., and intro. by J. B. Thompson. Cambridge: Cambridge University Press.

Ricoeur, P. 1991. *From Text to Action: Essays in Hermeneutics, II*, tr. K. Blamey and J. B. Thompson. Evanston, IL: Northwestern University Press.

Riddell, P. 2001. 'Blair as prime minister'. In A. Seldon (ed.), *The Blair Effect.* London: Little, Brown: 21–40.

Riddell, P. 2005. *The Unfulfilled Prime Minister: Tony Blair and the End of Optimism* London: Politico's.

Rimington, S. 2001. *Open Secret: The Autobiography of the Former Director-General of MI5.* London: Hutchinson.

Roberts, J. M. 1988. *Decision-Making During International Crises.* Houndmills, Basingstoke: Palgrave-Macmillan.

Roe, E. 1994. *Narrative Policy Analysis*, Durham, NC: Duke University Press.

Rogers, S. (ed.) 2004. *The Hutton Inquiry and its Impact.* London: Politico's-Guardian Books.

Rorty, R. 1980. *Philosophy and the Mirror of Nature.* Oxford: Blackwell.

Rose, R. 1987. *Ministers and Ministries.* Oxford: Clarendon Press.

Rose, R. 2001. *The Prime Minister in a Shrinking World.* Cambridge: Polity.

Royal Institute of Public Administration 1987. *Top Jobs in Whitehall.* London: RIPA.

Salamon, L. M. (ed.) 2002. *The Tools of Government: A Guide to the New Governance.* Oxford: Oxford University Press.

Sanderson, I. 2002. 'Evaluation, policy learning and evidence based policy making', *Public Administration* 80 (1): 1–22.

Sanjek, R. (ed.) 1990. *Fieldnotes: The Making of Anthropology.* Ithaca, NY: Cornell University Press.

Sanjek, R. 2000. 'Keeping ethnography alive in an urbanizing world', *Human Organization* 59 (3): 280–8.

Saunders, D. 1995. 'Behavioural analysis'. In D. Marsh and G. Stoker (eds), *Theories and Methods in Political Science*, London: Macmillan: 58–75.

Savage, S. P. and Atkinson, R. (eds) 2001. *Public Policy under Blair.* Houndmills, Basingstoke: Macmillan-Palgrave.

Scammell, M. 2001. 'The media and media management'. In A. Seldon (ed.), *The Blair Effect: The Blair Government 1997–2001.* London: Little, Brown: 509–33.

Schon, D. 1973. *Beyond the Stable State. Public and Private Learning in a Changing Society.* Harmondsworth: Penguin.

Schram, S. F. 1993. 'Postmodern policy analysis: discourse and identity in welfare policy', *Policy Sciences* 26 (3): 249–70.

Scott, D. 2004. *Off Whitehall: A View from Downing Street.* London: Tauris.

Sear, C. 2002 *Modernisation of the House of Commons: Sitting Hours.* Research Paper 02/41. London: House of Commons Library, Parliament and Constitution Centre, 27 June.

Sedgemore, B. 1980. *The Secret Constitution.* London: Hodder & Stoughton.

Seidman, H. 1975. *Politics, Position and Power*, 2nd edn. Oxford: Oxford University Press.

Seldon, A. 1995. 'The Cabinet Office and coordination, 1979–87'. In R. A. W. Rhodes and P. Dunleavy (eds), *Prime Minister, Cabinet and Core Executive*. London: Macmillan.

Seldon, A. (ed.) 2001. *The Blair Effect: The Blair Government 1997–2001*. London: Little, Brown.

Seldon, A. 2004. *Blair*. London: Free Press.

Seldon, A. (ed.) 2007. *Blair's Britain, 1997–2007*. Cambridge: Cambridge University Press.

Seldon, A. and Kavanagh, D. (eds) 2005. *The Blair Effect 2001–5*. Cambridge: Cambridge University Press.

Seldon, A. with P. Snowden and D. Collings 2007. *Blair Unbound*. London: Simon & Schuster.

Select Committee on Agriculture 1998. *Minutes of Evidence*. Memorandum submitted by the Ministry of Agriculture, Fisheries and Food, Annex A. 5 May 1998 Session 1998–9.

Select Committee on Foreign Affairs 1999. *Second Report. Sierra Leone. Report and Proceedings* (HC 116-I). *Minutes of Evidence and Appendices* (HC 116-II). Session 1998–9. London: Stationery Office.

Select Committee on the Constitution 2009. *Inquiry into the Cabinet Office and the Centre of Government. Interim Report*. Available at: http://www.parliament.uk/parliamentary_committees/lords_constitution_committee.cfm (accessed 15 October 2009).

Seymour-Ure, C. 2003. *Prime Ministers and the Media. Issues of Power and Control*. Oxford: Blackwell.

Shephard, G. 2000. *Shephard's Watch: Illusions of Power in British Politics*. London: Politico's.

Shore, C. 2000. *Building Europe: The Cultural Politics of European Integration*. London: Routledge.

Shore, C. and Nugent, S. 2002. *Elite Cultures. Anthropological Perspectives*. ASA Monographs 38. London: Routledge.

Shore, C. and Wright, S. (eds) 1997. *The Anthropology of Policy. Critical Perspectives on Governance and Power*. London: Routledge.

Short, C. 2004. *An Honourable Deception? New Labour, Iraq and the Misuse of Power*. London: Free Press.

Smith, M. J. 1990. *The Politics of Agricultural Support in Britain*. Dartmouth: Aldershot.

Smith, M. J. 1993. *Pressure, Power and Policy*. Hemel Hempstead: Harvester Wheatsheaf.

Smith, M. J 1999a. 'Institutionalising the "eternal return": textbooks and the study of British politics', *British Journal of Politics and International Relations* 1 (1): 106–18.

Smith, M. J. 1999b. *The Core Executive in Britain*. London: Macmillan.

Smithers, A. 2005. 'Education'. In A. Seldon and D. Kavanagh (eds), *The Blair Effect 2001–5*. Cambridge: Cambridge University Press: 256–82.

Smithers, A. 2007. 'Schools'. In A. Seldon (ed.), *Blair's Britain, 1997–2007*. Cambridge: Cambridge University Press: 361–84.

Stanley, M. 2008a. *How to be a Civil Servant*. Available at http://www.civilservant.org.uk/ (accessed 6 October 2009). Also available as a paperback from Politico's, 2004.

Stanley, M. 2008*b*. 'Mandarin English Part 1'. Available at http://www.civilservant.org. uk/jargon.pdf (accessed 6 October 2009).

Stewart, J. 2004. *The Decline of the Tea Lady.* Kent Town, SA: Wakefield Press.

Stothard, P. 2003. *30 Days. A Month at the Heart of the Blair War.* London: HarperCollins.

't Hart, P. 1990. *Groupthink in Government: A Study of Small Groups and Policy Failure.* Amsterdam: Swets and Zeitlinger.

't Hart, P. 1991. 'Group think, risk taking and recklessness: quality of process and outcome in policy decision making', *Politics and the Individual* 1 (1): 67–90.

't Hart, P. 1993. 'Symbols, rituals and power: the lost dimensions of crisis management', *Journal of Contingencies and Crisis Management* 1 (1): 36–50.

't Hart, P., Stern, E. K., and Sundelius, B. (eds) 1997. *Beyond Groupthink. Political Group Dynamics and Foreign Policy Making.* Ann Arbor: University of Michigan Press.

Taylor, C. 1971. 'Interpretation and the sciences of man', *Review of Metaphysics* 35: 3–51.

Taylor, I. 2003. 'Policy on the hoof: the handling of the foot and mouth disease outbreak in the UK 2001', *Policy & Politics* 31 (4): 535–46.

Thatcher, M. 1993. *The Downing Street Years.* London: HarperCollins.

Thatcher, M. 1995. *The Path to Power.* London: HarperCollins.

Theakston, K. 1987. *Junior Ministers in British Government.* Oxford: Blackwell.

Theakston, K. 1999. *Leadership in Whitehall.* London: Macmillan.

Theakston, K. (ed.) 2000. *Bureaucrats and Leadership.* Houndmills, Basingstoke: Macmillan.

Thomas, R. 1978. *The British Philosophy of Administration.* London: Longmans.

Thomas, W. I. and Thomas, D. S. 1928. *The Child in America: Behavior Problems and Programs.* New York: Knopf.

Thompson, G. 1993. 'Network co-ordination'. In R. Maidment and G. Thompson (eds), *Managing the United Kingdom.* London: Sage: 51–74.

Toke, D. and Marsh, D. 2003. 'Policy networks and the GM crops issue', *Public Administration* 81 (2): 229–51.

Tomlinson, M. 2002. *The Inquiry into A-level Standards—Interim Report.* London: DfES, 27 September. Available at: http://news.bbc.co.uk/2/shared/spl/hi/education/02/tomlinson_report/html/part1.stm (accessed 24 November 2009).

Toynbee, P. and Walker, D. 2001. *Did Things Get Any Better? An Audit of Labour's Successes and Failures.* London: Penguin.

Toynbee, P. and Walker, D. 2005. *Better or Worse? Has Labour Delivered?* London: Penguin.

Travers, M. 2007. *The New Bureaucracy. Quality Assurance and its Critics.* Bristol: Policy Press.

Treasury 2005. *Corporate Governance in Central Government Departments: Code of Good Practice.* London: HM Treasury, July.

Treasury and Cabinet Office 2004. *Devolving Decision Making: Delivering Better Public Services: Refining Targets and Performance Management.* London: Stationery Office.

Treasury Select Committee 2000. *Minutes of Evidence,* Annex 1, Treasury Aims and Objectives, Session 2000–1, 11 May. Available at: http://www.publications.parliament. uk/pa/cm199900/cmselect/cmtreasy/492/0051103.htm (accessed 6 October 2009).

Treasury Select Committee 2001. *HM Treasury*, Session 2000–1 (HC 73-I). London: Stationery Office.

Turnbull, A. 2005. 'Valedictory lecture', 27 July. Available at: http://www.guardian.co.uk/politics/2005/jul/27/Whitehall.uk (accessed on 6 October 2009).

Turnbull, Sir Andrew 2007. Permanent Secretary, HM Treasury, 'Stalinist Brown', An interview by N. Timmins, *Financial Times*, 20 March.

Van Eeten, M. J. G., Van Twist, M. J. W., and Kalders, P. R. 1996. 'Van een narratieve bestuurskunde naar een postmoderne beweerkunde?' *Bestuurskunde* 5: 168–89.

Van Maanen, J. 1978. 'Epilogue: on watching the watchers'. In P. K. Manning and J. Van Maanen (eds), *Policing: A View from the Street*. Santa Monica, CA: Goodyear: 309–49.

Van Maanen, J. 1988. *Tales of the Field. On Writing Ethnography*. Chicago: University of Chicago Press.

Verney, D. 1991. 'Westminster model'. In V. Bogdanor (ed.), *The Blackwell Encyclopaedia of Political Science*. Oxford: Blackwell, corrected paperback edn: 637–8.

Vicchaeri, C. 1993. *Rationality and Co-ordination*. Cambridge: Cambridge University Press.

Vickers, Sir Geoffrey 1968. *The Art of Judgment: A Study of Policy Making*. London: Methuen University Paperback.

Wajcman, J. 1998. *Managing Like a Man. Women and Men in Corporate Management*. Cambridge: Polity.

Wakeham, The Rt Hon Lord 1993. 'Cabinet government'. Lecture delivered on 10 November, Brunel University, Uxbridge.

Walker, P. 1991. *Staying Power. An Autobiography*. London: Bloomsbury.

Walker, P. G. 1970. *The Cabinet*. London: Jonathan Cape.

Wass, D. 1984. *The Government and the Governed*. London: Routledge & Kegan Paul.

Watson, G. 1986. 'Make me reflexive—but not yet. Strategies for managing essential reflexivity in ethnographic discourse', *Journal of Anthropological Research* 43 (1): 29–41.

Weick, K. E. 1979 [1969]. *The Social Psychology of Organizing*. Reading, MA: Addison-Wesley.

Weick, K. E. 1995. *Sensemaking in Organizations*. Thousand Oaks, CA: Sage Publications.

Weller, P. 2003 'Cabinet government: an elusive ideal?' *Public Administration* 81 (4): 701–22.

Weller, P. and Rhodes, R. A. W. 2001.'Conclusion: "Antipodean exceptionalism, European traditionalism"'. In R. A. W. Rhodes and P. Weller) (eds), *Mandarins or Valets? The Changing World of Top Officials*. Buckingham: Open University Press: 214–39.

Wheare, K. C. 1955. *Government by Committee: An Essay on the British Constitution*. Oxford: Clarendon Press.

White, H. 1973. *Metahistory*. Baltimore, MD: Johns Hopkins University Press.

White, H. 1987. 'The question of narrativity in contemporary historical theory'. In H. White, *The Content of Form. Narrative Discourse and Historical Representation*. Baltimore, MD: Johns Hopkins University Press: 26–57 and 216–24.

Wildavsky, A. 1979. *The Art and Craft of Policy Analysis*. London: Macmillan.

Wilkinson, K. 2009. 'Heroes and villains in the bureaucracy: interpreting policy making in DEFRA'. Paper to the 59th Political Studies Association Annual Conference, 'Challenges for Democracy in a Global Era', 7–9 April. The Manchester Conference Centre, University of Manchester.

Williams, S. 1980. 'The decision makers'. In Royal Institute of Public Administration, *Policy and Practice. The Experience of Government*. London: RIPA: 79–102.

Wilson, Sir Richard 1998. 'Modernising government: the role of the senior civil service'. Speech to the Senior Civil Service Conference, October.

Wilson, Sir Richard 1999. 'The civil Service in the new millennium' Valedictory speech, May.

Wilson, Sir Richard 2003. 'Portrait of a profession revisited', *Public Administration* 81 (2): 365–78. Published version of a speech delivered on 26 March 2002 at Admiralty Arch, London.

Wilson of Dinton, Lord 2006. 'Tomorrow's government'. Lecture at the Royal Society of Arts, London delivered on 1 March. Available at: http://www.ucl.ac.uk/constitution-unit/publications/unit-publications/137.htm (accessed 6 October 2009).

Winter, M. 2003. 'Responding to the crisis: the policy impact of the foot-and-mouth epidemic'. *The Political Quarterly* 74 (1): 47–56.

Wittgenstein, L. 1972. *Philosophical Investigations*, tr. G. Anscombe. Oxford: Basil Blackwell.

Wood, M. 1997. 'John Wayne agonistes', *New York Review of Books*, 24 April.

Woodhouse, D. 2004. 'UK ministerial responsibility in 2002: the tale of two resignations', *Public Administration* 82 (1): 1–19.

Working Group on 14–19 Year Reform (The Tomlinson Report) 2004. *Curriculum and Qualifications Reform. Final Report of the Working Group on 14–19 Reform*. London: DfES.

Wright, V. and Hayward, J. E. S. 2000. 'Governing from the centre: policy co-ordination in six European core executives'. In R. A. W. Rhodes (ed.), *Transforming British Government*. Vol. 2: *Changing Roles and Relationships*. London: Macmillan: 27–46.

Wulff, H. 2002. 'Yo-yo fieldwork: mobility and time in multi-local study of dance in Ireland', *Anthropological Journal of European Cultures* 11: 117–36.

Yanow, D. 1999. *Conducting Interpretive Policy Analysis*. Newbury Park, CA: Sage.

Yanow, D. 2006. 'Dear reviewer, dear author: looking for reflexivity and other hallmarks of interpretive research'. Paper to the Annual Meeting of the American Political Science Association, 30 August–3 September, Philadelphia.

Yanow, D. and Schwartz-Shea, P. 2006. *Interpretation and Method: Empirical Research Methods and the Interpretive Turn*. Armonk, NY: M.E. Sharpe.

Yin, R. K. 2003. *Case Study Research: Design and Methods,* 3rd edn. London: Sage.

Young, D. 1990. *The Enterprise Years. A Businessman in the Cabinet*. London: Headline.

Young, H. 1990. 'GCHQ Memorial Lecture', *The Bulletin*, July: 1.

Name Index

Subject Index

Subject Index